Jewish Women and Their Salons

THE POWER OF CONVERSATION

Jewish Women and Their Salons

THE POWER OF CONVERSATION

Emily D. Bilski and Emily Braun

WITH CONTRIBUTIONS BY

Leon Botstein

Shira Brisman

Barbara Hahn

Lucia Re

THE JEWISH MUSEUM • NEW YORK

UNDER THE AUSPICES OF THE JEWISH THEOLOGICAL SEMINARY OF AMERICA

YALE UNIVERSITY PRESS • NEW HAVEN AND LONDON

This book has been published in conjunction with the exhibition *The Power of Conversation: Jewish Women and Their Salons*, organized by The Jewish Museum.

The Jewish Museum, New York
March 4–July 10, 2005

McMullen Museum of Art, Boston College
August 22–December 4, 2005
Presented by Boston College, Chestnut Hill, Massachusetts, and the New Center for Arts and Culture, Boston

Exhibition Curators: Emily D. Bilski and Emily Braun
Manager of Curatorial Publications: Michael Sittenfeld
Curatorial Assistant: Shira Brisman
Manuscript Editor: Anna Jardine
Exhibition Catalogue Assistants: Beth Turk, Ivy Epstein, Tamar Rubin, and Erica Stern
Exhibition Design: Carlos Guri and Carolina Casajuana, Barcelona

Publisher, Art & Architecture, Yale: Patricia Fidler
Assistant Editor, Art & Architecture, Yale: Michelle Komie
Manuscript Editor, Yale: Laura Jones Dooley
Production Manager, Yale: Mary Mayer
Photo Editor, Yale: John Long

Designed by Katy Homans, New York
Set in Fournier by Katy Homans and Matt Mayerchak
Printed in Italy by Conti Tipocolor

Jacket illustrations: (front) Florine Stettheimer, *Portrait of My Sister Carrie W. Stettheimer*, 1923. Columbia University, New York, Gift of the Estate of Ettie Stettheimer, 1967 (p. 132)

(back, left to right, top to bottom) Wilhelm Hensel, *Fanny Hensel née Mendelssohn Bartholdy*, 1829. Kupferstichkabinett, Staatliche Museen zu Berlin–Preussischer Kulturbesitz (p. 161); Umberto Boccioni, *Antigrazioso*, 1912. Private collection, formerly in the collection of Margherita Sarfatti (p. 100); Mario Nunes-Vais, *Anna Kuliscioff*. Istituto Centrale per il Catalogo e la Documentazione, Gabinetto Fotografico Nazionale, Collezione Nunes-Vais, Rome (p. 77); Madame D'Ora (Dora Philippine Kallmus), *Berta Zuckerkandl*, 1908. Bildarchiv, Österreichische Nationalbibliothek, Vienna (p. 86); Pablo Picasso, *Portrait of Gertrude Stein*, 1906. The Metropolitan Museum of Art, New York, Bequest of Gertrude Stein, 1947 (p. 114); Johann Karl Kretschmar, *Portrait of Amalie Beer*, c. 1803. Stiftung Stadtmuseum Berlin, Hans-und-Luise-Richter-Stiftung (p. 39)

Frontispiece: Man Ray (American, 1890–1976), *Gertrude Stein and Alice B. Toklas in the Atelier at 27 rue de Fleurus*, 1923. Yale Collection of American Literature, Beinecke Rare Book and Manuscript Library, Yale University, New Haven (p. 121)

The Jewish Museum
1109 Fifth Avenue
New York, New York 10128
www.thejewishmuseum.org

Yale University Press
P.O. Box 209040
New Haven, Connecticut 06520–9040
www.yalebooks.com

Library of Congress Cataloging-in-Publication Data

Jewish women and their salons : the power of conversation / [curated by] Emily D. Bilski and Emily Braun ; with contributions by Leon Botstein . . . [et al].
         p.   cm.
    Catalog of the exhibition, The power of conversation : Jewish women and their salons, held at The Jewish Museum, New York, March 4–July 10, 2005.
    Includes bibliographical references and index.
    ISBN 0-300-10385-9 (clothbound : alk. paper) —ISBN 0-300-10846-x (paperbound : alk. paper)
    1. Jewish women–Europe, Western–Intellectual life–Exhibitions. 2. Jewish women–Germany–Berlin–Intellectual life–Exhibitions. 3. Salons–Europe, Western–History–19th century–Exhibitions. 4. Salons–Germany–Berlin–History–19th century–Exhibitions. 5. Upper class–Europe, Western–History–19th century–Exhibitions. 6. Europe, Western–Intellectual life–19th century–Exhibitions. I. Bilski, Emily D., 1956– II. Braun, Emily, 1957– III. Botstein, Leon. IV. Jewish Museum (New York, N.Y.)
    DS135.E83J58 2005
    305.48'8924'00747471–dc22   2004023218

A catalogue record for this book is available from the British Library.

The paper in this book meets the guidelines for permanence and durability of the Committee on Production Guidelines for Book Longevity of the Council on Library Resources.
10 9 8 7 6 5 4 3 2 1

Contents

Donors to the Exhibition

We gratefully acknowledge the following donors for their support:

Andrea & Charles Bronfman Philanthropies • Dorot Foundation

Leo and Julia Forchheimer Foundation

The Lucius N. Littauer Foundation

Sara Lee Schupf and Tillie K. Lubin

Blanche & Irving Laurie Foundation

Susan and Roger Hertog

The Donald and Barbara Zucker Foundation

The Richard J. and Joan G. Scheuer
Family Foundation

The Nash Family Foundation

New York Council for the Humanities

Austrian Cultural Forum

Agnes Gund and Daniel Shapiro

The Abby and Mitch Leigh Foundation

Leni and Peter May

The Alex Hillman Family Foundation
Ellen Katz
Patsy Orlofsky
Carol and Lawrence Saper
The Judy and Michael Steinhardt Foundation
Goldberg/Nash Family Foundation
Fern K. Hurst
Alfred J. Grunebaum Memorial Fund
Patricia Lasakwy
The Evelyn and Leonard Lauder Foundation
Levenstein Family Foundation
Josephine and Thomas Linden
Geri Pollack
Nicki and Harold Tanner
Debra Black
The Daniel & Estrellita Brodsky Family Foundation
Englander Foundation
The Perry & Martin Granoff Family Foundation
Barbara F. Kleinberg
The Reiss Family Foundation
Patricia Abramson
Kathryn Steinberg
Arlyn Gardner
Joanne B. and Norman S. Matthews
Estate of Nina Poliakoff

The catalogue was made possible by the Dorot Foundation publications endowment.

Special thanks to Susan Lytle Lipton, Sara Lee Schupf, Ellen Katz, and Carol Saper.

Lenders to the Exhibition

Amedeo Porro arte moderna e contemporanea

Archivio Dudreville, Monza Galleria Antologia

Leo Baeck Institute, New York

The Baltimore Museum of Art

Bard College Library, Annandale-on-Hudson, New York

Beinecke Rare Book and Manuscript Library, Yale
University, New Haven

Brooklyn Museum of Art

Emily Braun and Andrew Frackman

John J. Burns Library, Boston College, Chestnut Hill,
Massachusetts

Philip V. Cannistraro

Columbia University in the City of New York

Cooper-Hewitt, National Design Museum, Smithsonian
Institution, New York

Dexia Crediop, Rome

Fogg Art Museum, Harvard University Art Museums,
Cambridge, Massachusetts

Fondazione Anna Kuliscioff, Milan

Edmund M. Frederick

Marina and Antonio Forchino

Daniel M. Friedenberg

Galerie St. Etienne, New York

Galleria Claudia Gian Ferrari, Milan

Germanisches Nationalmuseum, Nuremberg

Hans-und-Luise-Richter-Stiftung, Stadtmuseum, Berlin

Heinrich-Heine-Institut, Düsseldorf

Houghton Library, Harvard University, Cambridge,
Massachusetts

The Jewish Museum, New York

Jüdisches Museum der Stadt Wien, Vienna

Kunstbibliothek, Staatliche Museen zu Berlin, Stiftung
Preussischer Kulturbesitz, Berlin

Kupferstichkabinett, Staatliche Museen zu Berlin,
Stiftung Preussischer Kulturbesitz, Berlin

Mark Samuels Lasner

Leonard A. Lauder

Laura Mattioli

The Metropolitan Museum of Art, New York

Museum of Fine Arts, Boston

Museo della Permanente, Milan

Musikabteilung mit Mendelssohn-Archiv, Staatsbibliothek
zu Berlin, Stiftung Preussischer Kulturbesitz, Berlin

Musikinstrumenten-Museum, Staatliches Institut für
Musikforschung, Stiftung Preussischer Kulturbesitz, Berlin

Nationalgalerie, Staatliche Museen zu Berlin, Stiftung
Preussischer Kulturbesitz, Berlin

The New York Public Library

Peggy Guggenheim Collection, Venice

Philadelphia Museum of Art

The Pierpont Morgan Library, New York

Private collections

Harry Ransom Humanities Research Center,
The University of Texas, Austin

Robert Gore Rifkind

Rose Art Museum, Brandeis University, Waltham,
Massachusetts

Magalì Sarfatti-Larson

Sheridan Libraries, Johns Hopkins University, Baltimore

William Kelly Simpson

Smith College Museum of Art, Northampton,
Massachusetts

Staatsbibliothek zu Berlin, Stiftung Preussischer
Kulturbesitz, Berlin

Stiftung Stadtmuseum Berlin

Wien Museum, Vienna

Francis Wyndham

Emile Zuckerkandl

Foreword

The salons of Jewish women have been a tantalizing subject for The Jewish Museum for nearly two decades. The integration of histories—social, art, feminist, Jewish—held the promise of a unique opportunity for new scholarship and a visually rich exhibition, exploring a 150-year history of influence on modern thought and major art movements. Yet a challenge persisted: how to create a visual experience about a medium—conversation—so different from the traditional basis of an exhibition. We were fortunate to have the enthusiastic involvement of exhibition curators Emily Bilski and Emily Braun, who tackled the challenge of communicating the public resonance of a selected group of private gatherings, in particular the influence of the salons of Jewish women in Europe and the United States. The curators were immeasurably assisted by Jewish Museum staff and outside scholars, and they received the vital support and participation of numerous donors and lenders. What resulted after many years of research and thought was a remarkable exhibition presented in New York by The Jewish Museum in 2005 and at the McMullen Museum of Art, Boston College, in the same year. This beautiful publication, with four essays offering an in-depth intellectual and visual journey, provides context and added meaning to this engaging subject.

The historical basis for the project is the emergence of the phenomenon of the salon and the role of the salonière between 1780 and 1950. By focusing on Jewish salonières, the curators illuminate the remarkable fact that Jewish women hosted a high proportion of salons. The exhibition and publication delve into the biographies of twelve of these women and their milieus so that the museum visitor and reader of this book encounter dozens of artists, writers, musicians, and politicians as well as the salonières themselves, each of whom is both a creative talent and a nurturer of others. Beginning with salons in Berlin that tested the ideals of Emancipation, the exhibition moves on to music salons in Vienna and Berlin, literary salons in Paris and London, the modernist salons of Vienna, Milan, and New York, and a salon of a European exile community in California. Cumulatively, these explorations demonstrate several essential themes: the egalitarian function of the salon as it boldly cut through the hierarchies and mores of society; the salon as a primary locus of the democratization of culture before the development of mass media; and the salon as an arena for the exercise of creativity and social action on the part of Jewish women, who had less mobility than men. In general, the salons are seen as both a means and a source of social, sexual, and religious emancipation.

The creation of both the exhibition and the catalogue entailed extensive curatorial research, impressive scholarly writing, and conscientious administration. It also necessitated the cooperation and support of a multitude of lenders and donors. I congratulate the co-curators and catalogue editors, Emily Bilski and Emily Braun. Their prodigious and thoughtful work has yielded a highly informative, beautifully constructed, and inspiring exhibition and catalogue. In addition, my warm thanks to everyone on the museum's staff who worked on the project, as well as those consultants whose expertise in media, design, graphics, exhibition interpretation, and music so greatly enhanced the experience of visitors and readers. Many of these individuals are acknowledged in subsequent pages. To this, I add personal thanks to those colleagues at the McMullen Museum of Art and the New Center for Arts and Culture who were responsible for producing the exhibition in Boston.

With this book, the reader can find an expansion of many of the themes and ideas of the exhibition beginning with the essay by Emily Bilski and Emily Braun as they provide captivating accounts of the salonières and the spirit of their times. Barbara Hahn penetrates the intellectual atmosphere of early Berlin salons through her research of letters, diaries, and archival materials. Leon Botstein explores music salons and their effect on nineteenth- and twentieth-century composers, performers, and audiences. In the final essay, Lucia Re focuses on the salon conversation as a new form of egalitarian and liberating communication and its influence on literary modernism.

This ambitious endeavor required years of work and substantial financial support. The museum's exhibitions committee and trustees gave encouraging advice and support from the earliest stage. From planning to implementation, the responsiveness of contributors to the exhibition was gratifying and impressive. Those who supported the project are noted on page vi of this catalogue. Among them are women who opened their homes to promote the idea of the exhibition to potential supporters. Collectively, the exhibition's sponsors responded to the timeliness of the subject, and found it compelling to consider these historic gatherings in our own time, when humanist ideals still fall short, feminism still needs to be nurtured, the avant-garde often remains marginalized, and anti-Semitism still exists in the world. Particular thanks are extended to the Andrea and Charles Bronfman Philanthropies, the Dorot Foundation, and the Leo and Julia Forchheimer Foundation, with added appreciation to the Lucius N. Littauer Foundation, Sara Lee Schupf, Tillie K. Lubin, and the Blanche and Irving Laurie Foundation. My thanks also to the large number of collectors, colleagues, and institutions listed on page vii who provided loans for the exhibition. Their willingness to participate in this exploration and celebration of the salon enabled us to borrow manuscripts, photographs, furniture, paintings, drawings, prints, and books in order to create a powerful presentation for both the New York and Boston venues.

Salons were private events that had broad public effect. They were gatherings where disenfranchised and marginalized people achieved power and influence and where a basic form of communication—conversation—allowed for extraordinary thought. What indeed would be the ideal salon in today's world? This project inspires us to think anew about our own social, professional, and domestic spheres and the possibility of creating congenial havens for new ideas that might have an incremental effect on changing the world. Perhaps this is a form of fantasy and wishful thinking, but the women celebrated in *The Power of Conversation*, and the fascinating results of their talents and convictions, remind us of the power of our own humanity.

JOAN ROSENBAUM
Helen Goldsmith Menschel Director
The Jewish Museum

Acknowledgments

Research for this project took place over four years, three continents, nine countries, and more than a dozen cities. Along the way we drew on the goodwill of colleagues, curators, librarians, archivists, and scholars, and personal friends and descendants of our salonières. We wish to extend our appreciation to Joan Rosenbaum, Helen Goldsmith Menschel Director of The Jewish Museum, who has always supported the idea of an exhibition on Jewish salonières and gave us the opportunity to organize it together. We redouble the gratitude expressed in her foreword to the lenders and sponsors who made it possible. In addition, we note our indebtedness to the following individuals and institutions.

In Austria: Karl Albrecht-Weinberger and Felicitas Heimann-Jelinek, Jüdisches Museum, Vienna; Ursula Storch, Wien Museum; Elizabeth Schmuttermeier and Christian Witt-Döring, MAK, Vienna; Peter Prokop, Österreichische Nationalbibliothek-Porträtsammlung, Bildarchiv und Fideikommissbibliothek, Vienna. In Belgium: Daniel Dratwa, Jewish Museum, Brussels. In England: Julia Rosenthal; Merlin Holland; Library of the National Portrait Gallery, London. In France: Françoise Balard; Henriette Guy-Loé; Chantal Bischoff; Gabriel Badea-Päun; Bibliothèque Nationale de France, Paris. In Poland: Biblioteka Jagiellońska, Kraków.

In Germany: Hermann Simon and Chana Schütz, Centrum Judaicum, Berlin; Kurt Winkler, Alice Uebe, and Christine Waidenschlager, Stiftung Stadtmuseum, Berlin; Sven Kuhrau; Günter and Ingrid Oesterle; Hans-Günter Klein, Mendelssohn-Archiv, Staatsbibliothek, Berlin; Bernhard Purin, Jüdisches Museum, Munich; Sigrid Achenbach, Kupferstichkabinett, Berlin; Angelika Wesenberg, Nationalgalerie, Berlin; Werner Sudendorf, Gero Gandert, Peter Latta, and Gerrit Thies, the Filmmuseum Berlin–Stiftung Deutsche Kinemathek; Conny Restle, Musikinstrumenten-Museum, Berlin; Anne Bohnenkamp-Renken, Freies Deutsches Hochstift, Frankfurter Goethe Museum; Beate Dannhorn, Filmmuseum Frankfurt; Deutsches Literaturarchiv, Schiller-Nationalmuseum, Marbach am Neckar.

In Israel: Dominique Bourel; Yfaat Weiss; Paul Mendes-Flohr; Shimshon Zelniker and the staff of the Van Leer Institute, Jerusalem, and the members of the salons discussion group; the staff of the Jewish National and University Library, Jerusalem.

In Italy: Amedeo Porro; Elisabetta Seeber; Giovanna Ginex; Antonio Forchino; Margherita Gaetani; Maria Diletta Rigamonti; Paola Mola; Francesca Morelli; Marie Andrée Mondini; Walter Galbusera and Marina Cattaneo, Fondazione Anna Kuliscioff; the Fondo Sommariva, Biblioteca Nazionale Braidense, Milan; Fondazione Primoli, Rome; and the Archivio Nunes Vais, Gabinetto Fotografico Nazionale, Rome. Claudia Gian Ferrari worked tirelessly on our behalf to obtain several loans, as did Philip Rylands and Jasper Sharp of the Peggy Guggenheim Collection, Venice. Much appreciation is due to Laura Mattioli, who gave of art, dialogue, and hospitality.

In the United States: Jane Kallir; Bernard Goldberg; Richard Feigen; Jeffrey Deitch; Franck Giraud; Daniella Luxembourg; Francis Naumann; John Richardson; James Melo; Donald T. Sanders; Constance Olds; Mary Gibson; Tim Zinnemann; Brigit Wertheimer; Laura Schor; Ruth Gay; Leora Auslander; Leslie Brisman; Peter Paret; Timothy Barringer; Dan Kershaw; Caroline Milbank; Elizabeth Frank; Susan Kohner; Gavin Lambert; Jack Larson; Sybille Pearson; Nicola Lubitsch; Peter Rippon; Linda Gertner Zatlin; Richard Dellamora; Adrian Kahan Leibowitz; Elizabeth Kujawski; Vlasta Odell; Jennifer Raab; Judith Friedlander; Yehuda Nir; Karole Vail and Vivien Greene, The Solomon R. Guggenheim Museum, New York; Valerie Steele, Fashion Institute of Technology; Colin Bailey, The Frick Collection, New York; Ida Balboul and Andrea Bayer, The

Metropolitan Museum of Art, New York; Sarah Elliston Weiner, Miriam and Ira D. Wallach Art Gallery, Columbia University, New York; Elizabeth Easton, Brooklyn Museum of Art; Katherine Rothkopf, The Baltimore Museum of Art; Christine Vigiletti, Robert Gore Rifkind Center, Los Angeles; Susan Edwards, Frist Center for the Visual Arts, Nashville; George Shackleford, Museum of Fine Arts; Boston; Barbara Bloemink, Cooper-Hewitt, National Design Museum, Smithsonian Institution, New York; Carol Eliel, Los Angeles County Museum of Art; Barbara Haskell, Whitney Museum of American Art, New York; Renée Price, Neue Galerie, New York; Christine Nelson, The Pierpont Morgan Library, New York; Peter Nisbet, Busch-Reisinger Museum, Harvard University; Marje Schuetze-Coburn, Feuchtwanger Memorial Library, University of Southern California; Frank Mecklenburg, Renate Evers, Renate Stein, Leo Baeck Institute, New York; Patricia Willis and Nancy Kuhl, Yale Collection of American Literature, Beinecke Rare Book and Manuscript Library, New Haven. We would like to thank the staff at the following institutions: Prints and Drawings Study Room, Fogg Art Museum, and the Houghton Library, Harvard University; The William Andrews Clark Memorial Library, University of California, Los Angeles; Thomas J. Watson Library, The Metropolitan Museum of Art.

The kindness and intellectual largesse of Magalì Sarfatti-Larson and Emile Zuckerkandl allowed us to realize the sections on their respective grandmothers, Margherita Sarfatti and Berta Zuckerkandl; Francis Wyndham provided invaluable material on his grandmother, Ada Leverson; and Thomas Viertel, and his wife, Ruth, graciously shared information and their recollections of his mother, Salka Viertel.

Much research and writing took place at the Lewis and Dorothy B. Cullman Center for Scholars and Writers at the New York Public Library (and in the library's superb collections), where Emily Braun was the Mel and Lois Tukman Fellow in 2002–3. Discussions with Thomas Bender, Elisheva Carlebach, Jeremy Treglown, and Stacy Schiff were essential to ideas and approaches developed in the exhibition. Our deepest

appreciation to Peter Gay, mentor and friend, who kept pace with the project all along, perused the manuscript, and stepped in to secure us a critical loan.

A project of this magnitude could not have taken place without the dedication of the Jewish Museum staff: Ruth Beesch, deputy director for program; Al Lazarte, director of operations; Anne Scher, director of communications; and Aviva Weintraub, director of media and public programs. Jane Rubin, head registrar, and Lauren Smith, assistant registrar, masterfully administrated a complex loan enterprise with extraordinary efficiency. In addition, we thank Mary Walling, chief operating officer, Sarah Himmelfarb, associate director of development, and Susan Wyatt, senior grants writer, who worked way beyond their normal duties. We benefited from the indefatigable interest of Beth Turk, Adina Loeb, Rebecca Sandler, and Leah Citron. Judith C. Siegel, interpretative consultant, was an essential part of our team in ways too numerous to enumerate here. Above all, Shira Brisman, research and curatorial assistant, deserves credit for bringing the exhibition together, serving as chief coordinator of loans, photographic materials, and installation. She did so with unfailing grace and good humor. Her central role cannot be overstated, nor can our gratitude.

We are fortunate that the exhibition will be seen by other audiences outside New York, and for this we thank Nancy Netzer, director, and Alston Conley, chief curator, of the McMullen Museum of Art, Boston College, and Shoshana Pakciarz, executive director of the New Center for Arts and Culture.

In this beautiful book copublished by Yale University Press and its professional staff, we inscribe our gratitude to Michael Sittenfeld, manager of curatorial publications at The Jewish Museum, who worked under immense pressure of deadlines and quality. We had the privilege of working with designer Katy Homans and editor Anna Jardine, who did not mince our words but whipped them into shape, and whose assiduous fact-checking saved face more than once.

This book has been immeasurably enriched by the contributions of Leon Botstein, Barbara Hahn, and Lucia Re, who were exceedingly generous with advice and research. We thank Deborah Hertz and Philip Cannistraro for many informative conversations. Mark Samuels Lasner shared his bountiful knowledge and enthusiasm for nineteenth-century London and the circle of Ada Leverson. Without the unstinting cooperation of the Hans-und-Luise-Richter-Stiftung at the Stiftung Stadtmuseum, Berlin, its board, and especially Kurt Winkler and Alice Uebe, there would have been no presentation on Amalie Beer.

The exhibition's designers, Carlos Guri and Carolina Casajuana, found the way to conceptualize our ideas in three dimensions, and we want to emphasize how much their remarkable vision has contributed to bringing the installation to life. The same is true of our other key artistic collaborators: Sandy Goldberg of Antenna Audio, who devised the acoustic theater; and Eve Wolf and the Ensemble for the Romantic Century, who advised on the music salons and authored the audio narrative on Fanny Hensel. We are especially indebted to Andrea Simon of Arcadia Pictures for the extraordinary films she created on the salons of Geneviève Straus and Salka Viertel.

Susan Lytle Lipton, former chairman of The Jewish Museum Board of Trustees, and Agnes Gund and Evelyn Lauder gave us constant encouragement. A special acknowledgment is due to Carol Saper, who devoted her boundless goodwill and energy to gathering a network of support for the exhibition.

We have been blessed with family members who offered not only counsel but also professional and scholarly assistance: Berthold Bilski, Gabriel Motzkin, and Andrew Frackman. We dedicate this book about women and the beauty of dialogue—informed, spirited, and respectful of others—to our sons, Theodore and Alexander Motzkin and Jacob and Daniel Frackman.

EMILY D. BILSKI AND EMILY BRAUN

The Power of Conversation: Jewish Women and Their Salons

EMILY D. BILSKI AND EMILY BRAUN

Introduction

In the numberless books I had read about social life in France . . . I had been told that the salon *had vanished forever, first with the famous* douceur de vivre *of the Old Régime, then with the downfall of the Bourbons, then with the end of the House of Orléans, and finally on the disastrous day of Sedan. Each of these catastrophes doubtless took with it something of the exclusiveness, the intimacy and continuity of the traditional* salon*; but before I had lived a year in Paris I had discovered that most of the old catchwords were still in circulation, most of the old rules still observed, and that the ineradicable passion for good talk, and for seeing the same people every day, was as strong at the opening of the twentieth century as when the* Précieuses *met at the Hôtel de Rambouillet.*

—EDITH WHARTON, *A BACKWARD GLANCE*, 1933

Conversation was not the reproduction of listening and talking and this was said and when there was more there was some understanding of that.

—GERTRUDE STEIN, *G.M.P.*
(*MATISSE PICASSO AND GERTRUDE STEIN*), 1912

Say the word *salon* and most Americans will think of the bohemian gatherings of Gertrude Stein. The French, in whose country the salon originated, would cite the drawing rooms of any number of illustrious women from the seventeenth and eighteenth centuries— Madame Madeleine de Scudéry, Madame Marie-Thérèse Rodet Geoffrin, or Madame Germaine de Staël, for example. But Parisians could also invoke the name of Stein, since she held court in their city, perpetuating into the modern era the salon tradition of *femmes auteurs* and *femmes savantes*. Stein was an American living abroad, who attracted avant-garde outsiders as ambitious and marginalized as their hostess. She turned her domestic space into the center of a vibrant subculture that eventually became mainstream, in no small part because of the marketing function of the salon itself. Although Stein presented herself as an innovative writer and unusual personality, she was but the culmination of a long line of salon women, and Jewish ones at that, who exerted their influence from inside the home. The Jewish salonières emerged in Europe at the end of the eighteenth century, when Enlightenment ideas of tolerance and universality allowed them to test the freedoms and limitations of emancipation—as both women and Jews. This is the story of the most powerful among them and of the private conversations that changed public life.

Salons were among the first institutions of modern culture. From the seventeenth to the early twentieth centuries they fostered the decline of aristocratic castes and the rise of new egalitarian elites. Cash-poor nobles made wealthy matches with individuals of lesser rank, and intellectuals found patrons and cachet. The arrivistes assumed many conventions of the aristocracy, not only out of pretense (though that was often the case) but also because stylized grace, better known as tact, allowed for the negotiation of difference among strangers. The ethics of salon reciprocity banned aggressive behavior in the pursuit of mutual tolerance, and women—perceived as having greater equanimity than men—were expected to take the lead.

The authoritative salonière couched matters of public importance in the nonthreatening language of open inquiry, soliciting and dispensing counsel in equal measure. Listening meant anticipating and pre-empting with the calibration of a military operation, while *bons mots* had to be lobbed with the grace of a surprise engagement—no appearance of ponderous premeditation. She provided for her guests the model of a rational, exhilarating, discursive style. Fine food, elegant dress, and the ostentatious display of wealth went only so far: the pretty could be boring and the nouveau riche vacuous, whereas the homely novice often emanated genuine depth of spirit or rallied with a blade-sharp wit. The most influential salonières were extraordinarily charismatic. Not all were obliging—certainly not to all of the people, all of the time. Nor did they have to be: they were after a place in history, not necessarily in etiquette books.

Today, when oral culture has been devalued for a culture of images, it is difficult to imagine the bygone skills of repartee or the delicate balance between self-effacement and self-aggrandizement. We tend to forget that before the advent of the mass press, let alone the free press, information divulged confidentially in private shaped ideas and their reception at large. Opinion evolved through collective voices; it was not dispensed in prepackaged formulas.[1] The power of conversation—the ability to publicize and arbitrate, to shape consensus, to unite in dialogue those who would not normally meet—was key to the political politesse of the salon. As a result, the salon tradition of egalitarian sociability doubled in importance for Jewish women who had not only their gender but also religious and ethnic difference to overcome.

The word *salonière*, like *muse*, conjures a stereotype of seductive femininity, with the added taint of class snobbery. But the salon could be much more than a showcase for charm—a word that makes our post-feminist moment wince. The apparent social elitism of the salon belies its actual progressive function. Precisely because the salon was private, it enabled people of different economic standing, religion, rank, and nationality to exchange ideas and be recognized both as individuals and as part of common humanity. To know the "other" it was vital to erode stereotypes of class,

gender, sexuality, and ethnicity. Further, salons marketed high culture for a larger world by launching individual talent and aptitude into the broader fabric of civic life. In the seventeenth century, the salon infringed on church and court as a site of literary and musical production and patronage; by the end of the nineteenth, it challenged the artistic tastes of nation-state institutions. Finally, the salon granted women a singular means for education, professional identity, and personal empowerment. Over time, the myth of the salonière grew almost as powerful as the reality, for it bequeathed a rare example of ambition and intellect to subsequent generations of women.

Strictly speaking, salons, or "at-homes," occurred weekly, on a *jour fixe*, on the same day, at the same time. Invitations, if needed, were sent by personal messenger, word of mouth, or, after the mid-eighteenth century, through urban postal services. Much later, a telephone call was not out of the question, even if the propriety of social correspondence and the traditional bond between salon conversation and letter writing died hard. Either midday dinner or evening supper was served, although a formal meal was not the focus of activity.[2] Salon sociability prospered, instead, on flexible seating arrangements—ad hoc pairs and small clusters, open circles for the enjoyment of a performance—save for the commandeering centrality of the salonière, who often presided on a daybed or divan. Food and its presentation nonetheless added to the tone. Over time and in different European capitals, elaborately prepared, multicourse delicacies or reverse chic, such as stew and polenta, offered nourishment and deliberate allusions to class and ethnicity.

Even more than the formality of a *jour fixe*, a successful salon depended on a core group of habitués, a combination of close friends and persons of renown. The last, along with the hostess herself, gave the salon its exclusive appeal. The most celebrated attendees frequented various salons, their role in each changing according to the communicative dynamic of the group. No less important were new recruits and occasional visitors, whose novel presence and perspectives staved off ennui, variegating the degree and kind of exchange.

Fig. 1. *Portrait of Rahel Levin Varnhagen*. Engraving, 9 x 7¼ in. (23 x 18.5 cm). Varnhagen Collection, Biblioteka Jagiellońska, Kraków

part of the hostess, in addition to scheduling rehearsals for music, a theatrical performance, or a literary reading. But effort had to be dissimulated, for the effervescence of sociability relied on spontaneity and free flow. Bound to be mistress of the house, the salonière excelled as master of ceremonies.

Aside from the learned hostesses of seventeenth- and eighteenth-century France, few salonières have been writ large in the historical narratives, as were most of their prestigious male guests—and not only because of their gender. Despite their aristocratic origins, salons suffer the distinction of being a kind of underground of high culture—with all the fascination and neglect that marginality implies. An ephemeral event whose study falls under the rubric of microhistory, the salon evolved over time in different nations with varying traditions of political democracy, relationships between the sexes, and commercially available culture. Knowledge of salons and salonières depends on letters, memoirs, autobiographies, and romans à clef—all of whose truth value must be constantly ascertained. These texts are imbued with fiction as well as fact, with a self-conscious fashioning for audience and legacy. Scholarship, with its focus on the unprecedented status of women during the Enlightenment, has created the impression that authentic salons died out after the French Revolution.[4] The salon has never been studied comprehensively as a vehicle of female emancipation and assimilation for Jews, as an institution of modern secular culture that spread throughout Europe after 1789 and lasted until World War II.

Jewish women form a disproportionately large number of the most influential and discussed salonières from Rahel Levin in early 1790s Berlin (fig. 1), to Salka Viertel in 1930s Los Angeles.[5] Aristocratic politesse found its finest heir in Marcel Proust's Duchess of Guermantes, a fictional character based in large part on the contemporary Jewish salonière Geneviève Straus (fig. 2). The salons of Jewish women form part of a larger development: the importation and domestication of French aristocratic sociability into Western and Central Europe, Russia, and America. At the same time, they made heterogeneous a tradition based on a

Depending on the era, one gained entrance through letter of introduction or vouchsafed word of mouth. Appearances were tricky and dissembling was a social art; spies, bores, and ne'er-do-wells might infiltrate temporarily. Rivals and usurpers were inevitable. "The salonière's supreme talent," writes Benedetta Craveri, "lay in knowing how to create a harmonious gathering of people who differed not only in temperament and intelligence but also in their social background, whilst allowing them all to express their own personalities and to show themselves at their best."[3] Preparations for an evening often entailed practice and self-scripting on the

Fig. 2. Paul Nadar (French, 1856–1939), *Madame Émile Straus (Geneviève Halévy)*, 1887. Archives Photographiques, Centre des Monuments Nationaux, Paris

sphere appeared all the more remarkable and, for their detractors, threatening. Symbols of highly contested difference and eventual success, Jewish salonières symbolized the ultimate outsiders on the inside. The women under discussion here made a difference: they were exceptional women and exceptional Jews, and could have been neither without the salon.

THE ORIGINS OF EGALITARIAN SOCIABILITY IN FRANCE

Salons began in early-seventeenth-century France as an offshoot of the court; by the mid-eighteenth century, they generated a form of critical discourse in opposition to absolute monarchy. They were instrumental to the rise of civil society, to the theory and practice of educated persons assembling in private to debate politics and culture. Like coffeehouses in England or literary societies (*Tischgesellschaften*) in Germany, salons were a prototype of what Jürgen Habermas has termed the bourgeois public sphere.[6] Here, parity based on intelligence displaced inherited privilege, and reasoning individuals challenged the monopoly of interpretation by church or king.[7] In addition, the new liberal elite drew a novel division between private life and public sphere: the world of family life, labor, and property declared itself morally and legally beyond the purview of state control; conversely, governmental authority was to derive its legitimacy from the reasoned judgment of private people, as a body representative of common concern.

Among these earliest examples of convivial associations, only the model of "French sociability"—the salon—allowed for the mixing of the sexes.[8] Around 1618, the Italian-born Catherine de Vivonne, Marquise de Rambouillet (1588–1665) withdrew from the rituals of the court to welcome persons of her choice in her private Parisian residence, the Hôtel de Rambouillet. There, she initiated the art of conversation according to principles of delight and decorum, to the end of discovering oneself through direct social contact with the personality and thoughts of another. The Marquise de Rambouillet further broke with convention by moving

Christian and aristocratic constituency and in doing so invigorated old elites and formed new ones. Assimilating Jewish women who had negotiated many boundaries readily embraced the role of social arbiter and cultural catalyst. Yet they also experienced the painful chasm between social power and racial prejudice, individual accomplishment and political disenfranchisement. The renown of these dual "noncitizens" in the public

Fig. 3. François Chauveau (French, 1613–1676), *Exaltation de la Ruelle,* mid-seventeenth century. Bibliothèque Nationale de France, Département des Estampes, Paris

F. Chauveau in. et fecit

loveless unions, legal subordination, and diminished, largely religious education.[10] The salon gave them autonomy and the right to adjudicate behavior: aggression, pedantry, and obsequiousness would be banished, while the status of fine conduct would replace celebration of rank.[11] Amid cards, verbal games, and recitations, conversation became a realm of ludic brilliance and expressive sincerity. Speech, gesture, and facial expression bespoke the quality of the *honnêtes gens,* of the new aristocratic publicity or the honed presentation of self in public. Along the way, women shaped the most buoyant stereotype of the French—civility. In the words of Immanuel Kant, who recognized the "true humaneness" of feminine sociability, "The French nation stands out among all others by its taste for conversation, in which it is the model for all the rest."[12]

No longer restricted to members of the court, *le monde* included venal officeholders, financiers, moral philosophers, scientists, actors, bastard sons, and disgraced daughters. The salon encouraged merit over birth, manners over money as criteria for an expanded nobility that included leavened haute bourgeois. Already in the seventeenth century, contemporaries either hailed or decried the weakening of social stratifications, with the question of female power at the center of the debate. Feminine intrigue and new money, it was argued, led to the proliferation of legal ennoblements; the salon promoted misalliances between noble and bourgeoisie (in most cases, with women rising from the lower estate); and salon women cultivated the new social standards that permitted upward mobility.[13] The *précieuses* ("precious ones"), as the first salon women were pejoratively named, threatened to destabilize the institution of marriage, with their desire for learning and self-determination, their practice of chastity or free love outside the legal unions made by arrangement or for mere compatibility. They emulated aristocratic speech and comportment, playing havoc with the distinguishing signs of caste. The feminization of men was linked to dissolute traits of aristocracy, and social chaos with women's violation of the "natural" order.

In fact, by the mid-eighteenth century the salon no longer promoted leisurely conversation for its own sake

her actual bed in an adjacent wardrobe alcove and receiving company in her grand, blue bedchamber (*chambre bleue*)—a prestigious rite of self-presentation formerly reserved for the king. The establishment of the *ruelle,* or the space between the bed and wall, predated the move into the large reception room, and bequeathed the symbolism of bodily ease, confidentiality, and immunity (fig. 3). Launched from the privacy of the lady's bedroom, the salon became an intimate yet sexually neutral domain, dedicated to the virtues of platonic love between men and women and the integration of masculine and feminine traits.[9]

In seventeenth-century salons, women established the ideals of self-betterment and its altruistic corollary, human progress. They pacified an estate once feudal and armed and gave purpose to nobility in transition and now largely idle with dwindling resources. Though titled from birth or marriage, the first salonières were well aware of the precariousness of their own existence:

but became a school of intellectual ambition. With women of the third estate now leading the salons and with eminent writers in attendance, serious study replaced serious play, even among functionless nobles. The salon became the institutional base for the Enlightenment, giving the philosophes independence from the Académie Française and court, a space of uncensored operation where rational inquiry could undermine the unsustainable tenets of both autocracy and theocracy.[14] The directed inquiries of the Enlightenment salons, as Habermas has shown, "turned conversation into criticism and *bons mots* into arguments."[15] Women were integral to this new Republic of Letters: the most famous, such as Madame Geoffrin, Mademoiselle Julie de Lespinasse, and Madame Suzanne Curchod Necker, governed in the spirit of politesse, attracted patronage, and in some cases contributed financial support.[16] But learned *femmes savantes* and *femmes philosophes* were not just facilitators, serving the needs of men, or accruing prestige by sitting next to celebrity: they also served

themselves, speaking and writing, creating erudite identities, holding their own. The intellectual status of women gave proof to the Cartesian dictum that the "mind has no sex." Nor did civility. The salon was a microcosm of Enlightenment universality, of a mixed citizenry without sovereignty, whose reasoned independence *and* obliging equanimity were exemplary qualities for the public at large.[17]

In her colloquy *De la conversation* (*On Conversation*), Madame Madeleine de Scudéry (1607–1701; fig. 4) demonstrated the ground gained by women through the dictates of sociability. To engage and please another meant policing oneself and avoiding self-centered talk. If men dwelled on their business or their properties, and women their clothes or their children, the collective dynamic would be lost. Though located in the home, the salon shunned the domestic as subject.[18] By declaring the professional concerns of men and the maternal duties of women off-limits, conversation created an ideal forum, where the politically disadvantaged could earn distinction. In the eighteenth century, the power of conversation established the model of an *aristocratic feminism*, to use Daniel Gordon's term: "a critique both of the domestic sphere to which women were relegated and the professional sphere from which women were excluded."[19] In theory, ulterior motives held no quarter, but the salonière's achievements as interlocutor, author, scientist, or musician proved correct those feminists of both sexes who claimed that only inferior education held women back.

The salon enacted polite theater with moral and pedagogical dimensions: it forbade contempt and humiliation of the weaker or lower in rank. The discursive space of the salon could not ignore its female constituency, nor at this time did it want to. Characteristics associated with femininity—refinement, indulgence, tolerance, agreeableness—defined the basis of intellectual exchange. Feminine difference was valued positively, and not merely for the mutual benefits of gender complementarity. Enlightenment thought was not necessarily democratic, but through the salon it sustained an egalitarian commerce of ideas that by necessity embraced all of its participants.[20] If truth were no longer divined or dictated, it could be arrived at solely through open dialogue with others, from multiple points of view. "The only truly liberal subjects of conversation," Germaine de Staël believed, "are thoughts and actions of universal interest."[21]

To this end the salon formed the center of an information network: through letters and newsletters it distributed and absorbed new ideas. From the beginning, the functions and conventions of personal correspondence and salon conversation intertwined. Letters, similar to spoken exchange, were a means of communication but also a creative genre. Reading and writing allowed the subjective self to develop by addressing and responding to another (real or fictional) in conversational form.[22] The psychology of character carefully elaborated and gently revealed in epistolary sketches developed into literary portraiture, autobiography, and the novel.[23] Like the salon, letter writing blurred the lines between private and public, since it formally represented, or publicized, the individual self in relation to the world outside. Though addressed to one person, letters were commonly read aloud to others, even collected and published in journals or volumes. Correspondence augmented what was at first a small public, allowing for exchange outside the city, into the provinces, beyond national borders. In turn, letters secured the infusion of new perspectives. Snippets of conversation and the gist of an argument could be disseminated, while incoming letters were dissected *in camera*. Literary newsletters, based on the emission of information (and paid subscription), started in early-eighteenth-century salons as a group endeavor of the habitués, who wrote, edited, and had their valets transcribe.[24] The network grew through early periodicals, whose publishers and editors frequented the salons and enjoyed their counsel and protection.

Salons trafficked in the innovation and distribution of cultural forms. They hosted musical or theatrical performances, creating more intimate versions of court spectacles and a discerning audience rather than a merely obedient one. Through the private patronage of art, music, and literature, the salon was a laboratory for the new—failures and successes alike. It preceded and supplemented publications, as well as the works heard in concert halls or seen in galleries, and it offered an insulated trial space for debuts. No longer considered the sacrosanct emblems of church or monarchy, music and art were "profaned" by the same rational critical public that questioned absolute authority. The modern institution of art criticism was born in the salon, educating amateurs, begetting connoisseurs. Discursive reasoning formed the standards of quality; a lay audience was empowered to determine new standards. As one of the first institutions of the public sphere, the salon made art and its appreciation accessible to people outside the court, the church, and the upper classes, initiating the widespread "democratization" of culture.[25]

Favors and favoritism, however, continued to characterize the behind-the-scenes power of salons, where the vetting of talent attracted and influenced patrons, government officials, and free-market impresarios. Given that the domestic, feminine space was perceived as apolitical, and men were presumed to curb their public ambitions, politicking could proceed apace. With their connections to court, ennobled bourgeois, and decorated intellectuals, salonières brokered appointments to the academy, procured prestigious commissions, promoted new talent, and influenced reception. As literary or theatrical agents they wielded unprecedented influence, forming, in the Baron de Montesquieu's opinion, "a state within a state; and anyone at court, in Paris, or in the provinces, who sees the activities of the ministers, the magistrates and the prelates, if he does not know the women who govern them, is like a man who sees a machine at work, but who is ignorant of the springs that move it."[26]

PICTURING CONVERSATION

Literature was the privileged medium of record for the early salons. Few images exist of these gatherings, save those depicting musical rehearsals and performances; conversation was, arguably, resistant to visualization. Intellectual pursuits and the suspension of hierarchy were removed from the content of the "conversation

Fig. 5. Johan Zoffany (German, 1733–1810), *John, Fourteenth Lord Willoughby de Broke, and His Family*, c. 1766. Oil on canvas, 49¼ x 58⅞ in. (125.1 x 149.54 cm). The J. Paul Getty Museum, Los Angeles

Fig. 6. Jean-François de Troy (French, 1679–1752), *The Reading from Molière*, c. 1728. Oil on canvas, 28¾ x 35⅞ in. (73 x 91 cm). Private collection

Fig. 7. Carle Vanloo (French, 1705–1765), *The Reading*, 1761. Oil on canvas, 64¾ x 50¾ in. (164 x 129 cm). State Hermitage Museum, Saint Petersburg, Russia

piece"—a genre that developed in northern Europe under the bourgeoisie.[27] Here men and women appear together as family, not as peers, with children by their sides. Conversation pieces, with their emphasis on the accumulation of material things, represent the autonomy of the private sphere as conjugal home and personal property, not as an independent discursive space. By the mid-eighteenth century, in the works of Johan Zoffany (fig. 5) or William Hogarth, pictorial virtuosity enlivens the poses and commemorative purpose, but the transient pleasures of wordplay escape the materiality of the brush.

Jean-François de Troy's *La Lecture de Molière* (*The Reading from Molière*, c. 1728; fig. 6) is one of few paintings of French sociability, but it captures the artifice of aristocratic leisure and politesse between the sexes, not spirited conversational exchange. Distracted, with their glances flitting around the rococo finery, the participants are more aware of seeing and being seen than absorbed in reading the dialogues of Molière (whose play *Les Précieuses ridicules* [1659] ruthlessly satirized Madame de Rambouillet and her lot). The Enlightenment virtue of intellectual absorption, of paying attention rather than merely being amused, resides instead in such images of the rococo *fête galante* as Carle Vanloo's *La Lecture* (*The Reading*, 1761; fig. 7). These depict a small group, typically out-of-doors, listening in sincere concentration, unaware of scrutiny by the beholder, who is invited to enter the experience through like contemplation.[28] Yet these pastoral idylls of tranquil pedagogy lack the number and diversity of guests, the presence of renowned intellectuals, and the public dimension of the urban salon.

The iconic image of the French Enlightenment, Anicet-Charles-Gabriel Lemonnier's *Une Soirée chez Madame Geoffrin en 1755* (*An Evening at Madame Geoffrin's in 1755*), relinquishes the expression of gallantry for the documentary efficacy of a re-created, largely symbolic mise-en-scène (fig. 8). The haute-bourgeois patron of the *Encyclopédie* (the multivolume compendium of knowledge) sits erect at the head of the illustrious gathering, which pictures the *philosophes* Jean-Baptiste le Rond d'Alembert, Bernard le Bovier de Fontenelle, Denis Diderot, and Jean-Jacques Rousseau among other luminaries. Geoffrin (1699–1777) hosted men of letters on Wednesdays and painters and connoisseurs on Mondays, but personalities of both worlds appear on this evening, including the painters Carle Vanloo and Joseph Vernet. The actors Mademoiselle Clairon and Lekain, at center left, read Voltaire's *L'Orphelin de la Chine* (*The Orphan from China*); a sculpted bust of the author oversees the proceedings. Paintings that Geoffrin commissioned or purchased, including Vanloo's *La Lecture*, genre scenes by Jean-Baptiste Greuze, and works by Vernet and Joseph-Marie Vien, adorn the walls and attest to her

Fig. 8. Anicet-Charles-Gabriel Lemonnier (French, 1743–1824), *An Evening at Madame Geoffrin's in 1755*, 1812. Oil on canvas, 50¾ x 77⅛ in. (129 x 196 cm). Musée Nationale du Château de Malmaison, Reuil-Malmaison, France

role as leading patron of the arts. Her salon functioned also as an exhibition space and salesroom.[29] Although the men far outnumber the women (among the seven women is the salonière Julie de Lespinasse), the composition and the air of male deference leave no doubt as to who is in charge. A woman was needed "to guide us, organize us, *Geoffrinise* us," bemoaned one former habitué, the abbé Ferdinando Galiani, bereft of the French salons in distant Naples.[30]

The salonière herself was duly recognized in images ranging from encomium prints to allegories of versatile intellect and *honnêteté*. Engraved series included decorous fashion plates that acknowledge rank and wealth, and more realistic portrait busts that forsake prettified visages to commemorate women of distinction in literature, the arts, and science.[31] Large ceremonial

portraits of the *belle savante* were reserved for women of the royal entourage, such as Mesdames de Montespan and de Pompadour, consorts of Louis XIV and Louis XV, respectively, who are publicized amid attributes of their learning—books, globes, and musical instruments (fig. 9). Overall, the eighteenth-century salonière emerges as muse and patron, and only secondarily as *femme savante* or *femme auteur*. Her goddess-like demeanor, combined with the attitude of convivial engagement, inspired poet, philosopher, and viewer. She embodies the achievements of humanistic culture, not the lower realm of nature, with which woman and her biological destiny were normatively linked. Likenesses of salon women rendered by artists who were also habitués tended to capture their subjects with studied immediacy in the act of reading or singing. They perform effortlessly, while natural grace

mitigates the potential threat of their independence
and accomplishment. In Jean-Etienne Liotard's *Portrait
de Madame d'Épinay* (*Portrait of Madame d'Épinay*;
c. 1757–59), the sitter is outwardly demonstrative,
embodying in her pose and gaze the obliging reciprocity that characterized salon dialogue (fig. 10).[32]

By the early nineteenth century, representation of
the salonière as exceptional woman crystallized in the
figure of Germaine de Staël (1766–1817). Her father
was the Swiss-born finance minister to Louis XVI, and
she was groomed as a child prodigy in the famous gatherings of her mother, Suzanne Curchod Necker.[33] A
poet, novelist, and correspondent, de Staël created, in
her novel *Corinne* (1807), her own feminist heroine,
who is betrayed in love by a man too weak to support
her intellect and independence. (De Staël's marriage
to the Swedish diplomat Eric Magnus Baron de Staël-
Holstein faltered early, and she bore children from several different liaisons.) She was an important conduit
for the spread of Romanticism into France, through her
book *De l'Allemagne* (*Germany*, 1810). Painted by her
peer Élisabeth Vigée-Lebrun as her alter ego, Corinne,
de Staël is garbed in the neoclassical tunic and chiton

typical of a muse but with a difference (fig. 11). A cre-
ator herself, she is represented with a lyre and her eyes
raised upward—a deliberate allusion to the ancient poet
Sappho.[34] As the most renowned salonière and woman
writer of her time internationally, de Staël established
the modern depiction of female genius as an introspec-
tive, breeze-blown sibyl for decades to come. Only later
in the nineteenth century, under the July Monarchy
(1830–48), did the professional woman of ideas replace
the aristocratic woman of accomplishment, with a
sphinxlike gaze or masculine features not always
intended to be flattering.[35]

A PUBLIC WORLD IN A PRIVATE SPACE

With the French Revolution, the salon tradition paid
dearly for its aristocratic and feminist identities.[36]
Ideological reaction against the cultured woman, one
who forsakes her duty as mother and wife—her natural
being—for the artifice and publicity of *le monde* had
begun under the pen of Rousseau: "Women in general,
do not like any art, know nothing about any, and have
no genius." Characterizing women's speech as frivolous, he attacked salon gallantry, for it forced men to
"lower their ideas to the range of women."[37] Following
Rousseau, bourgeois critics of polite society maligned
the artificiality and effeteness of the salon and claimed it
to be the site of social decadence rather than regeneration. Gender opposition conquered gender complementarity: a weak and dissolute aristocracy, self-interested
and pandering, had characterized the feminized ancien
régime; masculine strength and reason now guaranteed
the virtuous republican order. Despite the ideal of an
inclusive public sphere, women were denied political
rights and excluded from representation in the new
constitutional assembly. The bourgeois regime legitimized exclusive power for Christian men of property
under the rubric of Enlightenment universality and
drew strict divisions between the private dwelling and
the political arena. Family life was sovereign, with the
father at the head; women were relegated to the hidden
realm of the household, and citizenship in the visible
polis was reserved for men.

The gendering of the private sphere as feminine did not eradicate the salon tradition; indeed it was strengthened in new quarters and its constituency enlarged.[38] Most women had no more or less political or judicial standing than they had had under the monarchy (some women nobles actually lost power with the abolition of feudal rights).[39] The salon allowed women to maneuver outside the univocal identity of their "inferior" sex, to operate visibly within and against patriarchal authority, and to challenge openly the asymmetrical power relations between men and women. The continued importance of the salon as an institution of modernity owes specifically to its unique relation to the public and private spheres. It belonged wholly neither to one nor the other, overcoming binary oppositions of space and gender.[40] The salon was private by way of property and limited access, beyond the eye of government surveillance or the intrusion of state bureaucracy. Like a home, the salon offered the security of kinship—one not of blood or inheritance but of common humanity and like-mindedness. Despite the supposed neutrality of the domestic realm, pure of marketplace motive and profit, the salon took on financial and managerial roles in the business of culture and ideas. Within its genteel walls individuals competed to make their mark on the world but could also unite in a common effort or movement.[41] Women fraternized and men found themselves handmaidens to culture.

As the relationship between public and private shifted from the age of liberalism to that of modern mass society, so too did the progressive role of salons. From spaces of open learning they became sites of professional careers for women; from disinterested conversation, salons turned to utilitarian agendas, becoming centers for party politics and organized dissent. By the late nineteenth century, they boosted avant-garde movements in conflict with the academy; aestheticism and bohemia flourished in flagrant disregard of Victorian morals and materialism. Once autonomous in relation to the court, the salon seceded from the bourgeois public sphere and, eventually, mass culture. And as the state increasingly infringed on private mores, salons offered refuge from the public policing of behavior. At the same time, the private happenings of the salon became publicized in the mass media. Salon circles encouraged fame and celebrity, inculcating new forms of publicity—self-promotion and image management.

Salons thrived on stereotypically feminine wiles—intrigue, mediation, pacification, and parrying—all the while building careers and agendas for innovative movements. The salonière, to use an anachronistic term that applies to the ancien régime and the early twentieth century alike, was a *powerbroker*. True, men could host salons, even if the word and the space were identified as feminine; but these same men had other opportunities in civil society. They could assume the role of dealer, impresario, and host in the gallery, concert hall, club, and café. The salon was the unique terrain for women as "middlemen"—those crucial figures in the development of modern music, literature, and art, which depended on the evaluation of the new, on the expansion of taste, and on free-market enterprise. Beyond the salon, a few women had access to a worldly forum as novelists and journalists (often under pseudonyms), but their relationship to their potential audience did not entail face-to-face encounters with people of contrary position, politicians with de facto power, or artistic avant-gardes. To be aware of the new obliged reconnoitering in the salon for pundits of both sexes.

The salonière provided other women with intellectual sustenance and access, even as men outranked them as guests in number and renown. Salons functioned as a university for women—a forum not just to nurture great men but also to compete with them. Mothers instructed daughters and the childless mentored eager neophytes: dynastic lineages of custom and guests were established. The company of professionals, moreover, afforded female writers, critics, musicians, and artists a platform for their own creativity and subject matter for their work. Excluded from academies of art and science, women established careers among formidable persons of their own choosing, even though it rendered them no pay. As authors of letters, literary portraits, epigrams, novels, and critical reviews, they received invaluable appraisals from peers. Composers and artists, men and women, had a place to perform and exhibit when suitable public venues were nonexistent or inaccessible. Gossip and exegesis, the collusion and collision of personalities, not to mention character and fame, contributed the raw material for a grand portrait of human nature and behavior. The salon was woman's muse.

Salon women were literate and highly educated or became so through these gatherings, and all but a few were relieved from the hard labor of making ends meet. (In the late 1940s, Salka Viertel was so hard up that she considered opening a goulash stand on the beach in Santa Monica, California.) Some inherited money, while others married into it, although frequently the husbands of famous salonières gained wealth or prestige from their alliance with these women notables. Like men of their class, salon women needed to be free of drudgery to be ready for action, even as they continued to fulfill the sophisticated organizational tasks of the *maîtresse de maison*. But unlike men of property, they could not work in universities, the military, bureaucracy, or civil service, or hold office or vote.[42] They were as legally and politically disenfranchised as the economically disadvantaged women on whose domestic help they depended for entertaining and professional fulfillment. (The Socialist leader Anna Kuliscioff, alone among recorded salonières, spent twenty-five minutes every morning scrubbing the bathroom herself.)[43] Only a small minority of salonières used their platform specifically to fight for female enfranchisement across class lines; instead, they seized the opportunity to compete and create as individuals in ways otherwise denied them. Privileged but restricted, salonières could merely bring the public world into their private domain, temporarily lessening the divisions between the two.

Salons and salonières embodied the paradox of their historical origins: levelers of caste in the age of absolutism, exclusive coteries that encouraged tolerance and social fusion through intellectual parity.[44] Although it reinscribed class difference, the aristocratic model had liberating potential: it had always publicized the private realm, disdained domesticity as parochial, presented opportunity for female action, cultivated feminine qualities in men, and considered wit the standard-bearer. Neither inwardly hierarchical nor outwardly democratic, salon elites thrived on independence from the majority and mainstream for their superior tone.[45] Not all salons were progressive or even influential—most were not. As we know from Proust's precious excoriations of class prerogatives, salons could close rank as much as tear it asunder. The door that could be shut in one's face was just as easily opened to an individual who had never crossed the threshold into salon meritocracy. A temporary theater of equality, the salon instigated a dialectic of equality and difference that set the stage for freedom and acceptance at large.

THE SALONS OF JEWISH WOMEN

Salons held by Jewish women first appeared in 1780s Berlin, with the dissemination of French Enlightenment ideas into Germany. Factions within the Jewish community proposed gradual modernization to relieve isolation, ignorance, and persecution; a secularized Christendom offered to alleviate personal and professional restrictions and promised eventual citizenship. In the same way that woman was perceived as inferior only because of disadvantage and oppression, by the late eighteenth century, the status of the Jews was posed, by their supporters, as a matter of nurture, not nature. Education and dialogue were the means to self-betterment and social parity. "The mind is a powerful equalizer," Henriette Herz (fig. 12), the first Jewish salonière, optimistically affirmed.[46]

Proponents of the eighteenth-century Jewish Enlightenment, or Haskalah, dreamed of being "a man on the street and a Jew at home"[47]—a concept that constituted a notable disadvantage for the Jewish woman, who had to observe strict domestic rites and could hardly stroll the cobblestones alone. As with their Christian counterparts, the first Jewish salonières were from wealthy families, many of their ancestors enjoying positions as court Jews and financiers. Once again, female power owed to economic privilege, but the Jewish upper class had its own caste features, encouraged by state restrictions. It was separate within the

community and without, distinct from ghetto coreligionists, and from the Christian nobility who were forbidden to engage in money lending. Jewish women socializing with noblemen and Christian intellectuals comprised the early salon mix and led to a high percentage of intermarriage, as the women rebelled against their still restrictive faith and the caste system of arranged unions. Through the "feminine" arts of personal friendship, conversation, and self-divulgence, these women challenged the restrictions of both mainstream and minority.

In the same way that women of the French court "tamed" the feudal nobility, the first Jewish salonières were "civilizing" ambassadors for their people. In Berlin society, they gained new status for women and Jews, as well as personal emancipation from their Orthodox households. In Germany, they were among the first literary women to publish, and they drew unprecedented gatherings of aristocrats, scholars, writers, and civil servants.[48] As arbiters of change, the salons of Jewish women were later credited with importing French sociability into a stiff and stodgy Germany.[49] Though often viewed nostalgically as temporary "miniature utopias," these early Berlin

examples were no more idealizing or ephemeral than any progressive salon, which reigned with acute awareness of the inequality of the status quo.[50]

The reasons for the phenomenon of the Jewish salonière are many. Denied the opportunity of studying Jewish law, the Jewish daughters of ambitious fathers were schooled at home (not in inferior convent schools like their Christian counterparts), learning music and foreign languages. In addition to the superior home education, the Talmudic tradition of hermeneutic interpretation—the value of intellectual life—permeated the household and influenced the Jewish woman's propensity for dialogue and debate.[51] The salonière also drew from the long-standing function of Jews as financial middlemen (one of the few professions open to them), not to mention strength of surviving by wit, negotiation, and improvisation. For a biblical nation "wandering in exile" and deemed "rootless" by host countries, the salon granted a secure domicile and a sense of belonging—a home of one's own. Yet it was simultaneously a worldly place—a center for cosmopolitans, who, like the hostess, came from other lands and identified with the international comportment of *le monde*. Centuries of ostracism and ignorance can also explain the Jewish salonière's desire to follow a tradition based on humanist education, reasoned discourse, open dialogue, and collectively determined truth.

More to the point, holding a salon, like being baptized, was the ticket to the mainstream: personal association with the upper class and intelligentsia was the swiftest means of arriving, of mastering Western European high culture, and the finest forum for achievement. Illustrious home gatherings demonstrated the assimilating Jew's commitment to *Bildung* (the fashioning of the self through classical learning) and *Sittlichkeit* (moral respectability), that is, to upholding the stalwart values of the ascending bourgeoisie.[52] Intellectual ambitions and economic freedom allowed Jewish women to excel as *femmes auteurs* in German language, literature, and music. Rahel Levin attained fame for her epistolary talents (some ten thousand letters), which epitomized the German Romantic movement's quest for self, at the same time that her

Fig. 13. Two chairs with needlepoint seats and backs by Alice B. Toklas after designs by Pablo Picasso. Yale Collection of American Literature, Beinecke Rare Book and Manuscript Library, Yale University, New Haven

correspondence propagated a Goethe cult. The Jewish salonière Fanny von Arnstein was credited with importing the Christmas tree custom to Vienna in 1814, while the Berlin music salons of Sara Levy and Fanny Mendelssohn Hensel nurtured the Bach revival. Still, as Peter Gay writes, "It took two to make Germanness credible: the actor saying his loyal lines and the audience appraising his public performance."[53]

By the late nineteenth century, with Reform Judaism established and integration advanced by generations, Jewish salonières played another role, but one equally motivated by their difference. They gained unusual prominence as artists, writers, and impresarios of modernism and the avant-garde, since they could not lay claim to the classical European heritage.[54] Felicie Bernstein's salon in the 1880s introduced French Impressionism to Berlin society, and Ada Leverson's in the 1890s partook of the rebellious British aesthetic movement. In the early twentieth century, Jewish women led concerted efforts to modernize national cultures: Berta Zuckerkandl, in whose salon the Vienna Secession was born, and Margherita Sarfatti, who single-handedly promoted the Novecento as the official Fascist style. As prominent art critics with their own bylines (a rarity for women), they extended their agendas into the mainstream press. In Moscow, Lily Brik's salon—the center of a ménage à trois she conducted with her husband, Osip Brik, and the poet Vladimir

Mayakovsky—drew the Russian Futurists and Formalists, and later the radical photographers of the *Novyi Lef* magazine.[55] The cross-fertilization of modernist currents was fostered by American salonières who lived and traveled extensively abroad—among them Gertrude Stein and Florine Stettheimer. Both produced startlingly innovative portraiture, inspired by the unorthodox ideas and the gender identities performed in their own salon ensembles.

Like generations of non-noble women before them, Jewish salonières throughout Europe emulated the tradition of French sociability, adopting its customs, language (most were fluent in French), and attributes, notably the sofa—which symbolized for Diderot the jurisdictional seat of impartial dialogue.[56] The model of aristocratic feminism and eighteenth-century style held sway in earnest homage or, by the twentieth century, in parody. To be sure, Louis XV flourishes and profiles became the stuff of mass production for those who could not afford antique originals, a sign of "taste" and pretension in bourgeois homes.[57] But for the salonière, the daybed or sofa symbolized her consensual authority and confidentiality while encouraging a relaxed intimacy and the eroticism of a conversational tête-à-tête. "On my divan Austria comes alive," boasted Berta Zuckerkandl, with no exaggeration.[58] Expatriates in Paris, Gertrude Stein and Alice B. Toklas owned two miniature Louis XV fauteuils, with their coverings in needlepoint by Toklas after designs by Pablo Picasso (fig. 13). The Stettheimer sisters dressed up their New York salon interiors with over-the-top rococo touches as they assumed the roles, according to one habitué, art critic Henry McBride, of "Madame du Deffand, Madame Geoffrin and Mademoiselle de Lespinasse" (fig. 14).[59] Even Anna Kuliscioff in Milan received on a modest reproduction Louis XV divan, functionally upholstered in green velvet; there she listened to the woes of anonymous women workers and debated parliamentary strategies with male Socialist deputies (fig. 15).

Unlike her aristocratic predecessors, however, the Jewish salonière did not dismiss her role as mother or disdain bourgeois values of family loyalty. She united the feminism of the ancien régime with the virtues of

Fig. 14. Florine, Carrie, and Ettie Stettheimer in Berne, Switzerland, c. 1914. Photographic collage with postcard. Yale Collection of American Literature, Beinecke Rare Book and Manuscript Library, Yale University, New Haven

Fig. 15. Anna Kuliscioff's divan. Wood and green velvet, 31½ x 55⅛ x 22⅞ in. (80 x 140 x 58 cm). Fondazione Anna Kuliscioff, Milan

republican parenting. George Mosse has shown that assimilating Jews benefited from one positive stereotype—an exemplary patriarchal tradition and familial pedagogy instrumental to the health of the modern state.[60] The salon promoted the accomplishments of sons and daughters, schooled them in refinement, and allowed them access to professional peer judgment and contacts at a young age. Familial alliances were extended through salon networks as sisters, daughters, cousins, and nieces perpetuated across generations and national borders what became an upper- and middle-class Jewish tradition. And Jewish salons became home bases for foreigners and refugees, significantly Stein's expatriate community in Paris and Salka Viertel's temporary domicile for German and Austrian exiles in 1930s and 1940s Hollywood.

The parents of the salonières considered here were Jewish on both sides, and resistance to intermarriage formed the self-conscious limits of assimilation. Only the "apostates" of the first generation broke with their arranged Jewish marriages to move "upward" with ennobled Christian men.[61] Reform Judaism and modernization within the faith eased earlier pressures to convert. Later, many Jews broke with all religious observance in the name of secularization, abandoning Judaism for Jewishness in culture, ethnicity, or family tradition. Nonetheless, the salonières paired with Jewish partners or, if they "misallied," did not change their religious affiliation. The strength of the bonds between salonières and their fathers, and to a lesser extent their mothers, contributed to these women's ambitions, resolve, and confidence. Many depended on parental money, long after they left home and rejected patriarchal authority, substituting both with the salon. The salonières who married achieved unions of mutual respect, with supportive husbands who took second place (or were absent) in the salon arena, achieving their own professional status outside the home. Their partners, from Karl August Varnhagen von Ense to Alice B. Toklas, accepted, even promoted, their fame and their careers (figs. 16, 17).

The Jewishness of these women was subsumed by their status as women of ideas and by their membership in the salon community, which aimed at dissolving the restrictions of any group identity in favor of individuality and pluralism. Yet the Jewish salonière inevitably became a beacon for political, cultural, and sexual renegades, for those who were refused entry into high society or were shunned by the bourgeoisie. Not by coincidence, two scandals that erupted in British and French society in the 1890s, the Oscar Wilde and Dreyfus affairs, played out in the salons of Jewish women—Ada Leverson and Geneviève Straus, respectively. Inevitably the fact of their Jewishness, in positive or negative terms, came to bear on these salons, in the minds of the women themselves, their guests, and their adversaries. They were taken as evidence of human progress and modernization or, conversely, as signs of social chaos and the feminine pliancy of the Jewish "other." Even

Fig. 16. Wilhelm Hensel
(German, 1794–1861),
*Portrait of Karl August
Varnhagen von Ense*, 1822.
Pencil on paper, 5 x 4¼ in.
(12.6 x 10.8 cm). Kupferstich-
kabinett, Staatliche Museen
zu Berlin–Preussischer
Kulturbesitz

Fig. 17. Arnold Genthe
(American, 1869–1942),
Portrait of Alice B. Toklas,
c. 1906. Bancroft Library,
University of California,
Berkeley

when they severed their ties to Judaism, these salonières were seldom permitted to forget their roots by a society that kept many ingrained prejudices.

PARVENU AND PARIAH

The salon tradition of human communion and respectful dialogue enabled Jews one generation out of the ghetto to prove "I am like you" and to insist, "therefore accept me as I am." But the latter half of the equation did not always apply. The social mask of propriety, when donned by Jews, carried an especially negative connotation; the ability to mimic Christian customs and culture prompted accusations of rootlessness and lack of authenticity. The "money-grubbing" association had stinging resonance with successful Jews, since commerce and industry were two of the few areas open to them. While prejudicial commentary issued perforce from uneducated masses, anti-Semitism also showed itself among salon habitués. Cohorts within the private realm repositioned themselves in public, following other social pressures and circumstances. "I hear . . . that Varnhagen has now married the little Levy [sic] woman," Rahel Levin's former salon guest Wilhelm von Humboldt remarked, "So now at last she can become an Excellency and Ambassador's wife. There is nothing the Jews cannot achieve."[62] Jewish salonières were an easy target for petty jealousies, class-based antagonisms, professional rivalries, and ethnic jokes at their expense. Though it may not have been intended as a personal invective against the salon hostess, a "best friend," the diffused acceptability of Jew-bashing and the stigma of new money perpetuated a class-based anti-Semitism. Seemingly respectful relationships were colored by incident, pained by secondhand gossip and open snubs.

With the rise of political anti-Semitism in the late nineteenth century, Jews were viewed as parasites or subversive forces in adopted lands and were attacked, like women, for being "a state within a state."[63] Science, medicine, and criminal anthropology established new categories of "otherness" based on race and sex.[64] Perceived as biologically inferior and culturally subversive, the figures of woman, Jew, and homosexual amalgamated into a potent "megatype" of degeneracy. Under Jewish auspices, the cosmopolitanism of *le monde* implied dangerous liaisons of miscegenation and treason. The salons of Jewish women became the target of anti-Semitic invective, seen as centers for cosmopolitanism (the code for Jews as social rummagers and congenital wanderers), subversive discourse, and debauchery. One notorious Nazi publication set out to denigrate the contributions of the early Berlin salons of Jewish women (a perverse testament to the historical importance of their gatherings), while National Socialists in Vienna decried Zuckerkandl's home as a breeding ground for "Jewish Bolshevik conspiracy."[65]

In her classic study of anti-Semitism, Hannah Arendt claims that the Jew in Western European society could not escape the condition of parvenu or pariah, imposter or reject.[66] She focuses on Jews in high society with a critical eye to what she perceives as their parvenu aspirations and self-delusion: their acculturation and class privilege failed to protect them from persecution. The salon dynamic of social belonging and exclusion accentuated the uneasy position of Jews who disowned their own heritage to mimic those of others, only to be treated as perennial outsiders. Salon Jews were "exceptional Jews" in Arendt's negative estimation; they ascended through the ranks only by leaving "ordinary Jews" behind. Nothing could be further from the squalor and insularity of the Eastern European ghetto pariah (whose population was constantly visible in migration to the West) than the aesthetic refinement of salon society. Arendt leads her discussion of French anti-Semitism through the drawing rooms of the Faubourg Saint-Germain with Proust as her witness. In search of something new, the jaded aristocracy embraced the fashionable "vice" of Jewishness, now associated with inverts and homosexuals. To please and pander, the Jew as freak or exotic induced "the complicated game of exposure and concealment, of half confessions and lying distortions."[67] More to the point, Arendt accuses economically privileged Jews of having neglected the political dimension of their difference and their persistent social inequality while

foolishly drawing attention to their seemingly inordinate wealth.

Arendt's thesis on society Jews owes much to one of her first books, a biography of Rahel Levin. In many ways a projection of Arendt's misgivings about her own assimilated identity, this biography, subtitled *The Life of a Jewess*, was completed in 1938, during the catastrophic conclusion of German Jewish symbiosis.[68] With the benefit of hindsight and the understandable anger of the personally betrayed, Arendt castigates Levin for denying her true predicament as "Jewess and schlemihl," and for the self-deceptive fraud of pandering to a society not hers by birthright.[69] Consumed by her need to be validated by others, Levin missed the outcast's only chance to live life freely: admit that she could never be one of them and refuse to disavow her essence. She failed to cultivate the self-conscious awareness of the pariah, epitomized by the critical irony of her friend Heinrich Heine: "If stealing silver spoons had been within the law, I would not have had myself baptized."[70] The conscious pariah, Arendt writes, gathers strength from marginality, scoffs at conformism, demands equality under the law, and builds his self on his own terms.[71] Only at the end of Levin's life, and of Arendt's book, does the author concede that her subject accepted her fate and her people, thus finding "her place in the history of European humanity."[72]

To say "accept me in all of my otherness" was personally and historically impossible for any woman, let alone a Jewish woman, in late-eighteenth-century Europe. It is nonetheless instructive to apply Arendt's binomial model—parvenu or pariah—to those women who came after Rahel Levin and the first generation of German Jewish salonières, whom she did not consider or did not know. To be sure, these women could be labeled overambitious arrivistes, even when they were born near the top of the economic ladder. After all, social climbing as well as social slumming, the permeation of strict and repressive boundaries, are essential to democracy. The charge of *arrivisme* takes on negative connotations only when leveled by those who want to keep those barriers in place. No longer recent arrivals, declining to convert, proud of or indifferent to their backgrounds, prominent Jewish salonières chose their own peers and did not crave acceptance by those who would judge them—only professional acclaim. Parvenus perhaps, but unapologetic.

Impervious to the dictates of either the Jewish or the Christian religious communities, these salonières fall into the category of "conscious pariahs," to use Arendt's own ideal type: female powerbrokers within the patriarchy, satirists in the press, family rebels, avant-gardes, unmarried mothers, and lesbians. The public-private space of the salon proved the finest theater for determined and establishment rebels, be they the hosts or guests. The modernist salonières lived their lives with disregard for what people might think of their domestic arrangements, outré consorts, controversial art, or politics. In the history of modern times, it is difficult to find individuals who flouted convention and societal norms more than Gertrude Stein or Anna Kuliscioff. What counted was the judgment of the self-selected illustrious circle, with its influential reach. While the prestige and friendships of their salons did not protect them from loss and persecution, they did, as Arendt would have it, leave the women's inner self and work intact.

As heads of new elites, Jewish women also had, for the first time, the power to exclude others. Nor did they fritter away their time without working for political change: many of these salons created party agendas (on both the political left and right), worked for international diplomacy, and openly defended the Jews and other oppressed groups. Within the salon, Jewish women, like their Christian counterparts, created a space of self-achievement and collective action, akin to the virtuous civic polis, which Arendt has extolled in her studies on political theory and philosophy.[73] The rise of anti-Semitism and then totalitarianism politicized these salons to an unprecedented degree—and also revealed the fragility of their networks.

The notion of failed assimilation must also be revisited. Zuckerkandl, Sarfatti, and others were driven from their native lands, but the art, music, and literature produced by and through them have remained

signature styles, and their salons became the cradles of national identities. Arendt maintained that works of art guarantee permanence in the polis, transcend physical life, and "make something immortal achieved by mortal hands."[74] What could be more French than Straus's Proust, more British than Leverson's *Punch*, more Austrian than Zuckerkandl's Viennese Secession, more Italian than Sarfatti's Novecento, more avant-garde Paris than Gertrude Stein, or more vintage Hollywood than Salka Viertel? They established legacies on their own terms, defined certainly by their gender and their Jewishness, but foremost as individuals who refused to be limited or circumscribed. The tradition of egalitarian sociability empowered, in particular, the conversation of Jewish salonières. "Politeness conforms to the principle of equality that is so often spoken of," wrote Suzanne Curchod Necker. "It is the rampart of those who cannot defend themselves."[75]

The Romance of Emancipation

HENRIETTE HERZ: A JEWISH GODDESS

In 1778, shortly before her marriage, a girl of fourteen sat for her portrait. Henriette de Lemos (1764–1847), the daughter of a prominent Berlin doctor of Portuguese ancestry, was betrothed to Markus Herz, a physician seventeen years her senior.[1] The artist, Anna Dorothea Therbusch, employed a rococo palette of pastel hues to portray the young bride as Hebe— goddess of youth and cupbearer of the gods, daughter of Zeus and Hera (fig. 18). Henriette's long, dark tresses, which cascade down her back, her pale skin, full lips, and dark eyes conform to the image of the beautiful Jewess.[2] Indeed, Henriette was appreciated from an early age for her physical charms: as a child she was called on to appear in "a blue dress with colorful flowers" when the Jewish community received royal visitors, and her extraordinary beauty reportedly distracted young men when they saw her on the street.[3]

Therbusch conveys Henriette's chaste seductiveness by means of the garland of flowers that extends downward from the pitcher to caress her thigh, and the diaphanous gown that slips coyly from her shoulder, revealing part of her breast. Henriette/Hebe serves nectar from a jewel-encrusted cup resting on a cloud, against which she leans as though it were a plush sofa; these attributes appear to prefigure the role of hostess Henriette would soon assume. Her face, which has not yet shed its baby fat, is dominated by luminous black eyes crowned with thick, dark eyebrows. These eyes, and the straightforward gaze, belie the coyness of the dress and accoutrements, which recall the props and

costumes of the theatrical performances in which Lemos participated as a child.[4]

Allegorical depictions of young women as Hebe were not uncommon in the last quarter of the eighteenth century, especially as a prelude to marriage. The French artist Jean-Marc Nattier had favored the subject as early as the 1730s, portraying royalty, aristocrats, and the daughters of the upper bourgeoisie in this guise.[5] Although it was no longer particularly fashionable in France by the 1770s, this allegorical representation was chosen when the eighteen-year-old Marie-Antoinette had her portrait painted by François-Hubert Drouais in 1773, a few years into her marriage with the future Louis XVI (fig. 19). In Britain, artists including Sir Joshua Reynolds painted numerous allegorical portraits of brides-to-be as Hebe.[6] Although Hebe—unlike Aphrodite, with her many amorous conquests—was a palatable guise for a still-virginal if seductive young woman before marriage, choosing the mantle of pagan antiquity to clothe a young Jewish woman from a traditional family seems a remarkable leap.[7] Whereas Hebe became the bride of Hercules after his apotheosis, Henriette was fated to marry the traditional Jewish hero, a man who distinguished himself by erudition rather than brawn. It was through her husband's intellectual activities that the young wife would embark on her social career, earning distinction as the first Jewish woman to host a salon[8] and, in fact, the first salon hostess in Berlin generally.[9] Markus Herz (1747–1803) had studied medicine and philosophy in Königsberg and was an author and a disciple of Kant.[10] He gave private lectures at home in philosophy and the natural sciences, which were attended by a varied audience that included the brothers Alexander and Wilhelm von Humboldt, several young members of the Prussian royal family, and the future French revolutionary Honoré de Mirabeau, an enthusiastic supporter of Jewish rights.[11] From these private lectures, Henriette's social gatherings blossomed in the late 1780s and the 1790s.

The gatherings would have been inconceivable without the new attitudes that developed during the Enlightenment and the movement toward Jewish acculturation embodied in the portrait of Henriette as

Fig. 18. Anna Dorothea Therbusch (German, 1721–1782), *Henriette Herz as Hebe*, 1778. Oil on canvas, 29½ x 23¼ in. (75 x 59 cm). Nationalgalerie, Staatliche Museen zu Berlin–Preussischer Kulturbesitz

Fig. 19. François-Hubert
Drouais (French, 1727–1775),
Marie-Antoinette as Hebe,
1773. Oil on canvas, 37¾ x
31½ in. (96 x 80 cm). Musée
Condé, Chantilly, France

reform of Jewish education, as well as general education for Jews so that they could integrate into mainstream culture. But he remained loyal to Judaism,
insisting that Jewish religious law was of divine origin
and continuing to observe Jewish rituals. The *maskilim*
promoted a revived Hebrew—as opposed to Yiddish—
and High German as the languages to be used by Jews.
Mendelssohn's translations of the Hebrew Bible into
German helped a generation of young men moving
out of the ghetto to master the language skills required
for acculturation.[12]

The Jewish Enlightenment was supported by a
new Berlin Jewish elite that had emerged as a result of
the Seven Years' War (1756–63). Since Jewish financiers were of use to the crown, they were granted a
privileged status that, though falling short of citizenship, eliminated most economic restrictions. Having
amassed tremendous wealth, their families pursued a
new cultural orientation; they adopted a lifestyle similar
to that of their Christian counterparts, assuming the
dress and language of the surrounding culture, educating their children in secular subjects, acquiring lavish
homes, forming art collections—including works with
mythological and Christian subjects—and entertaining
on a grand scale.[13] Others in the Jewish community followed suit, even if they could not afford to attain the
same luxurious style.

Concomitant with these developments in the
Jewish community, a debate on the status of the Jews
was taking place within segments of the Prussian
bureaucracy. Inspired by Enlightenment philosophy
and the example of the newly independent United
States, and motivated by the practical desire to integrate
Jews into the body politic, some liberal German thinkers
advocated going beyond the king's "privileges" to
grant Jews citizenship and civil rights. Most influential
was a pamphlet published in 1781, *On the Civic Improve-
ment of the Jews*, by Christian Wilhelm von Dohm, a
legal scholar, Prussian civil servant, and friend of
Mendelssohn's. Dohm wanted to award Jews "equal
rights with all other subjects," and thereby make them
"better men and useful citizens."[14] Jews should no
longer be subjected to punitive taxes and humiliating

pagan goddess. Abandoning centuries of isolation,
Jews evinced an interest in becoming part of mainstream German culture, while the dominant German
culture began to be receptive to the integration of
Jews: these were developments that had been percolat-
ing in the decades before Henriette Herz received her
guests. The Jewish Enlightenment movement, or
Haskalah, matured in Berlin with the writings of Moses
Mendelssohn and his circle, known as the *maskilim*
(enlightened ones). Mendelssohn argued that Judaism
was not incompatible with the rationalist philosophy
of the Enlightenment. In order to reconcile Jewish life
with contemporary German culture, he advocated

Fig. 20. Anton Graff (German, 1736–1813), *Portrait of Henriette Herz*, 1792. Oil on canvas, 32¾ x 25¾ in. (83 x 65 cm). Nationalgalerie, Staatliche Museen zu Berlin–Preussischer Kulturbesitz

resulted in wide, if gradual, reforms of Jewish religious practices by segments of the Jewish community. The first social gatherings hosted by Jewish women in Berlin represent a response to these Enlightenment movements: the gatherings provided a means for acquiring knowledge of general German and Western culture and for moving beyond the confines of the Jewish community.

Around 1783, Henriette Herz again sat for a portrait, a chalk drawing executed by her friend Johann Gottfried Schadow (see fig. 12). She looks young, her expression fresh and open to the world, but the elaborate turban covering her head indicates her status as a married Jewish woman.[16] In her memoirs, Herz expressed her dismay at having to cover her hair and mentioned a religious ruling, which permitted women to don wigs, but eventually she abandoned the wig as well.[17] During the 1780s she hosted a small weekly reading group in her home, and she was a member of the Tugendbund (League of Virtue), a secret society founded in 1787. Its members—Wilhelm von Humboldt and his future wife, Caroline von Dacheröden; Moses Mendelssohn's daughter Dorothea (Brendel) Veit;[18] and Karl von La Roche, son of the novelist Sophie—created a cult of friendship, corresponded with one another in code, and engaged in sentimental rituals.[19] These forays of Herz's into a mixed—Jewish and Gentile—sociability would intensify in the following decade.

By 1792, the date of Anton Graff's portrait (fig. 20), Herz's luxurious black hair was once again proudly displayed.[20] She was now twenty-eight years old and in possession of a radiant mature beauty, which her husband no doubt wanted to celebrate by commissioning the portrait, which he hung in his study.[21] The rococo palette and the theatricality of playing the goddess have given way to the sober image of an imposing woman in shades of black and white. Graff's rendering of the nebulous background and the simplicity of Herz's dress provide no clues as to her social status; the emphasis is on the face that charmed Berlin's most illustrious personalities. Her statuesque figure fills the space—Herz was known for her height—as she calmly gazes out at the viewer. What have not changed since Therbusch's

laws that restricted their livelihood and place of residence. Dohm claimed that the "supposed greater moral corruption of the Jews is a necessary and natural consequence of the oppressed condition in which they have been living for so many centuries."[15] Integration should be furthered by obligating Jews to keep their communal records in the language of the land they lived in instead of Hebrew. Dohm's argument made it clear that emancipation would require Jews to change customs thought to impede their integration. His pamphlet initiated a period of reevaluation of the Jews' status that culminated in the Edict of Emancipation, issued by King Frederick William III of Prussia in 1812, which also portrait are the intelligent expression in the eyes and the physical allure; despite the austerity of pose and dress, the thin gauze of the bodice is sufficiently transparent to reveal the flesh of her breast and offer intimations of sensuality.[22] Contemporary observers described Herz as "Junoesque"; she had transformed herself into Hebe's mother, from the goddess of youth to the mother of the gods.[23]

Beauty enhanced by intelligence determined Herz's success as a hostess. And beauty was not only in the eye of the beholder; it was intrinsic to her self-image, as many passages in her memoirs make clear.[24] Her physical attributes shaped the way her social contacts were realized: "As young and unknowledgeable as I was, the guests spoke a great deal with me since they assumed I was intelligent because I was pretty; certainly these conversations were not without use for me, for the people who conversed were, in general, astute, and if they couldn't always speak *with* me, then they spoke *to* me."[25] Thus Herz's education continued apace after her marriage, aided by her husband and by her guests. Her self-presentation was never as an intellectual but rather as an intelligent and kind listener. Indeed, Wilhelm von Humboldt offered her as an example of the problem of knowledge disconnected from thought: whereas she was widely read and knew many languages, he found she had nothing interesting to say.[26]

While Markus Herz excelled in the rigors of philosophical thought, his wife came into her own during the 1790s, once the realm of the emotions became privileged, as the Romantic impulse began to eclipse rationalism. She recalled in her memoirs that her husband would send visitors to her if they wanted to speak about contemporary literature: "Go see my wife; she understands the art of explaining nonsense."[27] While she embraced works by Johann Wolfgang von Goethe—she specifically mentions *Götz von Berlichingen* and *Die Leiden des jungen Werthers* (*The Sorrows of Young Werther*)—her husband remained devoted to Gotthold Ephraim Lessing. The generation gap between Markus and Henriette became even more pronounced when it came to writers with mystical inclinations, such as Novalis.

Henriette's gatherings developed alongside her husband's,[28] attracting younger guests with an orientation toward Romantic literature. Alexander and Wilhelm von Humboldt, whom Henriette tutored in Hebrew, gravitated to her.[29] The artist Schadow, who was part of her circle, recalled:

> *[In the] salon of the lady of the house, several young men . . . who were devoted to German poetry . . . put forward, discussed, recited, and criticized newly published works. Of the many names, few are remembered: the Swede [Karl Gustav von] Brinckmann, whose poems appeared in print; [Karl Ludwig von] Woltmann, who also wrote historical works . . . and the brothers Counts Dohna; the older count became Minister of State, the younger was posted to several embassies. The famous Schleiermacher only joined the group several years later.*[30]

Friedrich Schleiermacher, the most influential Lutheran theologian in Germany in the first half of the nineteenth century, became an intimate of Herz's after he settled in Berlin in 1794, and remained close to her throughout her life. In contrast to Wilhelm von Humboldt, Schleiermacher valued Herz's intellect, to the extent that he sent her his manuscripts to read and comment on. He wrote his sister in 1798 about the Herz gatherings: "No person of importance comes to Berlin without visiting them."[31] His anonymously published treatise "Versuch einer Theorie des Geselligen Betragens" (Attempt at a Theory of Social Behavior, 1799) presented an ideal of social interaction free of considerations of social rank that was clearly beholden to the aspirations of Henriette Herz, Rahel Levin, and other Jewish hostesses.[32]

Henriette Herz's gatherings came to an abrupt end when Markus died in 1803; their generous entertaining had depleted their resources, and without her husband's income she could not continue hosting her open house. When she described these gatherings years later, she noted how difficult it had been to transcend class and religion, how vast the gulf had been that separated the nobility from the Jewish bourgeoisie, so that even when they mixed socially it was not as equals. Then she qualified—perhaps with the golden glow afforded by

Fig. 21. Christian Friedrich Tieck (German, 1776–1851), *Portrait of Rahel Levin*, 1796. Bronze, 10¾ x 10⅞ in. (27 x 27.5 cm). Nationalgalerie, Staatliche Museen zu Berlin–Preussischer Kulturbesitz

retrospection—that these obstacles were to some extent surmounted: "To be sure, though, the relationships changed within our circles soon enough. The mind is a powerful equalizer, and love, which now and then does not refrain from meddling, often entirely changes pride into humility."[33] It was the particularly potent combination of intellect and eros as great levelers that would be the hallmark of many salonières who followed in her footsteps.

RAHEL LEVIN VARNHAGEN: "A CONVIVIALITY THAT IS UNIQUE IN ALL OF GERMANY"

Rahel Levin Varnhagen (1771–1833; see fig. 1) aspired to create a new sociability that would serve to remake society, and also reinvent her place in the world. For more than two centuries, she has exerted a powerful hold on the imaginations of writers and historians as a model for the modern Jewish intellectual woman, reflecting the complexities inherent in those three signifiers. In her struggle to be taken seriously as a human being and as an intellectual—despite being a woman and a Jew—Rahel Levin mobilized two weapons: the gatherings she hosted and her writing, consisting primarily of thousands of letters.

One of the young men who attended her gatherings

was the sculptor Christian Friedrich Tieck (1776–1851). He arrived there via a chain of introductions: the Swedish diplomat and poet Karl Gustav von Brinckmann (see Hahn essay, fig. 3) introduced the young Prussian nobleman Wilhelm von Burgsdorff, who brought along Ludwig Tieck, who would achieve fame as a Romantic author, dramatist, and translator of Shakespeare and who in turn brought his younger brother.[34] In 1796, Christian Friedrich Tieck executed a bronze portrait medallion of Rahel Levin (fig. 21); he used the same format to depict several other members of his circle. She is seen in three-quarter profile, looking out to the right with lively eyes, as if into a brighter future. The smooth planes of the face contrast with the animated treatment of the hair; the swirling curls are alive with movement, drawing the eye away from the rather plain face, focusing attention on her head.[35] Tieck presents Rahel Levin as a woman who thinks, a woman of ideas.

Apart from dating and signing the work, Tieck inscribed it "Rahel." No family name seems to have been necessary.[36] Tieck could not have known that his subject would embark on a series of name changes, reflecting her troubled quest for identity, acceptance, and love.[37] After her fiancé Count Karl Finck von Finckenstein broke off their engagement, and after another romance, with the Spanish diplomat Raphael d'Urquijo, had failed, Rahel converted and married the author and diplomat Karl August Varnhagen von Ense (1785–1858; see fig. 16) in 1814. When he published her collected correspondence in 1834, the volumes were simply titled *Rahel: Ein Buch des Andenkens für ihre Freunde* (*Rahel: A Book of Reminiscence for Her Friends*), and no family name appeared on the title page. The single name, employed first by Tieck and then by Varnhagen, imparted a special aura: "Rahel" evoked the biblical matriarch and indicated the extent of her fame—her given name was enough to identify her. But it also served to sever her from her history and her family, from the name "Levin," indicating a member of the house of Levi, the priestly class of ancient Israel. Rahel is presented sui generis, an intellectual and spiritual woman.

Unlike most other Jewish women in Berlin who opened their homes to visitors, Rahel Levin possessed neither great wealth nor beauty. Her plainness is evident in Tieck's depiction; though she thought he had created an accurate likeness, she was unhappy with the treatment of her chin.[38] This "plainness," this lack of beauty, has become a trope in descriptions of her, in her own writings as well as those of contemporaries. Writing to Karl Varnhagen after her death, Brinckmann recalled how "the unassuming middle-class girl, without brilliant connections, without the universal entry ticket of beauty, and without a significant fortune, succeeded gradually in gathering an important social circle around her."[39] Her accomplishments are thus deemed all the more astounding as she managed everything without beauty: how great her intelligence, wit, depth of understanding and gift for friendship, in order to compensate for her lack of beauty and wealth—this is a recurring motif in texts from the period. The matter of her Jewish identity is seldom ignored. Count Karl von Nostitz, adjutant of Prince Louis Ferdinand, described her as "a small, not pretty, but very clever Jewess." She was "natural, unforced, good-natured, full of an as it were instinctive discernment. Although her body had inherited little of the delicate and beautiful figure of her kinfolk [fellow Jewesses], her spirit did not deviate from the piquant splendor of her Oriental lineage."[40] Rahel Levin had many unusual qualities that drew people to her: penetrating intelligence, wit, tremendous curiosity about people and the world, kindness, empathy, openness, tolerance, and an almost reckless lack of fear when it came to expressing emotions. She functioned like an exquisitely sensitive seismograph for her own and others' feelings. Above all, she was a passionate and original thinker.

As with Henriette Herz's gatherings that developed from the visits of her husband's students and patients, Rahel Levin's socializing was rooted in her family and took place in the quarters at Jägerstrasse 54 that she shared with her mother and siblings. Her father, Markus Levin, a banker and jewelry merchant, had entertained a mixed group of business associates including actors, nobles, and musicians in the family home. After his death in 1790, his daughter continued this practice; although business interests no longer con-

nected the guests, they were drawn to Rahel Levin by a shared desire for open sociability and a common interest in contemporary literature, philosophy, theater, and music. The "Goethe cult," which spread throughout Germany, is thought to have originated with her, and the conversations she spearheaded in her home, furnished with a "green sofa . . . the piano between the windows . . . a small table with a few select books," and a bust of Gotthold Ephraim Lessing, reflected the Enlightenment ideals that inspired the gatherings.[41]

Gleaning an accurate impression of these social encounters is extremely difficult because of the nature of the historical documents that have come down to us. The canonical source for Rahel Levin's gatherings in the years before 1806—her so-called first salon—is a description offered by a Count S**** (Salm), which was first published in 1859 by Varnhagen, Rahel's widower. Salm described an evening in 1801: a varied group of guests consisting of nobles and commoners, military officers, actors, writers, and men involved in state affairs. Although the refreshments served were modest, the company was illustrious. Salm had been introduced to Rahel's gatherings—as had so many others—by Karl Gustav von Brinckmann. Other guests who appear in Salm's narrative are Peter von Gualtieri, an officer in the service of King Frederick William III; the actress Friederike Unzelmann; the writers Friedrich Schlegel and Ludwig Robert (Rahel's brother); Friedrich von Gentz, the statesman who began as an admirer of the French Revolution but became increasingly conservative and is now best known as the right-hand man of Prince Metternich and thus one of the architects of the post-Napoleonic reaction; and Prince Louis Ferdinand, a nephew of Frederick the Great.

Salm recalled the conversation that night: "The talk was of the theater, of [the actor] Fleck, of [Vincenzo] Righini, whose opera at the time met with the greatest applause, about August Wilhelm Schlegel's public lectures, which even the ladies were attending. The most daring ideas, the keenest thoughts, the cleverest wit, the drollest games of the imagination followed in casual and general sequence."[42] Rahel's skill as a hostess was recounted admiringly: her ability to engage all in conversation so that none felt left out, to smooth over awkward moments through humor, and to keep conversation going despite silences or lapses in good manners on the part of her guests. In short, the success of her evening was predicated not only on her own conversational skills and intellect but also on her tact and ability to manage those assembled. Salm makes it clear, however, that her empathy and concern were hardly reciprocated; the following morning Rahel commented that her guests were interested not in her but in seeking her understanding.[43]

The authenticity of Salm's text and the identity of the author have recently been questioned; Barbara Hahn suggests that the text was written, or at least revised, by Varnhagen.[44] Moreover, even if the text was solely or in part the work of this Count Salm, the author explicitly states that he wrote the text as a reminiscence after receiving the news of Rahel's death, and so it partakes of an elegiac mood. The guests mentioned in the account are all known to have frequented Rahel Levin's gatherings (except for the count himself), yet the impression created of the company is distorted. We also know of many guests who attended her gatherings from contemporary letters—although some can no longer be identified—and these intimates have been omitted from the narrative of her "salon." Although we cannot draw a complete picture of the gatherings held by Jewish women in Berlin around 1800, Hahn's essay in this volume presents a picture of what can be said with confidence about these interactions on the basis of reliable contemporary sources.

These sources highlight a number of features of Rahel Levin's gatherings that bear consideration. The poet Clemens Brentano, who after 1806 would become increasingly nationalistic, anti-Semitic, and anticosmopolitan, earlier wrote to his wife, Sophie Mereau:

Yesterday I visited the famous Mademoiselle Levi [sic], who has a not unpleasant tone in her society, it could be very agreeable if the conversation were not so slovenly; she is over thirty years old, I would have guessed twenty-five, rather short but graceful; she is without pretension, permits the conversation to take

any turn, even to the point of uncivility, to which she reacts with merely a smile, she herself is extremely kind and yet strikingly witty. That Prince Louis Ferdinand and Prince Radziwill visit her causes much envy, but she doesn't care any more than if they were lieutenants or students, if these had as much spirit and talent as those, they would be equally welcome to her.[45]

Here Rahel Levin does not smooth over awkward moments, one assumes, in the interest of authentic social discourse. Sincerity and genuine talent were privileged over social rank, despite the status of several of her guests. And as Brinckmann recalled to Varnhagen after Rahel's death, she understood that much could be learned from "bad company":

[Rahel] once reproached [Friedrich] Schleiermacher that he visited her so seldom, and [he] answered jokingly: "If only you did not keep such bad company . . ." She replied with a smile: "But that is precisely your mistake. A thinker must be able to make something of everything, in his own way. Would you yourself, with your powerful mind and all your excellent talents, have become such a great scholar and erudite man, if you had not read very many bad books. Not through these books, but by considering and working through their stupid and dull contents have you developed your specific genius. . . . Why don't you judge my bad company in the same way? Just ask Brinckmann, I have finally taught him to read and leaf through all kinds of people."[46]

"All kinds of people" of course included Jews. The relationship between Rahel Levin's Jewish birth and her salon was ever present in the minds of her guests, including her greatest admirers. If Brinckmann was on his best behavior in writing to Varnhagen, he was far more candid in a letter he wrote to Countess Luise von Voss, a non-Jewish confidante: "I can assure you that in the presence of this Jewish sofa, more wit, understanding, and flashes of brilliance are squandered in an evening than in three of our gatherings."[47] Brinckmann's admiration for what Rahel Levin accomplished—her gatherings represented a true cultural

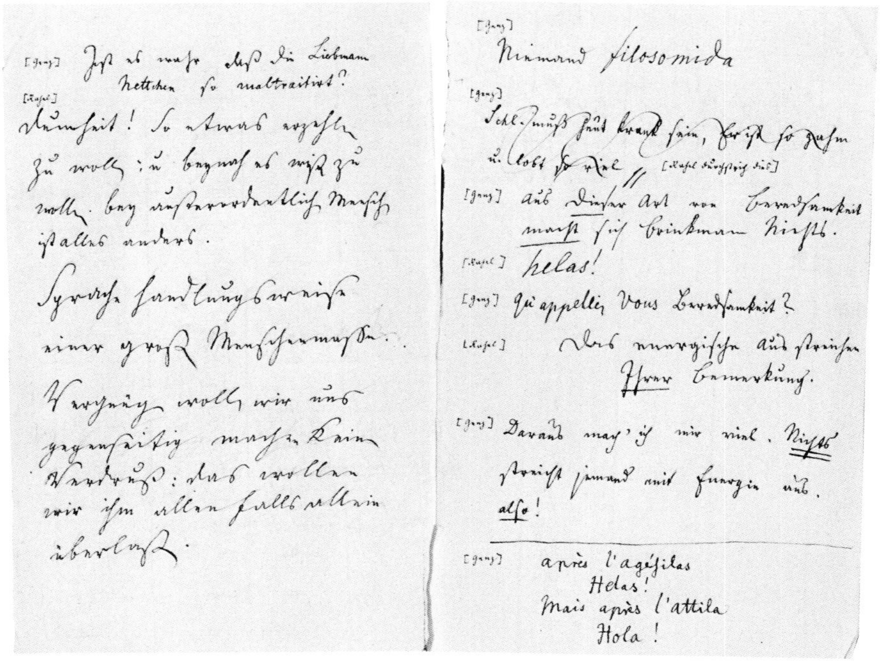

Fig. 22. Rahel Levin's notes from "August W. Schlegel's Berlin Lectures," with comments by Friedrich Gentz, 1802. Ink on paper, 4½ x 7¼ in. (11.3 x 18.5 cm). Varnhagen Collection, Biblioteka Jagiellońska, Kraków

achievement—is palpable, yet it is tinged with an insistence on confirming her enduring outsider status, not just in the singular construction "Jewish sofa," but more bitingly in the cruel exclusion of the phrase "our gatherings." Furthermore, he implies that there is something improper in the excess of ideas—a profligate intellectualism—"squandered" in Rahel Levin's rooms.

The attitudes represented by Brinckmann's delineation of "our" and its implied "their" or by Nostitz's insistence on the "Oriental" paradigm did not escape Rahel Levin's attention; on the contrary, she poignantly expressed her pain in a searing letter of 1795 to her friend David Veit:

> I have a strange fancy: it is as if some supramundane being, just as I was thrust into this world, plunged these words with a dagger into my heart: "Yes, have sensibility, see the world as few see it, be great and noble, nor can I take from you the faculty of eternally thinking. But I add one thing more: be a Jewess!" And now my life is a slow bleeding to death. By keeping still I can delay it. Every movement is an attempt to staunch it—new death; and immobility is possible for me only in death itself. . . . I can, if you will, derive every evil, every misfortune, every vexation from that.[48]

If in this same letter she defiantly proclaimed, "I shall never accept that I am a *shlemihl* and a Jewess," elsewhere she expressed resignation and the desire to make the best of it: "One will have to make do with the great necessity principle and, because nothing *else* can be done, wrap oneself respectfully in one's cloak and remain a Jew."[49] In her struggle to reinvent herself, to go beyond *shlemihl* and "Jewess," Rahel mobilized her social gatherings, as would the Jewish salonières who followed. Her explicit tool was conversation, as a means of probing her own psyche and challenging the conventions of a society that insisted on ostracizing her. This form of human communication was her primary outlet and production, in the conversations with her guests and intimates and in her vast epistolary oeuvre.[50] One can "see" the dialogue at play in notes that were passed between Rahel Levin and her friends Gentz and Prince Louis Ferdinand during a series of lectures given by August Wilhelm Schlegel in Berlin in 1802 (fig. 22): a mixture of serious engagement with the speaker's philosophical discussion, and gossip and flirtatious wit.[51]

Although one cannot claim that Rahel Levin Varnhagen's correspondence imitates the spoken conversation at her gatherings, it does provide a sense of her original use of language and of how intrinsic the principle of dialogue was to her entire project. Both of these qualities are evident in a letter she wrote to Gentz. In it she recalled his characterization of her language: "My writing often resembles aromatic strawberries, to which sand and roots still cling: you said this once to me; and I am in agreement. Nonetheless, I consider myself one of Germany's premier critics." That this natural, unspoiled state of her writing is related to spoken communication is made clear in the lines that follow: "I must express one more thing about my way of writing. . . . I would never like to write a speech, rather I prefer to write down conversations, as they actually take place among people full of life."[52] For her, writing, like conversation, must acknowledge the other, the reader-listener, the dialogical partner, without whom true communication is impossible. The letter to Gentz, like many of her epistles, opens with a precise delineation of the time and weather conditions—"drizzling rain in misty weather"—as if to bring her correspondent into the room with her through the sociable acts of writing and reading.

That Rahel Levin's original use of language was part of her effort at self-reinvention is obvious from other letters, as one to Wilhelm Bokelmann: "Language is not at my command, not [even] German, my own; our language is our lived life. I have invented my own [life], therefore I could make less use than many others of the existing phrases, that is why mine are often rough and flawed in all sorts of ways, but always genuine."[53] Rahel Levin had a healthy regard for her own literary worth. As she told the Romantic writer Friedrich de la Motte Fouqué, "I know well that I write things that are worth reading." She went on to construct a striking metaphor to express the difference between Fouqué's use of German and her own: his words are ordered, like "drilled soldiers in beautiful uniforms," whereas hers resemble an unruly gathering of "rebels with cudgels."[54] In numerous texts she marshaled the language of battle to describe her struggles, and her writing. Her words may be undisciplined and unconventional, but they are fierce combatants nonetheless. She fought to be taken seriously, to be accepted, and for a more egalitarian society, with the weapons at her disposal, namely her salon and her writing.

When actual war came and Napoléon's armies defeated Prussia, the invading forces effected the destruction of Germany's ghettos. Long-overdue reforms were enacted, including, eventually, the Edict of Emancipation of 1812. Paradoxically, these reforms and greater liberalization spurred a conservative reaction, a dramatic shift in attitude and political orientation on the part of many young German intellectuals, some of whom had been among Rahel Levin's regular guests. The aristocratic opposition to reform was epitomized by Friedrich August von der Marwitz—brother of Rahel Levin's friend and correspondent Alexander—who in 1811 warned of what the emancipation of the

Jews would bring: he argued that the Jews already possessed masses of money and that if they were to be allowed also to acquire property without restriction, then "our old honorable Brandenburg-Prussia will become a newfangled Jewish state."[55] The new nationalist, anti-Semitic, and anticosmopolitan attitudes espoused by many Romantic writers led to the establishment of the Christian German Eating Club in 1811, which excluded "women, Frenchmen, Philistines, and Jews," meaning also converted Jews. Among its members were guests of Henriette Herz and Rahel Levin: Gentz, Brentano, the writer Ludwig Achim von Arnim, and even for a time Rahel's future husband, Varnhagen.

The new mood left Rahel Levin isolated, and this situation was exacerbated by her deteriorating financial situation as a result of the war. In January 1808, she wrote Brinckmann: "At my 'tea table,' as you call it, I sit alone with my dictionaries; tea is not being served, except every eight or ten days, when Schack, who has *not* deserted me, asks for it. Everything is different. Never was I so alone. Absolutely."[56] Her problematic status as a single Jewish woman was further complicated when conflicts with her mother prompted the older woman to move out later that year: "With the opinion that I should be a queen (not a reigning one) or a mother, I experience that I am actually *nothing*. No daughter, no sister, no beloved, no woman, not even a citizen."[57]

With her marriage to Varnhagen in 1814—and the conversion to Christianity that was a prerequisite— Rahel entered a new phase in her life. The couple traveled for a number of years in connection with Varnhagen's work as a diplomat, and when they returned to Berlin in 1819, she resumed her entertaining, first in rented rooms at Französische Strasse 20 and then, from 1827, in their own home at Mauerstrasse 36 (fig. 23). In place of Lessing's bust, which had graced the Jägerstrasse dwelling, there were now busts of Prince Louis Ferdinand and Schleiermacher. Rahel's "second salon" was held in the atmosphere of decreased tolerance and conservative retrenchment after Napoléon's defeat. Varnhagen was an ardent democrat, and he and Rahel found themselves on the

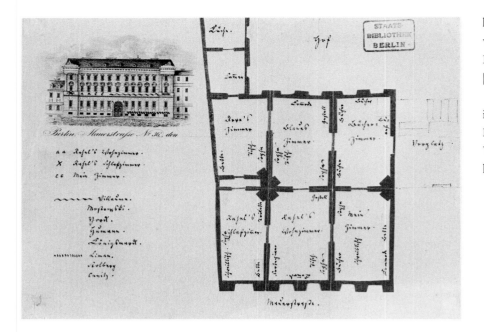

Fig. 23. Karl August Varnhagen von Ense, *Plan of the Varnhagen Home at Mauerstrasse 36.* Brown ink and green paper pasted on card, 5¼ x 7¾ in. (13.5 x 18.8 cm). Varnhagen Collection, Biblioteka Jagiellońska, Kraków

margins not only because of her origins but also because of their politics. On her return to Berlin in 1819, the year of the anti-Jewish "Hep! Hep!" riots, Rahel Varnhagen lamented the "dissipation" of her previous gatherings, "the remnants of a conviviality that is unique in all of Germany."[58] But her passion for ideas and literature ensured that she would again surround herself with talent. Her entertaining became more sumptuous, in keeping with the new style of open houses as practiced by the Beer and Mendelssohn families; she hosted one particularly elegant dinner in honor of the marriage of Fanny Mendelssohn and Wilhelm Hensel in 1829. She still drew famous guests, many of them now professional intellectuals attached to Berlin's new university, founded in 1810. Her passion for social justice attracted her to the writings of Claude-Henri de Saint-Simon, and his ideas were debated at her gatherings, which were attended by the young American Saint-Simonist Albert Brisbane. That Rahel and her gatherings could still inspire fresh ideas is attested to by the devotion of one regular in the 1820s, the radical young poet Heinrich Heine, who dedicated his cycle *Die Heimkehr* (*The Homecoming*) to her. Writing to her husband about this dedication, which initially displeased Rahel Varnhagen, who had not been consulted

beforehand, Heine admitted, "It seems to me as if I wanted to express with it that I belong to someone. . . . I shall always have written on my collar: *j'appartiens à* [I belong to] Madame Varnhagen."[59]

To some extent, Rahel had become a walking institution. Eduard Devrient, a friend of Felix Mendelssohn's, described the presences of Rahel and Varnhagen at gatherings in the Mendelssohn family home:

> *Rahel often enlivened the circle. In appearance and address plain and natural, speaking at all times frankly what her ready insight and warm feelings suggested, she yet was fully aware that her sayings were noted, and by no one more than by her husband. It could not escape observation that Varnhagen was ever watching her; even when he was at a distance he would approach when any laughter or sounds of approbation came from the quarter where she was and ask: "What did she say then?" The future recorder of her sayings was plainly visible. Thus there was a halo of self-consciousness about this couple.*[60]

Recollections of this kind contributed to the idea that Varnhagen was the chief architect of the "Rahel cult," whereas it is clear that she herself was engaged in preserving her legacy for posterity. Already in 1800, before leaving for Paris after her break with Finckenstein, she wrote with characteristic military allusions to Wilhelmine von Boye, a lifelong Jewish friend: "You see, I who never wanted to *must* retreat. I must *leave* everything that I know, that I love, all that angers and offends, stimulates and pleases me.—For nothing! Without any hope. It is a kind of death. . . . I must die; but I will not be dead."[61] Rahel further indicates her keen awareness of the value of her letters: "And, if I die, search for *all* my letters—through cunning perhaps—acquire from *all* my friends and acquaintances and tell Finckn [Finckenstein] that I *command* him, as a dead and murdered person to do it—not just from him—that he gives them and arranges them with Brinckmann. It will be an original story, and poetic. Adieu! *This,* Boye, I impose upon you this *duty.* I *will* it. One can after all demand it from a friend."[62] If

Henriette Herz was depicted as Hebe and reminded contemporaries of Juno, Rahel Varnhagen was likened to the goddess of wisdom, but also of war. In a review of the volumes of posthumously published letters that appeared in 1834, she was hailed as "a marvelous gift from heaven, the German Pallas Athena."[63]

As a project of integration and a model of enlightened tolerance, recent scholarship has made us aware of the ways in which the Berlin salons in the last decades of the eighteenth century and the first decade of the nineteenth fell short. The persistent anti-Semitic views expressed in private (and sometimes in public) by non-Jewish guests, the lack of social reciprocity—Rahel Levin Varnhagen and her fellow hostesses were seldom, if ever, welcomed into the homes of many of their regular guests—and the nationalist, anti-Semitic, anti-cosmopolitan, anti-Enlightenment reaction in Germany after 1806 all point to the failure of this experiment in egalitarian sociability and intellectual engagement. Yet, seen another way, Rahel Levin Varnhagen's aspirations set a standard: she inspired an ideal of sociability and integration, and a model for the role that Jewish women could play in shaping intellectual and cultural life in the modern world. The myth of these early "utopian" salons does not negate their legacy but rather constitutes a central part of it, especially as it was to a degree their own making. Henriette Herz's memoirs already contain many of the seeds of the idealization. And Rahel Levin Varnhagen, having played an active role in preserving and preparing her epistolary legacy, began a task that her husband continued after her death. What they could not realize in life, in their social gatherings, these women attempted to accomplish through constructing the idealized image of sociability that conformed to their aspirations. From this perspective, the early Berlin salons are not merely an all-too-brief flowering—and disappointing even at that—but the beginning of a long process and history, of Jewish women who shaped culture and politics through their salons.

FANNY VON ARNSTEIN AND CÄCILIE VON ESKELES: "SCANDALOUSLY PRUSSIAN"

The open sociability introduced by Jewish women in Berlin was exported to Vienna by two of the daughters of Daniel Itzig (1723–1799), private banker, master of the mint, and court Jew to Frederick the Great, and in 1791 the first Jew in Prussia to be granted full citizenship.[64] Franziska, known as Fanny (1758–1818), moved to Vienna in 1776 upon her marriage to the Viennese Jewish banker Nathan Adam Arnstein, who would be ennobled with her in 1798. Fanny introduced her divorced younger sister, Cäcilie (Zippora, 1760–1836), to Nathan's Jewish business partner, Bernhard von Eskeles, and the two were married in 1800.

The eight and ninth of the fifteen Itzig children who survived into adulthood, Fanny and Cäcilie received an excellent education, especially in music; another sister, Sara Levy, became a virtuoso pianist, hosted an important music salon in Berlin, and played a leading role in the Bach revival.[65] It was partially through their musical talent and connoisseurship that the two sisters established themselves in the social world of a city where Jews were shown less tolerance and enjoyed an even lower legal standing than in Berlin.[66] The emancipation of Jews in the Austrian monarchy was initiated in 1781, when Emperor Joseph II issued the Edict of Toleration. Rahel Levin's husband, Karl Varnhagen von Ense, credited Fanny's "penetrating influence" with breaking down the barriers that had plagued Vienna's Jews and enabling them to attain a "free and honored position."[67] Some have likened her role in pleading with the emperor for the rights of her people to the biblical queen Esther.[68]

In a portrait by Vincenz Georg Kininger, Fanny is depicted in the French neoclassical style (fig. 24).[69] She is seated sideways to emphasize her swanlike neck and dressed in revealing Empire fashion, with her curls piled high on her uncovered head; no details of clothing or deportment identify her as a married Jewish woman. Indeed, in pose and dress Fanny resembles contemporary female portraits by Jacques-Louis David and his students (fig. 25).[70] The most telling difference is that

Fig. 24. Vincenz Georg Kininger (Austrian, 1767–1851) after Jean Urbain Guérin (Alsatian, 1760–1836), *Portrait of Fanny von Arnstein*, 1804. Mezzotint, 6¼ x 4⅞ in. (16 x 12.5 cm). Jewish Museum, Vienna

Fig. 25. Marie-Guillelmine Benoist (French, 1768–1826), *Mme Philippe Desbassayns de Richemont and Her Son, Eugène*, c. 1803. Oil on canvas, 46 x 35¼ in. (116.8 x 89.5 cm). The Metropolitan Museum of Art, New York, Gift of Julia A. Berwind, 1953

while David's sitters eschew jewelry and ornament, Fanny wears a three-strand pearl necklace and enormous pearl earrings.[71] Though not exactly ostentatious, this jewelry signified the phenomenal wealth of the Arnsteins, which Fanny used wisely to achieve social prominence, through both her lavish entertaining and her generous philanthropy. Karl Varnhagen described her as "radiant with beauty and grace, of elegant manner and tone, of vivacious and fiery expressions, combining a sharp mind and wit with a gay disposition, well read and a master of foreign languages as well as her own . . . a most striking and strange phenomenon in Vienna."[72] Diplomat and statesman Friedrich von Gentz, referring to the Treaty of Amiens (1802), wrote that peace was superior to many things, but was "truly not more splendid than the neck of Frau Arnstein."[73]

Varnhagen noted that Arnstein's home was "open every day to numerous guests of all classes."[74] Her style of entertaining was far more luxurious than that of Henriette Herz or Rahel Levin Varnhagen; still, it enlivened the ossified customs of Vienna's old aristocratic elites. A Bavarian traveler described the refreshing graciousness of the Arnstein home: "From midday, about 12 o'clock, until late after midnight, one meets the most sought-after society here, to which one has daily entrance without a special invitation. In order to make available the 'honors' of her house without interruption, [Arnstein] never or seldom goes out, truly no small sacrifice, the gravity of which the foreigner cannot gratefully enough acknowledge. One comes without great ceremony and goes without taking leave; every burdensome etiquette of the 'higher circles' is banned; the spirit, released from the restraints of propriety, breathes freely here."[75]

This freedom did not sit well with all observers, however; much of what we know of Fanny's and Cäcilie's salons is based on secret police reports. In Austria, a far-reaching system of surveillance kept the government informed of any subversive activities on the part of the population, with the extensive use of police informants. Even some of the guests who enjoyed the women's hospitality expressed ambivalence, as revealed in a letter of 1803 from Gentz to

Swedish diplomat Karl Gustav von Brinckmann: "As much as I hold both sisters in esteem, the society in these two houses verges too closely on *mauvaise société* [bad company]. Now that I have oriented myself in Vienna in order to find better, I go there with reluctance; but it would be crass ingratitude if I were to neglect them. And of this I will never be guilty."[76] Gentz's feeling of unease suggests the diversity and lack of conformity in both salons, while his care not to offend either woman bears witness to their social power.

Fanny was renowned for her Tuesday evening musical soirées, hosted in the various residences the Arnsteins occupied over the years.[77] Contemporary sources indicate that her musicianship was much admired but that by 1796 she was no longer performing for guests: "The most difficult and complex compositions are the ones she prefers to play. . . . She seems to have lost her taste for playing because she touches the pianoforte only rarely."[78] The musician Johann Friedrich Reichardt described an evening at the Arnsteins' in 1809—comparing it to the gatherings of Madame Récamier—and noted that Henriette, Fanny's daughter, performed a double sonata "masterfully" for three or four hundred guests.[79] The Arnstein and Eskeles salons were important venues for visiting musicians. Ignaz Moscheles, a Jewish prodigy from Prague who arrived in Vienna in 1808 at the age of fourteen, performed at the Eskeles home and benefited from Fanny's connections when she arranged for the publication of his piano variations in 1810; the piece was dedicated to her.[80]

Wolfgang Amadeus Mozart and Ludwig van Beethoven were part of the Arnstein and Eskeles orbit; Mozart lived for eight months in the Arnstein house before his marriage, during which time he composed *The Abduction from the Seraglio;* Fanny attended his subscription concerts.[81] Beethoven composed a song to a text by Goethe, "Der edle Mensch sei hülfreich und gut," and inscribed it with a dedication to Cäcilie von Eskeles in her family album, a testament to the esteem in which she was held, and perhaps also a nod to her friendship and correspondence with Goethe.[82] Both

women were patrons as well as collectors and subscribers of music.[83] Fanny's most lasting contribution to the musical life of Vienna was her role in establishing the Gesellschaft der Musikfreunde (Society of Music Lovers), a charitable institution that sponsored public concerts and that remains central to the city's cultural life today. Apart from her musical talent, Cäcilie was appreciated for the exquisite cuisine in her home, which, a contemporary said, "until now one could [find only] in Paris."[84] In Friedrich von Amerling's portrait of her at seventy-two (fig. 26), she is still strikingly handsome and, judging from the books at her side, still involved in the world of ideas. Cäcilie is shown poised between her domestic interior and the larger world of the city, depicted in her hat as if having just returned home or about to depart, an allusion to her importance in Viennese public life.

As an institution, the salon was a powerful agent of cultural transfer; curiously, the Jewess Fanny von Arnstein introduced the northern German Protestant custom of the Christmas tree to Catholic Vienna in 1814. The importation of the custom was not a sign of her abandoning Judaism. The Arnsteins were particularly successful in constructing an identity composed of several comfortably coexisting strands—a strikingly "modern" achievement. Fanny, Cäcilie, and their husbands not only remained Jews but were active in Jewish philanthropies; their donation of a number of Jewish ceremonial objects to the community points to their involvement in Jewish ritual practice.[85] An account of one Christmas tree party describes many of the salient features of Fanny's gatherings—the Berlin customs; the distinguished guests; the mix of nobility, men of state, Jews and non-Jews—albeit in a condescending tone:

> At the Arnsteins' the day before yesterday there was a very well attended Christmas tree celebration. . . . Present were State Chancellor Hardenberg, the privy councillors Jordan and Hoffmann, Prince Radziwill, Mr. Bartholdy, all the baptized and circumcised relations of the household. All of the invited individuals received gifts or souvenirs. . . . Comical songs were sung, according to Berlin custom; Frau von Münch

*sang Punch and Judy songs. A procession was held
through all the rooms with distributed objects taken
from the Christmas tree. Hardenberg amused himself
no end.*[86]

This evening took place during the Congress
of Vienna (1814–15), when Fanny's salon reached its
zenith. As political leaders met after Napoléon's defeat
to reconstitute Europe, international celebrities and
powerbrokers descended on the city. Fanny managed
to attract them, including Tsar Alexander I of Russia,
with her legendary hospitality. One evening several
guests performed a *tableau vivant*: "No effort was
spared regarding preparation, decorations and lighting.
It was very successful; there were almost more people
than the space permitted: the Princes of Prussia,
Cardinal Consalvi, Prince Trauttmannsdorf, Prince
Hardenberg, Prince Hessen-Homburg, Count Capo
d'Istria, Count Keller, Count Solms. . . . They say
[that] Frau von Arnstein had the goal of surpassing the
tableaux . . . of the Court; she succeeded." Among the
other guests identified in the police report were "Lord
Wellington accompanied by the Portuguese ambassador, Prince Beauharnais (with M. Méjean) . . . Baron
Humboldt . . . old Prince Metternich."[87]

The surveillance reports imply that Fanny's and
Cäcilie's gatherings were perceived as threatening to
the authorities, not only because of the freedom of the
social interactions but also for the conversations and
opinions expressed, not least by the hostesses themselves. The sisters' abhorrence of the French and their
loyalty to the Prussia of their birth were causes for
concern: "Your Excellency! The ladies Arnstein and
Eskeles do scandalous things, hold scandalous gatherings in order to influence public opinion in favor of
Prussia. . . . In short, these women are scandalously
Prussian."[88]

Their self-identification as Prussians exemplified
the patriotic feelings of many Jews. Yet the partial
integration of accomplished families inspired a new
type of anti-Jewish discourse. Gentz's break with the
Arnsteins came after he had read—with appreciation—
the anti-Jewish pamphlet by Berlin jurist Karl Wilhelm

Grattenauer, *Wider die Juden* (*Against the Jews*), originally published in 1803.[89] Unlike earlier diatribes that
had castigated the Jews for clinging to their backward
ways and refusing to assimilate, Grattenauer took aim
at the modernizing enlightened Jews, with particular
venom directed at wealthy Jewish women who enthusiastically embraced Western culture: "They read many
books, speak several languages, use many arguments,
draw in a variety of styles, paint in all colors, dance in
all fashions, and have distinct abilities, but not the ability
to unite all these elements into a total attractive femininity. They do not learn the refined tact of the wide
world, neither in Paris, nor in Berlin, nor in Vienna, no
matter how long they spend time with princes, counts,
and other gentlemen."[90] Grattenauer set forth the insidious argument that there was nothing Jews could do—
not even convert—to remove the taint of their Jewishness. As the romance of emancipation gave way to the
hard realities of political gains tempered by crushing
disappointments, the next generation of the Berlin
Jewish elite reacted to unfolding events with various
strategies of acculturation, assimilation, and conversion. The salons were an example of these strategies for
negotiating identity, attaining social position and professional success, and achieving personal fulfillment.

The Music Salon

The language of music was key to the acculturation of German Jews, for it overcame barriers of speech and even allowed for human communion through listening together, rather than social discourse.[1] Performances that featured celebrated composers and musicians also brought people inside a Jewish home who otherwise would not have approached the door. Two of the foremost music salons of the Berlin Biedermeier period were hosted by Jewish patrons and musicians.

Amalie Beer (1767–1854) was the daughter of the richest Jew in Berlin,[2] and her husband, Jacob Herz Beer (1769–1825; fig. 27), amassed his own huge fortune as a sugar refiner and financier, so that by 1815 he had become the wealthiest man in the city. She used her wealth and influence to benefit her compatriots and Berlin's Jews, to modernize Jewish religious practice through her support of the Reform movement, and to promote the careers of three of her four sons.[3] Jacob Meyer (1791–1864), as Giacomo Meyerbeer, became one of the nineteenth century's leading composers; Wilhelm (1797–1850), a businessman and banker, made significant discoveries as an astronomer; and Michael (1800–1833) achieved success as a poet and playwright.[4] Her second son, Heinrich (1794–1842), was a notorious spendthrift, known largely for his friendship with Georg Wilhelm Friedrich Hegel.[5] None of the family converted, and Beer alone among Jewish hostesses played a role in the modernization of the Jewish religion. Beer's sense of civic responsibility, noblesse oblige, and royal hospitality, combined with her maternal devotion, earned her the epithet "The Queen Mother."[6]

Johann Kretschmar's portrait (c. 1803; fig. 28) shows her seated in a landscape—a departure from the typical depiction of hostesses in domestic interiors. The pose, with one hand raised to the shoulder and fingers caressing the shawl, is a variation on the Roman figure of Pudicitas, which, as a personification of modesty and virtue, was a fitting antique prototype for a portrait of a young matron with a strong sense of family and civic duty.[7] Beer's contemplative expression and the dramatic landscape with its distant vista reflect a new expressive mode, similar to that in Pierre-Paul Prud'hon's *Portrait of the Empress Josephine* (1805; fig. 29). The Romantic image of woman in nature projects Beer out of the drawing room and into the wide world, eager to take her place on a broader stage.

The desire to venture forth was not without considerable risk, as the fate of another family portrait makes clear. Amalie and Jacob Beer's firstborn son made his public debut as a pianist in 1801. To commemorate opposite page:

Fig. 27. Attributed to Johann Heinrich Schröder (German, 1757–1812), *Portrait of Jacob Herz Beer*, c. 1797. Pastel on parchment, 25¾ x 20⅞ in. (65 x 53 cm). Stiftung Stadtmuseum Berlin, Hans-und-Luise-Richter-Stiftung

Fig. 28. Johann Karl Kretschmar (German, 1769–1847), *Portrait of Amalie Beer*, c. 1803. Oil on canvas, 38¾ x 28 in. (98.5 x 71 cm). Stiftung Stadtmuseum Berlin, Hans-und-Luise-Richter-Stiftung

this triumphal event, his parents commissioned a life-size portrait of him from the court painter Friedrich Georg Weitsch, who depicted the elegantly attired prodigy standing before a piano with scores by Mozart and Franz Lauska (1802; fig. 30). When the portrait was exhibited publicly at the Academy of Arts, the anti-Jewish propagandist Karl Wilhelm Grattenauer raised a protest, and the Beers removed the painting to their home at Spandauer Strasse 72.[8] Grattenauer was affronted by the Beers' attempt to realize the promise of emancipation—to live privately as Jews but to play a visible role in the city's public life. If this was not to be permitted, Jews like the Beers would have to carve out a new sphere for their family; they did not simply retreat to the private sphere of the home but rather transformed it, through the salon, into a liminal space, poised between controlled visibility and social discretion.

Amalie Beer organized a splendid salon where many of the best European musicians and singers of the day performed, among them Carl Maria von

Weber, Muzio Clementi, Johann Nepomuk Hummel, Ignaz Moscheles, Friedrich Kalkbrenner, Louis Spohr, Niccolò Paganini, Henriette Sontag, Angelica Catalani, and Wilhelmine Schröder-Devrient (fig. 31). The luminaries of Berlin's musical life—Carl Friedrich Zelter, director of the Singakademie and Giacomo's composition teacher; Johann Friedrich Reichardt, the opera orchestra concert master; Bernhard Anselm Weber, a composer and the director of the Royal Opera; and the court musician Vincenzo Righini, who gave singing lessons to Amalie and her sons—all participated in the salon. An imposing hall for concerts that could accommodate large audiences was enlarged and paneled in pine in the Beer home in 1811.[9] While music was Amalie's primary passion—she was a member of the Singakademie, aside from having studied singing and supervising her sons' musical training—theater was also presented at the salon. Jacob Beer was a founder of the Königstädtische Theater, and the Beers, like many Berlin Jews at the time, were theater enthusiasts.[10] The

renowned actor August Wilhelm Iffland gave readings during the French occupation of the city.[11] Together with musicians, actors, and theater directors, salon guests included statesmen, diplomats, aristocrats, artists, and writers. Apart from the first-class cultural offerings, it was the Beers' famous hospitality that drew guests, as noted by one noble, the Prince Pückler: "There is far more discernment, talent and knowledge to be found there, and also the food is better, since these people have more money than our impoverished aristocracy."[12]

In Amalie Beer's salon, her talented sons were afforded the opportunity of performing for prestigious audiences in a sheltered environment, of making contacts and testing their mettle; once they had achieved fame, they became part of the attraction. Michael (fig. 32) read his early writings to guests, and his success in having his first play, *Klytemnestra*, produced when he was not yet twenty is evidence of the excellent connections he forged. His one-act tragedy *Der Paria*, which premiered in Berlin in 1823, dramatizes the fate of an

Indian ostracized by the cruel caste system; the work's plea for an end to prejudice was understood by many contemporaries as a reference to the plight of the Jews. When the pariah declares, "Would that I could only be a human among humans!—Alas! . . . Treat me as an equal and see if I am like you! I have a fatherland and will defend it,"[13] audiences heard an echo of the patriotism of Jews—Wilhelm Beer among them—who had volunteered to fight in the Wars of Liberation against the French.[14]

By the time Michael Beer wrote *Der Paria*, the obstacles to full Jewish equality had become clear. The "Hep! Hep!" riots of 1819, though they did not reach Berlin, were nonetheless deeply disturbing. Likewise, the theatrical farce *Unser Verkehr* (*Our Business*), which attacked Jewish acculturation through mean-spirited stereotypes, had been presented in Berlin in 1815. More devastating than the play were the popular prints based on it that caricatured Jews, including cultivated Jewish women, which were displayed prominently in book-store windows (fig. 33).[15]

Fig. 33. Popular print with anti-Semitic caricature illustrating the theatrical farce *Unser Verkehr*, Germany, c. 1815

Fig. 34. Drawing of the Reform Synagogue in the Beer home at Spandauer Strasse 72 by Isaak Markus Jost in a letter to S. M. Ehrenberg, September 30, 1817. Ink on paper, 9½ x 7¾ in. (24.2 x 19.5 cm). Aa: entrance for men; Ab: entrance for women; a: window; B: organ and choir; C: seating for men; D: seating for women; F: seating for the magnates; G: baldachin; and H: altar. Leo Baeck Institute, New York

Like her son Wilhelm, Amalie demonstrated her patriotism during the wars against the French, organizing benefit concerts, performances, and exhibitions to raise money for wounded Prussian soldiers. In recognition of her service, she was awarded the prestigious Luisenorden in 1816 by King Frederick William III. The decoration normally took the form of a cross, but the king presented a medal with an alternative design to Amalie. Although this may have been a sign of respect for the feelings of a Jewish woman who would not want to wear a cross, it seems that discrimination rather than cultural sensitivity lay behind the gesture; the king felt that a Jew should not be allowed to wear a cross. Indeed, the Beers interpreted the "special" medal as a humiliating reminder of their difference.[16] Nevertheless, as she was the only Jew in Berlin to be admitted to an exclusive group of women with close connections to the court, the Luisenorden greatly increased Amalie's social standing.

Despite the many conversions in their milieu—among salon guests and other hostesses—the Beers remained loyal to Judaism; they played a critical role in the controversy over religious reform that gripped the Berlin Jewish community during the second decade of the nineteenth century.[17] Spandauer Strasse 72 may be the only residence that hosted a salon and a synagogue simultaneously. Jacob Beer invested an immense sum of money in late 1815 to transform a space in their home into a synagogue, in order to accommodate the growing number of Berlin Jews who preferred the new Reform services, characterized by organ, choir, and sermons in German. In an account of the Yom Kippur service held in the "Beer Temple" in 1817, the Jewish scholar Isaak Markus Jost described the arrangement and the synagogue furnishings (fig. 34), the lavish decoration donated by the Beers: "The central section is romantically adorned, abounding in golden tassels, gold-covered columns, gold-embroidered silk curtains, golden crowns."[18] The silk Torah curtain that was later passed down for generations in the Beer/Meyerbeer family may have hung in the synagogue (fig. 35). Meyerbeer and two Christian composers connected to the Beer salon, Zelter and Weber, composed music for the services.[19] Apart from the Beer family, the only person known also to have attended both the salon and religious services at the Beers' is Heinrich Heine. With the capacity to hold a thousand worshippers, the temple —like the salon—straddled the border between private and public. The synagogue was closed down in 1823 by royal decree, as the king sought to discourage religious reform in the Jewish community and thereby exercise more pressure on Jews to convert.

Around 1820, the Beers moved their residence to a luxurious villa away from the city center in the Tiergarten district, on "in den Zelten," at the edge of the park. The villa had originally been their summer residence—Weber had been a guest there in 1816—but was winterized by 1818; over the years additional wings were added, with a large reception room measuring nearly 460 square feet. After his father's death in 1825,

Fig. 35. Torah Curtain, nineteenth century. Silk embroidered with metal threads and appliqué, 72½ x 49¾ in. (184 x 126 cm). Stiftung Stadtmuseum Berlin, Hans-und-Luise-Richter-Stiftung

Fig. 36. Cup and Saucer with Monogram A[malie] B[eer], c. 1840. Porcelain. Cup: diam. 3¾ in. (9.2 cm); saucer: diam. 5⅞ in. (15 cm). Stiftung Stadtmuseum Berlin, Hans-und-Luise-Richter-Stiftung

Wilhelm and his family joined Amalie in the villa, where he installed a state-of-the-art observatory on the roof; his presence ensured that the Beer gatherings now included scientists.[20] The salon seems to have been conducted with more pomp after Amalie became a widow; certainly the gala reception rooms on the ground floor were suited to entertaining large assemblies.[21] One guest, Felix Eberty, recalled: "When we entered the rooms where [Amalie Beer] received her visitors, which considering the period were extremely ornate, we felt very festive. From the small boudoir, dimly lit through colored-glass windows, a set of open steps led to a well-kept glasshouse full of flowering exotic plants. Attached to that were baths and delicate interior gardens with glass cupolas . . . all things which in those years could not be found in private homes."[22] All that is known to survive of the villa's magnificent furnishings are a cup and saucer in neo-rococo style, bearing Amalie Beer's monogram (fig. 36).

Despite the opulent surroundings, many of the old attractions of the Jewish salons—the diversity of the guests, the basic informality—remained: "I prefer to be at the Beers', because one is received there so naturally and amiably . . . Jewish good-natured liberalism holds sway to a high degree . . . one sees people from all walks of life; everyone can do what he wants: play, sing, or recite."[23] Not all impressions were positive, however; Ludwig Börne described Amalie Beer as "an old Jewess with a nasal twang" and wrote a mocking report of an evening at the villa in 1828: "Today there was a so-called smaller party, and yet there were thirty people at table . . . officers, actresses, and hangers-on of all kinds. They live in the Tiergarten, far from the city. [Marianne] Saling said to me that she emancipated herself from this house, since it was a long way [to get] there and not much to brag about."[24] Börne's snide remarks suggest the tensions between Jews who had converted—such as Börne—and those who had not.

Amalie also hosted musical soirées on a grand scale, such as an evening in February 1840 described by the artist Johann Gottfried Schadow, with more than two hundred fifty in attendance, printed programs, and singers performing "enchanting" music.[25] The following

Fig. 37. Eduard Magnus
(German, 1799–1872),
*Portrait of Felix Mendelssohn
Bartholdy*, 1840. Oil on can-
vas, 24 x 18 in. (61 x 45.7 cm).
Leo Baeck Institute, New
York

Fig. 38. Moritz Daniel
Oppenheim (German, 1800–
1882), *Portrait of Fanny
Mendelssohn Hensel*, 1842.
Oil on panel, 16½ x 12¾ in.
(42 x 32.5 cm). Collection
of Daniel M. Friedenberg,
New York

year, Baroness Willmar, the wife of a Belgian diplomat,
reported: "Comfort, that which is pleasant, and that
which is useful are all united here. Frau Beer is already
advanced in age, she loves the great wide world, luxury,
and, above all, music."[26] Marianne Spohr, wife of Louis,
described a dinner in July 1845 of more than twenty
courses, in the garden pavilion, with lively conversation
in the "Berlin style, full of wit and wordplay."[27]

Amalie Beer did not rule via intellect.[28] She created
one of Berlin's most brilliant salons by using her wealth,
love of music and literature, beneficence, and fundamental kindness to attract the best artists and to provide
her guests with warmth and generous hospitality. Her
goodness impressed even the cynical Heine, who noted:
"No day passes without her helping the poor; it even
appears as though she could not go to sleep without
having done a noble deed. In the process she does
not discriminate between religions, giving to Jews,
Christians, Turks, and even infidels of the worst kind."[29]

FANNY HENSEL, NÉE MENDELSSOHN: THE SALON AS MUSE

> *I cannot tell you, my dear Fanny, how pleased I am
> by your plan for the new Sonntagsmusik. It's a bril-
> liant idea and I implore you in God's name not to
> let it slip into oblivion; instead you must ask your
> nomadic brother to compose something new for you.*[30]

With this letter of 1831, Felix Mendelssohn (1809–1847;
fig. 37) encouraged his sister Fanny Hensel (1805–
1847; fig. 38) in her plan to revive the family's Sunday
musicales, which had been discontinued in 1829 when
Felix left home and Fanny married. The piece he was
inspired to compose—*The First Walpurgisnacht*, based
on Goethe—would be one of the most frequently performed during the years of Fanny's *Sonntagsmusiken*.
Fanny built on the family legacy: her mother, Lea
Salomon Mendelssohn, was a granddaughter of the
prominent banker Daniel Itzig, and several of Lea's
aunts—among them Fanny von Arnstein (see fig. 24)
and Cäcilie von Eskeles (see fig. 26), for whom Fanny
Cäcilie Mendelssohn had been named—had organized
important music salons. Her paternal aunt Dorothea
Mendelssohn Veit Schlegel had been part of the circle
of Henriette Herz and Rahel Levin Varnhagen. Fanny's
parents had hosted a weekly musical salon where both
she and Felix performed; here Felix had the chance to
gain wider exposure for his compositions.[31] For Fanny,
who was as gifted as her younger brother, her parents'
gatherings were crucial to her musical education and
development. Perhaps following this example, she conceived of the family's Sunday music salons as an opportunity for her own musical self-expression. Assuming
responsibility for the salon in 1831, she programmed
each concert, played the piano, conducted, and composed
music. She derived great satisfaction from the musicales;
as she wrote in her diary on October 4, 1831: "My
Sonntagsmusiken are really thriving and bring me great
joy. Yesterday a new [piece] of mine was rehearsed."[32]

Fanny Hensel's talent and energy guaranteed that
her musicales became one the most important sites for
music-making in Berlin, and for hearing unusual repertoire superbly performed. Perhaps even more significant

for the history of the salon, she harnessed the power of this institution to stimulate her artistic development as composer; and in playing, conducting, and programming she assumed the role of impresario—perhaps the first woman to do so. Fanny Hensel transformed the salon into her muse.

Although she faced restrictions of gender, class, and family background, Fanny brilliantly mined the potential of the salon to realize her ambitions; the constraints on her may, paradoxically, have provided the freedom to experiment, without the demands and vulnerability that come with public scrutiny. Fanny received an excellent general and musical education, studying first with her mother and then with the best musicians in Berlin, Carl Friedrich Zelter for composition and theory, Ludwig Berger for piano. She developed into an accomplished pianist and composer, yet her family deemed a public career in music unacceptable.[33] In an oft-cited letter addressed to his fifteen-year-old daughter, Abraham Mendelssohn expressed his conviction that music could never be Fanny's profession, even though he thought she had adequate talent: "Music will perhaps become a profession for him [Felix], while for you it will and should always be only an ornament, never the foundation of your being and doing."[34] On her twenty-third birthday he reminded her, "You must shape yourself more seriously and diligently for your real profession, for the only profession of a girl, that of a housewife."[35]

In 1816, Abraham and Lea had all four of their children baptized; they would wait until 1822 to convert. Many Berlin Jews were converting during these years, in what has been called a "crisis."[36] Whereas his sister Dorothea converted for love and out of conviction, Abraham's actions reflect the strains facing the Berlin Jewish community in the wake of emancipation. By converting their children to Lutheranism, the dominant confession in Prussia, and adopting the name Bartholdy, the elder Mendelssohns were, perhaps naively, seeking to make sure that they would be unfettered by legal restrictions and anti-Jewish prejudice. Though the 1812 Edict of Emancipation had granted Jews new civil rights, these were incomplete and soon came under

threat in the aftermath of the Napoleonic Wars. Indeed, in 1816, prominent Prussian officials had increasingly attacked the edict, advocating that it be rescinded, and popular opinion, as seen in the success of the play *Unser Verkehr*, was not sympathetic to acculturating Jews.

That Abraham and Lea saw conversion as a question of societal demands and not of religious conviction is evident from the letter Abraham sent to Fanny on the occasion of her confirmation in 1820; he tells her that she was baptized because Christianity "is the creed of most civilized people, and contains nothing that can lead you away from what is good, and much that guides you to love, obedience, tolerance, and resignation, even if it offered nothing but the example of its founder, understood by so few, and followed by still fewer. . . . By pronouncing your confession of faith you have fulfilled the claims of *society* on you."[37]

Fanny Hensel demonstrated a sense of loyalty and pride to the Mendelssohn name and family history, and jokingly referred to herself as "a soul of Jewish descent."[38] More relevant for the choices she made in pursuing her music and shaping her salon, the family was still perceived as Jewish by contemporaries. Abraham's sensitivity to this appears in a scolding letter he sent to Felix after he performed in London as "Mendelssohn" rather than "Mendelssohn-Bartholdy," or "Bartholdy": "There are as few Christian Mendelssohns as there are Jewish [Confuciuses]. If you are called Mendelssohn you are *eo ipso* a Jew and that does not suit you, if only because it is not true."[39] Even though Felix and Fanny had converted, they were still subjected to anti-Jewish sentiment. A particularly hurtful instance occurred when Zelter's correspondence with Goethe was published in 1833–34, and Zelter's disdainful remarks concerning the Mendelssohns' Jewish roots were made public. The disappointment was considerable, especially as Zelter had been Fanny and Felix's teacher and friend. Zelter said of Felix: "While he is certainly the son of a Jew, he is no Jew himself. . . . It would really be a rare thing [*eppes Rores;* Yiddish] for the son of a Jew to become an artist."[40] Fanny and her sister were described as "the Old Testament's youngest grandmothers." Fanny told Felix that the publication

Fig. 39. Wilhelm Hensel (German, 1794–1861), *Self Portrait*, 1829. Pencil on paper, 8¾ x 6¾ in. (22.2 x 17.1 cm). Kupferstichkabinett, Staatliche Museen zu Berlin–Preussischer Kulturbesitz

Fig. 40. Fanny Mendelssohn Hensel, *Der Maiabend* (*May Evening*). Song on a text by J. H. Voss. Autograph with a watercolor vignette by Wilhelm Hensel. Mendelssohn-Archiv, Staatsbibliothek zu Berlin–Preussischer Kulturbesitz

of the letters had "completely and forever poisoned my feelings for a man that I was truly fond of and would have gladly continued to respect."[41]

Felix's Jewish birth also harmed his professional advancement.[42] By restricting herself to playing music within the shelter of her home, Fanny avoided confronting much anti-Jewish sentiment. She sang in the chorus of Felix's legendary conducting of J. S. Bach's *Saint Matthew Passion* in Berlin in 1829. On another occasion she performed her brother's music at a benefit concert. Apart from these rare public appearances, her music-making took place in the grand house at Leipziger Strasse 3, which the Mendelssohn family had occupied since 1825. After her marriage to the court painter Wilhelm Hensel (fig. 39) in 1829, the couple lived there with her parents. Wilhelm encouraged Fanny to create: "My husband has given me the duty of going to the piano every morning immediately after breakfast, because interruption upon interruption occurs later on. He came over this morning and silently laid the paper on the piano, and five minutes later I called him over and sang it to him exactly as it [later] appeared here on the paper."[43] Many of the sheets of Fanny's compositions are tangible expressions of an artistic collaboration between husband and wife, with Wilhelm Hensel providing vignettes that illustrate and complement his wife's work. On the autograph sheet of Fanny's lied "Der Maiabend" ("May Evening"; fig. 40), to a poem by Johann Heinrich Voss, which she composed two years before their marriage, Wilhelm's drawing of young lovers seated beneath a tree illustrates the song's opening lines and evokes its concluding phrases: "Enveloped by the perfumes of May, / Under the blossoming tree's luminous shade . . . In sweet thoughtfulness the maiden sat / And whispered, shall we go, and went not."[44] The tree that shades the couple also spreads its protective leaves over the musical composition and buttresses the first bars of the song, unifying the three lines of music for voice and both hands of the piano.

Conversations of music, word, and image were reflected as well in Fanny's salon, in the performances of lieder, oratorios, instrumental music, and tableaux vivants. Wilhelm Hensel collaborated on the visual

aspects of performances, which were often quite complex in costume, setting, and size of the chorus, and he made portraits of performers and guests. His delicate pencil renderings, filling more than a thousand sheets in numerous albums, constitute a who's who of culture, politics, and society, of both Berliners and those who visited the Hensels while passing through the city.[45] Perhaps influenced by the dialogical principle of the salon, most of the drawings bear not only Hensel's signature and the date but also an inscription by the sitter. On the sheet where Hensel drew his portrait (fig. 41), Heinrich Heine wrote, "Eh bien, cet homme c'est moi!";[46] and the poet Michael Beer added rhyming lines: "Wenn dies Gesicht / Mit Freundes Augen zu dir spricht / so lügt es nicht" (When this face speaks to you with friendly eyes, it is not lying).

The Sunday musicales took place between eleven in the morning and two in the afternoon. Saturday evening was usually devoted to rehearsals. Fanny played the piano and conducted. Her letters and diary entries suggest how varied the programming was, in terms of the music performed and the nature of the

audience. On several occasions, the musicales attracted such large audiences that although they remained private—by invitation only—they took on the flavor of concert performances and had a measurable impact on Berlin's cultural life. Fanny's diary entry of July 8, 1839, relates activities of early 1838: "I regularly made music and kept notes on my repertoire. These morning entertainments reached their greatest brilliance in the winter; it is incredible how people pushed in and we regularly had to turn some away because our rooms were always overcrowded. Often the singers had no room to sit, barely could stand. Novello sang a number of times; Fassmann introduced herself to me and offered to sing; Decker was in excellent voice. A performance of Titus in which these three and Curschmann sang, had the greatest resonance. That winter I also played in public, in the so-called amateur concert. Altogether we had more company than ever before."[47]

If there were many guests, the performances took place in a spacious room bordering the garden (fig. 42), which measured 46 by 25 feet and could accommodate up to three hundred people. Over the years, a glittering array of musical celebrities came to listen, from Clara Schumann and Charles Gounod, whom Fanny and Felix had befriended during their sojourn in Rome (1839–40), to Franz Liszt and the singer Giuditta Pasta. The composer Johanna Kinkel recalled: "During the warm seasons the glass doors were left open, and during the intermissions singers and guests wandered beneath the . . . large trees, which stretched nearly to the city wall. Hensel's atelier was adjacent to one side of the music room, and through the French doors one could see several of his historical paintings."[48] Thus Hensel's art was part of the experience of Leipziger Strasse 3–for salon guests and residents as well.

For a smaller number of listeners and musicians, a more intimate venue in the home would be chosen.[49] Fanny described the summer of 1838 as a period of making music only with family and close friends: "We actually made music; but only among ourselves, since because of Wilhelm's absence I did not want Sunday parties. A few times we had a choir in the evening, when Felix's new psalms were sung and he frequently

played."[50] In contrast to the large *Gartensaal*, Fanny's music room provided privacy for her daily composing, rehearsing, and playing with a small group in attendance (fig. 43). This room derived its warmth from the wood floors, green walls and plants, light streaming through large windows, and the many paintings on the walls. The simple furnishings—a piano, a desk, a few chairs—and the cross on the table directly opposite the piano impart a sense of seriousness of purpose.

Fanny programmed a great deal of her brother's music, even if he was not there to perform. His *Saint Paul Oratorio* received its Berlin premiere at a *Sonntagsmusik*, and Fanny supervised rehearsals for a subsequent public performance at the Singakademie. Her frequent scheduling of works by Beethoven has been linked to the universal aspects of his music that transcend any specific religious faith, what Beatrix Borchard has called "a supraconfessional world religion."[51] Works by Mozart, Bach, Franz Joseph Haydn, and to a lesser degree Louis Spohr were also performed regularly.

Fanny died suddenly, at the age of forty-one, a few hours after collapsing while conducting one of her favorites, Felix's *Walpurgisnacht*, during a *Sonntagsmusik* rehearsal.[52] Her place in Berlin's musical life was acknowledged in the obituaries that appeared in the press: "Fanny Hensel was an artist in the most exalted sense of the word. . . . Just as she shone as a gifted and accomplished pianist, so do the works only recently published under her own name testify to that heartfelt depth of feeling . . . fundamental to a lofty and noble creation."[53]

Fig. 42. Sebastian Hensel (German, 1830–1898), *Garden House at the Mendelssohn Residence at Leipziger Strasse 3*, 1851. Pencil and watercolor on paper, 8¼ x 11 in. (21 x 28 cm). Mendelssohn-Archiv, Staatsbibliothek zu Berlin– Preussischer Kulturbesitz

Fig. 43. Julius Helfft (German, 1818–1894), *Fanny Hensel's Music Room at Leipziger Strasse 3*. Watercolor and pencil on paper. Collection of Frau Dr. Luise Hackelsberger, Ebenhausen, Germany

The Literary Salons
of the Belle Époque

ADA LEVERSON:
"THE SPHINX OF MODERN LIFE"

On the morning of May 19, 1897, Oscar Wilde was released from prison, after having served two years with hard labor for "gross indecency." He was greeted by a small group of loyal friends, among them Ada Leverson (1862–1933; fig. 44), whom he addressed with the nickname he had given her: "Sphinx." "Sphinx, how marvelous of you to know exactly the right hat to wear at seven o'clock in the morning to meet a friend who has been away! You can't have got up, you must

Fig. 44. Ada Leverson, 1890s. Collection of Francis Wyndham, London

have sat up."[1] Whereas most of Wilde's acquaintances —and many of his friends—had deserted him after his arrest, Ada and her husband, Ernest, had offered him a place to stay when no hotel would take him. In the nursery at their home at 2 Courtfield Gardens in South Kensington, Wilde found temporary refuge between the opening of his second criminal trial on May 20, 1895, and his conviction for committing homosexual acts on May 25. For a woman who once claimed that the thing she especially feared was scandal,[2] Ada Leverson demonstrated social courage, unshakable loyalty, a gift for friendship, and strength of character. These human qualities, enlivened by an extraordinary wit, had attracted glittering figures from London's art and theater worlds to her salon during the 1890s. As her publisher Grant Richards recalled:

> To the young man of the 'nineties, one of the most important things that could happen was a meeting with . . . Ada Leverson, the Egeria of the whole 'nineties movement, the woman whose wit provoked the wit in others, whose intelligence helped so much to leaven the dullness of her period, the woman to whom Oscar Wilde was so greatly indebted, the authoress of a half-dozen novels which the world should not let die, so truly do they mirror their years.[3]

Anxious to liberate herself from parental control, nineteen-year-old Ada Beddington had married Ernest Leverson, a diamond merchant twelve years her senior. Although Judaism seems to have played a very minor role in their upbringing, the couple married within the faith and according to traditional rituals. Ernest's father "believed that Jews who were lucky enough to be born in England should not intermarry but should be assimilated."[4] In the opening pages of her biography of her mother, Violet Wyndham née Leverson traces Ada's Sephardi heritage with evident pride and the conviction that it influenced her high standard of integrity.[5] It did not take long for Ada to see that Ernest was an unsuitable marriage partner. Aside from discovering that his young ward living in France was actually his illegitimate daughter, she realized that they shared few interests. Ernest's compulsive gambling led him to abandon

her for the gaming tables and strained their finances. Ada sought consolation in a number of lovers, but friendships with artists and writers with whom she had an affinity and her own writing became more effective ways to generate meaning in her life and stave off loneliness and boredom. Her salon proved a boon to both pursuits.

Despite their emotional estrangement, Ernest Leverson supported his wife's literary endeavors and was gracious to her guests. He not only joined her in standing by Wilde but helped the writer financially after his arrest. Ernest's cousin and Ada's friend Marguerite Leverson was married to Brandon Thomas, the author of the popular comic play *Charley's Aunt,* and they introduced the Leversons to theater people and bohemian friends who eventually became regulars at Ada's salon. Many of the scintillating personalities who made up the aesthetic movement and defined London style in the 1890s attended. In addition to Wilde and his lover, Lord Alfred Douglas, known as "Bosie" (fig. 45), Ada welcomed the artists Aubrey

Beardsley (fig. 46), Max Beerbohm, Walter Sickert, John Singer Sargent (see Re essay, fig. 11), Charles Ricketts and Charles Shannon (fig. 50), William Rothenstein (fig. 47), and Charles Conder; the publisher John Lane; the writers John Gray, Frank Harris, and Henry Harland; the composer Paolo Tosti; the Duc d'Orléans; Wilde's friends Robert Ross and Reginald Turner; the actors Mrs. Patrick Campbell and George Alexander; and the actor-producers Charles Hawtrey and Herbert Beerbohm Tree, Max's half brother.

Ada Leverson met Wilde in 1892; they were drawn to each other by their gift for lighthearted witticisms that could reveal unsettling truths, and a sense of fun. Sketches, the dialogue in Wilde's plays, and the *bons mots* that have come down to us reveal something of the witty banter in Leverson's drawing room. "When Wilde boasted of an apache in Paris who had become so attached to him that he accompanied him everywhere with a knife in one hand, it was characteristic of Ada Leverson to reply, 'I'm sure he had a fork in the other!'" When a guest of hers excused himself from a party by

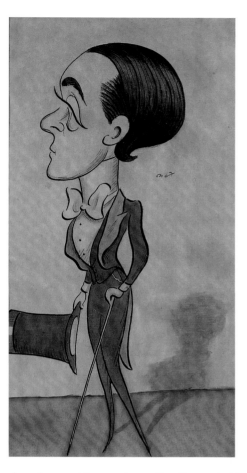

saying that it "was only by going to bed early that he
could keep his youth, she answered, 'I didn't know you
were keeping a youth.'" [6] Her charm and flirtatious wit
nearly persuaded Robert Ross to be a "mulierast."[7]

By all accounts, Wilde's writings do not do justice
to his wit; Leverson described "a spectacular genius,
greater, perhaps, as an improviser in conversation than
as a writer."[8] Rothenstein recalled that "Wilde talked
as others painted or wrote; talking was his art."[9] But
the cult of the dandy required verbal prowess as an
attribute of self-presentation, and most of Leverson's
habitués rose to the occasion. Beardsley quipped that
he once caught a cold by inadvertently leaving the tas-
sel off his cane.[10] The salon banter found its way into
the writing of Leverson and her guests, and their appreciation of her talents encouraged her in her writing.[11]
Beerbohm's caricatures of many in Ada's circle provided
a visual counterpart to the verbal wit and repartee,

though not without a tinge of malice, as in his depiction
of Wilde as a monstrous incarnation of fleshy over-
indulgence and unkempt hair, his bulk filling the page
(fig. 48). In contrast, Beerbohm's self-presentation is
one of wasp-waisted trimness, sharp features, slicked-
back hair, and elegant attire (fig. 49).

Leverson's guests were friends, collaborators,
and rivals—often all three simultaneously. Several
were involved in the production of Wilde's plays. She
and others contributed to Lane's *Yellow Book*, with
Harland as literary editor and Beardsley as art editor.
In *The Dial*, Ricketts and Shannon (fig. 50) published
literature and original prints, with a preference for
works related to French Symbolism. Wilde, who was
particularly sensitive to the physical qualities of his
books, worked with Ricketts—illustrator, designer of
books, sets, and costumes, wood engraver, painter, and
sculptor—on almost all his first editions.

Fig. 50. William Rothenstein (British, 1872–1945), *Charles Ricketts and Charles Shannon*, 1897. Lithograph, 13½ x 8½ in. (34.3 x 21.6 cm). Collection of Mark Samuels Lasner, Washington, D.C.

By the 1890s, Leverson was becoming known for the "wonderful, witty, delightful sketches"[12] she contributed to *Punch* and *Black and White*. In these frothy texts, she gently parodied the writings of friends with a "suggestive . . . intellectual sympathy," which nevertheless provided a female perspective and corrective to the misogynistic tendencies of many aesthetes.[13] Her sketches were appreciated by her friends, as they offered free advertisement for their own expensively produced works and kept them in the public eye in more accessible publications with large circulation. More important, her writings demonstrated her inherent understanding of their art, as Wilde wrote: "No other voice but yours is musical enough to echo my music."[14] By the time *The Green Carnation*—which satirized the circle around Wilde and Alfred Douglas and made explicit the nature of their relationship—was published anonymously in 1894, Leverson was a prime suspect as author.[15] Her satires attest to the fame of the members of her circle, which the media promoted. Her

parodies, like Beerbohm's caricatures, presupposed a degree of celebrity: the public had to be familiar with the figures being parodied.

Many of Leverson's habitués existed on the margins of Victorian bourgeois society; in their writings, art, and way of life, they challenged the norms of that society, including its definition of gender roles, sexuality, fashion, taste, and morals. The aesthete's desire to liberate art from ethical considerations and from the task of imitating nature, and the dandy's transformation of the self into a work of art through dress and self-presentation, were enacted in her drawing room and refracted in the pages of the literary magazines and sumptuous volumes of poetry and prose published by her associates. Leverson recalled: "Where in those days, was the strong silent man? Nowhere! Something weaker and more loquacious was required."[16]

As Anglo-Irish among the British, as Catholics and Jews in Anglican England, and as homosexuals, many of her habitués, whatever their success, were outsiders. Male homosexual acts had been criminalized only in 1885, and the purported intent to protect "public decency" in fact made private as well as public acts illegal. It was during the 1890s that homosexual identity—as opposed to homoerotic desire or forms of sexual behavior—was emerging and that effeminate manners, dandyism, and sexual practice began to define the "homosexual."[17] With the public exposure brought by the Wilde trials, Leverson's gatherings offered a safe and nonjudgmental haven. Yet the anxiety produced by society's condemnation of "deviance" could not be eradicated. Beerbohm's caricature "*Had Shakespeare asked me . . .*" (fig. 51) depicts a naked Frank Harris with his back turned and a clothed Shakespeare sneaking up behind him. Harris was known for both his aggressive heterosexuality—he would write the famous erotic memoir *My Life and Loves*—and his obsession with Shakespeare. Beerbohm once heard him remark: "Unnatural vice! I know nothing of the joys of unnatural vice. You must ask my friend Oscar Wilde about them. But, had Shakespeare asked me, I should have had to submit!"[18]

The Leversons are not known to have suffered directly from anti-Semitism, but popular sentiments—

Fig. 51. Max Beerbohm (British, 1872–1956), *"Had Shakespeare asked me . . ."*: *Caricature of Frank Harris*, c. 1896. Ink and wash and paper, 21 x 5 ½ in. (53.3 x 14 cm). Collection of Mark Samuels Lasner, Washington, D.C.

"Had Shakespeare asked me . . ."

expressed in contemporary novels among other arenas—that conflated Jews, dandies, and homosexuals as threatening to the fabric of solid English society would not have escaped their notice.[19] Although Ada reportedly flirted with the idea of conversion to Catholicism in the wake of the Wilde crisis and at a time when acquaintances had abandoned the Anglican Church for Rome, nothing came of it.[20]

Leverson's recounting of an anecdote encapsulates the aesthetic stance and the collaborative nature of much of her circle's artistic production, while acknowledging, with typical subtlety, its members' marginal position vis-à-vis society. After viewing a new book of poetry by John Gray, where she "saw the tiniest rivulet of text meandering through the very largest meadow of margin," she suggested to Wilde that he "publish a book *all* margin; full of beautiful unwritten thoughts, and have this blank volume bound in some Nile-green skin powdered with gilt nenuphars and smoothed with hard ivory, decorated with gold by Ricketts (if not

Shannon) and printed on Japanese paper." Wilde approved: "It shall be dedicated to you, and the unwritten text illustrated by Beardsley. There must be five hundred signed copies for particular friends, six for the general public, and one for America."[21] Leverson repeats Wilde's description of a volume of Charles Baudelaire's *Les Fleurs du mal* (*The Flowers of Evil*), and the unusual word "nenuphar"—a type of water lily—appears in Wilde's poem "The Sphinx," for the publication of which as a book Ricketts had created a luxurious binding and illustrations (fig. 52).[22] Beardsley's drawings for Wilde's play *Salome*, one of which belonged to Leverson, had provoked some people but had delighted others with their elegance, erotic wit, and caricatures of Wilde and company.

Leverson's guests convened in a drawing room adorned with exquisitely delicate fans painted by Charles Conder (fig. 53). In form and decoration, these convey nostalgia for a bygone era of French sociability —a reminder of the salon's origins. Depicting a languorous realm of pleasure, "an Arcadia peopled by dreamy capricious figures who lead lives of luxurious idleness,"[23] and with a refined use of watercolor inspired by Jean-Antoine Watteau, Conder's fans evoke elegant social interactions enlivened by erotic intrigue, the *fêtes galantes* as refracted through Paul Verlaine's poetry.[24] They provided a counterpoint to the barbed wit that animated Leverson's drawing room and to the stark black-and-white decadence of Beardsley's drawing from *Salome* (fig. 54), showing the Judean princess kissing the severed head of John the Baptist.[25]

The climactic scene of Wilde's play (banned from the stage in June 1892) inspired Beardsley's drawing, which was published in the first issue of *The Studio* in 1893. Wilde, impressed with the young man's talent, gave him a copy of the original French edition with the inscription: "For Aubrey: for the only artist who, besides myself, knows what the dance of the seven veils is, and can see that invisible dance."[26] Beardsley was commissioned to create a series of drawings to illustrate an English edition of the play that appeared in 1894.[27] The book was a succès de scandale, forever linking playwright and artist in the public mind. Whereas

Wilde resented the acclaim awarded his young collaborator for drawings that threatened to overshadow the play, Beardsley came to rue the notoriety his association with Wilde conferred on him. In the wake of Wilde's trials he was dismissed as artistic editor of *The Yellow Book* by a panicked John Lane.[28] Leverson summed up the difference in artistic temperament between her two intimates: "Oscar loved purple and gold, Aubrey put everything down in black and white."[29]

That Leverson owned the Beardsley drawing was appropriate. She believed that *Salome* was the only play important to Wilde, in which he "expressed *himself* in his innate love of the gorgeous and the unique."[30] Yet, with her golden hair and light eyes, Ada Leverson was far removed from the image of the sultry, exotic, and "Oriental" Jewess who captivated the fin-de-siècle imagination in the guise of Judith, Delilah, and above all, Salome, "goddess of Decadence."[31] Salome, with her aggressive, predatory sexuality, was a fascinating—and amusing—alter ego for a Jewish hostess of such understatement and subtle humor. But Wilde had transformed the traditional character in ways that would have appealed to Leverson. Unlike the subsequent literary incarnations, Wilde's Salome acts not out of obedience to her mother but from her own carnal desire: "Ah! Thou wouldst not suffer me to kiss thy mouth, Jokanaan. Well! I will kiss it now."[32] Wilde's Salome is independent, "an assertive modern woman."[33] When she describes her physical passion for John's body after she has been handed his head, the verbal imagery establishes a disturbing echo of the love poetry of the Song of Songs.[34] If Jokanaan's body was "a garden . . . of lilies of silver," the blood dripping from his severed head now nourishes a monstrous lily growing at the bottom of Beardsley's drawing.

Wilde employed another favored fin-de-siècle symbol of the dangerous and devouring female, the embodiment of female sexuality, "at once enigmatic and cruel."[35] In his poem "The Sphinx" (1894), he conjured a monstrous creature, "half woman and half animal," who has survived millennia and "mutilated" countless lovers, the product of the overheated imagination and libido of a student contemplating the statue of a sphinx: "In a dim corner of my room for longer than my fancy thinks / A beautiful and silent Sphinx has watched me through the shifting gloom."[36] Wilde's extravagant use of language, for the pure pleasure of invoking sounds and images, and the artificiality and bravado of his style have the paradoxical effect of muting the tale's horror. Leverson grasped this, and in her parody "The Minx" she declawed the Sphinx with charm and humor.[37] In her "poem in prose," Wilde's aroused and terrified student has been transformed into a poet, who behaves more like a brash young journalist interviewing a contemporary celebrity or society lady about her amorous past. The Sphinx's response is at once evasive and self-promoting:

> POET: No doubt you have talked with hippogriffs and basilisks?[38]
> SPHINX (MODESTLY): I certainly *was* in rather a smart set at one time.
>
> . . .
>
> POET: In my opinion you are not a Sphinx at all.
> SPHINX (INDIGNANTLY): What am I, then?
> POET: A Minx.

J'AI BAISÉ TA BOVCHE
IOKANAAN
J'AI BAISÉ TA BOVCHE

AVBREY BEARDSLEY.

Fig. 54. Aubrey Beardsley (British, 1872–1898), *J'ai baisé ta bouche, Jokanaan*, 1894. Illustration for *Salome* by Oscar Wilde. Ink on paper. Aubrey Beardsley Collection No. 97, Manuscripts Division, Department of Rare Books and Special Collections, Princeton University Library, Princeton, New Jersey. Formerly in the collection of Ada Leverson

Fig. 55. Edward Tennyson Reed (British, 1860–1933), *The Minx*, 1894. Illustration for Ada Leverson's satire, published in *Punch*, July 21, 1894. Ink on paper, 14 ½ x 11 ½ in. (36.8 x 29.2 cm). Collection of Mark Samuels Lasner, Washington, D.C.

Fig. 56. Illustration for Ada Leverson's spoof, "From the Queer and Yellow Book," *Punch*, February 2, 1895, 58

Published in *Punch*, the sketch was accompanied by a caricature of Ricketts's illustrations by E. T. Reed (fig. 55), which depicted a sphinx exhausted rather than alluring, more hag than femme fatale. Wilde found Leverson's sketch "delightful and the drawing a masterpiece of clever caricature. I am afraid she really was a minx after all. You are the only Sphinx."[39] The Sphinx of old was lethal because she harbored a secret; failure to guess the answer to her riddle resulted in death. In modern life, according to Wilde, women have no secrets, and so must pretend to have them—this is the theme of his story "The Sphinx Without a Secret" (1887); Lord Henry Wotton in *The Picture of Dorian Gray* comments that women are "sphinxes without secrets." Leverson turns the idea on its head in the first of her sketches published in *Punch*, "An Afternoon Party," which is structured as conversations of characters taken from contemporary theater, and where a Lord Henry says, "Women are secrets, not sphinxes."[40] If the "Sphinx of modern life"—another of Wilde's monikers for Leverson—poses riddles, it is not to

destroy men but to amuse them; a witty response is all that is required to avoid social death. In the same sketch, Leverson parodied the princess Salome: "There is no harm in her. She's only a little peculiar. She is particularly fond of boar's head." To which Lord Illingworth responds: "The uninvitable in pursuit of the indigestible." The scene ends with a comment crystallizing Leverson's inclusive vision of sociability and sets it against English exclusivity and stodginess: "The fact is, society is getting a great deal too mixed. Now, I like to go away from an afternoon party feeling a purer and better man, my eyes filled with tears of honest English sentiment."[41]

Leverson's parodies were not limited to Wilde. She followed with pleasure the developing career of Beerbohm, who had been her friend since he was a boy. Her Jewishness was part of her attraction for him.[42] Beerbohm was infatuated, and wrote her quite ardent letters.[43] In "From the Queer and Yellow Book," she presented "1894" by "Max Mereboom," a spoof of Beerbohm's "1880," which had been published in

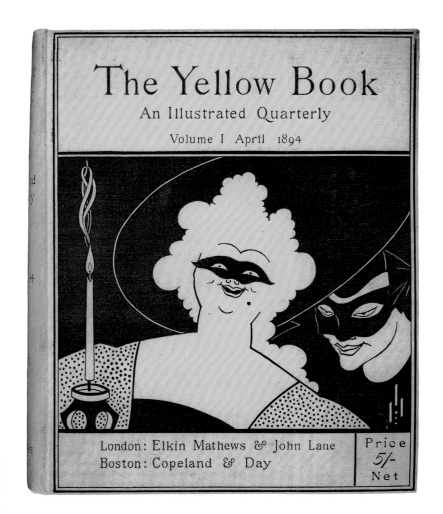

social interaction diametrically opposed to the ideal of sincerity—"wahr sein"—espoused by Rahel Levin. "In point of fact what is interesting about people in good society . . . is the mask that each one of them wears, not the reality that lies behind," Wilde wrote. He advocated cultivating "the lost art of lying" because "the cultured and fascinating liar . . . was the true founder of social intercourse. For the aim of the liar is simply to charm, to delight, to give pleasure."[46] The mask provided the freedom to reveal a different level of truth. Lying was an integral part of fashioning life as art. Ada Leverson's salon, in this performance of life as art, was one of the main stages on which this drama—part comedy, part tragedy—unfolded.

GENEVIÈVE STRAUS: "SHE WAS A PARISIAN JEWESS, THAT IS TO SAY, A PARISIAN TWICE OVER"

Woman was the Muse and counselor of the writer, the judge and the sovereign public of letters. . . . Without her patronage, without the recommendation of her enthusiasm, no one could get plays played, applauded or even read. Every mode of literature, every sort of writer, every pamphlet, every volume, even a master-piece, required that she sign its passport and open a way to publicity. . . . From 1700 to 1789, woman was not only the magnificent spring that set all in motion; she seemed a power of a superior order, the sovereign of all thinking France.[47]

Replete with nostalgia for a long-gone aristocracy and their own up-to-the-minute misogyny, the brothers Edmond and Jules de Goncourt immortalized the French salonière in *La Femme au XVIIIème siècle* (1862). The female sex—which reigned with despotic flair over the culture of the ancien régime—overcame inferiority of mind through the supremely feminine skill of leading men on, and upward, in the arts. "Woman . . . the most admirable of laying machines," the two opined on another occasion, "is an evil, stupid animal unless she is educated and civilized to a high degree."[48] Alas for the brothers Goncourt, whose contempt for women

The Yellow Book; in it she reviews the previous year from the vantage point of history, reporting on friends, musing that "perhaps I have fallen so deeply beneath the Spell of the Age, that I have tended to underrate its unimportance," describing the "Decadents" and "a Sketch of a lady with a Mask on, playing the piano in a Cornfield, in a low dress, with two lighted Candles, and signed '*Aubrey Weirdsley.*'"[44] Indeed, the accompanying illustration (fig. 56) caricatures Beardsley's *Yellow Book* covers, with their masked women sporting lascivious demeanors and low-cut gowns (fig. 57).

The mask appears frequently as a motif in Beardsley's art and as a theme in Wilde's writings on aesthetics. Wilde once asked Leverson: "When you are alone with [Beerbohm] does he take off his face and reveal his mask?"[45] Behind this quip lay a philosophy of

Fig. 58. Giuseppe Primoli
(Italian, 1851–1927), *Edmond
de Goncourt on the Steps of His
House*. Archivo Fotografico,
Fondazione Primoli, Rome

Fig. 59. Geneviève Straus,
1889. Bibliothèque Nationale
de France, Département des
Estampes, Paris

was exceeded only by their anti-Semitism: several of
the most influential salonières of the Third Republic
(1871–1940) were Jewish. The Goncourts rubbed
shoulders with these silk-clad doyennes in public at
the same time that they maligned them in the pages of
their private diaries. How aggravating that one of their
favorites, Princess Mathilde, sister of Napoléon III (and
niece of the first emperor), ecumenically surrounded
herself with "juiverie" who, in turning French society
upside down, "behave just like madwomen from La
Salpêtrière let loose by Charcot."[49] What an unpleasant
pill for Edmond (fig. 58) to swallow when he realized
that Madame Geneviève Straus (fig. 59) drew more
titled nobility to her salon than did any other hostess
in Paris.[50] With embittered sarcasm he conceded, "The
Jewish women of society are, at the moment, the great
readers, and they alone read—as they dare to admit—
those young talents held in contempt by the Academy."[51]

The inverted lens of the Goncourts puts the con-
tortions of Jewish-Gentile relations into sharp focus.
As Michael Marrus has observed, upper-class Jews
could "maintain a certain element of Jewishness as a
family distinction . . . which did not, at the same time,
commit one to avoiding the anti-Semitic salons of the
aristocracy."[52] Acculturated French Jews (self-named
israélites versus Eastern European *juifs*) and those of
foreign extraction hobnobbed with Catholic royalty,
inspired the most prestigious creative figures of the
day, and added their own talents in painting, theater,
opera, and journalism to the grand French tradition.
That so many prominent salonières were Jewish testifies to the amazing degree of acceptance in the haught-
iest quarters. "During the Republic, the Jewesses held
a place in high society that is hard to imagine today,"
wrote the Belle Époque portraitist Jacques-Émile
Blanche in 1949.[53]

Although they remained proud of their heritage,
upper-class French Jews had largely forsaken Judaism
and considered themselves steadfastly patriotic. Yet
the more they achieved in the decades after emancipation under Napoléon (1791), the more they bore
the stigma of capitalist parvenus. As in the popular
press, the powerful Rothschilds fare the worst in the

Goncourts' text, where they are degraded by common stereotypes: miserly, lecherous, bereft of innate taste, and indifferent to the French nation. Their ilk could insinuate themselves into the drawing rooms of the Faubourg Saint-Germain, but the ambiguity of their identity reigned supreme with every nuance of behavior, turn of phrase, revealing accent, and aesthetic judgment. They were inevitably perceived as either Jews *déracinés* or Frenchmen manqués. In his history of the Dreyfus Affair (1894–1906), which he witnessed firsthand, Léon Blum commented that contemporary anti-Semitism found its true expression in the art and literature of the era, not in violent pogroms—which had not occurred in France but had in colonial Algeria. Anti-Semitism emerged "in the exclusive circles of Parisian society, in *le monde*, and in the professions; it was the direct outcome of the seemingly brusque intrusion of newly rich Jews or the too rapid ascent of Jewish academics. It did not manifest itself at all in persecution, but rather in forms of exclusion."[54]

Fueled by the economic vulnerability and xenophobia of the middle classes, as well as by indiscriminate journalism, French anti-Semitism, which had been largely dormant under the July Monarchy (1830–48), regrouped under the Third Republic with the publication of Édouard Drumont's inflammatory *La France juive* (*Jewish France*) in 1886.[55] Like Drumont's invectives, the novels and social satires of Gyp (the Comtesse de Martel; fig. 60) targeted the infiltration of Jews into the upper crust and their deleterious effects. "Anti-Semitism became a fashion which suited certain jealousies remarkably well," recalled Élisabeth de Gramont, Duchesse de Clemont-Tonnerre (later the lover of the American-born writer and Parisian salonière Natalie Barney).[56] But with the Dreyfus Affair, it was the accusation of actual treason, not merely age-old usury, that threatened the pampered security of acculturated French Jews. The suture between private and public burst open as the fight over truth and justice politicized conversation and salon culture to an unprecedented degree. Egalitarian sociability fell by the wayside, as witnessed in the salon of Geneviève Straus.

No better document of the tensions and hypocrisy of French salon society exists than Marcel Proust's *À la recherche du temps perdu* (*In Search of Lost Time*, 1913–27). From his own enlightened, if precarious, position as half-Jew (on his mother's side) and homosexual, Proust's acute vision reveals all the intricacies that the Goncourts' myopia obscures. That known anti-Semites such as the Goncourts, Alphonse and Léon Daudet, Gyp, Paul Bourget, Jean-Louis Forain, and Edgar Degas readily mixed with the dreaded "other"—Proust, Charles Haas (the main model for Charles Swann in *Recherche;* fig. 61), Reynaldo Hahn, Georges de Porto-Riche, Charles Ephrussi (the editor of the *Gazette des Beaux-Arts*), the Halévys, Sarah Bernhardt—and the salonières Straus, Ernesta Stern, Marie Kann,[57] Léontine-Charlotte Arman de Caillavet— reveals that the salon continued to function as social mediator and foremost arena for self-promotion. Racism, in other words, could be tolerated for the sake of career advancement, or in many cases, real friendship

Fig. 61. Paul Nadar (French, 1856–1939), *Charles Haas*, 1895. Archives Photographiques, Centre des Monuments Nationaux, Paris

Fig. 62. Madame Arman de Caillavet. Bibliothèque Nationale de France, Département des Estampes, Paris

prevailed over hostile preconceptions—at least until the Dreyfus Affair. Proust's characters are based on single or composite models of real-life intimates and acquaintances, to the end of a larger social commentary on the mesmerizing vacuity of *le monde* and the internecine warfare between "two Frances" unleashed in salon culture.

The distanced narrator in *Recherche* frames the Semite's social predicament in the opposing profiles of Bloch and Swann, respectively, the gauche interloper and the Jew too good to be true. Bloch, who early in the novel bears his race like a calling card, "remained for a lover of the exotic as strange and savory a spectacle, in spite of his European costume, as a Jew in a painting by Decamps."[58] Swann dons a gray topper made exclusively for him and a select group from the Faubourg Saint-Germain. He is accepted by those anti-Semites "who have a fit if they see a Jew a mile off" because they think him—the epitome of aristocratic breeding—"the natural grandson of the Duc de Berry."[59] By contrast, Proust portrays none of the

salonières in *Recherche* as Jewish, even though they and events around them are drawn in good measure from the actual figures of Léontine-Charlotte Arman de Caillavet, Rosalie de Fitz-James, Ernesta Stern, and above all, Geneviève Straus. In this schism between art and life, Proust mirrors the dominant cultural bias under the Third Republic: in French literature and legend, male characters carried the stigma of the "ugly Jew," whereas women, for the most part, escaped anti-Semitic malice, becoming personifications of virtue and bravery.[60]

Madame Léontine-Charlotte Arman de Caillavet (1844–1910; fig. 62) was the mistress, muse, and driving force behind the career of the writer Anatole France (see Re essay, fig. 3). "From devotion she tyrannized over the indolent Master," recalled Élisabeth de Gramont, "and shut him up to compel him to write."[61] Born Léontine-Charlotte Lippmann into an assimilated family (her father was a banker of German descent), she married the son of a successful shipbuilder from Bordeaux in

Fig. 63. Paul Nadar (French, 1856–1939), *Comte Robert de Montesquiou*, 1895. Archives Photographiques, Centre des Monuments Nationaux, Paris

Fig. 64. Paul Nadar (French, 1856–1939), *Comtesse Adhéaume de Chevigné*, 1885. Archives Photographiques, Centre des Monuments Nationaux, Paris

1868. They never divorced, despite her open relationship with Anatole France and her husband's anti-Dreyfus position. She held her literary salon at 12 avenue Hoche every Sunday (giving smaller dinners on Wednesdays). "The faithful," as Proust called them, included the writers Alexandre Dumas *fils*, Robert de Montesquiou (Proust's Baron de Charlus; fig. 63), Jules Lemaître, Anna de Noailles, Georges de Porto-Riche, Georg Brandes, and the young Colette; the actress Sarah Bernhardt (see Re essay, fig. 7); the historian Ernest Renan; and the politicians Raymond Poincaré and Georges Clemenceau. More than one contemporary noted the salonière's pretense to re-create the rarefied atmosphere of the seventeenth-century Hôtel de Rambouillet.[62] Her clear ambition to rule the literary firmament was reflected in the formidable figure of Madame Verdurin in *Recherche*, while the typology of the "one-man show" was mimicked in the gatherings of Madame Swann, which existed solely to promote Bergotte (Anatole France). Yet Madame Arman de

Caillavet's salon mixed generations, offering young writers contact with potential mentors and establishing networks for patronage and support.

Proust did not sketch the Comtesse Rosalie de Fitz-James, but she was critical to his novel nonetheless. The young Proust's infatuation with the Comtesse Laure de Chevigné (fig. 64), the model for the cruel edge and angular beauty of the fictional Oriane, Duchesse de Guermantes, led him to hound her on her daily walks.[63] When, in May 1892, he finally ventured to stop and speak with her, she angrily cut him off with: "Fitz-James is expecting me." This actual scenario inspired the treatment of the fictional duchess's aloofness and the narrator's pathetic love. Fitz-James, on whom the Comtesse de Chevigné was making her call that fateful day, was nicknamed "Rosa Malheur" (a pun on the name of the painter Rosa Bonheur) because of her nasty and unfaithful husband, another anti-Dreyfusard. Née Gutmann, the Viennese-born Fitz-James was "plain and melancholy," but, as one Proust biographer notes, "she was said to keep a secret weapon in her desk: a list of all the Jewish marriages in the noble families of Europe."[64] Through habitué (and anti-Semite) Paul Bourget, Edith Wharton met Fitz-James, then widowed, who, Wharton said, "had the easy cosmopolitanism of a rich Austrian Jewess" and was eager to welcome foreigners, including the novelists Henry James and Matilde Serao, the art historian

Bernard Berenson, and the philosopher Count Hermann Keyserling. In her memoirs, Wharton presents Fitz-James's salon as the most prestigious in Paris, with allusions to the agreeable conversation, well-designed mélange of personalities, and social authority of the eighteenth-century salonière. Yet, as Wharton astutely observes, "there were still, among the irreducibles of the Faubourg, a few who held out, declined to risk themselves among such international promiscuities, and received the mention of the hostess's name with raised eyebrows and the affectation of hearing it for the first time."[65]

Although the literary salons of Belle Époque Paris revolved around male writers, some Jewish salonières went beyond the role of hostess and muse, creating their own novels and works of literary criticism. Madame Louis Stern (born Ernesta de Herschel in Trieste; her husband was a banker) published mildly titillating novels under the pseudonym Maria Star. Whereas her literary efforts inspired Robert de

Montesquiou to write a review so insulting that Stern's son challenged the offending critic to a duel, her salon met with great success.[66] The eclectic décor of her home at 68 rue du Faubourg Saint-Honoré—Chinese, Indian, and Persian objects alongside medieval Madonnas and Renaissance furniture—paralleled the diversity of visitors to her salon: "heads of state, artists, priests or Freemasons, over whom she ruled like a sorceress."[67] Reynaldo Hahn (fig. 65) introduced Proust to the salon that may have inspired Madame Verdurin's, and it was here that Proust first met Gabriel Fauré.[68]

Madame Guillaume Beer (1864–1949) successfully combined the roles of salonière, muse, and serious woman of letters. Born Elena Goldschmidt-Franchetti in Florence, she married Guillaume Beer, a great-grandson of the Berlin salonière Amalie Beer (see fig. 28). Her paternal grandfather was the Frankfurt banker Benedict Hayum Goldschmidt, whose children married into some of the wealthiest and most powerful Jewish families in Europe.[69] Her mother, Sophia, came from the Italian Franchetti family of barons. Both Elena and her sister, Isabella Errera (1869–1929), married foreign Jews and hosted salons in their adopted cities, Elena in Paris and Isabella in Brussels.[70] As Madame Guillaume Beer, Elena presided over literary soirées on the rue des Mathurins that were celebrated as "always a true artistic delight."[71] Often featuring poetry readings and song, her gatherings attracted Proust, Geneviève Straus, Rosalie de Fitz-James, Charles Ephrussi, and various Rothschilds, as well as the writers Matilde Serao and Gabriele D'Annunzio.[72] In spring and summer Madame Beer welcomed guests to the family's Château de Voisins in Louveciennes.

Tall, blonde, and strikingly beautiful, Madame Beer was famous as the muse of the aged poet Charles-Marie-René Leconte de Lisle in the last three years of his life. He immortalized her as the "rose of Louveciennes" and died at her château.[73] For Proust, who figured her not in *Recherche* but in a literary portrait, she united "Italian grace with the mystery of women of the North," the charms of "two climates and two races."[74] In a portrait by Antonio de La Gandara (1896; fig. 66), she faces away from the viewer, evincing

a regal hauteur.[75] After the death of Leconte de Lisle, Beer became a prolific woman of ideas under the nom de plume Jean Dornis. In *Le Voile du temple* (*The Veil of the Temple*, 1906), the story of a love affair between an idealistic young Jewish woman and a young Catholic lieutenant, she explored metaphysical questions and examined the tradition, ossification, and reformation of contemporary religious practices.[76] Her incisive studies of contemporary French and Italian literature—written from the perspective of an Italian long residing in France and familiar with many writers who had frequented her salon—attest to an intellectual rigor that earned her the title "Princess of Letters."[77]

From the mid-1880s to the late 1890s, however, all who counted, or wanted to count, appeared chez Madame Geneviève Straus. Born to a middle-class family of artists and musicians, "she was a Parisian Jewess, that is to say, a Parisian twice over," in the words of one contemporary.[78] Straus perpetuated the cultural legacy of her worldly father, the opera composer Fromental Halévy, permanent secretary of the Académie des Beaux-Arts. Her uncle Léon Halévy was a respected dramatist, political writer, and educator. Fromental Halévy's phenomenal success *La Juive*

(1835) expressed his generation's militant belief in religious tolerance—on all sides. The Halévys' degree of assimilation extended to Fromental's decade-long liaison with a Catholic mistress, which produced three children, and Léon's marriage to the Catholic Alexandrine Le Bas.[79] The Halévys forsook Orthodox Judaism because they considered it backward and superstitious, but also to advance in their careers without prejudice. This did not always happen: George Sand, for one, wrote that Fromental's compositions were "the ugliest, most hooked-nosed and most stupid music there ever was."[80] The brothers Halévy epitomized the dual identity and equivocations of first-generation *citoyens* and *israélites*, determined to regenerate both Judaism and the French nation through liberalism and secular achievement. When asked why she never converted, Geneviève Halévy Straus pragmatically replied: "I have too little religion to change it."[81]

Geneviève's mother, Léonie Rodrigues-Henriques, was a Sephardi Jewess from a wealthy Bordeaux banking family. An amateur sculptor, she drew Eugène Delacroix and other artists to her own salon and amassed a notable collection of artwork, which Geneviève inherited. Her side of the family also bequeathed a debilitating mental illness. Léonie spent long periods away from her children in the private asylum of Dr. Antoine Blanche (father of the painter and salon habitué Jacques-Émile Blanche). Her depression was aggrieved by the death of her husband in 1862, and that of Esther, Geneviève's older sister, two years later, at the age of twenty-one, under obscure circumstances at the clinic of Dr. Blanche. Geneviève endured these losses and, further, a tortured and estranged relationship with her mother.[82] After the Dreyfus Affair and the dénouement of her salon, Geneviève battled unrelenting anxiety, often withdrawing into isolation or becoming bedridden for weeks at a time. Her only child, Jacques Bizet, suffered morphine addiction, alcoholism, and a troubled marriage until he committed suicide in 1922.

In addition to her status as a Halévy, Geneviève earlier garnered fame, and sympathy, as the young widow of Georges Bizet, her father's pupil, whom she had married in 1869. Bizet died in 1875 shortly after the

Fig. 68. Edgar Degas (French, 1834–1917), *Charles Haas, Geneviève Straus, Albert Boulanger-Cavé, and Émile Straus*. Private collection

Fig. 69. Edgar Degas (French, 1834–1917), *Edgar Degas, Geneviève Straus, Albert Boulanger-Cavé, and Étienne Ganderax*. Private collection

disastrous Paris debut of *Carmen*. Although their marriage had been filled with strife (his struggling career, their poverty during the siege of Paris in 1870–71, his presumed infidelity, her nervous condition), it was later mythologized by many, encouraged by Jules-Élie Delaunay's portrait of a liquid-eyed Geneviève in black veils of mourning and with beguiling curls (fig. 67). The painting caused a sensation when exhibited in the Salon of 1878. To draw herself out of isolation and placate numerous admirers, Geneviève began to greet writers and artists on Thursdays at 22 rue de Douai, where she and Bizet had lived along with other members of the Halévy clan. Her cousin Ludovic Halévy was a leading librettist (especially for the music of Jacques Offenbach) and was immortalized behind the scenes at the opera in drawings by Degas, who became a salon regular. While some women hosted salons out of social ambition or professional need, for Geneviève it was a question of survival, of warding off not mere ennui but psychological demons. It also allowed her to break free of her identity as Bizet's widow and a dark,

gypsy-spirited Carmen. Royalties from the works of her late father and husband fostered her newfound independence.

Among her suitors was the persistent Émile Straus, a wealthy lawyer for the Rothschilds (Edmond de Goncourt spread the rumor that Straus was actually the illegitimate son of the elder Baron de Rothschild).[83] Amiable, but short-tempered if provoked, Straus was recognized for narrow, half-shut eyes, which had been injured—it was said—during the siege of Paris (fig. 68). Straus, who would be profiled in the elegant sociability of Proust's Swann, introduced Geneviève to the upper crust of the Faubourg Saint-Germain. Influential and rich, he shared her religious background; and in 1886, after eleven years of widowhood, Geneviève finally said yes.[84] That same year, Drumont's *La France juive* made assimilated *israélites* suddenly self-conscious of an identity previously taken for granted. The couple moved into a luxurious townhouse at 134 boulevard Haussmann, bringing with them the aristocracy who had once flocked to Geneviève's more bohemian

Fig. 70. Edgar Degas (French, 1834–1917), *Six Friends*, c. 1885. Pencil and chalk on paper, 45¼ x 28 in. (114.9 x 71.1 cm). Museum of Art, Rhode Island School of Design, Museum Appropriation

quarters: Princess Mathilde and her nephew, the photographer Giuseppe (Joseph) Primoli; Comte Othenin d'Haussonville, grandson and family archivist of Germaine de Staël; Marquis Boni de Castellane, the profligate husband of the American heiress Anna Gould; and Prince Edmond de Polignac, whose American wife, Winaretta Singer, held a famed music salon.[85] Joining them were old cohorts from the rue de Douai— Ludovic Halévy, Degas (fig. 69), the librettist Henri Meilhac, Albert Boulanger-Cavé, and the editor Louis Ganderax. This close group of artists and writers vacationed together, along with Jacques-Émile Blanche and

Ada Leverson habitué Walter Sickert, in the resort town of Dieppe on the Normandy coast, not far from Straus's summer residence in Trouville (fig. 70).[86]

Straus first fascinated Proust when he was a schoolmate of her son at the Lycée Condorcet, whose parent body included liberal supporters of the republic and many Jews and half-Jews well placed in society. Gently dismissive of his romantic infatuation, she became instead a lifelong friend and correspondent. Proust transferred his love for Jacques onto his mother, and Geneviève displaced her maternal love onto her "cher petit Marcel."[87] In 1908 she gave Proust five narrow notebooks (fig. 71) in which he jotted down his initial ideas for *Recherche*, and she later helped with contacts for its publication.[88] She was never scandalized by his sexuality, and correspondence between the two suggests that as confidants they discussed it.[89] Her salon did not discriminate: Geneviève welcomed heterosexual dandies, renowned homosexuals (making the anti-Semitic association of Jew and invert inevitable), as well as "manly" writers of the naturalist school, socialists and monarchists, actresses and academicians. After the turn of the century, as her salon and health declined, she and Proust, "perhaps the two most thorough neurasthenics in Paris," rarely saw each other.[90] Céleste Albaret, Proust's faithful housekeeper, recorded their "remarkable intellectual intimacy," which endured "right up until the end."[91] In 1913, when *Swann's Way*, the first volume of *Recherche*, appeared, Straus's copy carried this dedication: "To Mme Straus, the only one of the beautiful things I already loved at the age where this book begins, for whom my admiration has not changed."[92]

Straus inspired details for the Duchesse de Guermantes—not the heartless, superficial side of Oriane but the infallible *bons mots* and expertise on Victor Hugo.[93] "Tell him to wait five minutes—I'll be down in half an hour," was one favorite recorded by Giuseppe Primoli.[94] When friends expressed their dismay that she had finally succumbed to the marriage entreaties of Monsieur Straus, she retorted, "What else can I do? It's the only way to get rid of him."[95] At once blithe and piercing, "with an evenness and simplicity

Fig. 71. Marcel Proust's note-books, 1901–18, given to Proust by Geneviève Straus. Bibliothèque Nationale de France, Département des Estampes, Paris

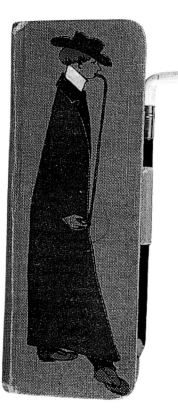

Fig. 72. Paul Nadar (French, 1856–1939), *Comtesse Élisabeth Greffulhe*, 1896. Archives Photographiques, Centre des Monuments Nationaux, Paris

afternoons. Just like the Goncourts' classic woman of the eighteenth century, Madame Straus assembled those in the know, who brought, "piping hot, like a dish, the effluvium of what was going on in the Law Courts, in Parliament, in the Government offices, in the big newspaper offices, and especially in the theatres. Abel Hermant brought her his first novels, Paul Hervieu theater boxes for his first-nights; *Le Figaro*, that eminently Parisian paper, and *La Revue de Paris* were annotated at her parties."[97]

At other salons, themes for discussion were assigned by the hostess, as with the despotic Madame Verdurin, based on the real-life Madame Lydie Aubernon de Nerville (1825–1899), who called on guests to speak as she saw fit.[98] At Madame Straus's, the conversation was eclectic, free, and spontaneous, though evenings often featured scheduled readings and performances. And by contrast to the fictionalized salon of Oriane de Guermantes, from which most women were excluded in order to make the duchess shine more brightly, Madame Straus welcomed women, and women of talent, different ethnicities, and social status. Nor did she need to fend off the two most beautiful hostesses in Paris, the Comtesse de Chevigné and the accomplished Comtesse de Greffulhe (fig. 72), who filled out the other, contrasting facets of Proust's Duchesse de Guermantes.[99] Not only men but also women esteemed Madame Straus, for she "had the rare and delightful gift of fastening with her delicate feminine antennae on the latent desires of the mind and heart. She knew what you loved, what you were waiting for, what preoccupied you; she flattered and caressed."[100]

Madame Straus's impeccable clothing was as pointedly chosen as her words. Degas often accompanied her to her dressmaker.[101] Encouraged by her husband's indulgence, she was a fashion buff known for her elegant bonnets (see figs. 2 and 59). A stunning red ensemble of hers inspired a central satirical vignette in *Recherche*, when the Duc de Guermantes insists his wife change her black shoes to match the color of her red gown.[102] As a young woman, Geneviève developed a nervous tic in her left eye, which droops ever so slightly in Delaunay's portrait. With age, her features

of tone," hers was "poetry allied with gamine intellect," recalled the writer Robert Dreyfus, "and she never dwelled on something she considered in bad taste."[96] In *Recherche*, the spirit of the real-life librettists Meilhac and Halévy presides over the Guermantes' receptions, with obvious allusions to Geneviève: Meilhac and her cousin Ludovic were celebrated comedic talents, they both wrote for Bizet, and she herself was a Halévy. Men and women of the theater gave the Straus salon a particular esprit that distinguished it from the mundanities of the bourgeois and the formalities of the aristocracy. The dramatists Paul Hervieu and Georges de Porto-Riche gathered with others in their crowd and in operatic circles, including Sarah Bernhardt, Réjane, Lucien Guitry, and Emma Calvé, for improvised and scripted

Fig. 73. Giuseppe Primoli (Italian, 1851–1927), *Geneviève Straus, Colette Dumas Lippman, and Guy de Maupassant in Triel (Seine-et-Oise), June 1889*. Archivo Fotografico, Fondazione Primoli, Rome

thickened and her famously sonorous eyes sank further into their depths. Later in life, her lower lip would protrude involuntarily and her head tilt abruptly, leading one acquaintance to describe her face as "a sky disordered by summer lightning."[103]

The awe in which Proust's narrator initially holds Oriane de Guermantes and her place at the summit of society reflects the author's actual engagement with the personalities in orbit around Straus's star. Her salon thrived on the mix of *gratin* and *bohème*. Secure with the social competition, she invited whom she pleased, not whom she ought to: the formula was winning for its uncalculating vigor. The aristocrats and the men of money and business remained mostly in the background, for the real players were the intellectuals, such as the philosopher Henri Bergson (who married a cousin of Proust's), theater personalities, and literary stars including D'Annunzio, Bourget, Lemaître, and, when visiting from London, Oscar Wilde and George Moore. Well known to be enamored of her, Guy de Maupassant (fig. 73) rendered Madame Straus in the character of the high-society hostess Michèle de Burne in *Notre coeur* (*Our Heart*, 1890). The luminaries at the salon humored the younger writers, old school friends of Jacques Bizet's—Proust, Robert de Flers, Robert Dreyfus, and Fernand Gregh. Among Straus's regulars

were Charles Haas, Robert de Montesquiou, and Anna de Noailles. Her musical family's tradition continued with Claude Debussy, Charles Gounod (who had taught the young Geneviève piano), Gabriel Fauré, the pianist Léon Delafosse, and Proust's lover the composer Reynaldo Hahn (see fig. 65).

The Straus salon was held in an oval-shaped entresol. Lunch was served for a dozen or so selects, with other guests arriving in the afternoon. The house was overfilled with terra-cotta figurines and marble statuary from the estate of Geneviève's mother, and eighteenth-century French furniture acquired by Émile, who also made sure that his wife received her company surrounded by bouquets of fresh roses. The salon displayed his two passions: the salonière herself and his art collection. Aside from the Delaunay portrait (whose sphinxlike *éternel féminin* represented a Geneviève long past), works by François Boucher, Jean-Honoré Fragonard, and Georges de La Tour hung on the walls. But the showpieces were by contemporaries—Camille Corot, Eugène Boudin, Camille Pissarro, Georges Seurat, Eugène Carrière, Édouard Vuillard, and Gustave Moreau (a frequent visitor, initially brought by Degas).[104] Here Proust saw Claude Monet's canvases for the first time (the Impressionist incarnated in *Recherche*'s fictional Elstir). Paul Nadar and Degas, the caricaturist Jean-Louis Forain, who kept Madame Straus in stitches, Édouard Detaille, who did the sets for *Carmen*, and Jacques-Émile Blanche were faithful guests. Madame Straus's portrait was painted by Moreau, Giovanni Boldini, and possibly Degas (fig. 74), although none of these images has been securely identified.[105]

Émile Straus's success in collecting was equaled by his triumph with Geneviève's apotheosis. Like the Duc de Guermantes, who disingenuously brags of his wife, "She lives surrounded by a court of superior minds— I'm not her husband, I'm only the senior valet," Monsieur Straus took great pride in his wife's wit and did everything to further her social standing.[106] Their marriage endured periodic crises—possibly because of Geneviève's romantic liaisons. It is speculated, though unsubstantiated, that she may have dallied with Samuel Pozzi, the gynecologist and surgeon whose dashing

portraits by John Singer Sargent and Nadar gave cre-
dence to his nickname "Dr. Love" (fig. 75). Despite
the occasional negative observation, most intimates
approved of Émile and of a marriage clearly founded
on mutual respect and affection. Moreover, it is clear
from reading the comments of her so-called male
admirers that Monsieur Straus had little control over
their blind desire to see her as a femme fatale, in line
with the misogynist literary conventions of the period,
including the seductive figure of *la belle juive*.

Even Edmond de Goncourt could not help admiring Madame Straus, with her reputation for comedic
recitation, the aplomb of her eighteenth-century décor,
and her "Jewish nonchalance," as she lounged deep in
her pillows, dressed in black silk with fluffy bows, to
complement the black poodle on her lap.[107] He typically
projected his anti-Semitism onto her husband, rubbing
salt into the wound by claiming he could think of her

only as Bizet's widow and alluding to marital dishar-
mony. Although Goncourt approved of Straus's amiability and "Jewish humility," he observed that "in a
novel he would be the perfect type for a satanic eye-
glasses merchant with his bestial eyes that appear para-
lyzed. . . . He has a damned mephistophelian air about
him that makes me distrust my inclination to like him."[108]

One must search through lost time to find remnants of Madame Straus's conversational zest, but political events secured her salon's place in recorded history.
Her ephemeral gatherings were inscribed in the facts—
and fictionalization—of the Dreyfus Affair. The salon at
134 boulevard Haussmann became nothing less than the
"general headquarters" of pro-Dreyfus intellectuals.[109]
To begin with, it was at her summer house in Trouville,
in August 1897, that the lawyer Joseph Reinach (another
admirer) revealed that Captain Alfred Dreyfus had
been framed. Accused of espionage for the German

Fig. 76. Madeleine Bizet, Paul Hervieu, and Geneviève Straus reading *L'Aurore* during the Dreyfus Affair, 1898. Photograph, 3½ x 4¾ in. (9 x 12 cm)

government, Dreyfus had been convicted in December 1894 and sent into exile. With Madame Straus's orchestration, Reinach announced that Major Ferdinand Walsin-Esterhazy was the real spy, to the disbelief of her guests at the salon that October, before the exposé had reached the press. Lemaître, Degas (whose intimacy with Geneviève and the Halévys is recorded in several of his photographs; see fig. 69), Forain, and the historian Gustave Schlumberger immediately left the room in outrage, and for good.[110] The complicity of government and army in the ensuing cover-up caused many to deny the truth out of allegiance to the Third Republic. Others could not imagine Dreyfus innocent, simply because he was a Jew, and hence a born traitor. With every mounting piece of evidence in Dreyfus's favor, the government delayed revising its stance, thereby deepening the crisis.

In January 1898, after the acquittal of Esterhazy and imminent imprisonment of the noble whistleblower, Colonel Georges Picquart, Zola published "J'Accuse," a denunciation of the French military and government. Proust, his brother Robert, Straus's son, and her nephews Daniel and Élie Halévy solicited signatures for a "Manifesto of the Intellectuals." They secured the invaluable name of Anatole France to start it off (Madame Arman de Caillavet fretted that he

would be jailed as a result).[111] The Straus salon gathered other Dreyfusards, including the young Léon Blum and the circle of Thadée and Alexandre Natanson, editors of *La Revue Blanche* and *Le Cri de Paris*. Straus used her extensive network to lobby for signatures at the behest of Anatole France when he led a petition to support Picquart in the fall of 1898, and she convinced personal friends (Hervieu, Porto-Riche, and Pozzi) to join the revisionist cause. Several photographs capture Straus and her colleagues attentively reading the papers—posed to be sure, but an accurate assessment of their awareness of the role of journalism in inflaming conspiracy theories and anti-Semitism (fig. 76).[112] Georges Clemenceau (whose journal *L'Aurore* published "J'Accuse") and Jean Jaurès led the revisionist press and now spoke strategy at Madame Straus's. They were drawn together with others in a profoundly sad flurry of activity, the salon now functioning as information network and moral ground. Robert Dreyfus witnessed that Madame Straus's "physical languor became toned with determination," yet never did fanaticism "corrupt" the liberal attitude of her salon.[113]

Delafosse, Debussy, and Detaille also hastily departed from Madame Straus's. The academician and long-standing habitué Othenin d'Haussonville began to pronounce her name with a German intonation, "*Sch*traus," and Gustave Schlumberger insulted her in public. Others avoided her hospitality but refrained from personal invective. Every new development and betrayal occupied Straus in her correspondence. As she wrote to her beloved cousin: "The despicable [Henri] Rochefort gives me a dirty look whenever he sees me strolling with Alphonse de R. [Baron de Rothschild]."[114] Yet Straus's honor was defended by some, who found intolerable the behavior of former guests, such as Forain, who "would not know how to draw but for her," and who started his anti-Semitic journal *Pssit . . . !* "after living off her bread."[115] Straus managed the social slights but despaired of the criminal actions of the state.

"It was true that the social kaleidoscope was in the act of turning and that the Dreyfus Affair was shortly to relegate the Jews to the lowest rung of the social ladder," thinks the narrator in *Recherche*. These were not the exotics like the fictional Bloch but those who had become "Gallicised . . . limbered up by the gymnastics of the Faubourg."[116] Blanche, a treacherous gossip, recounted with some pleasure how he and Maurice Barrès bantered about which salon to visit after dinner: "What about the Jewesses? They would be the best to amuse us. But no, these Oriental fruits are now forbidden!"[117] Because of the affair, Proust and his fair-weather friend Blanche did not speak to each other for thirteen years. Social casualties accumulated, as the aristocracy closed ranks with Catholics, monarchists, right-wing nationalists, and most of the academy, carrying along anti-Dreyfusards of Jewish origin who had married into the nobility. The majority of important bourgeois salons were revisionist—those of Madame Arman de Caillavet, Madame Aubernon (see Re essay, fig. 5), and the publisher Georges Charpentier, for instance—or neutral, as was Madame Lemaire's (1845–1928; see Re essay, fig. 6). Opportunists seized the day, since either condemning or supporting Dreyfus might elevate the mediocre. The Straus salon was polarized with that of the Comtesse de Loynes, who, with her lover, Lemaître, and the extremists Barrès, Drumont, Léon Daudet, and Gyp (see fig. 60), founded the Ligue de la Patrie Française. Habitués of both salons switched loyalties. Straus moved to a newly built *hôtel particulier* at 104 rue de Miromesnil in 1898, and her salon, in spirit and presence, was never the same.[118]

In the "social kaleidoscope" of the affair, revisionists could be anti-Semitic, like Colonel Picquart himself, and Jews anti-Dreyfusards, like the editor Arthur Meyer, another guest who marched out of the Straus salon; the Jewish Bergson, among others, remained noncommittal. In contrast to his sons, Proust's father, Adrien, was an ardent nationalist, exemplifying a rift not uncommon within families and proving that not all anti-Dreyfusards were anti-Semitic, as many Jews believed. Madame Straus's friend Haas signed for Zola, but not for Picquart, while Montesquiou refused to lend his name to either side, though he seems to have thought, like his cousin the Comtesse de Greffulhe, that Dreyfus was innocent. Nor did Jews necessarily fight

for Dreyfus because of their race or religion; indeed, this was a spurious explanation often leveled by the opposition.[119] Dreyfusards united against injustice and the blind adhesion of ideologues and racists, as evidenced by the shocked disbelief of Proust, years earlier, at the chatter of anti-Semites in his literary crowd: "They account for character and genius by physical habits or race. . . . And that is most unintelligent."[120] The history of the Straus salon and its habitués demonstrates the barriers still existing in public affairs between groups seemingly "at home" together. Face-to-face exchange tempered, but did not always eradicate, ingrained beliefs or irrational fears, while individuals could not always counter the force of mindless typecasting.

Undoubtedly, the chic, sublimely clever, and egalitarian Madame Straus helped Proust alleviate personal insecurities about his own half-Jewish heritage.[121] In *Recherche*, Swann's features, emaciated by cancer during the Dreyfus ordeal, changed profoundly: he "was returning to the spiritual fold of his fathers," like Madame Straus and other acculturated Jews.[122] Geneviève could recall with pride and indignation that her grandfather Élie Halévy cofounded the first Jewish journal in France, *L'Israélite Français: Ouvrage Moral et Littéraire*. German-born, he befriended Moses Mendelssohn through the Haskalah before settling in Metz. His poem "Ha Shalom," a commemoration of Napoléon's peacemaking efforts with the British in 1801, was recited or sung in Hebrew in the Great Synagogue of Paris and then performed in churches across France. And in 1820, Fromental Halévy composed a funeral march based on a Hebrew psalm for a service held at the rue Sainte-Avoye synagogue after the assassination of the reactionary Duc de Berry.[123] Straus may have had "too little religion" to change it, but she was also too French to sit back and watch her country—and that of her forbears—shame itself. The Duchesse de Guermantes selected few and rejected many, building her exclusive salon on what she perceived as "the corner-stone of sacrifice."[124] After the Dreyfus Affair, Straus's salon lost its social stature, but as one habitué testified, she "accepted sacrifice for the cause of truth."[125]

The Political Salon

ANNA KULISCIOFF:
THE SUBVERSIVE SALONIÈRE

The following is an official description of Anna Kuliscioff (c. 1855–1925; fig. 77), a subversive of "notable education" and "elegant oratory," filed by the Milan police in 1899:

> Stature: short. Physique: slender. Hair: blond. Brow: low. Nose: pointed. Eyes: light blue. Mouth: regular. Chin: rounded. Face: thin. Skin color: pale. Deportment: self-possessed. Countenance: personable. Manner of dress: scrupulous.[1]

Among the salonières, Russian-born Kuliscioff bears the distinction of having served time in prison (where she contracted tuberculosis) for her political activities. The empirical classifications used in her Milanese police record were a standard type developed into a dubious science by the nineteenth-century Jewish-born criminal anthropologist Cesare Lombroso. Lombroso's influential studies also argued that the physiognomy of criminal women paralleled that of nonwhite races, who were deemed atavistic and hence biologically and intellectually inferior.[2] Kuliscioff's luminous, "Pre-Raphaelite" beauty blatantly contradicted such stereotypes, as did her intimidating, "magnificent mind."[3] In a twist of history, Lombroso and his two daughters had befriended her in Turin in 1885, when she was finishing medical studies in gynecology. Because of her, "Socialism entered the Lombroso household," and, despite his sexist theories, Lombroso went on to support female suffrage.[4] For her part, Kuliscioff dismissed the "conclusive" evidence of women's smaller brain size in her treatise "Il monopolio dell'uomo" ("The Monopoly of Man," 1890), and made it her life's work

to change the economic and social inequalities that led to women's oppression.

Born near Simferopol in the Crimea around 1855, Anja Moiseevna Rozenstein hailed from a well-to-do Jewish merchant family who sent her to study engineering at the Zurich Polytechnic in 1871, where she also took courses in philosophy.[5] In Switzerland, political exiles introduced her to the anarchism of Mikhail Bakunin and the populism of Pyotr Lavrov, and she married a fellow revolutionary of noble birth, Pyotr Macarevich. Like other Eastern European radicals of her generation, she rejected her privileged upbringing in favor of solidarity with the peasantry subjugated by the tsarist regimes. Her attraction to revolutionary ideologies was typical of many Jewish women from Orthodox families (there was no Reform Judaism in Eastern Europe), who having being exposed to secular culture through their trades or university education, rebelled against rabbinical and patriarchal authority. Kuliscioff, like Rosa Luxemburg and Emma Goldman, embraced a new religion of social justice with equal devotional fervor. "They had far less to discard doctrinally than men," argues Naomi Shepherd in her study of Jewish women radicals, "and far more freedom to gain."[6]

Returning to Russia in 1873, Kuliscioff and Macarevich worked for revolutionary factions in the orbit of Zemlya i Volya (Land and Liberty), first in Odessa and then in Kiev.[7] The activities of the group included propagandizing among the peasants and terrorist strikes against authorities. Her husband was arrested in 1874 and sentenced to five years of hard labor; she would never see him again. Kuliscioff escaped capture several times and lived clandestinely in constant flight from the Tsarist police. At one point in 1876, she took refuge in Kharkov and earned enough to survive by singing in the town park.

The fascinating fugitive with the long golden braid fled Russia for good in April 1877 and first appears as "Kuliscioff" in the Paris police records from that year. Although the origins of her new surname have never been explained, in all likelihood Anna Rozenstein Macarevich chose it as a symbolic gesture

Fig. 77. Mario Nunes-Vais (Italian, 1856–1932), *Anna Kuliscioff*. Istituto Centrale per il Catalogo e la Documentazione, Gabinetto Fotografico Nazionale, Collezione Nunes-Vais, Rome

of her allegiance with the lowest of the working class: *kuli* in Russian (as *coolie* in English) refers to an unskilled worker from the Far East. Kuliscioff rejected all luxury associated with her moneyed background, while her proud, if despotic, father continued to send her funds. She also buried any trace of her Jewish background, although she identified with the relentless persecution of the Jews (from personal knowledge of the Russian pogroms) and in 1917 hailed the prospect of a state for Jews in Palestine. Tellingly, the young Kuliscioff's favorite writer was Heinrich Heine, none other than Hannah Arendt's epitome of the conscious pariah.[8]

Kuliscioff was unique among her radical Russian sisters, first, for surviving intact through periods of political persecution, and second, for eventually immigrating to Italy, where she continued the fight for workers' emancipation in an entirely different cultural context.[9] Though she began as an anarchist, she had turned to scientific Marxism and more pragmatic agendas by the time she met Andrea Costa, the founding father of Italian Socialism, while they were both exiles in Switzerland. Their passionate relationship, begun late in 1877, was foiled by their frequent imprisonment and deportation: between 1878 and 1882, Kuliscioff was repeatedly expelled from Italy (for inciting class hatred and revolt against the state) and sought refuge in Lugano. In December 1881, she gave birth to their daughter, Andreina, in Imola, Costa's hometown. Costa proved more progressive in his politics than in his attitudes toward women's emancipation, and after years of living apart and lacking a sense of parity in the relationship, Kuliscioff left for Bern, Switzerland, with her two-month-old baby and enrolled in medical school. She would be among the very first women to practice medicine in Italy: she eventually graduated from the University of Naples in 1886 and opened a clinic in Milan.[10]

In 1885, Kuliscioff met lawyer and political centrist Filippo Turati (1857–1932; fig. 78); under her influence, he absorbed Marxist doctrine and emerged as the leader of the reformist wing of the Italian Socialist Party (PSI). Viewed by their contemporaries as the stronger, sharper, and more politically savvy of the two, Kuliscioff became his closest adviser, most unsparing critic, and the chief strategist of the reformist PSI. From the founding of the Partito dei Lavoratori Italiani (the first incarnation of the PSI) in 1892, to her death in 1925, the year Benito Mussolini outlawed oppositional parties, Kuliscioff weighed in on all critical matters. And she did not take a private role behind the public figure. A political celebrity, she was highly visible in national and international party congresses (fig. 79), as a union organizer, and in the press. "There is only one man in Italy—and she is a woman," her colleague Arturo Labriola wrote to Friedrich Engels in 1893.[11]

Without question, as a woman unable to vote or hold office, Kuliscioff felt the bitterness of having to operate through another, not to mention the frustration of lobbying for women's suffrage only to have it rejected in 1912 by a parliament of men elected solely by men. Yet all politicians maneuver behind the scenes, and in Kuliscioff's case, a salon afforded her the means to direct policy and advance a legislative agenda. The salon tradition arrived in Italy in the late eighteenth century with the influx of French exiles and expatriates.

Fig. 79. Mario Nunes-Vais (Italian, 1856–1932), *Congress of the Italian Socialist Party, Florence*, 1908. Istituto Centrale per il Catalogo e la Documentazione, Gabinetto Fotografico Nazionale, Collezione Nunes-Vais, Rome. Anna Kuliscioff is seated in the second row, third from the left. Filippo Turati is beside her.

As revolution swept Europe in 1848, certain salons of wealthy elites served as bases of resistance against the restoration of monarchical and clerical power. The Milan salon of Contessa Clara Maffei (1814–1886), for example, was a focal point of Lombard patriotism and liberalism during the Italian Risorgimento.[12] Kuliscioff's gatherings inherited the mantle of political avant-gardism, but she propagated the ideology of the left in a rapidly industrializing and mostly illiterate young nation. For three decades, hers was "the salon that led Italy," originating "the resolutions of the party leaders and the parliamentary motions, giving directives for the Socialist congresses, the local sections, legislative chambers, the leagues, and the strikers, and organizing the

propaganda campaign in the newspapers and the 'red' press."[13] In short, Kuliscioff was dedicated to the overthrow of those privileged classes who had bequeathed the salon tradition, yet she upheld the practice of reasoned negotiation and critical dialectic, as opposed to demagogy. Although the use of the salon as a militant base for the rights of the economically downtrodden may seem contradictory, Kuliscioff drew a straight line from the Enlightenment discourse of universality to the Marxist doctrine of a classless society.

From 1891, Kuliscioff and Turati lived on the fifth floor of Portici Galleria 23, above the Galleria Vittorio Emanuele II, the bustling commercial center of modern Milan. Their apartment door displayed two nameplates

—one plain and white that read "Dott. Anna Kuliscioff" and the other an ornate plaque engraved "Turati." The salon began as Socialists naturally gravitated to the home and office of the two PSI leaders, being further compelled by Kuliscioff's legendary reputation as a Russian revolutionary and her warm, if authoritative hospitality. Large windows in the apartment gave an unobstructed view across the piazza del Duomo to the magnificent Lombard cathedral, exactly on eye level, Kuliscioff liked to point out, with the sculpted figures of the Christian martyrs. A large image of Karl Marx hung on the wall, books filled shelves from floor to ceiling, and the drawing room contained the couples' desks: Kuliscioff's the smaller and less tidy of the two, stacked with letters and papers, and crowned by at least one vase of flowers never left empty by visitors.[14] They arrived in shifts, twice daily, after lunch and in the evening before dinner. Kuliscioff would sit against a corner of a small green velvet divan (see fig. 15) to brace her body, increasingly contorted by a degenerative disease—either rheumatoid arthritis or tuberculosis of the bone. Turati referred to the divan as "the confessional," where seamstresses, telephone operators, and rice pickers from the countryside came to ask for advice and young members of the party could speak to "Signora Anna" in confidence.[15]

Kuliscioff smoked incessantly, using her knobby fingers to snap her cigarettes in two—a habit born years earlier out of prison deprivation. She affectionately referred to the physically imposing Turati as "the bear" and her animated, shriveled self as "the monkey."[16] A picture of elegant severity, with a diaphanous, otherworldly presence, she avoided both the dour attire of her fellow "Russian agitators" and any display of bourgeois finery (see fig. 77).[17] She never wore pants (as did feminist figureheads like George Sand), nor did she disguise her femininity. "The fact is that woman is neither inferior nor superior," Kuliscioff publicly affirmed. "She is what she is; and that being so, and with all of her differences from the other sex, there is no reason for woman to find herself in a subordinate condition."[18] Contemporary descriptions of her relied inevitably on binary oppositions: at once tough and caring, instinctively perceptive and rigorously empirical, Kuliscioff had "a masculine brain, a maternal heart."[19] Her Italian comrades perceived her otherness, if they did at all, in certain of her "Slavic qualities," but for the most part she took on the mythic stature of a zealous missionary, having attended to the poor and sick in the "most inelegant" surroundings as only a "true lady" could.[20]

"At far remove from high society and gossip," Kuliscioff and Turati received visitors in what was together a drawing room and the working space for the "basic blueprint of democratic socialism," a "smithy continuously forging ideas."[21] The pair had founded *Critica Sociale*, the preeminent journal of the PSI, in 1891, and produced the bimonthly from their desks. Their editorials and those of other politicians derived from the salon interchange, as one witness recounted, evolving "little by little from an unbiased analysis of information, maturing through the contrast of ideas and opinions, until they reached definitive written form."[22] Numerous articles were joint efforts, signed with their initials "t.k." or with "Noi" (Us), although Kuliscioff used her own name for essays on women's emancipation. She was one of the first female journalists in Italy, at a time when most Italian women were illiterate.[23] Responsible for the content, layout, and distribution of the journal, Kuliscioff also solicited foreign contributors, such as Engels, Karl Kautsky, August Bebel, Jean Jaurès, and Émile Vandervelde. Her facility with languages and her prestigious international contacts broadened the reach of Italian Socialism and, as she intended, broke through its provincialism.[24] Salon regulars wrote for other presses, including the official Socialist daily *Avanti!*, with columns and features that bore the imprint of the influential hostess.[25]

Through her salon, Kuliscioff mediated—and sometimes encouraged—frequent ideological schisms with the PSI. Maximalists, those in favor of violent insurrections, sparred with minimalists, like herself, who advocated legislative compromises with the shrewd liberal prime minister, Giovanni Giolitti. As she wrote to Engels in 1894: "It would certainly not be possible to talk of a socialist revolution in a country that is two-thirds medieval."[26] She took her own positions according to the issue and the historical moment, and did not always side with Turati; the salon dynamic, like that of the party, shifted over the years. Insiders included the moderates Ivanoe Bonomi and Leonida Bissolati, as well as Claudio Treves and Giuseppe Emanuele Modigliani (the brother of the artist Amedeo), both of whom shared Kuliscioff's militant bent. As a hotbed of activism, the salon attracted the labor leader Angelo Cabrini, Milan's Socialist mayor Emilio Caldara, and such intransigents as Arturo Labriola and Angelica Balabanoff (like Kuliscioff a Russian Jew), who had been romantically involved with a young renegade named Benito Mussolini. With strategic equanimity Kuliscioff engaged these divisive factions within the PSI and for decades served as a mentor to a younger generation of the political left. The poet Ada Negri and the writer Filippo Tommaso Marinetti (who was also involved in anarchic syndicalism) attended the salon, and it was a required stop for many foreigners, among them Russians (the exiled Marxist Georgij Plechanov, for example) and Germans with whom Kuliscioff shared an anarchist past.[27]

More than one commentator has attempted to reconcile the apparent discrepancy between Kuliscioff's radical feminism—devoted above all to the female worker—and her facility in the art of the salon. Hers was the "salon among salons" in a city filled with aristocrats such as the Visconti holding court and grand bourgeois vying for social supremacy.[28] Yet for Kuliscioff these social encounters represented not a pastime or frivolity but viable labor, a fruitful expenditure of time, energy, money, and organizational skills that operated directly into the public sphere. She extended the principle of salon egalitarianism, receiving anonymous members of the lower class as well as bourgeois parliamentarians and upper-class Milanese women. From ambassadors to maids, Kuliscioff knew how to "put herself at the level of any interlocutor" and make others feel at ease. A master of "arcane, ladylike" skills, she avoided clichés like "What a nice surprise," when welcoming newcomers, and did not engage in superfluous flattery or intrusive questions. Instead, "she made

it seem as if she had always known that person and that they were resuming a conversation interrupted the night before." More than anything, witnesses esteemed her "virile" speaking style, elaborated analytically, without meandering, equivocation, or playful artifice. She disarmed opponents with irrefutable facts and statistics mustered in midsentence. On her death, hagiographers extolled Kuliscioff for understanding the arguments of others better than they did themselves, forcing them to recognize any weakness in their own positions.[29] But during her lifetime, Kuliscioff knew that she was infamous among her intellectual peers for "always having the last word."[30]

Colleagues spoke of the salon as Kuliscioff's, both out of gender convention and because she was increasingly immobilized and confined to the apartment. She frequently received alone, since Turati traveled around the country and, as of 1906, took up part-time residence in Rome as a parliamentary deputy. In later years she felt "enslaved" by the constant stream of visitors, but she never complained, except to Turati.[31] They began a twenty-seven-year correspondence when they were both arrested and temporarily jailed for inciting the widespread workers' unrest of 1898; their epistolary exchange—which continued during Turati's absences from Milan—is considered one of the most important documents of modern Italian political history. It also contributed to the venerable connection between the salon and letter writing, for Kuliscioff reported on who attended and what was discussed, and thereby involved Turati in an almost daily quarrying of information, and of reports and opinions in the press. Their dialogue then informed party strategy in the salon. "Our letters are a long-distance conversation," she confirmed, "our ideas, sentiments, and our projects meet as if we had only one brain and one soul."[32] Ideologically opposed to marriage as a form of female servitude, Kuliscioff held up her own arrangement as a model of equal partnership, further eradicating any dichotomy between her private and public life. During the Socialist Congress in Zurich in 1893, she overheard a party neophyte refer to her as "the woman of Turati," and turned around to correct him: "I am the woman of no one. I am simply

Fig. 80. First issue of *La Difesa delle Lavoratrici*, January 7, 1912, with an article by Anna Kuliscioff on August Bebel

and children resulted directly from her efforts. Influenced by Bebel's *Women and Socialism* (translated into Italian in 1891), Kuliscioff insisted that the fight for female emancipation was one and the same as class struggle: "The vote is the weapon of labor, and labor has no sex."[34] From 1909 to 1912, she led an arduous campaign for female enfranchisement (for all women, not just those of the middle and upper classes) in anticipation of the liberal government's bill for universal suffrage (or what Kuliscioff, ironically, called the "universal masculine").[35] Even after she overcame resistance within her own Socialist Party, including editorial polemics from Turati, the motion to give women the vote was overwhelmingly defeated in the Chamber of Deputies. Italian women would gain suffrage only after World War II.

Although Kuliscioff was often the only woman among men, her salon was "the pillar of feminist groups in Milan"[36] bringing together an older generation of proselytizers, such as Anna Maria Mozzoni (the translator, in 1870, of John Stuart Mill's *Subjection of Women*), with younger recruits to the PSI. The militant labor organizers Maria Giudice and Argentina Altobelli mixed with upper-class women who devoted their energies to philanthropic institutions, notably Alessandrina Ravizza and Ersilia Maino, head of the Milanese Unione Femminile (Women's League). In 1912, Kuliscioff launched the bimonthly *La Difesa delle Lavoratrici* (*The Defense of Female Workers;* fig. 80) with PSI backing; several feminist habitués of her salon served on the editorial board and contributed articles. A blend of dogma, reports about the political battlefield, and personal advice columns, the journal aimed to galvanize, rather than merely educate, its working-class readership on matters of rights and party solidarity.[37]

As a salonière, Kuliscioff was said to have defused potential envy from other women across class lines, but in fact she often clashed with suffragists and bourgeois feminists, such as Ravizza and Maino, who also held important Milanese salons. With their substantial marital wealth, these women promoted feminist causes through social networking and welfare programs, instead of investment in militant Socialism.[38] Even

Anna Kuliscioff." "Don't take it personally," Turati told the flustered young man. "These Russians are lively, you know!"[33]

If Kuliscioff perpetuated the feminine authority of the salonière, she rejected the ideology of social gallantry upon which salon politesse was based. Uninterested in social pleasantries as a form of gender compensation for women of the upper classes, Kuliscioff ceaselessly campaigned in the drawing room to alleviate the appalling conditions of working women (sixty percent of the Italian industrial workforce), who were doubly exploited at home and on the job. Key labor legislation passed in Italy in 1902 protecting women

Fig. 81. Crowds assembling on the piazza del Duomo, underneath Anna Kuliscioff's apartment, in anticipation of her funeral procession, December 1925

though she commended their initiatives, Kuliscioff, the orthodox Marxist, judged them to be misguided capitalist exploiters, just like their male counterparts. Women in the factories, she believed, had a more realistic understanding of gender equality than did rich matrons without the dignity of salaried jobs (even though some legitimately "worked" through their salons). One ambitious and well-to-do disciple who admired and envied Kuliscioff's power was Margherita Sarfatti, whom the ʒarina once belittled in her drawing room for wearing lavish jewelry.[39] By 1922, Sarfatti had eclipsed Kuliscioff and her political hegemony, conducting her own salon under the aegis of Fascism.

With the outbreak of World War I, the Socialist Party split decisively over the issue of Italian intervention in the European conflict. Mussolini led the breach in the ranks against Turati, agitating for war versus the party's official pacifist stance. In 1914 he resigned as editor of *Avanti!* and five years later, in a right-wing revision of Marxist principles, founded the Fascist movement. Once Italy entered on the side of France and Britain in 1915, and began to endure humiliating defeats against the Austrians, Kuliscioff's salon became the center for the patriotic reformists of the PSI.[40] She watched the mass demonstrations on the piazza del Duomo and twice heard glasses rattle in the apartment from small explosions set off in the nearby Caffè Biffi.

Like an eager parvenu, Mussolini had once tried to gain approbation from Kuliscioff, whom he deemed

"worth even more than a good man." She quickly sized him up as "a cheap poet who has read a bit of Nietzsche."[42] In 1924, Fascist thugs assassinated the Socialist deputy Giacomo Matteotti, who had been one of her salon's devotees, and in the ensuing crisis Mussolini seized dictatorial power. When Kuliscioff died, at the very end of 1925, crowds quietly filled the piazza del Duomo to pay their respects (fig. 81) and then followed the funeral cortege to the cemetery, but not before the procession was disrupted, the flowers and wreaths torn and strewn, by Fascist violence. "Fascism did far worse things," commented the historian Luigi Salvatorelli, "but perhaps nothing revealed more clearly its irrevocable moral repugnance."[43] Many key figures associated with *Critica Sociale* and the now defunct salon became ardent anti-Fascists and found themselves in life-threatening danger: Labriola, Modigliani, Claudio Treves, Gaetano Salvemini, Pietro Nenni—and Turati—fled to Paris within a year.

The Salons of Modernism

In the late nineteenth century, the salon acquired an added dimension as a means of advancing and disseminating new art movements. As collectors, critics, and exhibition organizers, Jewish salonières were the agents who brought together creative talents from various countries and disciplines to exchange ideas. A number of salons offered unique opportunities for viewing art in domestic spaces conducive to contemplative enjoyment and engaged discourse. When the collections of the salonières featured examples of the latest art, particularly art from abroad, to which access was otherwise nonexistent or severely limited, the impact could be enormous. A weekly salon afforded the possibility of exposure over time to novel and often difficult images, and the discussions that took place around them increased the effect of these artworks and their makers on society.

The salon most critical for the dissemination of modernism in Germany was held by Felicie Bernstein, née Rosenthal (1850–1908), together with her husband, Carl (1842–1894), in their grandly furnished Berlin home during the 1880s and 1890s.[1] The painter Sabine Lepsius described the hostess's talents, which distinguished this salon in Wilhelmine Berlin: "[She] possessed that engaging quality that unites opposites, encourages clever and amusing conversation—in short, that nourished intellectual competence and flexibility. . . . Around the year 1880 the first Impressionist pictures to arrive in Berlin appeared on these walls; passionately admired or ridiculed, but always discussed, they provided the occasion for plans, which were later realized in the founding of the Secession"[2]—the independent artists' association established in 1898 to exhibit modern German and international art in Berlin.

As wealthy Francophile Russian Jews living in Berlin, the Bernsteins were outsiders several times over. They attracted Germans and foreigners, controversial young artists like Max Klinger and established painters like Adolph Menzel, émigrés and refugees, and many figures in the art world who would be irrevocably influenced by the encounter with the Bernsteins' collection of French Impressionism. The couple had acquired these paintings in Paris, advised by Carl's cousin Charles Ephrussi, editor of the *Gazette des Beaux-Arts*, collector of Impressionist works, friend of Pierre-Auguste Renoir and Marcel Proust, and habitué of Geneviève Straus's salon, among others in Paris. The Bernsteins installed the works in their music room (fig. 82), where they were seen by an international group who frequented the Wednesday evening gatherings, instigating a quiet but significant revolution in artistic taste, practice, and patterns of collecting.[3] The encounter with works of Édouard Manet, Claude Monet, Alfred Sisley, and Camille Pissarro in Berlin, at a time when these artists were not yet accepted in France, elicited some of the earliest writings and commentaries on Impressionism. The French Symbolist poet Jules Laforgue, who had gone to Berlin as reader to Empress Augusta of Prussia with an introduction to the Bernsteins from Ephrussi, wrote a treatise on the physiological and aesthetic explanation of the Impressionist formula in response to these paintings that has become a canonical early text on the movment.[4] The Danish literary critic and salon regular Georg Brandes (born Morris Cohen) observed that the collection would be "a useful element of fermentation" to the German art scene, as "artistically, the distance between Paris and Berlin is such that not one out of forty painters here [has] seen an Impressionist painting."[5] This proved prophetic, especially in regard to the painting of one salon guest, Max Liebermann, who would be the chief proponent of the new painting in Berlin, a founder of the Berlin Secession, and a major collector of Impressionist works.[6]

Many of the younger generation of German museum directors and curators saw their first Impressionist works at the Bernsteins' salon, including Alfred

Fig. 82. Music room in the Bernsteins' home, showing some of their collection of Impressionist art. Among the artworks in the room are: on the left wall, Édouard Manet's *White Lilacs in a Vase* (c. 1882, fig. 83); to the left of the doorway, top, Alfred Sisley's *Seine at Argenteuil* (1875); and to the right of the doorway, top, Manet's *Departure of the Folkestone Ferry* (1869), now in the collection of the Philadelphia Museum of Art. Harvard University Fine Arts Library, Cambridge, Massachusetts

Fig. 83. Édouard Manet (French, 1832–1883), *White Lilacs in a Vase*, c. 1882. Oil on canvas, 21¼ x 16½ in. (54 x 42 cm). Nationalgalerie, Staatliche Museen zu Berlin– Preussischer Kulturbesitz, Gift of Felicie Bernstein

Lichtwark, who became director of the Hamburger Kunsthalle in 1886, and Hugo von Tschudi, who as director of Berlin's Nationalgalerie and then the Neue Pinakothek in Munich would be among Germany's great institutional champions of international modernism.[7] Shortly before her death, Felicie Bernstein, who had remained childless, donated art and furnishings from her home to habitués of her salon—a Monet landscape to Liebermann, Manet's *Lilacs in a Vase* (fig. 83) to Tschudi's Nationalgalerie, and so on. The works in her collection thus went on to carry her message of cosmopolitan taste and openness toward the avant-garde.

BERTA ZUCKERKANDL: "ON MY DIVAN AUSTRIA COMES ALIVE"

If the seeds of the Berlin Secession were planted quietly in the Bernsteins' salon, the Vienna Secession was born in that of a more publicly vocal Jewish woman, the journalist Berta Zuckerkandl (1864–1944; fig. 84). Throughout her long life, she was at the center of a salon, beginning with the Vienna gatherings hosted by her parents, the liberal journalist and newspaper owner Moritz Szeps and his wife, Amalie (1864–1944; fig. 85), "which attracted statesmen, parliamentarians, and financiers, along with poets, actors, aristocrats, women of the world and simple folk," and where there was "no room for snobbism and arrogance."[8] As with many other Jewish salonières, her upbringing was decisive both for the social connections she forged and for the egalitarian education and professional example she received from her father. Not only did Moritz Szeps give his daughter an inside track to a career as a journalist, but before her marriage Berta traveled extensively as his secretary and, most important for the development of her salon, met many prominent figures in European culture and politics, notably in France. She never abandoned the liberal politics espoused by her father, for which he was both much admired and reviled.

Berta Szeps married the anatomist Emil Zuckerkandl in 1886; it was difficult for the Jewish Zuckerkandl to become a full professor in the capital, and the couple moved to Graz before he received an

Fig. 84. Madame D'Ora (Dora Philippine Kallmus) (Austrian, 1881–1963), *Berta Zuckerkandl*, 1908. Bildarchiv, Österreichische National-bibliothek, Vienna

Fig. 85. The Szeps family, c. 1882–84. Photograph. *From left:* Amalie Szeps, Julius Szeps, Ferdinand Bryndza (an editor of the *Neues Wiener Tagblatt*), Moritz Szeps, Leo Szeps, Sophie Szeps, Emil Zuckerkandl, Ella Szeps, Berta Szeps (Zuckerkandl), and the family governess. Private collection, Palo Alto, California

Fig. 86. Madame D'Ora (Dora Philippine Kallmus) (Austrian, 1881–1963), *Arthur Schnitzler*, 1908. Bildarchiv, Österreichische National-bibliothek, Vienna

appointment as professor in Vienna in 1888.[9] They settled into a house in the Nusswaldgasse, in the Döbling section; in their garden were walnut trees beneath which Ludwig van Beethoven had once composed. "It did not take long for our house to become the center of a circle of friends, a mixture of the artistic, scientific and academic worlds."[10] Johann Strauss the younger liked to tease his hostess that he visited to be inspired by those walnut trees, but clearly he came in order to be in the orbit of "the most marvelous and witty woman in Vienna."[11]

The scientists and doctors from Emil's milieu were distinguished by their pioneering spirit and desire to reform medicine in Austria; this also involved the admission of women to university medical studies, of which Emil was a prime advocate. Berta Zuckerkandl's guests included Emil's medical colleagues Richard Krafft-Ebing and Julius Wagner-Jauregg, along with Arthur Schnitzler (fig. 86), better known for his novels and plays that dissected the empty conventions of bourgeois society and morals, and exposed the sexuality beneath the surface. Schnitzler was part of the group

of mainly Jewish writers known as Jung Wien (Young Vienna); among other members were Richard Beer-Hofmann, Peter Altenberg, Felix Salten, Stefan Zweig, Hugo von Hofmannsthal, and the author and critic Hermann Bahr, all of whom became part of Berta Zuckerkandl's circle. Joining them were painters, designers, and architects who rebelled against the staid historicism of the academy and sought to rejuvenate Austrian art and design: Gustav Klimt, Otto Wagner, and Josef Hoffmann.

In 1897 these artists founded the Vienna Secession, an independent association that offered an alternative to the official exhibitions mounted by the Künstlerhaus. The Secession presented innovative Austrian and international art, and its members designed all aspects of the exhibitions—invitations, posters, catalogues, and installation. The critic Ludwig Hevesi claimed that "the idea for the Secession was first discussed [in Zuckerkandl's salon]. Here the small group of moderns who gave expression to this idea first met and began the fight for the revivification of art in Vienna."[12] Klimt, who was elected president of the Secession, designed for the first exhibition in

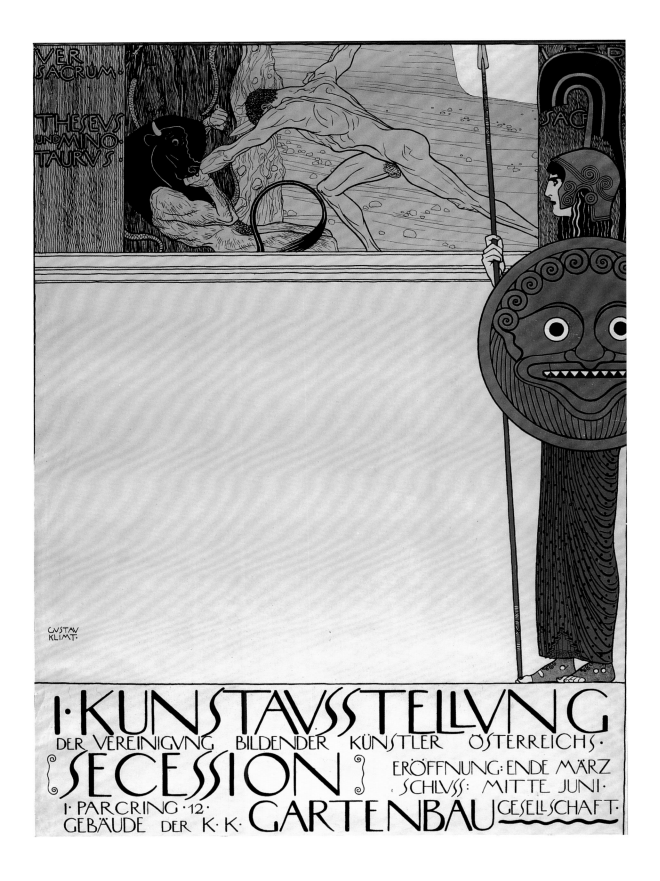

ARCHITEKT DAGOBERT PECHE—WIEN.   MODESCHAU—WIEN »RAUMGESTALTUNG«

DIE WIENER MODE-AUSSTELLUNG.

Nach einer von Regierungsrat Professor Hoff-mann gegebenen Anregung schlossen sich verschiedentliche, Kunst und Mode angehören-den Genossenschaften, zu einer Mode-Schau zusammen, die besonders der Originalart des Wiener Kleider- und Hutputzes, der Wiener Textile und der Wiener Spitzentechnik dienen sollte. Im Säulenhof des österreichischen Mu-seums wurde vom Architekten Dagobert Peche ein reizvoller Rahmen eingebaut, der sozusagen den engen Zusammenhang, welcher in Augen-blicken schöpferischer Kultur-Phantasie Mode mit Kunst stets eng verbindet, symbolisieren sollte. Denn es ging in dieser Ausstellung um die künstlerische Stellungnahme zu dem Problem „Wiener Mode". Im Gegensatz zu den gewerb-lichen und den genossenschaftlichen Schneider-Ausstellungen war hier eine Aktion zur künst-lerischen Beeinflussung des Modegewerbes ins Werk gesetzt, durch die Herstellung eines un-mittelbaren Verkehres zwischen Künstlern und gewerblichen Unternehmern. Daran muß fest-gehalten werden, um den Stil, Sinn und Zweck dieser Vorführung richtig zu verstehen. Sie war eigentlich eine Materialschau über Auf-putz, Stoffe, Stickereien, Batiken, gemalten Bändern, Posamenten, Spitzen aller Arten, die ganz frei von französischer oder anderer fremdländischer Beeinflussung zeigen sollte, wie die seit einem Jahrzehnt von der Wiener Kunst-gewerbe-Schule vorbereitete und in die Ge-werbe geleitete Modekunst nun zu einem wirt-schaftlichen Faktor von großer Bedeutung emporwächst. Die Kleider, vielfach von Kunst-gewerblerinnen und meist nur aus billigem Ma-terial verfertigt, wollen nicht als Modelle für Schneider gelten. Sie sollen nur dazu dienen, einen Hintergrund abzugeben für die dekorative

Fig. 87. Gustav Klimt (Austrian, 1862–1918), *"Theseus and Minotarus 1": Poster for the First Secession Exhibition* (before censorship), 1898. Color lithograph, 37 x 26¾ in. (94 x 68 cm). The Robert Gore Rifkind Collection, Beverly Hills, California

Fig. 88. Berta Zuckerkandl's article on the Vienna Fashion Exhibition ("Die Wiener Mode-Ausstellung") in *Deutsche Kunst und Dekoration* 37 (April–September 1916), with illustration of exhibition design by Dagobert Peche (Austrian, 1887–1923)

March 1898 a poster that depicted Theseus in battle with the Minotaur, symbolizing the struggle for the new art, with Pallas Athena presiding as defender of the Secession (fig. 87). A censor later insisted on the addi-tion of a tree to conceal the hero's genitalia. By the second exhibition, in November 1898, the Secession had its own building, designed by Joseph Maria Olbrich, and emblazoned with the words of Hevesi: "Der Zeit ihre Kunst, der Kunst ihrer Freiheit" (To every age its art, to art its freedom).

The causes that Zuckerkandl energetically advo-cated all her life—the creation of an Austrian avant-garde in art, literature, and theater, liberal democratic politics, and social reform—found expression in her salon and in her journalism: "In this fight my weapon

was my pen, my battlefield the *Wiener Allgemeine Zeitung*."[13] Zuckerkandl's columns exemplify the Viennese feuilleton, which had "developed into a chatty essay on any topic written to match the verve and sparkle of conversation,"[14] and which had a disproportionate number of Jewish practitioners. In the newspapers she cajoled her fellow citizens to demand high-quality design, and to appreciate the art created by members of her circle, especially Klimt, Hoffmann, and the designer Koloman Moser; for the popular German art publica-tions *Die Kunst für Alle* and *Deutsche Kunst und Dekor-ation* (fig. 88), she reported on current exhibitions and developments in the Viennese art scene. Her articles were carefully calibrated according to local or interna-tional readership, and she served as critic, booster, and public relations wizard.

The second issue of *Ver sacrum*, the luxuriously produced journal of the Vienna Secession, contained her article "Wiener Geschmacklosigkeiten" ("Viennese Lack of Good Taste"). Here she touched on most of the themes that would occupy her in her writings on art, and the style and method of argumentation are characteristic of her approach. "The Viennese like to complain about themselves," Zuckerkandl begins, "but it has to be in a tenderly admiring fashion, like that of a mother admonishing the amusing misbehavior of a child. They do not take well to serious criticism."[15] She then proceeds to proffer serious criticism, but in a gen-tle, dare one say "maternal" style, a delicate balance of chiding mixed with compliments. Lamenting the deplorable state of Viennese art, design, architecture, and fashion, she tempers her criticism with praise of the natural gifts of the Viennese: "In habits and customs, in architecture, art, and closely related crafts one would expect a strong individualistic feeling. But no; in spite of the existing natural gifts and talents, Vienna has lost its sense of beauty. Who would have thought that Berlin would beat us even in this regard." Zuckerkandl's sense of competition with Germany, and her insistence on differentiating Austrian creative sensibility from German art, permeates much of her writing. In par-ticular, she relates to the advances made by Alfred Lichtwark and others in the Bernstein circle in bringing

For Zuckerkandl, the crisis in art and design is symptomatic of a larger malaise, which extends to fashion and social interaction:

From art and crafts the general lack of taste passes into other expressions of life. Our women, who are the most graceful in the world, do not know how to dress anymore. They confuse individuality with eccentricity and have adopted a certain uniform elegance that is possibly correct but very boring. Correct and boring is also the manner in which Viennese social life plays out. Is there a Viennese salon, that is to say a meeting place for all intellectual stirrings, a rallying point for all modern thinkers and strivers? A neutral ground where every opinion is respected and yet discussed with poetry and grace? By no means.[17]

"Wiener Geschmacklosigkeiten" can be read as Zuckerkandl's manifesto, and as such, it illuminates her vision of the salon as part of a reform of all aspects of life. By the time the article was published, she had set out to establish the ideal salon she described, and with it to achieve her goals for Vienna. As art, design, and fashion are to be integrated into a total vision of life, sociability—the salon—is part of the *Gesamtkunstwerk*, the total work of art. This concept motivated the establishment of the Wiener Werkstätte (Viennese Workshops), founded by Josef Hoffmann and Koloman Moser in 1903, which rendered designs for buildings and everything in them—painting, furniture, decorative arts, cutlery, wallpaper, even the clothing and accessories of the residents—unifying interior and exterior into an expressive aesthetic totality. While Zuckerkandl never had the financial means to indulge in a complete Wiener Werkstätte environment, she owned objects conceived by the workshops, and sported their fashion and accessory designs (fig. 89). She publicized Werkstätte projects in the press and was responsible for brokering the first important commission. At Berta's instigation, her brother-in-law Viktor Zuckerkandl engaged the Werkstätte to design the Purkersdorf Sanatorium, a combination spa and hospital near Vienna, and all its furnishings (fig. 90).

Though the new art benefited from enlightened

Fig. 89. Stand at the Kunstschau Vienna 1908 with society ladies in Wiener Werkstätte clothing and jewelry. Berta Zuckerkandl is at far right. Photograph by Josef Justh. MAK—Austrian Museum of Applied Arts/ Contemporary Art, Vienna

Fig. 90. Josef Hoffmann (Austrian, 1870–1956), *Chair for the Dining Room of the Purkersdorf Sanatorium*, Austria, 1904–6. Manufactured by Thonet Brothers. Beechwood, leather, and metal, 99 x 46 x 43 in (39.6 x 18.4 x 17.2 cm). Cooper-Hewitt, National Design Museum, Smithsonian Institution, Museum Purchase from Combined Funds and Crane and Co., 1968-6-1

modernism to Germany; by comparison she finds Vienna wanting. She discusses architecture and "decorators and wallpaper designers," and finds them awash in "senseless orgies of brocade, velvet, and gold," endlessly perpetuating old styles that have lost any significance. She calls for a "modern national style," which can be achieved by "assimilating foreign accomplishments technically and materially."[16]

right:
Fig. 91. Gustav Klimt
(Austrian, 1862–1918), *Study
for "Philosophy,"* c. 1898–99.
Pencil and crayon on paper,
35¼ x 24⅞ in. (89.6 x 63.2
cm). Wien Museum

below:
Fig. 92. Gallery view of the
Tenth Exhibition of the
Vienna Secession with
Gustav Klimt's *Medicine*.
Exhibition architecture and
design by Koloman Moser.
From *Ver Sacrum* 4, no. 9
(1901): 159

far right:
Fig. 93. Gustav Klimt
(Austrian, 1862–1918),
*Transfer Drawing for
"Jurisprudence,"* 1902–3.
Black chalk and pencil on
paper, 32½ x 23¾ in. (84 x
61.4 cm). Private collection

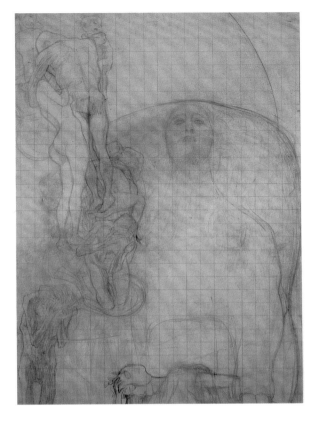

patrons and even enjoyed state support, it was also
much vilified by conservative critics, with Zuckerkandl,
like the Pallas Athena in Klimt's poster, always its
staunch defender. The public controversy surrounding
Klimt's university paintings, which were commissioned
to decorate the ceiling of the aula, or Great Hall, representing *Philosophy* (1900; fig. 91), *Medicine* (1901; fig. 92),
and *Jurisprudence* (1903; fig. 93), spurred Zuckerkandl
to defend him in print, while he was being viciously
attacked by the popular press. Criticized for their amor-
phous forms and nudity, Klimt's paintings offended
mainly because of their philosophical pessimism.
Instead of celebrating the triumphs of the university
faculties, with knowledge, science, and progress tri-
umphing over ignorance, sickness, and injustice,
they depicted a chaotic and cruel world with humans
enslaved by passions and haunted by the inevitability of
death. Nationalists perceived the paintings as evidence
of an insidious Jewish influence, a view characteristic
of the tendency to associate Jews with the avant-garde.

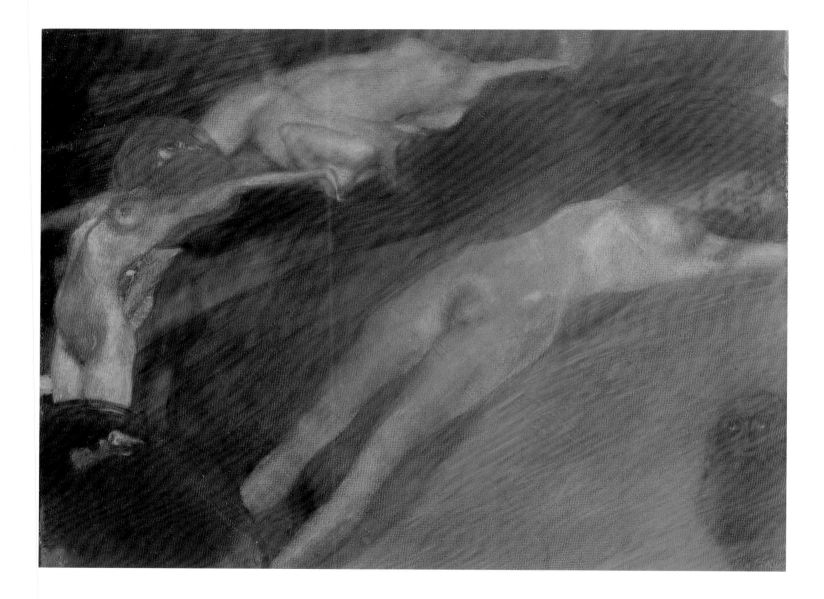

Fig. 94. Gustav Klimt (Austrian, 1862–1918), *Moving Water*, 1898. Oil on canvas, 21 x 26⅛ in. (53.3 x 66.4 cm). Private collection, courtesy of Galerie St. Etienne, New York

Fig. 95. Martha Alber, *Jewish New Year Greetings*, 1910–11. Postcard of the Wiener Werkstätte, 3½ x 5½ in. (8.9 x 14 cm). Leonard A. Lauder Collection, New York. The pattern in this postcard—called *Blätter* (*Leaves*), which was designed by Martha Alber for the Wiener Werkstätte—is the same as that of the dress worn by the sitter in Gustav Klimt's *Portrait of Johanna Staude* (1917–18; Österreichische Galerie Belvedere, Vienna)

The newspaper *Deutsches Volksblatt* declared: "We know Jewish effrontery. To feed their poison into the people they have made it their principle to proclaim the lowest and meanest."[18] In a journalistic coup in 1905, Zuckerkandl interviewed the protagonist of the "Klimt Affair," and published Klimt's call for artistic freedom and his letter to the ministry of education announcing his intention to buy back his paintings from the state.[19]

Though Klimt was not Jewish, for his detractors, his art epitomized "le goût juif," for its ornamental, "superficial" style and purported decadence (fig. 94), and because of his many Jewish patrons, sitters, and supporters, chief among them Zuckerkandl and Hevesi. But the connections among Klimt, the Secession, the Wiener Werkstätte, and Jewish patrons raised as well the question of recasting identity through aesthetics (fig. 95). Karl Kraus, the brilliant, caustic, and anti-Semitic Jewish cultural critic—and perhaps Berta Zuckerkandl's only real enemy—wrote in his publication *Die Fackel:* "Just as every aristocrat used to keep his Jew-in-residence, so today every stockbroker has a Secessionist about the house. . . . Herr Klimt initiates Frau Lederer into the art of Secessionist painting. This rapport between modern art and idle-rich Jewry, this rise in the art of design, capable of transforming ghettos into mansions, occasions the fondest of hopes. . . . Those who had the opportunity to admire the burgeon-

ing of the celebrated *goût juif* at the recent Secessionist Exhibition will not dismiss such dreams as merely idle."[20] Kraus sensed that Vienna's Jews were adopting the new style to promote assimilation, reinventing themselves—remaking the "ghetto"—by commissioning Secession and Wiener Werkstätte interiors; yet by supporting this style, they continued to mark their difference—or as the architect Adolf Loos commented, they merely replaced the old caftans of the ghetto with the new caftans of the Werkstätte.[21]

Zuckerkandl—who combined a cosmopolitan worldview with patriotic devotion to Austria—insisted that what was being created was a specifically *Austrian* style, one that would reflect the diversity inherent in the empire, with its Czechs, Jews, Moravians, Germans, Slavs, Magyars, Romanians, and other ethnic groups: "It was a question of defending a purely Austrian culture, a form of art that would weld together all the characteristics of our multitude of constituent peoples into a new and proud unity. For to be Austrian did not mean to be German; Austrian culture was the crystallization of the best of many cultures."[22]

Zuckerkandl saw French culture as the catalyst that would assist Austrian art in achieving its individual identity. Her ties to France went back to her days as her father's travel companion and her friendship with Georges Clemenceau, whom she credited with introducing her to much of the new art. These relationships were cemented and intensified when Sophie, her older sister, married the younger Clemenceau brother, Paul. Sophie's salon in Paris and Berta's in Vienna were a mechanism for cultural diplomacy, with the habitués of one sister welcome in the home of the other. Through Sophie, Berta met the French artist Eugène Carrière, who painted both sisters (figs. 96–97). While he chose to depict Sophie's elegant attire, a symphony of frothy pale fabric,[23] he emphasized Berta's pensive appearance and expressive hands, which, with her face and neck, are the only areas of light emerging from a murky background. When Berta first saw her likeness and noted how "sad and thoughtful" she looked, Carrière responded that it might have been a reflection of his own depression over the Dreyfus Affair.[24]

Fig. 96. Eugène Carrière
(French, 1849–1906), *Portrait
of Sophie Clemenceau*, n.d.
Oil on canvas. Private collection, Palo Alto, California

Fig. 97. Eugène Carrière
(French, 1849–1906), *Portrait
of Berta Zuckerkandl*, 1894.
Oil on canvas, 34½ x 27 in.
(87.6 x 68.6 cm). Private collection, New York. Formerly
in the collection of Berta
Zuckerkandl

Many of the contacts that Berta facilitated between French and Viennese artists originated with meetings at Sophie's. Zuckerkandl's abiding interest in fashion as an art form (see fig. 88) led her to arrange for the couturier Paul Poiret to show his designs in Vienna in 1912; she introduced him to Klimt, Hoffmann, and other artists of the Wiener Werkstätte, which inspired Poiret's collection for 1912–13, and his use of fabrics designed by Hoffmann and Dagobert Peche.[25] Zuckerkandl orchestrated Auguste Rodin's visit to Vienna in 1902, and his meeting with Klimt and other members of the Secession.[26] The composer Maurice Ravel and the mathematician-turned-statesman Paul Painlevé were other salon guests whom Berta first met at her sister's in Paris. It was also because of Sophie that Berta first hosted Gustav Mahler: "My sister . . . had gathered a little circle of music lovers around her, and, carrying on the tradition of her father's house, she continued to work for a cultured rapprochement between Austria and France. . . . From 1900 to 1908 this little group was present at nearly every concert that Mahler gave."[27] Sophie and Paul Clemenceau would later persuade Auguste Rodin to accept the commission to sculpt Mahler's portrait (fig. 98).

Perhaps the most romantic meeting that took place at Berta Zuckerkandl's was between Mahler and Alma Schindler (fig. 99). The young beauty, who had been involved with Klimt and with her music teacher Alexander Zemlinsky, confided to her diary one of the descriptions of salon conversation recounted immediately after the event:

*This evening at the Zuckerkandls'.
Met Mahler.
Present were: Frau Clemenceau, [Max] Burckhard, [photographer Friedrich] Spitzer, Mahler and his sister a[nd] Klimt. With the latter I barely spoke two words—was perfectly calm. Nor with Mahler at first—but then: a highly interesting controversy arose concerning Alex's [Zemlinsky's] ballet—about artistic cross-fertilization in a time of cultural decay. He denied the justification of ballet as an art form in its own right etc. Klimt, Carl [Moll, painter and Alma's stepfather], he and I led the discussion. Then it turned to Alex personally. [Mahler] described him as restricted—in a certain sense he's right too. He described the ballet [by Hugo von] Hofmannsthal as unperformable.*[28]

Not only did Mahler meet his future wife at Berta Zuckerkandl's, but his encounter with artists there led to fruitful collaboration with Alfred Roller, a cofounder of the Secession and the designer of *Ver sacrum*, who went on to design sets and costumes for Mahler's productions at the Vienna Royal Opera. Mahler conducted his arrangement of the choral portion of Beethoven's Ninth Symphony as part of a private viewing of the fourteenth Secession exhibition in 1902, created around Max Klinger's Beethoven sculpture.

Berta Zuckerkandl was widowed in 1910 and moved in 1916 to a four-room apartment in the center of Vienna, at Oppolzergasse 6, where she would remain until she fled for Paris in 1938. The new residence's proximity to the Burgtheater signaled a shift as her salon acquired a more theatrical bent; actors, producers, and writers for the theater could stop by after an evening's performance. Zuckerkandl herself became increasingly involved in translating French plays into

Fig. 98. Auguste Rodin (French, 1840–1917), *Bust of Gustav Mahler*, 1909. Bronze, 13⅜ x 11 x 9¾ in. (34.0 x 27.9 x 24.8 cm). Brooklyn Museum of Art, Ella C. Woodward Memorial Fund, New York

Fig. 99. Madame D'Ora (Dora Philippine Kallmus) (Austrian, 1881–1963), *Alma Mahler*, c. 1915. Bildarchiv, Österreichische National-bibliothek, Vienna

German and promoting their production for Viennese audiences—yet another example of her role as cultural emissary. Through her excellent contacts, she arranged for Schnitzler's plays to be translated and performed in Paris. Her most significant theatrical contribution was as herald and advocate for the Salzburg Festival, founded by her habitués Max Reinhardt and Hugo von Hofmannsthal to rejuvenate Austrian culture in the wake of the empire's defeat and dismemberment after World War I.[29] Their goal of creating an Austrian the-atrical idiom paralleled her efforts in the visual arts. She offered Hofmannsthal her salon as the site to gauge the response to a new work, *Das grosse Welttheater* (*The Great Theater of the World*), before its debut at the Salzburg Festival: "a modest reading for a few old and new acquaintances and strangers in this informal neu-tral place." In the end, more than one hundred attended the reading.[30]

Josef Hoffmann designed the interior at Oppolzer-gasse, in what Berta called "the sign of the modern, which is also my sign." The collection of Chinese fans

amassed by her late husband imparted "an unusual magic of color" to the black-and-white wood paneling and the white lace curtains with animal motif designed by Dagobert Peche that decorated the living room.[31] Koloman Moser's distinctive high-stemmed liqueur glasses, which had previously graced the Döbling resi-dence, served as a topic of conversation, for the glasses all differed slightly in color and shape (fig. 100).[32] An oversize divan that easily sat ten people was the phys-ical and emotional center of the room: "The divan, which has seen so many things, listens to the politicians with understanding; it knows many poets who sounded their laments on it. . . . On my divan Austria comes alive."[33] The salon focused more on politics in the postwar years, uniting conservatives and liberals, such as Chancellor Ignaz Seipel and the Socialist Julius Tandler.[34] Still, the guest books reveal a fascinating variety of visitors, as does one spread for 1932, where Albert Einstein faces Colette (fig. 101).

Zuckerkandl never tired of using French contacts to support Austria and promote social justice. In 1917

Fig. 100. Koloman Moser (Austrian, 1868–1918), *Five Liqueur Glasses*, 1900. Clear, green, yellow, and violet glass, 12⅛, 12⅜, 12¾, 13, 13½ in. (30.7, 31.5, 32, 33, 34.2 cm). Private collection. Formerly in the collection of Berta Zuckerkandl

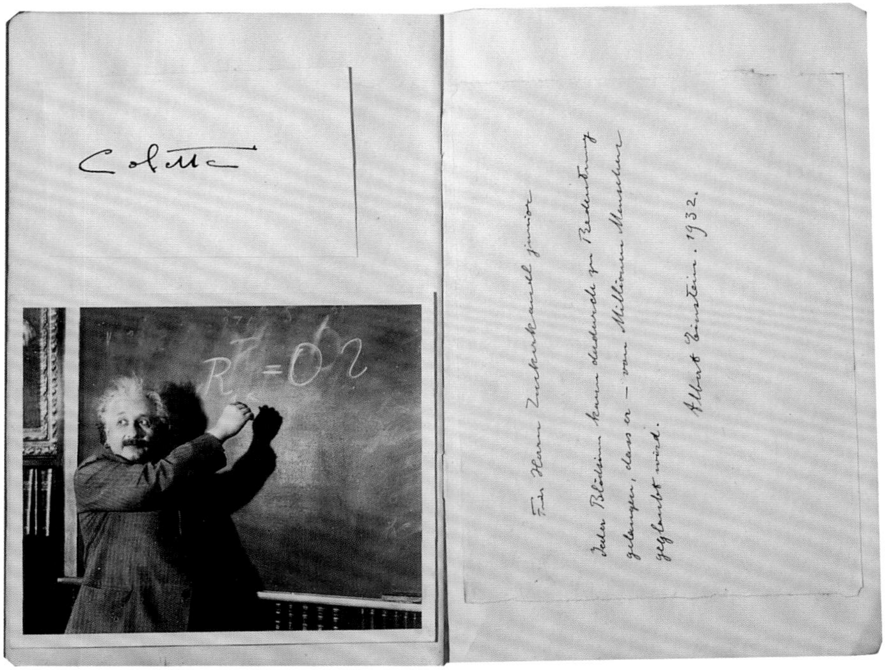

Fig. 101. Guest book of Berta Zuckerkandl and her grandson, Emile, 1932. Pages with signatures of Colette and Albert Einstein. Private collection, Palo Alto, California

she held secret meetings in Switzerland to try to negotiate a separate peace between Austria and the Allies during World War I.[35] She later interceded on Austria's behalf with the Hoover Commission in the United States to aid her country. Jewish causes also moved her to action; during the war she worked to alleviate the suffering of Jews in Galicia in central Europe and of the many immigrants—mainly Jews—who descended on Vienna from the eastern reaches of the empire. She used her excellent political connections in Austria and France to help secure the release of Philipp Halsmann, a young Jew who in 1928 was falsely accused by anti-Semites of murdering his father and subsequently imprisoned, in a case known as the "Austrian Dreyfus Affair."[36] As Philippe Halsman, he went on to become a recognized portrait photographer and contributor to *Life* magazine. Even in exile, Zuckerkandl continued to hold a salon, both in Paris and in the tiny apartment she shared with her son, daughter-in-law, and grandson in Algiers, at 30 avenue Clemenceau. At eighty she still captivated her guests, among them American and British soldiers and officers, and the French writers Paul Géraldy and André Gide.[37]

Berta Zuckerkandl's career as salonière and journalist encourages us to reevaluate some of the assumptions about fin-de-siècle Viennese culture. Scholars such as Carl Schorske have presented a view of that culture dominated by a political paralysis, of men unable to act definitively, retreating into aesthetic culture as a response to the defeat of the liberalism of their parents: "The life of art became a substitute for the life of action."[38] This withdrawal from the public sphere is associated with taking refuge in interior, domestic spaces formerly associated with women.[39] The characters in Schnitzler's novel *Der Weg ins Freie* (*The Road into the Open*) epitomize this trait; they procrastinate and suffer from "a deep-seated cynicism that nothing will ever really change at all . . . that no road into the open is likely to lead anywhere."[40] Zuckerkandl is an alternative model, of a feminine mobilization of the interior for public and political engagement. In her salon and her journalism she was proactive, motivated by what Ludwig Hevesi called her "energetic idealism."[41]

Fig. 102. Gustav Klimt
(Austrian, 1862–1918), *Pallas
Athena*, 1898. Oil on canvas,
33 x 16½ in. (84 x 42 cm).
Wien Museum

German author Helene von Nostitz recalled: "One
was always optimistic with her, believing in a
future, regardless of how dark it appeared to be."[42]
Zuckerkandl never retreated and never abandoned
the liberalism of her father, represented by the tragedy
of Crown Prince Rudolf, with whose death the dreams
of a liberal Austria died. Zuckerkandl's approach was
in line with her salonière antecedents like Rahel Levin,
who believed in the utopian ideal of the salon and its
power to effect social—and in Zuckerkandl's case, artistic
—change. Rahel Levin, "the German Pallas Athena,"
like Zuckerkandl went into battle with her pen. Klimt's
Pallas Athena (fig. 102), defender and guardian of
the Secession, a painting that belonged to Viktor
Zuckerkandl, represents Berta Zuckerkandl's fighting
and crusading spirit.

MARGHERITA SARFATTI:
THE ANTECHAMBER OF POWER

In 1912 the Futurist Umberto Boccioni painted the
salonière Margherita Sarfatti (1880–1961), although the
image has never been officially recognized as her portrait (fig. 103). The given title of the work, *Antigrazioso*
(*Ungraceful*), refers to the style of pictorial ugliness that
the Futurists adapted to affront staid bourgeois tastes.
Amid misshapen masses a figure hunches over a desk,
pen in hand, poised over white paper. Boccioni distorts
the facial features beyond recognition, but the puffed
sleeves and front ruffle of the blouse confirm that the
writer is a woman. Her luminous red hair corresponds
to other portraits of Sarfatti by artists who enjoyed her
hospitality—Emilio Gola, Achille Funi, Mario Sironi,
and Carlo Socrate. Not only the distinctive coiffure
but also the iconography of the woman of ideas (she is
hard at work by the light of a lamp, seen at the upper
right) makes the identity unmistakable: no other female
critic belonged to Boccioni's intimate circle, let alone
one who had published on Futurism. Having begun her
career in 1901, at age twenty-one, Sarfatti wrote for
feminist and Socialist journals, and by 1909 earned
her own byline in the newspaper *Avanti!* of the Italian
Socialist Party.[43] She disliked the Futurists' experiments

with Cubist abstraction, but *Antigrazioso* entered
directly into her collection (she was one of the few
Italian patrons of avant-garde art). Sarfatti never sold
it, as she did with many other works she owned.

For his image of a formidable thinking woman,
Boccioni drew from Pablo Picasso's famous *Portrait
of Gertrude Stein* (1906; see fig. 117), which he saw at
Stein's salon during a visit to Paris in the fall of 1911.[44]
Both artists painted their subjects from the waist up:
intentionally or not, Boccioni positioned Sarfatti,
with similarly massive rounded shoulders, at the
opposite angle from Stein, so that they face each other
like pendants. While both artists created a masklike
visage, Boccioni augmented the savage distortions,
directly inspired by studies for Picasso's *Les Demoiselles
d'Avignon* (1907), which he likewise saw at the Stein
residence. The masking of the sitters' features marks
the modernist break with realist portraiture, but also
an about-face from the metaphoric "social mask" of
propriety developed in the eighteenth-century salons.[45]
Masking here is neither a protective means of delicately
revealing oneself to another—or a masquerade, the
false face of an insincere personality. Instead Picasso
and Boccioni incorporated the anticlassical deforma-
tions of primitive art, a potent symbol of racial and
cultural difference, to represent the impenetrable and
possibly threatening otherness of their two sitters, both
Jews, women, sexually unconventional, and the artists'
intellectual superiors.[46] Gone is the delicate grace of
the civilizing *belle savante*, replaced by the image of the
salonière as masculine force and primal nature. Just as
Picasso struggled over dozens of sittings to get Stein
right, Boccioni had tried before to paint Sarfatti but,
dissatisfied with the results, slashed the canvas with his
palette knife.[47]

Sarfatti may have thought of herself as the Italian
Gertrude Stein, but with her direct access to absolute
power, the comparison to Madame de Pompadour is
more apt.[48] In 1913, the year after Boccioni painted
her portrait, Sarfatti began a twenty-year relationship
with Benito Mussolini, whom she likely met at Anna
Kuliscioff's salon in Milan (see fig. 77). No mere consort,
Sarfatti helped plan Mussolini's ascent to power during

Fig. 103. Umberto Boccioni
(Italian, 1882–1916),
Antigrazioso, 1912. Oil on
canvas, 31½ x 31½ in. (80 x
80 cm). Private collection.
Formerly in the collection
of Margherita Sarfatti

Fig. 104. Emilio Sommariva
(Italian, 1883–1956),
Margherita Sarfatti, c. 1926.
Fondo Fotografico
Sommariva, Biblioteca
Nazionale Braidense, Milan

the founding years of Fascism and throughout the
1920s convinced many intellectuals, including herself,
that Fascism represented a rebirth for Italy. With the
racial laws of 1938, Sarfatti fled to Paris and then South
America, despite having written a best-selling biography of Mussolini, *Dux* (1925), that was translated into
eighteen languages. On her return to Italy shortly after
World War II she was treated as a pariah, but that did
not deter the indomitable Sarfatti from writing her own
story, *Acqua passata* (*Water Under the Bridge*) in 1955.
That the word "Fascism" appears only once in the book
testifies to her refusal, or inability, to account for her
role in Italy's totalitarian debacle. As her old friend
Bernard Berenson recalled, "We agreed about events,
occurrences, all that happened. She denied none, but
when we came to discuss how and why, we seldom
agreed about the how and never about the why."[49]

Sarfatti was well aware that posterity would seek
out the sensationalist story and overlook the intricacies
of a life lived on the inside of artistic and political revo-
lutions. She also wanted money and, given the precedent of Stein's *Autobiography of Alice B. Toklas* (1933;
see Re essay, fig. 14), knew that the public relished firsthand accounts of a "collector of celebrities."[50] Sarfatti's
memoirs give one pause, for the array of international
talents reveals the depth and breadth of her culture—
perhaps intended as an underlying defense—seemingly
at odds with the reality of Fascism as a politically oppres-
sive regime. She wanted to insist on her autonomy from
Mussolini (he had all but buried her in the 1930s) and
resist the taint on her legacy, but both attempts failed in
postwar Europe. Four decades after *Aqua passata*, biographers fully documented her role as "the intellectual
mentor to the Duce," as well as her independence when
it came to ruling culture under Fascism.[51]

Sarfatti's unsettling theories of nationalizing the
masses accompanied liberal ideas on creative freedom,
just as her modernist eye coexisted with blind chauvin-
ism. In her guest books progressive writers and artists
scrawled their names near the autographs of Fascist
ministers, establishment French writers, and American
and British diplomats. The Nazi Hermann Göring, a
voracious art collector, signed several pages after the

composers Alfredo Casella and Nino Rota (later known for his collaborations with Federico Fellini and the scores for Francis Ford Coppola's *Godfather* movies).[52] Alberto Moravia's name appears regularly, even though his novel of moral apathy, *Gli indifferenti* (*The Indifferent Ones;* 1929), openly spurned Sarfatti's Fascist rhetoric of motherhood and civic virtue. For almost two decades her salon ruled the cultural firmament: she was, according to the authority Alma Mahler, "the uncrowned Queen of Italy."[53] Sarfatti (fig. 104) determined successes or failures in her newspaper columns and had new talents published and exhibited in the journals and shows she commanded. Like the woman of the eighteenth century, she secured architectural commissions, Italian nominations for the Nobel Prize, and appointments to the Reale Accademia d'Italia (modeled on the venerable Académie Française). But Sarfatti's salon—which transformed the enlightenment institution to the ends of antiliberal politics—embodied contradictions of her own making. Hers was an elitist enterprise at the greatest distance from the masses she intended to edify and a one-woman show that put female emancipation back twenty years.

Sarfatti was, "if not the mother, then the incubator and nurturer of Fascism," commented the writer Virgilio Brocchi, "and was rewarded when the suckling showed his teeth and bit the breast that had nursed it."[54] That a Jew could have become Mussolini's political partner is less surprising in the Italian context than the fact that he, supremely contemptuous of the female sex, accepted a woman as his equal. Having overcome centuries of violent anti-Semitism to take a leading and respected role in the Risorgimento, Italian Jews had been highly assimilated since the late nineteenth century. In a young nation long factionalized by a diversity of regions, dialects, and political allegiances, Jews became Italians just like everyone else, or even more so, as outstanding generals, admirals, politicians, and heads of state. Most Italian Jews had supported the Fascist revolution of 1922 and then the regime. Anti-Semitism was not a part of official Fascist ideology and became so only opportunistically, after Mussolini's alliance with Adolf Hitler in the second half of the 1930s.[55] Jews were also among the first and most prominent anti-Fascists, including Sarfatti's cousin, the biologist Giuseppe Levi, and his daughter, the writer Natalia Ginzburg, whose circle of family and friends became a center of resistance in Turin and abroad.[56]

By contrast, Italian women were third-class citizens (after illiterate men) without the vote, full property rights, or the ability to sue for adultery. Impeded by the dogma of the Catholic Church, they received an inferior education under religious tutelage, if they had any formal schooling at all. As the daughter of an ambitious, religiously observant Jewish father, who did not concur with the popular notion that reading books made a woman less eligible for marriage, Sarfatti enjoyed innumerable advantages. Prestigious home tutors, all of them Catholic, taught her Italian literature, foreign languages, and art history and developed her notable discursive skills. One of them, Antonio Fradeletto, became the first director of the Venice Biennale (inaugurated in 1895). He had introduced the young Margherita to the writings of John Ruskin, which inspired her deep conviction that all art was perforce ethical and public, a spiritual force that inculcated civic consciousness and national pride. Sarfatti's sophistication far outranked the ill-bred Mussolini's, but so did the intellect of another of his Jewish lovers, the Socialist Angelica Balabanoff. Despite the identity of these two main political mentors (and Kuliscioff's position in the PSI), Mussolini never shook off his own ignorant, clichéd notions about women or Jews.[57]

Sarfatti's family, of Sephardi and Ashkenazi ancestry, was exceptional even among their acculturated coreligionists. Her father, Amedeo Grassini (a lawyer and developer of the Hotel des Bains on the Venice Lido), allied himself in local politics with Cardinal Giuseppe Sarto, the future Pope Pius X. During her youth they moved from a palazzo in the Venetian ghetto to a stately palace on the Grand Canal. Receptions in the family home groomed Sarfatti for her own social ascent; guests included British writer Israel Zangwill, whose "Chad Gadya" and "The Promised Land" she later translated for the Italian publishing house La Voce.[58] Physically attractive and supremely

self-confident, Sarfatti was no self-hating Jew, but she was an Italian first and foremost, passionately devoted to a new religion of the *patria*, largely of her invention. Undoubtedly a lingering sense of her own difference impelled her vision of a nation-state that subsumed conflicts of class, regionalism, and ethnicity into a total-izing ideology of *italianità*. Revealing a latent racism, she claimed the Jews to be an integral part of the same "white" Mediterranean civilization that defined the cul-tural boundaries of Fascism. With the underpinnings of messianic faith, Sarfatti ardently believed in a future nation of Italians, the chosen people of Western cul-ture, after centuries of parochialism and foreign subju-gation.[59] Unable to lead in synagogue, church, or state, Sarfatti undertook this mission from her salon.

Margherita moved from Venice to Milan in 1902, a few years after marrying Cesare Sarfatti (fig. 105)—a prominent lawyer, Socialist, and Zionist with political aspirations. They eventually resided on the Corso Venezia, an exclusive enclave in the center of the city. Through the circles of Alessandrina Ravizza, Ersilia Maino, and Kuliscioff, the Sarfattis made their entry

into the power base of Milanese progressives. Sarfatti wanted her own voice in the press, and a career, still unheard of for Italian women, in the opinion-forming, masculine spaces of editorial rooms and exhibition halls. Kuliscioff had succeeded in making her house a center for instrumental propaganda, but Sarfatti believed in the power of art to revolutionize proletarian conscious-ness—a concept Kuliscioff had no time for. In the first phase of her salon, from 1909 to 1915, Sarfatti created herself as an impresario, gradually claiming territorial rights over a new generation of artists and traveling to European capitals to broaden her professional con-tacts. She modeled herself after Filippo Tommaso Marinetti (fig. 106), who had founded the Futurist movement in 1909, which he subsidized with his sub-stantial personal income. An indefatigable promoter, Marinetti generated dozens of publications, instigated publicity stunts, and organized exhibitions from his "Casa Rossa" (Red House), also on the Corso Venezia, with the aid of his devoted housekeepers, Marietta and Nina Angelini. He invented a new form of attention-grabbing, diffused marketing that put modern Italian

right:
Fig. 107. Gaetano Previati (Italian, 1852–1920), *Young Girl with a Basket of Fruit*, 1916. Oil on canvas, 39⅜ x 31½ in. (100 x 80 cm). Private collection. Formerly in the collection of Margherita Sarfatti

below:
Fig. 108. Medardo Rosso (Italian, 1858–1928), *The Jewish Boy*, 1892–93. Wax over plaster, 9½ in. (24 cm). Signed and inscribed on the base, lower right: "Ciau Margarita tuo Rosso"; inscribed under the base "A Margarita, Cesare e Roberto mes amis Rosso 22/6/15." Private collection. Formerly in the collection of Margherita Sarfatti

far right:
Fig. 109. Adolfo Wildt (Italian, 1868–1931), *Bereavement*, 1919. Ink on vellum, 13½ x 11¾ in. (34.3 x 29.8 cm). Inscribed "A Margherita Sarfatti, gentile amica di tutti gli artisti /Adolfo Wildt, 1919." Private collection. Formerly in the collection of Margherita Sarfatti

opposite page:
Fig. 110. Luigi Russolo (Italian, 1885–1947), *Solidity in the Fog*, 1912. Oil on canvas, 39⅜ x 25¾ in. (100 x 65 cm). Gianni Mattioli Collection, Peggy Guggenheim Collection, Venice

art on the European map. Marinetti's "factory" also led the way in changing the aristocratic salon—a "bureau d'esprit"—into a prototype of the culture industry. Even the Parisian art world followed suit.[60]

With her father's death in 1908, Sarfatti came into a handsome inheritance that allowed her to expand her personal influence as an art collector who could make or break reputations. She acquired works by the first generation of Italian modernists whom the Futurists claimed as their forerunners—the Divisionist painter Gaetano Previati (fig. 107), the symbolist Alberto Martini, and the sculptor Medardo Rosso (fig. 108). She held her Wednesday evenings in what she termed the "study" rather than the "drawing room," because it sounded "less bourgeois" and, as in Kuliscioff's case, doubled as a professional writer's office.[61] Sarfatti soon learned that the combination of art critic and salonière produced lucrative results (and conflicts of interest), since ambitious artists frequently gave works in homage to their hostess (fig. 109).[62] Opportunely, she backed Marinetti's cadre of artists—Boccioni, Luigi Russolo (fig. 110), Carlo Carrà, and architect Antonio Sant'Elia (fig. 111)

—who were all habitués of her gatherings, unless they
failed to attend out of grievance for a less than favor-
able article by her. There she introduced them to
wealthy collectors, who bought pictures, ordered commissions, and provided working stipends. Her faithful
included the sculptor Adolfo Wildt (fig. 112), the
dramatist Sem Benelli, the writers Aldo Palazzeschi
and Alfredo Panzini, and the poet Ada Negri (fig. 113),
one of the few woman regulars and the only woman
whose career Sarfatti tenaciously advanced.

By 1912, Sarfatti stopped appearing at Kuliscioff's
salon. Her independence signaled a growing distance
from the reformist doctrine of the PSI, in favor of
the antipositivist philosophies she encountered through
La Voce and its French counterpart, *Cahiers de la
Quinzaine* (whose principal collaborators included
Daniel Halévy, Geneviève Straus's nephew). Sarfatti
hosted a series of conferences by dissident Catholic
priest Don Brizio Casciola, who shared her ideas on a
new mystic nationalism and the role of emotive collective rites as a means of mass persuasion. Though
Mussolini, now the leader of the revolutionary
Socialists, made frequent appearances, Sarfatti separated the cultural affairs of her private gatherings from
their editorial strategizing. These sessions occurred in
his offices at *Avanti!* or during private trysts. In late
1912, they founded a new political journal, *Utopia*—the
first of their many editorial and propaganda collaborations. The sequestering of their personal ambitions set
the long-term pattern of the Sarfatti salon, which put
Mussolini in his place as her social inferior and gave
her dominance over aesthetic issues but also ultimately
worked against her desired union of aesthetics and
politics.

In May 1915, when Italy entered World War I
against Austria-Hungary, the Futurists and many of
Sarfatti's habitués eagerly volunteered to fight in the
trenches. On the cultural front she began to reconfigure
the battle plan. She allied herself with the artists of the
Nuove Tendenze (New Tendencies), such as Leonardo
Dudreville and Achille Funi, who represented a conservative flank of Futurism, along with her other regulars,
Mario Sironi and Arturo Tosi. The deaths in 1916 of

Fig. 113. Mario Nunes-Vais (Italian, 1856–1932), *Ada Negri and Amelia Rosselli*. Istituto Centrale per il Catalogo e la Documentazione, Gabinetto Fotografico Nazionale, Collezione Nunes-Vais, Rome

Fig. 114. Mario Nunes-Vais (Italian, 1856–1932), *Gabriele D'Annunzio*, 1906. Istituto Centrale per il Catalogo e la Documentazione, Gabinetto Fotografico Nazionale, Collezione Nunes-Vais, Rome

Boccioni and of Sant'Elia, along with defections within the Futurist movement, left the artistic field open for regrouping. Sarfatti maneuvered in her columns and in her salon, constructing the ethos of a social and aesthetic regeneration, led by an intellectual elite who had experienced the struggle of war.[63] She herself embodied the spirit of patriotic sacrifice as a mythic *madre dolorosa:* in 1918 her eighteen-year-old son, Roberto, died heroically on the Alpine front in an assault against the Austrians. Her salon devotees, now the most famous personalities in Italy—Ada Negri, Gabriele D'Annunzio (fig. 114), and Mussolini—ritualized her private grief in public commemorations.[64]

From 1918 until 1925, Sarfatti's salon moved forward with programmatic initiatives for a postwar "return to order," in tandem with her behind-the-scenes planning for Mussolini's seizure of absolute power. She wrote regular Friday art reviews for *Il Popolo d'Italia,* Mussolini's newspaper and the mouthpiece of the nascent Fascist movement, which articulated her goals of discipline and hierarchy—in art as well as in politics. Her son Amedeo later recalled the lively deliberations led by Sarfatti and the writer Massimo Bontempelli as the salon collectively shaped a style in art and literature that combined Italian reverence for "constructive synthesis" with the innovations of European modernism. In 1920 her artists Russolo, Sironi, Dudreville, and Funi issued the manifesto "Contro tutti i ritorni in pittura" ("Against All Returns in Painting"), which disavowed both academic revivals and the "anarchic individualism" of prewar abstraction.[65] Sarfatti's salon functioned as an intermediary space between the antiquated ivory tower existence of Italian intellectuals and their new identity as nation builders. Meanwhile, Fascist *squadristi* pummeled

workers and political opponents in the streets, including several of Sarfatti's former Socialist colleagues,
whom she had frequented when she was an ingénue in
Milanese society.

The desire for power drew Mussolini and Sarfatti
together, but he continued to have many lovers, and she
took pleasure in reminding him of his inferior social
standing. Mussolini never felt at ease in salon society,
even in the company of Marinetti and Arturo Toscanini,
Sarfatti's frequent guests, who also ran on the first
Fascist ticket for national parliamentary elections in
1919. (Toscanini later became a vocal anti-Fascist.)
One evening that year Toscanini brought the young
Czech violinist Vasa Prihoda to give a recital at her
salon. After he performed brilliantly, Sarfatti turned to
Mussolini, a modest musician, and goaded him to play.
Mortified by the request, he declined, but she continued
to insist until finally, clenching his teeth in anger, he
whispered, "Cut it out, you louse!"[66]

In her personal ambition to originate culture
for the Fascist epoch, Sarfatti mustered her salon artists
into a new group called the Novecento (Twentieth Century), initially an entourage of seven led by Dudreville,
Sironi, and Funi (fig. 115). Sarfatti promoted them in
the press as "spiritual guides" for a "modern classicism." Her announcement of their program coincided
with the March on Rome in October 1922, and in the
following March, she arranged to have Mussolini, now
prime minister, preside over their inaugural exhibition in
a commercial gallery in Milan. Her brazen opportunism
had its price: many artists recoiled from Sarfatti's
attempt to control their work or align it with politics,
but nonetheless they fell into line. "La Sarfatti in
that period was a powerful force in artistic circles,"
Dudreville remembered, "and her power, always on the
rise, attracted arrivistes like a magnet."[67] She used them
and they used her, although Sarfatti later claimed she
suffered to learn just how many coasted along because
of her connections to Mussolini.[68] By contrast to the
confidentiality usually afforded by a salon, guests of
Sarfatti knew that no idea was off the record or protected
from use: she represented the public face of absolute
power and used her salon to publicize this authority.

By 1926 she organized the Novecento into a
national exhibition of more than one hundred artists
working in various styles, and appointed her personal
favorites to the organizing committee. The hub of a
Fascist propaganda enterprise, her study churned out
Novecento exhibitions for tour abroad, and *Gerarchia*, a
journal of political theory, whose executive staff included
two other Jewish fascists, her close friends Carlo and
Eloise Foà.[69] Marinetti resented her feminine influence
peddling and lobbied to have Futurism accepted as the
official Fascist art. But Mussolini shrewdly divided and
conquered the intellectual community by never imple-
menting a state art or dictating style.

Her salon showcased the art she promoted to the
nation: Symbolist and Futurist works she had acquired
earlier hung next to Novecento images in a Magic Realist
style (figs. 115, 116) and Italian landscapes painted in a
middle-of-the-road naturalism. Out of aesthetic conviction or pure strategy, she took few risks and aimed
for a *juste milieu* between the revolution of European
modernism and the restoration of innately Italian values. To her credit, Sarfatti, with her sophisticated tastes,
opportunistic eclecticism, and a salon where avant-
garde artists fraternized with the future Duce, laid the
groundwork for Fascism's incongruously liberal policy
in the arts. Yet she failed to imagine that her humanistic
brand of national culture and its distribution from on
high to the uneducated masses would be rendered obso-
lete by totalitarian consensus building.

After he became prime minister and moved to
Rome, Mussolini no longer attended Sarfatti's salon.
Immersed in governing and then dictatorship, he left
cultural matters to her, "And peace there was between
them," seethed a rival critic, Ugo Ojetti, "if none
for poor Italian art."[70] Out of propriety, Sarfatti and
Mussolini took care to be seen together only at selected
public events or in his press office; in this way too,
he placated antifeminist party officials and his wife,
Rachele, all jealous of Sarfatti's influence. Cesare
Sarfatti's view of his wife's philandering remains
unknown, though from the outside he tolerated it. He
had always been supportive of her ferocious ambitions
and continued to aid Mussolini with legal matters.

Fig. 116. Mario Sironi (Italian, 1885–1961), *Urban Landscape*, 1921. Oil on canvas, 34¾ x 26¾ in. (88 x 68 cm). Private collection. Formerly in the collection of Margherita Sarfatti

Cesare's death in 1924 freed Sarfatti to move to Rome, where, by 1926, she established her second salon.[71] In 1928 she moved into an elegant apartment on via Nomentana, across the street from Mussolini's official residence. He avoided her late Friday afternoon receptions, but his political omnipresence accounted for the assorted sycophants, journalists, Fascist Party officials, spies, and those desiring Sarfatti's imprimatur. "This is the antechamber of the one who commands," the novelist and anti-Fascist Corrado Alvaro commented when he was first invited to the salon. "This is playing with fire."[72] When the Duce arrived unannounced and in secret, demanding her urgent attention, excuses were made and guests abruptly bidden good evening. In the second half of the 1920s, Sarfatti became reckless and tactless about her supreme authority. She comported herself "with the air of a general," losing any semblance of a classic salonière's politesse and equanimity.[73] The appearance of reasoned dialogue reigned, as long as the reasoning was Sarfatti's.

By 1929, however, Mussolini had distanced Sarfatti from matters of government policy. Fascist fine-art syndicates and a centralized system of government exhibitions eliminated her ability to operate independently. Much to her disgust, Mussolini signed the Lateran Pact with the Vatican, making Catholicism the official religion of Italy. Nonetheless, Sarfatti positioned herself as an essential go-between, using the "open" venue of her salon—and her notable linguistic skills—for backroom diplomacy. She fashioned a positive image of Fascism abroad as a correspondent for the Hearst newspapers and brokered access to Mussolini on behalf of many foreign journalists. Thomas Morgan, the head of the Rome bureau of United Press and a Fascist informant; Anne O'Hare McCormick, a correspondent for the *New York Times;* and Alexander Kirk, the chargé d'affaires of the American embassy, sought out her confidences. Some may have disparaged salon chatter as a feminine pastime, but as Sarfatti wrote in her Mussolini biography, "I have read too much history to disdain gossip."[74]

In the early thirties, as Mussolini strutted his role as a decisive balance between Nazi Germany and the other European powers, Sarfatti proved a valuable source of inside information for high-level Americans. Fearful of Mussolini's growing interest in Hitler, she worked hard, also at the Duce's request, to forge secret contacts with Franklin Delano Roosevelt. She regularly entertained the novelist Fanny Hurst, Missy Meloney of the *New York Herald Tribune*, and Ambassador Breckinridge Long, all of whom were close to the American president. Sarfatti cultivated Columbia University president Nicholas Murray Butler, who appointed Giuseppe Prezzolini, her former editor at *La Voce*, to head the Casa Italiana in New York and promote the Fascist cause.[75] Though Mussolini remained conspicuous by his absence, other Fascist ministers, who also happened to like Sarfatti, regularly reconnoitered in her drawing room: Italo Balbo, Giuseppe Bottai, Dino Grandi, and Mussolini's brother, Arnaldo. A visit to Sarfatti was also de rigueur for such would-be Fascists as Oswald Mosley and Ezra Pound.

Sarfatti's physical relationship with Mussolini ended by 1931, and he increasingly shunned her, even pushing her off the staff of *Il Popolo d'Italia*, but he could not yet eradicate her network of personal contacts. At the end of that year she moved to a new residence on via dei Villini to keep a distance from her former lover and assert her role as a cultural attaché. The quality of her salon countered the regime's ever more bombastic rhetoric while also furthering the propaganda that "humane" Fascism differed from the brutal parochialism of Nazi Germany and the Soviet Union. Sarfatti upheld pluralism, artistic freedom, and her own creative style of coercion. Visits to her salon by Sinclair Lewis, Paul Valéry, André Gide, André Malraux, and her old friend Colette showed that different streams of European and American culture permeated the borders of Fascist Italy. Expatriate Italian artists from Paris also stopped by when in Rome—Giorgio de Chirico, Gino Severini, and Filippo De Pisis. The American artist George Biddle visited several times and met Mario Sironi, who along with Sarfatti spearheaded the Italian mural painting movement of the 1930s. One can imagine the conversations that took place after Sironi published his manifesto of mural painting in *Il Popolo d'Italia* in January 1932. When Biddle returned to the

United States at the end of that year, he persuaded Roosevelt to start a similar program for artists' employment and the decoration of public buildings: the Federal Art Project of the Works Progress Administration.

As the Fascist regime grew more rigid, autonomy and egalitarianism returned to Sarfatti's salon through the back door.[76] She welcomed officious courtiers, cultural dissidents, and the politically unaligned. Since some apparent Fascists who attended—Giovanni Ansaldo for one—worked clandestinely against the regime, Sarfatti's gatherings fostered a degree of subversion unknown even to her. Direct police surveillance stopped at her door, even though some incorrectly suspected her of spying and the Fascist police trailed several of her visitors and, later, the salonière herself. For her part, Sarfatti cared more about individual brilliance than Fascist affiliation and disdained any policy that reduced art to dogma. Perhaps that explains the appearance of the art historian Lionello Venturi, champion of the Turin-based Gruppo dei Sei (Group of Six), who overtly challenged the regime's increasing parochialism; in 1932, Venturi escaped a police dragnet and fled to Paris. The half-Jewish Alberto Moravia (and his sister, the painter Adriana Pincherle) also showed up at her salon, representing another potential political liability, as he was a cousin of the exiled resistance leaders Carlo and Nello Rosselli. Sarfatti regularly hosted the nonconformist young artists of the Scuola Romana, or Roman School, who were friends with Moravia, and their patron Countess Anna Laetitia Pecci-Blunt, a rival Roman salonière.[77] After the fall of Fascism, many pretended they had never known Sarfatti—yet her guest books tell otherwise.

As news of Sarfatti's public fall from grace in 1933 rippled through elite ranks, the signatures in her last guest book fell precipitously in number and status. Many who had resented her arrogance and self-serving machinations went elsewhere, though few places in Mussolini's provincial "Third Rome" offered the heady diversity of Sarfatti's lair. She traveled extensively in the United States, shoring up the faltering impression of the regime and still informing Mussolini on foreign affairs—when she was given an audience. After the imperialist conquest of Ethiopia in 1936 and the regime's alliance with Nazi Germany, several of her former habitués, now clandestine anti-Fascists, had to watch their steps or go underground. In the following two years the salon record shows a string of one-time visitors, mostly foreigners and unknowns. "The Manifesto of the Race" was issued in July 1938, the last month her book records visitors. When Sarfatti, now a "Jewish" salonière, could no longer invite whom she pleased, she knew it was time to leave. None of her prominent American friends could secure entry for a "Fascist sympathizer" into the United States. Butler consulted Prezzolini about hiring her at Columbia's Casa Italiana, but her colleague of thirty years demurred: "Better to save an Israelite who is of real value and is poor."[78]

Expatriates and Avant-Gardes

GERTRUDE STEIN:
UNCONVENTIONAL CONVERSATIONS

In *The Autobiography of Alice B. Toklas*, Gertrude Stein (1874–1946; fig. 117) recounts "the beginning of my life in Paris. It was based upon the rue de Fleurus and the Saturday evenings and it was like a kaleidoscope slowly turning."[1] Though speaking through Toklas, Stein implicitly acknowledged her coming into being as a person and as an artist with her birth as salonière. The allusion to the kaleidoscope—a prismatic overlay of fragmentary shards—may well refer to the Cubism of Picasso, described a few paragraphs later. As an optical metaphor for memory, it also suggests the present-day distortion of the past. But directly or subliminally, Stein lifts her key phrase from the pages of a literary rival, one whose writing had been similarly inspired by the protagonists and the goings-on of the French salon elite. "It was true that the social kaleidoscope was in the act of turning," wrote Marcel Proust, "and that the Dreyfus Affair was shortly to relegate the Jews to the lowest rung of the social ladder."[2] Writing her autobiography in the early 1930s, Stein could boast that her salon had again put a Jewish hostess at the apex of Parisian society, which had shifted from the aristocratic Faubourg Saint-Germain to the raucous chic of the Left Bank. By 1912, Jacques-Émile Blanche, a habitué of Geneviève Straus's salon and a friend of Proust's until the Dreyfus Affair, was bringing visitors to Stein's atelier to view the pictures. "Buying and making collections of objects which may catch people's fancy is a quality that the Jewish race has brought to the pitch of genius," he observed with his usual tone of crisp condescension.[3]

Stein and her brother Leo started their "at-homes" in 1906 to accommodate the aficionados and curiosity seekers who wanted to stare at the art they collected: "Little by little people began to come to the rue de Fleurus to see the Matisses and the Cézannes, Matisse brought people, everybody brought somebody, and they came at any time and it began to be a nuisance, and it was in this way that Saturday evenings began."[4] Her intimates and later biographers have thoroughly documented the astonishing numbers who passed through or repeatedly returned, as well as the international social constellations of artists and writers.[5] By 1910, Gertrude dominated the proceedings with Toklas beside her, "listening and loving," and fostering competition among the Parisian avant-garde.[6] After World War I, Stein's salon no longer served as a clearinghouse for innovation in the visual arts, and it diminished in importance, if not in reputation. She gathered mostly literary stars, accompanying the change in her public identity from patron to writer. Though most readers of Stein found her modernist prose unwelcoming, they were fascinated by her story of social ascent—a woman with a modest trust fund and ample girth, a lesbian, and a "Jewess once of San Francisco, but now of Paris."[7]

"Can a jew be wild," wrote Gertrude Stein in 1917.[8] If she was referring to her prose as the "new barbarism" or her role as the reigning hostess of the Fauve beasts and the savage Cubists, the answer was certainly yes. As a cultural icon, Stein was defined by her Jewishness and her lesbianism, but also by her American origins, which she privileged above the other two distinctions in the creation of her public persona. The French conflated her outsider status as Jew with the exotic appeal of an untamed American. More than one visitor appalled by the art on the walls attributed the tastes of the "Stein Corporation" (fig. 118) to American gullibility or to the ersatz culture of those without rooted history. Fernande Olivier, Pablo Picasso's lover and a fine diarist, wrote (favorably) of Leo Stein as an "archetypical *American*-German Jew."[9] In 1904 Gertrude and Leo were joined in Paris by their brother Michael and his wife, Sarah, who became avid collectors of Matisse, and held a rival Saturday evening

Fig. 117. Pablo Picasso (Spanish, 1881–1973), *Portrait of Gertrude Stein*, 1906. Oil on canvas, 39 ⅜ x 32 in. (100 x 81.3 cm). The Metropolitan Museum of Art, New York, Bequest of Gertrude Stein, 1947

Fig. 118. The Stein family and friends. Yale Collection of American Literature, Beinecke Rare Book and Manuscript Library, Yale University, New Haven. Sarah Stein is seated in the foreground, with her husband, Michael Stein, and their son Allan behind her; Gertrude Stein is to the left, with Leo Stein seated at back between two unknown friends

salon. (Toklas later disparaged Sarah as a provincial Madame de Staël.)[10] As foreigners abroad with no pretense to citizenship, the Stein clan did not represent the threat of the "internal other" posed by French or Eastern European Jews. "They are not men, they are not women, they are Americans," as Picasso liked to say.[11]

Whereas earlier Jewish salonières had stood out from the rest of upper-class society, diversity and difference were the calling cards of Stein's guests. She hosted a new, supranational collective bohemia, one defined by ambiguous social background, subversion, and social alienation—qualities long associated with a nomadic underclass.[12] Leo Stein once jokingly recalled the presence of "a lot of Hungarians, Turks, Armenians & other Jews."[13] Foreigners and expatriates encamped at 27 rue de Fleurus, which became the port of call for avant-gardes and conscious pariahs. "They were always there, all sizes and shapes, all degrees of wealth and

poverty, some very charming, some simply rough and every now and then a very beautiful young peasant."[14] Democratically open to anyone in the know ("On whose recommendation do you come here?" Stein asked by way of admission), the salon welcomed Germans, English, Americans, Italians, Swedes, Spaniards, and, later, a few slumming French aristocrats. "Really everybody could come in," she explained, "and as at that time these pictures had no value and there was no social privilege attached to knowing anyone there, only those came who really were interested."[15]

The perception of Stein as the ultimate outsider on the inside obscures the ways in which her salon extended a venerable practice. She was introduced to salon sociability in the late 1890s, at the Baltimore home of the Jewish sisters Etta and Claribel Cone. Stein's collection was avant-garde, but the incongruous assortment of people, the marketing of the new, and the careerism of the ambitious hostess had long characterized the public dimension of this domestic space. To see Stein sui generis is to ignore the fact that elitist salons had earlier undermined social stratification, legitimized marginality, and challenged gender conventions. Even though she strictly demarcated writing time from salon time, the two were inseparable, for her guests inspired her work, the art on the walls brought new personalities and protégés to her domain, and the ever-expanding network led her to publication and renown. In *Paris France*, Stein claimed that she found her métier in a country that gave her distance from her own, but she also co-opted a culture famous for the *femme auteur*.[16] In the same way that Rahel Levin Varnhagen shaped her own myth, so too did Stein let a selective memory speak in *The Autobiography of Alice B. Toklas* (see Re essay, fig. 14). A brilliant collector and writer, yes, but without her salon, Gertrude Stein would have been someone who was anyone, not one being remembered for being something.

In several key ways, Stein's childhood compares to that of other successful Jewish salonières. Raised by a despotic father and a passive, unprepossessing mother, with a parade of private tutors, Stein typically directed her inbred, overachieving drive into a powerhouse of

Fig. 119. Romaine Brooks (American, 1874–1970), *Natalie Clifford Barney (The Amazon)*, 1920. Oil on canvas. Musée Carnavalet, Paris

with "talk." Fortunately for Stein, she found a genius of a wife in Alice B. Toklas, who played the role of Madame Arman de Caillavet to her Anatole France. Toklas fanned Stein's fame, guarded her work time, and sorted the sycophants from the useful up-and-comers, replicating the gender inequality of most heterosexual unions. Gertrude was the husband and Alice the wife, whereas most illustrious salon women were wives of the aristocratic bent who refused the traditional domestic role. Stein also followed the norm by not converting, and settled down with Toklas, a Jewish American of Polish descent whose prominent Semitic features led Mary Berenson to call her "an awful Jewess, dressed in a window curtain."[18] In another link to salon history, Toklas had been trained as a pianist by her grandmother, who had been a pupil of Clara Schumann, a guest at Fanny Hensel's Sunday musicales.

Stein's lesbianism was neither flamboyant nor unusual in the context of Belle Époque soirées. Aristocrats and bohemians alike rebelled against bourgeois morality, and they did so in private spaces protected from police surveillance and sanctioned by their salon peers. As Proust's *À la recherche du temps perdu* revealed, homosexuality among the privileged was tolerated (not so among the middle and lower classes) and even cultivated in salons as a form of self-expression and aesthetic performance. Lesbians were at once less threatening to society than were male homosexuals and more constricted in their practices. The arrival of the American Natalie Clifford Barney (1876–1972; fig. 119) in Paris in 1902, a year before Stein, changed the public profile of lesbian activity: at her home on the rue de Jacob, she hosted women-only Sapphic gatherings in the back garden while maintaining, in her drawing room, one of the most important literary salons in Europe.[19] Stein did not hide her relationship with Toklas, but neither did she flaunt it by being part of Barney's coterie or by cross-dressing, supporting other women writers, or turning her sexuality into a political cause célèbre.[20] Early photographs and descriptions of Stein as salonière capture her feminine gaiety, sensuous earthiness, and womanly flesh. Only later did she come

creative human communion. Before the salon, "there was nothing to say," for Stein reacted to her brother Leo's early dominance over her with silence.[17] Much has been made of Stein's "masculine" genius, in no small part because of the self-promotional efforts of the woman herself. But salon keepers had come into existence centuries earlier precisely to hold the floor on their own intellectual terms; many of her predecessors were similarly hailed or maligned for their "unnaturally" agile or analytic minds and testosterone-infused ambition. Stein's writing was radical, but her gender attitudes were not; she bought into the idea that writing was a male prerogative and had little patience for the "wives of geniuses" who filled the space of her salon

Fig. 120. Marsden Hartley (American, 1877–1943), *One Portrait of One Woman*, 1916. Oil on composition board, 30 x 25 in. (76.2 x 63.5 cm). Collection of the Frederick R. Weisman Art Museum at the University of Minnesota, Minneapolis, Bequest of Hudson D. Walker from the Ione and Hudson D. Walker Collection

to resemble the salonier of Pablo Picasso's iconic portrait of 1906, with a masculine bearing and helmet of hair—just as the artist predicted she would (see fig. 117).[21]

The Stein salon became "one of the sights of Paris" by 1906,[22] the same year Gertrude resumed work on her monumental *The Making of Americans*, whose system of characters was based on the people who passed through the studio. In the following years she did "short portraits of everyone who came in and out."[23] Stein considered "talking and listening" to be the essence of the human enterprise, and the volatility of salon conversation inspired her radical experiments with language. Although she overturned conventions of readable writing—mimicking the fragmentation, flow,

interjection, and declaration of nonlinear speech—her choice of genre was steeped in tradition. Salon literary portraits originated in the seventeenth century as impromptu games or were incorporated into letters sent among guests. Unlike a commissioned work or an allegorical depiction, these forms of personal homage (like Stein's tributes to her salon devotees) were based on intimate knowledge between author and subject. Stein rejected the idea that an individual could be evoked by the recall or mimesis of personality traits. Instead, her destruction of syntax and her use of the gerund create the sensation of a continuous present and immediate presence, of the duration involved in making the acquaintance of someone, and that one here and now.[24] Her soirées offered the raw data for her portraits, for the "mixing and mingling and contrasting" of diverse human types. Narrative snippets of salon sociability—the comings and goings of guests—break through the verbal flow, while analogies to amusing salon repartee are made with Stein's own nursery-rhyme wit. As Wendy Steiner observes, "Stein's work is liveliest when read and heard, when our own oral/aural talents lift her words from the page and animate them in an informal or formal, private or public, theatrical environment."[25] At least one visitor, the American painter Stanton Macdonald-Wright, recalls Gertrude Stein reciting the portraits to an audience in the salon.[26]

Many artists rendered likenesses of Stein, but only a few guests understood her literary project and reciprocated with their own versions of nonrepresentational portraiture. The seeming redundancy and literalness of Stein's language led visual artists to evoke a person through inanimate attributes rather than detailed physiognomic description. Marsden Hartley's *One Portrait of One Woman* (1916; fig. 120) arose from many long conversations at 27 rue de Fleurus. "I feel as if I were really 'in' somewhere," he wrote Stein when accepting a dinner invitation, "whereas most places one goes one remains forever at the gate."[27] The title of Hartley's image derives from a signature style found in Stein's early portraits, such as "Five or Six Men" (1908) or "One. Carl Van Vechten" (1913), which categorically elaborate similarities and differences among standard

types and unique individuals. The word "one" is repeatedly used as a noun with adjectival attributes ("a fat one" "a skinny one") or with a particularizing pronoun adjective noun ("each one" and "that one"). By incorporating the descriptive adjective "one" instead of the generic article "a" (as in *A Portrait of a Woman*), Hartley makes clear that his is a unique portrait depicting not just any woman, but a singular one.

Hartley symbolizes Stein through the teacup and checkered tablecloth of her hospitality and captures her big ego with the script— *"MOI"* (me)—at the bottom of the composition. As part of a cryptic exchange, the object pronoun *moi* deliberately reverses and translates the first person singular *I* used in the title of Stein's play *IIIIIIIII* (1913), which contains, as it happens, her literary portrait of Hartley. In the painting, a large, abstract red, yellow, and white form dominates the center background, flanked by two smaller versions of a similar shape on either side. These have been interpreted as mandorlas (spiritual halos), but with the slit down the middle they more closely resemble female genitalia, and the flanking candles the flame of sexual passion.[28] Hartley, a homosexual, took comfort in Stein's open sexual orientation and, *one* might venture to say, celebrated it here with a domestic setting and iconography remarkably prescient of Judy Chicago's *Dinner Party* (1974–79).

Though it has never been identified as an object portrait of Stein, Juan Gris most certainly created *Flowers* (1914; fig. 121) as a bouquet for his hostess. Unique in Gris's usually somber oeuvre for its exuberant photographic-based imagery of rose blossoms pasted over florid wallpaper, the mixed-media collage reiterates in visual form "Rose is a rose is a rose is a rose." Stein's trademark phrase came from her text *Sacred Emily* (1913) and was highly visible around 27 rue de Fleurus as a signet on table linens and writing paper.[29] *Flowers* entered Stein's collection as part of her first purchase of Gris's work from the dealer Daniel-Henry Kahnweiler, just before the war. Whether she was in on the game or whether Gris simply made it in the hope that it would ring a bell and she would buy it (Stein famously wrote that Toklas heard bells when she

encountered genius), we will never know. Like Stein's metaliterary prose, Cubist collage makes its audience aware of the conventions of representation through fragmentation and repetition: photographic prints of roses have been cut, like flowers, from their source and placed in the vase of the still life, while underneath and around them are trompe l'oeil shadows of their blossoms and petals. In this game of real and fake, everything is and isn't a rose.

Stein's habitués joined in the parlor games and inside jokes. Picasso's *Au Bon Marché* (1913; fig. 122) takes its title from Stein's portrait "Flirting at the Bon Marché" (1908) and enlivens the theme with a peek-a-boo collage of wallpaper and newspaper copy and advertisements featuring the upper half of a woman and a lingerie label. The lower half of the collage parts open with the open parts of words and female anatomy, for when pronounced, the fragments make a puerile pun: "un / trou / ici" (a hole here), with a big letter B in between. Picasso picks up verbatim Stein's own lexical fun with the French *trou* and the English "true" from her exactly contemporary portrait, *Americans* (1913): "B r., brute says. A hole, a hole is a true, a true, a true."[30] Stein, like Picasso, her favorite artist, had a minimal command of French, and they both created by destroying the linguistic conventions of their respective media. She claimed that Americans and Spaniards shared a primitive otherness that contrasted with the European realist tradition. Being complicit with Stein in art as well as in public relations, Picasso painted his self-portrait of 1906 with the same masklike visage as his contemporaneous image of her, "mixing and matching" their features with those of archaic Iberian sculpture.

It is often noted that 27 rue de Fleurus was the first museum of modern art. The premises consisted of a two-story apartment with an adjacent high-ceilinged atelier, where the Steins hung most of the artworks and where the salon took place. Many of the pictures that they once owned have been canonized as masterpieces by the public institutions in whose collections they now reside (figs. 123, 124).[31] Like Madame Geoffrin in the mid-1700s, Gertrude Stein oversaw an exhibition

Fig. 122. Pablo Picasso (Spanish, 1881–1973), *Au Bon Marché*, 1913. Oil and pasted paper on cardboard, 9¼ x 12¼ in (23.5 x 31 cm). Museum Ludwig, Cologne

Fig. 123. Man Ray (American, 1890–1976), *Gertrude Stein and Alice B. Toklas in the Atelier at 27 rue de Fleurus*, 1923. Yale Collection of American Literature, Beinecke Rare Book and Manuscript Library, Yale University, New Haven

gallery, a salesroom, and a classroom for connoisseurship. Avant-garde art aimed at breaking with, rather than upholding, the grand French tradition, but fellow investors who bought from Stein, like the Cone sisters and Sergei Shchukin, viewed the risk in terms of even bigger returns. Yet in common with eighteenth-century salon taste, there were plenty of lascivious female nudes on the walls, by Pierre-Auguste Renoir, Félix Vallotton, Henri Matisse, Pierre Bonnard, and Picasso. The Steins often purchased from the artists themselves, and for several years their atelier was the only place the new art could be seen, aside from the annual independent exhibitions. Whereas some dealers allowed only potential buyers in, the Steins did not discriminate. Leo, and then Gertrude, supported modern French art but rarely acquired works by Americans, and almost never by women artists (who were, admittedly, very few). Exceptionally, Gertrude purchased a painting by Marie

Laurencin (the first the artist ever sold), which was but a group portrait of members of the salon's inner circle —Picasso, Fernande Olivier, Laurencin, and her lover, the critic Guillaume Apollinaire (fig. 125).

The Steins' collection circulated beyond the walls of the atelier, influencing the drunken colors and new pictorial concoctions of any number of international artists. Given the citizenship of the hostess, Americans formed a large contingent of guests, eager to discuss the language of modern French painting in their native tongue. "What made it lively was the presence of all the striking new young artists in Paris talking shop," reported the art critic Henry McBride, "the pleasantest kind of talk there is for those who talk it."[32] Marsden Hartley literally took notes, enclosing a small pen sketch based on Picasso's *The Architect's Table* (1912; fig. 126) in a letter to Alfred Stieglitz (fig. 127).[33] *The Architect's Table* was the first work to be purchased by

Fig. 124. Interior view of the atelier at 27 rue de Fleurus, c. 1913. Yale Collection of American Literature, Beinecke Rare Book and Manuscript Library, Yale University, New Haven

Fig. 125. Marie Laurencin (French, 1883–1956), *Group of Artists*, 1908. Oil on canvas, 25½ x 31⅞ (64.8 x 81 cm). The Baltimore Museum of Art: The Cone Collection, formed by Dr. Claribel Cone and Miss Etta Cone of Baltimore, Maryland. Formerly in the collection of Gertrude Stein

Stein on her own, without Leo (who disliked Cubism), and Picasso hedged his bets by including an image of Stein's calling card in the lower right, in clever homage to his patron.

Americans who could not gain entry into Picasso's and Georges Braque's studios saw Cubism unfolding from 1907 through 1913 in the examples Stein acquired: rare studies for *Les Demoiselles d'Avignon*, milestone Analytic Cubist canvases, and the mixed-media stratagems of collage. In the salon, foreign competitors such as the Italian Futurists keenly studied the Cubist works, but for Stein they could only be, like the habitué Robert Delaunay, faux practitioners of the "earthquake school." She alone in Paris found Filippo Tommaso Marinetti very dull. The Futurist Gino Severini countered with a put-down of her legendary soirées: "They were boring really, with their impossible *'petit-nègre'* French, but Miss Stein, although highly intelligent, was

probably unaware of how much more amusing she was in her books than at her parties."[34]

In common with Berta Zuckerkandl and Margherita Sarfatti, Stein was publicist and power-broker for modern art but availed herself of "general introducers" or "liaison officers," as Leo dubbed them, to further her own work in kind.[35] "Everybody brought somebody," in an ever wider network of circulating pronouns. The writer Mildred Aldrich brought the miniaturist Myra Edgerly, who introduced Stein to the publisher John Lane, who frequented Ada Leverson's salon, who issued the British edition of *Three Lives* in 1909. Stein's first published word portraits—"Picasso" and "Matisse"—appeared in the August 1912 edition of Alfred Stieglitz's *Camera Work* (fig. 128). Stieglitz, one of her earliest habitués, extended Stein's influence into the New York Dada scene, where Marius de Zayas and Francis Picabia developed her literary experiments into

Fig. 126. Pablo Picasso (Spanish, 1881–1973), *The Architect's Table*, 1912. Oil on canvas, mounted on oval panel, 28⅝ x 23½ in. (72.6 x 59.7 cm). The Museum of Modern Art, New York, William S. Paley Collection

Fig. 127. Marsden Hartley (American, 1877–1943), *Sketch of Picasso's "The Architect's Table,"* 1912. From a letter to Alfred Stieglitz, received July 12, 1912. Ink on paper, 7 x 5 in. (17.8 x 12.7 cm). Yale Collection of American Literature, Beinecke Rare Book and Manuscript Library, Yale University, New Haven

abstract, mechanistic, often nihilistic "object portraits."[36] Another key facilitator was Mabel Dodge, who started Wednesday evenings at her home in Manhattan in 1913, after Gertrude's example. Her article on Stein, timed to coincide with the Armory Show (to which the Steins lent works), turned the scandalous Gertrude and her collection into "good copy" in America.[37] Carl Van Vechten in the *New York Times* and Henry McBride in the New York *Sun* also profiled Stein and her salon, spreading the gospel of modernism by shocking the philistines. The American Alvin Langdon Coburn was the first "to come and photograph her as a celebrity and she was nicely gratified." Stein then sent him to photograph Matisse in his studio, and a portrait of the artist found its way into Coburn's book of world-famous

individuals, *Men of Mark* (1913; fig. 129).[38] Gertrude, being a woman, did not make the cut.

Matisse first met Picasso in 1906, chez Stein, and over time, their open rivalry played out at 27 rue de Fleurus. On one occasion Stein seated them at the dining table so each faced his own picture—a form of staged flattery that Matisse and others eventually saw through: "The world is a theatre for you, but there are theatres and theatres," he told Stein, "and when you listen so carefully to me and so attentively and do not hear a word I say then I do say you are very wicked."[39] But Stein knew that if she used some people, they used her as part of the ego-enhancing and career-building momentum of salon reciprocity. As she wrote in her novella *G.M.P. (Matisse Picasso and Gertrude Stein)* (1912): "Fortune and succeeding and coming again often is all of something and that thing is creating repeating, and creating something is gaining recognition, and gaining something is expecting some one, and expecting some one is pleasing one who is succeeding."[40] Tellingly, the pairing of "being" and "succeeding" occurs over and over in Stein's various portraits, referring to a being in succession (a living entity developing over time), and to a person who achieves renown. Stein measured her success through the success of others and viewed fame as the ultimate creative act.

Gertrude Stein's salon collected egos and masterpieces, and combined highbrow art with lowbrow

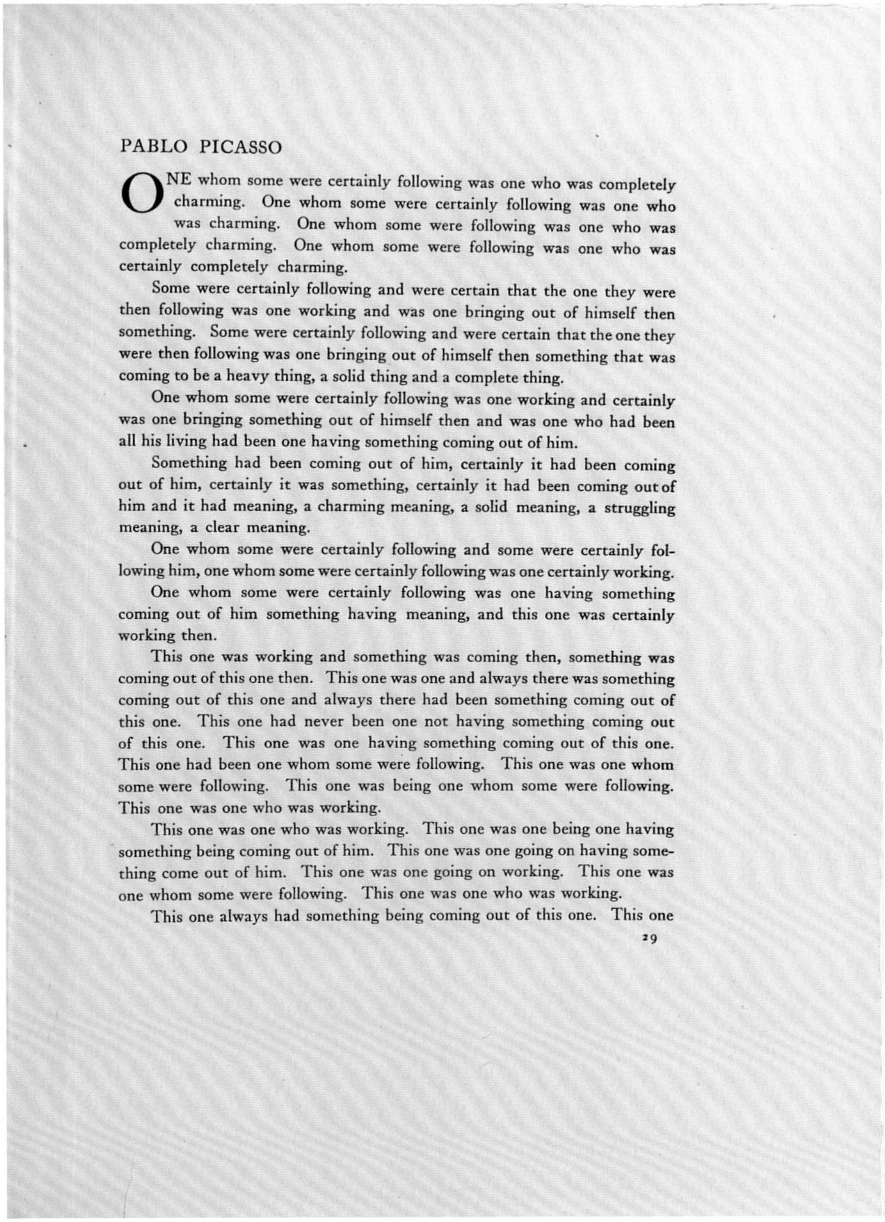

PABLO PICASSO

ONE whom some were certainly following was one who was completely charming. One whom some were certainly following was one who was charming. One whom some were following was one who was completely charming. One whom some were following was one who was certainly completely charming.

Some were certainly following and were certain that the one they were then following was one working and was one bringing out of himself then something. Some were certainly following and were certain that the one they were then following was one bringing out of himself then something that was coming to be a heavy thing, a solid thing and a complete thing.

One whom some were certainly following was one working and certainly was one bringing something out of himself then and was one who had been all his living had been one having something coming out of him.

Something had been coming out of him, certainly it had been coming out of him, certainly it was something, certainly it had been coming out of him and it had meaning, a charming meaning, a solid meaning, a struggling meaning, a clear meaning.

One whom some were certainly following and some were certainly following him, one whom some were certainly following was one certainly working.

One whom some were certainly following was one having something coming out of him something having meaning, and this one was certainly working then.

This one was working and something was coming then, something was coming out of this one then. This one was one and always there was something coming out of this one and always there had been something coming out of this one. This one had never been one not having something coming out of this one. This one was one having something coming out of this one. This one had been one whom some were following. This one was one whom some were following. This one was being one whom some were following. This one was one who was working.

This one was one who was working. This one was one being one having something being coming out of him. This one was one going on having something come out of him. This one was one going on working. This one was one whom some were following. This one was one who was working.

This one always had something being coming out of this one. This one

29

Fig. 128. Gertrude Stein's portrait "Picasso," which appeared in *Camera Work* in August 1912

Fig. 129. Alvin Langdon Coburn (American, 1882–1966), *Henri Matisse*, 1913. Gelatin on nitrocellulose roll film, 11 x 9 in. (28 x 23 cm). George Eastman House, Rochester, New York, Gift of Alvin Langdon Coburn

celebrity-sighting in a decidedly American way. It also signaled a profound shift in the nature of salon conversation. Whereas some remembered Stein as a vivid talker, others considered her more of a listener, or often oblivious of the discussions around her. Stein loved to gossip, and by several accounts there was much confusion and a lot of fun. By 1913, dozens came through on any given Saturday: "And everybody came and no one made any difference," Stein observed in her autobiography.[41] The countless numbers of strangers and the foreign tongues were hardly conducive to calm and lucid inquiry. Speaking in earnest gave way to the importance of seeing and being seen. Stein helped turn literature into sound bites and salons into show business. "She likes the adventure of a new one," she wrote about her painters and the art market, and "once everybody knows they are good the adventure is over."[42] With its rapid changes in style, discontinuous speech, and fleeting fame, 27 rue de Fleurus was just around the corner from Andy Warhol's Factory. In the modern salons of the art world, as Robert Hughes has surmised, "better to be Baby Jane Holzer than the Duchesse de Guermantes."[43]

FLORINE STETTHEIMER:
THE JEWISH ROCOCO

The painting of Florine Stettheimer does not in the general sense belong to the concert hall, it is distinctly chamber music meant to be heard by special, sympathetic ears; it has about it an eighteenth-century delicacy which has no place in the present-day broadcasting system; it is not art for the hundred millions any more than the novel of Proust is meant to be a common language for multitudes to feast upon. . . . It is the ultra-lyrical expression of an ultra-feminine spirit.[44]

Florine Stettheimer's *Soirée* (1917–19) catches the viewer looking in through the picture window and extends an invitation to join the party (fig. 130). The salons held by the "Stetties"—Florine and her sisters Ettie and Carrie—were distinctive in post–World War I New York for their aristocratic politesse and over-the-top Dada flair. The painting's interior replicates the faux lavish décor in their brownstone on West Seventy-sixth Street in Manhattan: red brocade upholstery, ormolu furniture, gold and pale gray boiserie, and pictures on the walls and on easels, all by Florine. *Soirée* depicts her sisters and Stettheimer habitués, including Leo Stein and the playwright Avery Hopwood at center, and the artists Gaston Lachaise and Albert Gleizes standing before the easel at lower left. Ettie convenes with Isabelle Lachaise and the artist Maurice Sterne under a corner of Florine's *Family Portrait No. 1*, while Carrie finds herself next to Madame Gleizes on a red and white settee. A still life at the bottom of the canvas gives a hint of the elaborate multicourse meals devised by Carrie (who also painstakingly typed up the menus). Rum cocktails or champagne was served, and standard fare included lobster in mayonnaise aspic, oyster salad, and ham mousse—hardly kosher, but very refined.[45]

The legs of a seated Harlequin on the right allude to the literal commedia dell'arte taking place in this particular viewing of Florine's works. The artist herself presides over the drawing room from her nude *Self-Portrait* (1915–16), a send-up of the cheeky courtesan depicted in Édouard Manet's *Olympia* (1863) and the

pictorial mise-en-scène among artist, model, and viewer. The stiff figure of the Hindu poet Sankar[46] prudishly covers the hostess's public display of her private parts, but from the shocked gesture of Madame Gleizes, the dismayed "Oh no" glances of Florine's sisters, and the awkward silence that seems to circle the room, one gathers that the picture must have been quite a conversation-stopper when first unveiled. In any event, the actual dialogue is between Florine and the viewer, whom she engages with genteel amusement and a knowing gaze. The posing of the dark-skinned poet against the ivory nude decidedly echoes the loaded opposition in *Olympia* between the white sex goddess and the black maid who holds a bouquet from an admiring client. In Stettheimer's witty visual repartee, the flowers have already found their way into the hand of the naked hostess, who thanks you, with a smile, for the thoughtful gift.

Soirée is a conversation piece, overstuffed with worldly things and displaying fashionable sitters typically mute, but Stettheimer put a new gloss on old veneer by making her pictures the actual subjects of discussion. She "amusingly" re-created "our parties / our picnics / our banquets / our friends" in her portraits of intimates and modern-day *fêtes galantes*.[47] Some of the guests recorded in *Soirée*, in addition to the regulars Edward Steichen, Alfred Stieglitz, Carl Van Vechten, Henry McBride, Marsden Hartley, and Charles Demuth, were also habitués of Gertrude Stein's. With the Great War, returning Americans and exiled Europeans made the Manhattan transfer, and the Stettheimer home, like the apartment of Louise and Walter Arensberg, was one among several where Yankee Doodle dandies and expatriates such as Marcel Duchamp produced an exhilarating social cocktail.[48] Like Stein, Florine Stettheimer depended on her salon for inspiration and audience, but the two women and their gatherings could not have been more different. Stettheimer was, as Duchamp ennobled her, "painteress to the King,"[49] and the effeminate milieu she favored blatantly mocked Stein's reverence of masculine genius. Whereas Stein adamantly courted the glare of publicity, Stettheimer did not stoop to conquer, and took pleasure

Fig. 130. Florine Stettheimer (American, 1871–1944), *Soirée*, 1917–19. Oil on canvas, 28 x 30 in. (71.1 x 76.2 cm). Yale Collection of American Literature, Beinecke Rare Book and Manuscript Library, Yale University, New Haven

too much of Eighth Street in his manner he was unlikely to reappear."⁵² With the comportment of nobility, the sisters always presented their public selves, even to their intimates. Florine, in particular, turned on her social "soft pink light," as she described it, out of courtesy and self-protection.⁵³ She inspired respect and admiration, wrote Van Vechten (fig. 132), but not warmth or affection.⁵⁴ The Stettheimer salon was a public world in a private residence, filled with guests of the sisters' choosing; Stein, by contrast, casually opened her door to dozens of people whom she had never met and many of whom would never return. As Florine revealed in one of her poems written to herself, with no other audience in mind: "The world is full of strangers / They are very strange / I am never going to know them / Which I find easy to arrange."⁵⁵

In a throwback to seventeenth-century sociability, the Stettheimer salon was an inner sanctum where conversation, rather than art world propaganda or agendas, held sway. In a nod to the French tradition, Florine re-created the alcove bed of the original salonières when the family moved to a new apartment in the Alwyn Court on West Fifty-eighth Street in 1926 (fig. 133). Madame de Rambouillet had conceived her *chambre bleue* and the other public spaces of her private *hôtel* in a comfortable, feminine design; Florine decorated her duplex atelier in the Bryant Park Studios, a Beaux Arts building on West Fortieth Street, in an ensemble of cellophane and lace curtains, gilt fringe, crystal flowers, and rococo commodes (fig. 134). Her aesthetic project was one of parody, not parvenu aspiration, but with a genuine affinity for ancien régime wit and femininity. She elaborated her fey taste in deliberate affront to the rigid standardization and antidomesticity of International Style modernism. Recent scholarship has hailed her as a precedent for gay camp aesthetics, pop art, and feminist subversion.⁵⁶ But the Stettheimer salon must also be considered a whimsical evocation of the historical French salon, a feminized space that abetted social fluidity and where tastemakers and the talented formed the new aristocracy.

in distancing herself from commerce and the crowd. Although they had many close friends in common, the two women did not meet until just after they collaborated on Virgil Thomson's opera *Four Saints in Three Acts* (1934), with the libretto by Stein and the set and costumes by Stettheimer.⁵⁰

The Stettheimer salon was a distinctly uptown affair, a theater of the world where propriety and appearances were maintained, if knowingly staged. "Your slightest desire has the authority of the Constitution itself. I'll present myself in one of the swellest dinner jackets you ever saw," H. L. Mencken responded to an invitation, in a handwritten note.⁵¹ "Occasionally a gifted refugee from Greenwich Village drifted in," recalled Henry McBride (fig. 131), "but if there were

Of course it helped to be to the manor born, and the Stettheimers were a product of that novel American

Fig. 133. Florine Stettheimer's canopy bed at the Stettheimer family apartment in the Alwyn Court, New York City. Furniture and décor by the artist. Florine Stettheimer papers, Rare Book and Manuscript Library, Columbia University, New York

Fig. 134. Interior of Florine Stettheimer's studio in the Bryant Park Studio, 80 West Fortieth Street, New York City. Furniture and décor by the artist. Florine Stettheimer papers, Rare Book and Manuscript Library, Columbia University, New York

caste—New York Jewish nobility. Their mother, Rosetta Walter, hailed from one of the grand German Jewish families, whose intermarriage among merchant bankers—Seligmans, Hellmans, Birnbaums, and Guggenheims—led to the establishment of the New York "One Hundred."[57] The Upper East Side German Jews stood one rank below the earlier settled Sephardim, and far above the Russian and Polish Jewish immigrants of the Lower East Side. From an early age, in their childhood parlor of "Nattier blue," the Stettheimers were introduced to a privileged, if still segregated, world of "heavily encrusted calling cards." Whereas two of their aunts married extremely well (the butler of their Aunt Addie Seligman was the envy of all Manhattan and allegedly retired a million-aire from guests' tips), their mother misallied, with Joseph Stettheimer.[58] He abandoned her and their five children when they were still young and living in Europe. In the early 1890s the fatherless family returned to New York; they returned to Europe for an extended sojourn in 1898.

Despite their fluent French, upper-class back-ground, and indifference to organized religion, the Stettheimers never pretended to be other than what they were. Florine disparaged "fashionable Jews" who chose to be baptized. In 1910, while she was traveling through France by train, a woman in her compartment "made it her business" to find out about her religion. As the artist gleefully recorded in her diary:

> I took the pleasure in telling her I was not a Christian —in fact a Jewess—and she could not believe it—I was not "le type" and was my mother a Jewess also—and were there other Jews in America. I told her all her saints and her Sauveur and her vierge were Jews—she did not believe it—and said the only one she knew was Judas le traitre Iscariot! . . . She tickled me under the chin! And said she would pray for a change of heart for me in Lourdes—I asked her how she would like me to pray for a change of heart in my church. I did not tell her I had never attended a service in that same church.[59]

Florine was over forty when she, her two sisters (the other siblings had married), and their mother

Fig. 135. Florine Stettheimer, *Portrait of My Sister Ettie Stettheimer*, 1923. Oil on canvas mounted on composition board, 40 x 26 in. (101.6 x 66.04 cm). Columbia University, New York, Gift of the Estate of Ettie Stettheimer, 1967

effete "our crowd." Their salon bore witness to the ways in which a domestic space—outlandishly so in the case of the Stettheimers' self-consciously feminine appointments—could house an entourage of male intellectuals and cultural impresarios.[60]

Like the seventeenth-century *précieuses*, the Stettheimers cultivated an autonomous female environment for their own edification and pleasure, where men were expected to oblige. They made no excuses for their spinsterhood, nor did they bemoan it. With acute awareness of her aging self, but also of the benefits of independence, Florine identified with the career *salonières* of early centuries, most of whom were past their sexual prime, if still flowing with the feminine graces needed to elevate brute nature into art. In her poem "The Civilizers of the World," she knowingly observed, "They like a woman / to have a mind / they are of greater interest / they find / They are not very young / women of that / kind."[61] In their haute couture dress, the Stettheimers made haute talk, free of partisan gender topics. "The conversation was such as never occurs in our salon," Florine wrote to Ettie about an evening away from home. "Child birth thoroughly gone into by the three women—when the men joined us —(sounds antiquated), stories of French-Paris brothel life."[62] Instead, chez Stettheimer, animated discussions skipped from the Holy Ghost to Mae West, the sort of "unexpected turns" that underlie *Soirée*. "The gift of delicate satire and iridescent wit" that, as Hartley noted, graced Florine's paintings also permeated the "airy and ornamental" salon spirit. Not surprisingly, this artist of salon life was a devoted reader of Proust's *À la recherche du temps perdu*.[63]

The three sisters each played a role. Ettie (1875–1955), the *femme savante*, with her doctorate from the University of Freiburg (her dissertation was on William James) and her learned coquetry, governed the conversational rules. (Duchamp punned her "Ettie-qu'êtès" / Etiquette.)[64] In Florine's portraits of herself and her sisters, which she conceived as a triptych, she places Ettie on the divan, as the figurehead of salon sociability and the firefly who lights up at night (fig. 135). In addition to the luminous orbs against the black backdrop,

returned to New York in 1914 and settled together on the less prestigious Upper West Side. They lived well through inheritances and shrewd investments and followed their wealthy Jewish clan custom in their summer exodus from the city to country houses and resorts. Since they came from a highly assimilated background, the additional freedom from Jewish patriarchal domination only encouraged the Stettheimers' emancipated "New Woman" style, with its distinct echoes of aristocratic feminism. As Jews who could not enter certain Gentile establishments and who did not want to belong to religious congregations that would have them as members, the Stettheimers formed their own elite and

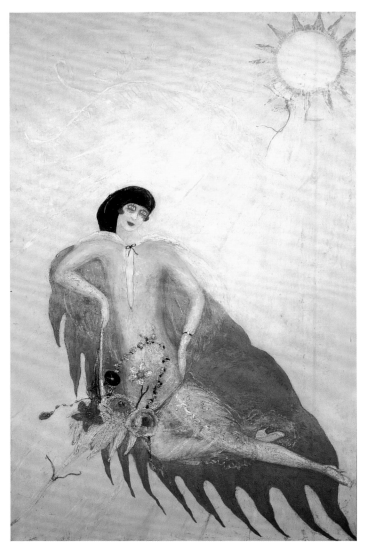

Fig. 136. Florine Stettheimer (American, 1871–1944), *Portrait of My Sister Carrie W. Stettheimer,* 1923. Oil on canvas, 37⅞ x 26⅛ in. (96.2 x 66.4 cm). Columbia University, New York, Gift of the Estate of Ettie Stettheimer, 1967

Fig. 137. Florine Stettheimer (American, 1871–1944), *Portrait of Myself,* 1923. Oil on canvas, 40 x 26 in. (101.6 x 66 cm). Columbia University, New York, Gift of the Estate of Ettie Stettheimer, 1967

the image is ablaze with a Christmas tree revealed as Moses' burning bush—a twinkling allusion to the Stettheimers' assimilated Jewish identity.[65]

Ettie entertained a brief career as a novelist under the name Henrie Waste—for *Henrie*tta *Wa*lter *Ste*ttheimer—an acronym inspired by Duchamp's word games. Duchamp was a central figure at the salon from 1916 to 1923, and kept up the effervescent dialogue with correspondence during his frequent trips abroad. In Florine's novel *Love Days* (1923), Duchamp appears in the character of Pierre Delaire (Pierre of the air and "stone of the air")—a pointed reference not only to one of his Dada ready-mades, the glass ampoule, *50 cc of*

Paris Air (1919), but also to his ethereal manner, his insubstantial romantic attachments, and his refusal to be pinned down by any fixed identity. Ettie and Duchamp conducted a highly intellectualized flirtation—wordplay as foreplay—congenial to the quick intelligence and linguistic brilliance of both parties. The discursive pas de deux in French and English and the idea of conversation as a perpetual state of play characterized the witty stylization of the Stettheimer salon. As in the seventeenth-century tradition, they delighted in pure verbal exchanges, or what Ettie, in a letter to Duchamp, called a "pensée-cadeau," a gift of thought.[66]

Carrie (1869–1944), the fashion plate and doyenne

of hospitality, did not pursue a career but held a full-time post as party planner. Anointed by Duchamp as "House Keeperin,"[67] she managed the German cook and maids with organizational efficiency; several images by Florine record her dutifully attending to guests. In her official portrait Carrie takes on the attributes of social butterfly (a term used by German Jewish high society to describe Mrs. William Waldorf Astor and *her* crowd),[68] with lacy wings and antennae topped by a beaded cloche. She stands between parted drapes on an Aubusson carpet, her monogram on the scalloped edges attesting to her signature role as the artful lady of the house (fig. 136). The metaphor is extended by the presence of Carrie's painstakingly crafted dollhouse (now in the Museum of the City of New York), which she points to with evident pride. A collective work of the salon, it contains miniature paintings, drawings, and sculpture by guests Gleizes, Duchamp, Lachaise, Marguerite Zorach, and Carl Sprinchorn, in addition to the layers of décor furnished by Carrie, such as the tiny Louis XV chair in her right hand.

Florine's self-portrait in the sisterly triptych has her in a diaphanous gown, floating on a capelike unfurled cocoon (fig. 137). In the family menagerie of delicate, flittering insects, Florine was the transparent dragonfly. Her winged *éphémère* veers too close to the sun on the upper right, a poignant commentary on the risks of social and artistic ambition. Florine once wrote caustically that her personal light "singed some," while others "tried to extinguish it."[69] By nature the least gregarious of the sisters, she also kept her distance in order to observe the social artifice that she then transformed into a pictorial comedy of errors or a garden of ephemeral delights. Here Florine captured her own shifting persona with the dandy's attributes of androgynous body and black artist's beret. Far from the matronly, social dowager type, she was none other than a "flutterby," the inconspicuous *femme auteur* as dispassionate flâneur: "Miss Butterfly / Sighed a sigh / 'My name does me belie / I shall change it to Flutterby / For I love the air / And to flutter / And I do not care / For butter.'"[70]

The Stettheimers emulated the sexually neutral space of the original salons, insofar as flirtation as high art could proceed apace without concern for actual consummation. Duchamp, who made it his life's work to pursue the erotic "delay" in art as well as in personal relations, found willing intellectual partners among the Stettheimer "ready maids."[71] Florine painted him in 1923, three years after he gave birth to his gender-bending alter ego Rrose Sélavy (Eros—that's life) in collaboration with the photographer Man Ray (fig. 138). With anything but erotic excitement, Florine accurately seizes on the mechanics of his female impersonation, for he cranks up the figure of Rrose, in her eponymous color, on a corkscrew-shaped device (a reference to sexual "routine" from his own work).[72] The bodies of the two personae are mirrored in their cross-legged pose, while the curves of their torsos are barely differentiated to connote their respective genders (fig. 139). Florine and Duchamp shared an aloof demeanor and sexually ambiguous (though not homosexual) identity; the prettily androgynous features of bob-haired Rrose are not too far from Florine's own. Indeed, the portrait of Duchamp may be considered a double portrait or a testament to the imaginative reciprocity of the salon circle.

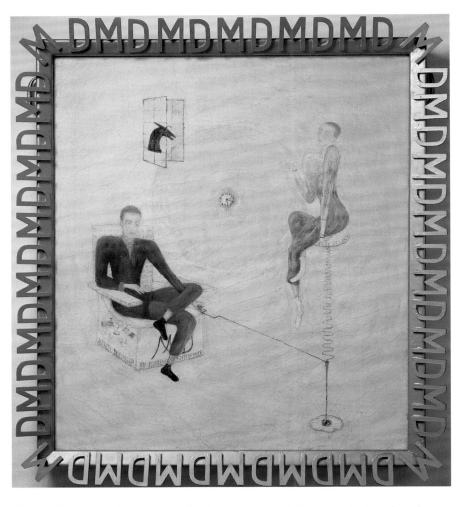

Fig. 139. Florine Stettheimer, *Portrait of Marcel Duchamp*, 1923. Oil on canvas, 30 x 26 in. (76.2 x 66 cm). William Kelly Simpson Collection

Duchamp recounted that when he first thought of changing his identity he considered using a Jewish name, but eventually decided on a female persona: in his immediate circle the Stettheimer sisters flamboyantly exhibited both marks of otherness.[73] During his association with their salon—and before Rrose Sélavy arrived on the scene—Florine often used the color rose and delighted in painting pink flowers, pink accoutrements, and hearts. Neither virginal white nor carnal red, rose is the in-between shade in the erotic spectrum. *Le Spectre de la rose* (*The Specter of the Rose;* first performed in 1911), a ballet about unfulfilled desire, inspired Florine's painting *Music* (1920), where Vaslav Nijinsky, a noted homosexual in the starring role of heterosexual desire, is depicted as simultaneously male and female. Who influenced whom we will, fittingly, never know,

but Duchamp and Stettheimer engaged in a complicated dance of gender doubling and transmutation. He referred to her as a bachelor—a pun on her unmarried status and the professional status conferred on a "bachelor of the arts." In a further gesture of complicity, Duchamp signed himself Rrose Sélavy in more letters to the Stettheimers than to any other correspondents.[74]

At the Stettheimer salon, the women could be ladies and so could the boys, as Florine emphasized in her unabashedly languid or daintily posed figures. Urbane New York between the wars was a "mecca for bachelors," and this facilitated the development of a more open, if still negotiated, gay world.[75] Several of the Stettheimers' habitués were distinguished public figures in the arts with private sexual identities, while others freely cultivated their "fairy" self-presentation. The Stettheimers hosted single homosexual men (Demuth, Hartley, Thomson, McBride), married ones (Van Vechten), and bisexuals (Cecil Beaton, Baron Adolf de Meyer), along with straight aesthetes (Stieglitz, Leo Stein). In her portraits of habitués, Florine does not discriminate, fashioning them all with svelte profiles, thin waists, and acquiescing doll-like limbs, emphasizing the fragility of all identities. Their physical bearing of languor and ennui belies the sharp faces alive with verve and whimsy.

Like Madame de Scudéry, who invented the game of salon portraiture, Stettheimer used her acute skills of observation and psychological acumen to draw out the distinguishing characteristics of her sitters. She unmasks the artificiality of their public faces with the telling petulant frown, pinched smile, arched eyebrow, or crooked wrist. She typically surrounds her sitters with a representational pageantry of their noble professions and favorite pastimes, as seen in the emblems and devices embellishing the McBride and Van Vechten portraits. In centuries past, salonières hung silhouettes or engraved images of their intimates to keep them company when they were apart.[76] Stettheimer similarly assembled a picture gallery of those who counted in her little world and in the sprawling culture of New York, portraits she did not sell or give away, but kept near—for herself.

When Stettheimer returned to the United States after years abroad, and was struck by its unconventional freedoms and brash exuberance, she decided to paint "America having its fling."[77] Skyscrapers, flashbulbs, garish parades, and George Washington memorabilia, Bendel's, Broadway, and Wall Street—all caught her precious eye. At the center of a subversively superior milieu, she cultivated a camp taste that played havoc with artistic hierarchies, elevating lowbrow glitz and effusion into high style.[78] As with the growing gay subculture that was welcome at the Alwyn Court, Stettheimer undermined traditional social demarcations while reinscribing her difference with exclusive visual and behavioral codes. The Stettheimer crowd despised the vulgarity of philistinism but could turn kitsch into the ultimate mark of a discerning sensibility with an aesthete's noblesse oblige. Only in America, the land of upward mobility and anything goes, could Stettheimer have contrived a style that was otherwise historically inconceivable—a Jewish rococo.

Stettheimer worked at a time when the social segregation of Jews still existed in many quarters. In 1920 she rendered the scene at Asbury Park South, a black beach resort down the New Jersey coast from the German Jewish colony at Sea Bright, where the Stettheimers vacationed. Florine respected and admired the difference of Afro-American culture, which she experienced through Van Vechten, a leading promoter of black music and frequenter of Harlem literary salons. He dedicated his novel *Nigger Heaven* (1926) to the Stettheimer sisters: the slang of the title refers to the uppermost seats of theaters, to which blacks were generally restricted.[79] Despite their economic fortune, the Stettheimers were aware of racial prejudice that permeated even the educated classes. Only in 1917 was a Jew, Otto Kahn (who had already served as the chairman of the board for years), permitted to buy a box in the "diamond horseshoe" of the Metropolitan Opera House.[80] Inevitably tinged with wry commentary, both playful and critical, Florine's view of "society" was that of someone whose immediate ancestors were once on the outside looking in. Redoubling her irony, with an air of religious complicity, the Jewish critic Paul

Rosenfeld characterized her festoonery and spangles as "Christmas-tree art," with a gentle dig at the tacky and commercialized rituals of mainstream Christian America: "gay decorations in colored paper, and lacquered red and blue glass balls, and gilt-foil stars and crepe streamers, and angels of cotton wadding, and tinted wax tapers."[81]

Although the Stettheimer sisters were not political activists (Ettie, however, had been a suffragist) and did not host a "colored salon," their liberal clique gently eroded stereotypes and pretension, in the best Enlightenment tradition. Their gatherings brimmed with swells and bookish types, gay men and tough-skinned newspaper columnists, Europhiles and American moderns, and several of their Jewish cousins and friends, including the social reformer Rabbi Stephen Wise, founder of the Free Synagogue in New York City. The Stettheimer salon accurately mirrored the sexual and social mobility of Manhattan and contained selected, glittering pieces of the American ethnic mosaic. It was the "open intellectual life of the place," recalled Rosenfeld, that made the guests "feel at home."[82] Amid the delicate finery of the Stettheimer boudoir, "hardy ideas" were shaped into words, witnessed Henry McBride, "which echoed sooner or later in other parts of the city."[83]

In addition to the dandies and social butterflies, the salon buzzed with Wasps—the dealer Kirk Askew, Jr., Everett "Chick" Austin, Jr., director of the Wadsworth Atheneum, Virgil Thomson, Monroe Wheeler of MOMA, and others. Indeed, the Stettheimer salon represented a new ethnic alliance of wealthy Gentiles and German Jews. Many guests overlapped with the similarly blended circles of Edward M. M. Warburg and Lincoln Kirstein, founders of the American Ballet Company (a precursor to the New York City Ballet), and the Harvard art historian Paul Sachs, who mentored a generation of museum directors, including Alfred H. Barr, Jr. As Thomas Bender has written, these constellations of uptown "civic intellectuals" were passionate about the visual arts, dance, and music. They were less active politically than their less wealthy and more radical downtown counterparts, who tended,

almost puritanically, toward literature and print.[84] Thanks to the Stettheimer salon connections, funding to produce *Four Saints in Three Acts* materialized when Askew, Barr, and Austin provided the sponsorship of their not-for-profit Friends and Enemies of Modern Music.[85]

With its ritualized formality, assimilated wealth, and talented habitués, the Stettheimer salon sustained a space for personal contacts and networking essential to the new institutions of New York City culture. Florine celebrated the ménage à trois of the old-boy network, new money, and uptown bohème in *The Cathedrals of Art* (1942–44; fig. 140), a mock allegory of the art world and its own dangerous liaisons with commerce and commercialization. In its grand design, the painting satirizes the rivalry and intrigue among the establishment Metropolitan Museum of Art, the avant-garde Museum of Modern Art, and the fledgling Whitney Museum of American Art. At the base of the Metropolitan's grand stairway, flashbulbs light up the baby "Art," cooed over by an adoring handmaiden. At the top of the stairs are the figureheads of the respective institutions: Francis Henry Taylor of the Metropolitan at center, the Modern's cerebral Alfred Barr, Jr., in self-chosen solitude at upper left, and the Whitney's Juliana Force, sidelined and clearly miffed about it, at upper right.[86]

Florine presents herself as the *comère* (godmother) to the newborn in this nativity scene, though by standing under her signature boudoir canopy she signals to her actual role as presiding salonière. The painting constitutes a group portrait of Stettheimer's habitués—the effete critics, artists, and dealers who make this world go 'round. Force was the first and last woman director of any of the big three New York museums, and intentionally or not, Stettheimer underlines the lagging prominence of women in the arts by not configuring herself among the artists. They are represented exclusively by men: the figures of Charles Demuth, Elie Nadelman, Pavel Tchelitchew, and George Platt Lynes; the inscribed names of Picasso, Joan Miró, and Salvador Dalí; and by Stettheimer's pastiche of museum masterpieces—those by Picasso, Franz Hals, and Henri Rousseau, for example. Women appear as muses, as objects of desire, or, in the group of blondes between Force and Stettheimer, as parasitic socialites. In another indication of still-existing barriers, the Jewish protagonists here play their traditional role of middlemen, like Stettheimer herself, and the dealers Stieglitz, Marie Sterner, and Julien Levy: it would be years before one of these three major institutions appointed a Jewish director. Yet her "soul" mates were ascending the stairs of the Metropolitan, just as Florine greeted the cultural firmament at her door. *The Cathedrals of Art—* religious metaphor notwithstanding—acknowledges just how far Jewish New Yorkers and salonières had scaled the heights.

The Salon in Exile

SALKA VIERTEL: THE SALON AT THE OTHER END OF THE WORLD

The gatherings held from the late 1920s through the 1940s in a modest house at 165 Mabery Road in Santa Monica, overlooking the Pacific Ocean, represent the farthest-flung incarnation of the European salon tradition. The writer S. N. Behrman called the hostess who presided "the greatest salonière of modern times."[1] Salka Viertel (1889–1978; fig. 141) arrived in Hollywood in 1928 with her husband, the Viennese writer and director Berthold Viertel (fig. 142), of whom Christopher Isherwood would observe, "[He had] the face of a political situation, an epoch. The face of Central Europe."[2] Like many leading European theatrical talents of the interwar period, Berthold Viertel had been lured by a Hollywood studio; Fox had invited him to write the screenplay for F. W. Murnau's second American film, *4 Devils*. Salka Viertel's trepidation about leaving Europe and her successful career as a stage actress, as well as her parents and siblings, was overcome by her husband's hopeful enthusiasm: "Fate is calling us and we must follow."[3] What was intended as a brief sojourn to improve their finances and experience something of the New World turned into an extended stay; Salka became an American citizen in 1939. Despite the difficulties of adjustment, Hollywood presented her with the opportunity for a second profession as a screenwriter, and a legendary career as a salonière. Over the years, she would host a mix of actors, directors, musicians, and intellectuals—European émigrés and refugees, and Americans as well. Most crucial, the decision to go to America meant that the Viertels—Berthold, Salka, and their three sons—were safe when the Nazis came to power, and Salka was in a position to help her elderly mother reach safety in the United States and to aid the refugee community through her salon.

The salon began informally: "Moving to Santa Monica did not impair our social life. On the contrary, our Sunday afternoons became very popular," Salka recalled with characteristic modesty.[4] In fact, during the Viertels' early years in Hollywood, their home was a key meeting place for European and British actors, writers, and directors who had been brought to Hollywood to impart sophistication to American films: Ernst Lubitsch, Max Reinhardt (a Zuckerkandl habitué) and his sons Wolfgang and Gottfried, William Dieterle, Murnau; Emil Jannings and Conrad Veidt; Charlie Chaplin, Charles Laughton, and Elsa Lanchester; Aldous Huxley. Among the American guests were Miriam Hopkins, Johnny Weissmuller, George Cukor, Harold Clurman, and Oscar Levant, and later, Irwin Shaw and Norman Mailer. Though the atmosphere was carefree, the situation was not without its tensions:

> In those first years in California I don't think I met anyone who had been born or raised there. The actors and writers, especially those from the East, were transitory, having come to make money and to get out as soon as possible. I also was counting the days till our return to Europe. I became aware that we were constantly explaining ourselves to our American friends, trying to convey our identity and what really possessed us, who we were. Berthold's futile efforts to communicate made me unhappy. . . . For a man so erudite and creative in his own language, it was torture to confine himself to . . . primitive vocabulary . . . and escaping to the men's room to read Kant and Kierkegaard was small relief. The only comfort was the sight of the sea and the happiness of our sons, who had become dedicated Californians.[5]

Given Berthold's difficulties, it is not surprising that he soon sought projects back in Europe, leaving Salka to manage their sons and life "at the other end of the world."[6] Salka, with her optimism and resilience, learned to drive, mastered English, and reinvented herself.

When Lubitsch invited the Viertels and Greta Garbo to his home on the same night, a connection was

made that altered Salka's life: "The next day we had just finished lunch when the doorbell rang and in the open window of the entrance appeared the unforget-table face. . . . Gaily she announced that she had come to continue the conversation of last night, and stayed all afternoon."[7] The two women each found a soul mate in the other, and they embarked on a fruitful collabor-ation. Garbo helped Viertel find something to do, as boredom had threatened: "The lunches and parties were getting me down. . . . To survive in Hollywood [I] had to work."[8] Viertel appeared in four films in Holly-wood, in one of them, a German-language version of *Anna Christie*, opposite Garbo. The English version was Garbo's first "talkie," and its success ensured her status as a star in the new economy of sound pictures. While the silents could play anywhere, spoken dialogue limited the market for Hollywood's English-language productions, so studios made versions of their hits for export. Salka assisted the French director Jacques

Feyder with the German dialogue, and she turned in a memorable performance as Marthy Owens, the old waterfront whore originally played by Marie Dressler. Seated in the women's section of the run-down bar, Marthy and Anna Christie regard each other warily (fig. 143), in a profound moment of on-screen commu-nication that mirrored the off-screen affinity between the two actresses. But film roles frustrated Viertel—"Acting in fragments is like drinking from an eyedrop-per when you are parched"[9]—so Garbo suggested she write screenplays instead. Viertel would collaborate on Garbo's scripts for MGM—among them *Queen Christina* (fig. 144), *Anna Karenina*, and *Conquest*—earning a rep-utation as a Garbo expert, and as a means for studios to gain access to one of Hollywood's hottest properties. Viertel thus had enormous clout, and although Garbo did not always show up at the Sunday gatherings in Santa Monica, her aura enhanced the hostess's prestige.

Salka Viertel brokered connections. She introduced

Fig. 143. Greta Garbo and Salka Viertel in the German-language version of *Anna Christie* (1931). Courtesy of the Academy of Motion Picture Arts and Sciences

Fig. 144. Poster for *Queen Christina* (1933), starring Greta Garbo. Salka Viertel collaborated on the story and the screenplay, and S. N. Behrman wrote the dialogue, for this Metro-Goldwyn-Mayer film. Courtesy of the Academy of Motion Picture Arts and Sciences

Tallulah Bankhead to Garbo—and a lasting friendship was born.[10] After Sergei Eisenstein was introduced to Viertel at a party given by Upton Sinclair in 1930, she made herself the avant-garde Soviet director's advocate in Hollywood, helping to raise funds for his ambitious Mexican film project and defending his artistic credentials in the face of uncomprehending business people. His screenplays for Paramount were never shot, and Eisenstein would later say that the only films he made in Hollywood were photographs taken with the Viertels on the beach (fig. 145).[11] But the most significant impact of Viertel's salon came in the years after the Nazi ascent

to power, with the influx of refugees to southern California. Gottfried Reinhardt (fig. 146), her lover during those years, described the meeting of European artistic and intellectual giants and Hollywood glamour:

The greatest contrasts collided in the salon of Salka Viertel. . . . It was a salon. In her house in Santa Monica, George Sand, Chopin, Liszt, Musset, Delacroix would have felt comfortable. Now it was where Greta Garbo elucidated to Max Reinhardt how she intended to play Hamlet; where Chaplin . . . recruited his musical ghostwriter, the brilliant

Fox – PARAMOUNT – Production
in two virgins:
S. M. EISENSTEIN
„ Des Meeres u. d. Liebe Wellen "

B.V.: „ Na Kinder! Ich
gehe jetzt ba-
den....
Ich hoffe, daß
ihr brav
sein werdet! "
(ab)

S.M.: „ Well, Zalka,
let us be
brave ?
Z : „ Ha! Ha! Ha!
Hi! Hi!
Hi! "
(they are brave)

(After being brave
for a little time)
Z : „ Quick! Quick!
He is coming
back! "
S.M.: „ He is! Shut
up, Zalka! "
(Zalka shuts up
see picture →).

Fig. 145. Edward Tisse, "Fox-Paramount Production in two virgins!" Photo album page with Salka Viertel and Sergei Eisenstein on the beach. Tisse was Eisenstein's cameraman. Private collection

Fig. 146. Gottfried Reinhardt. Archiv der Stiftung Deutsche Kinemathek Berlin

Fig. 147. Bertolt Brecht (seated left) and Charles Laughton (right) during a radio broadcast in Los Angeles, 1947. Archiv der Stiftung Deutsche Kinemathek Berlin

sycophant Hanns Eisler; where the happy-go-lucky virtuoso in the grand tradition, Arthur Rubinstein, was polite to the unhappy and unlucky, tradition-trampling Arnold Schönberg [sic]; where the brothers Heinrich and Thomas Mann, estranged for decades, were reconciled after many weeks of delicate . . . diplomacy . . . where Max Reinhardt, for the first time, made the acquaintance of his former Dramaturg *(literary adviser)—Bertolt Brecht.*[12]

Whereas Reinhardt had grown up in such an environment, for visitors like John Houseman, the

encounter with these luminaries was exceptional: "The town's most eminent émigrés continued to congregate and . . . you might find yourself sharing brilliant conversation or a sachertorte with Brecht, [the writer Lion] Feuchtwanger, [Max] Reinhardt, [the actor Fritz] Kortner, Thomas or Heinrich Mann among the literati and theatre people; [Ernst] Toch, [Erich Wolfgang] Korngold, Eisler, Schoenberg and [Salka's brother Eduard] Steuermann among the musicians."[13] Both these descriptions, however, belie the seriousness of what was transacted at the salon. Viertel used her connections to supply affidavits for desperate refugees and negotiate studio contracts for new arrivals, and if that was impossible, she helped them find domestic work; in one memorable case, she persuaded friends to hire the wife of an impoverished émigré lawyer from Berlin to wash their dogs. Through the European Film Fund, established with Liesl Frank (daughter of the Berlin singer Fritzi Massary and the comic actor Max Pallenberg, and wife of the writer Bruno Frank) and the Dieterles, performers donated a portion of their salaries to support refugees. By the time refugees escaped Europe—as did Alma Mahler, with her third husband, the writer Franz Werfel, and Heinrich and Nelly Mann, who fled occupied France on foot over the Pyrenees, and arrived in the United States in October 1940—whatever the hardships and their disdain for American culture, it was clear that poverty and lack of recognition in America were preferable to being hunted in Europe.

Not all of Viertel's attempted matchmaking succeeded. She arranged a meeting between Arnold Schoenberg and Irving Thalberg in the hopes of securing a contract for the composer to score the film of Pearl Buck's *Good Earth*, but Schoenberg's demand for artistic control and a fifty-thousand-dollar fee scuttled the deal. Her introduction of Bertolt Brecht to Charles Laughton (fig. 147), though, yielded a historic collaboration: the performance in Hollywood on July 30, 1947, of Brecht's *Life of Galileo*, with Laughton as the scientist appearing before the Inquisition—a metaphor for the procedures of the House Un-American Activities Committee and its investigation of Brecht and others in

Viertel's circle.[14] Three months later Brecht would testify before the committee in Washington, and the next day would leave the United States for good.

Apart from providing contacts, Viertel's salon was a touchstone, with the sounds and tastes of a continent that had once been home but that the émigrés could now regard only with ambivalence. At first they tried to inform the rest of the world about the severity of the Nazi menace; once the United States entered the war, many were subject to curfews as "enemy aliens." After Germany's defeat, they became suspect as Communist sympathizers and "premature anti-Fascists." Having survived in the United States, they experienced guilt—both the Jews who escaped the camps, and the non-Jews such as Brecht, who lost a son fighting in the German army. No wonder they longed to be among people who understood their plight. Brecht wrote: "Even in the backwoods of Finland I never felt so out of the world as here. Enmities thrive here like oranges and are just as seedless [groundless]. The Jews accuse one another of anti-Semitism, and the Aryan Germans accuse one another of Germanophilia."[15] Viertel's salon welcomed artists across the spectrum, from Thomas Mann to Bertolt Brecht, whose rivalry marked the émigré society. Mabery Road was the site of a meeting on August 1, 1943, attended by Berthold Viertel, Heinrich and Thomas Mann, Brecht, Feuchtwanger, Bruno Frank, the physicist Hans Reichenbach, and the philosopher Ludwig Marcuse, to draft a declaration supporting the struggle for a strong democracy in Germany and distinguishing between the Hitler regime and the German people; the next morning Thomas Mann withdrew his signature.[16]

If Mann noted several times in his diary the tastiness of Salka's Mitteleuropean cuisine and the quality of her coffee, it was the chance to hear Schoenberg perform his *Pierrot lunaire* or to discuss with Theodor Adorno the question of musicality in the novel that made the writer an enthusiastic regular, despite his complaint that the house was too hot and smoke-filled, even on a January evening.[17] Mabery Road was the logical site for an established ritual of German letters, the celebration of the birthdays of the brothers Mann.

On May 2, 1941 (weeks after the actual date), literary representatives of the "other Germany" congregated there to observe Heinrich's seventieth birthday; a decade earlier, his sixtieth had been celebrated at the Prussian Academy of Arts in Berlin. Alfred Döblin described the Santa Monica evening as being "like old times: [Thomas] Mann pulled a manuscript out of his pocket and read his congratulations. . . . Then [Heinrich] pulled a manuscript out of his pocket and likewise read his printed thanks. We sat over dessert, about twenty men and women, and listened to each other talk about German literature. Feuchtwanger, Werfel, [Walter] Mehring, the Reinhardts, and a few people from film."[18] In her memoirs, Salka Viertel characterized the guests as representing "the true Fatherland to which in spite of Hitler they adhered, as they adhered to the German language."[19]

Viertel's tact and generosity eased the way for many of her intimates as they navigated the business of the studios and the vicissitudes of daily life and complex interpersonal relationships. The distances and the inadequate public transportation system in Los Angeles proved vexing for many émigrés, who either had not learned to drive or, like the Brechts, were too poor to afford a car. Salka chauffeured Helene Weigel, Brecht's wife, from Santa Monica to the central market in Los Angeles, where she could buy food cheaply.[20] Brecht's collaborator and mistress, Ruth Berlau, who had been living in New York, came west to give birth to their child; the baby died after a few days and Berlau herself was seriously ill. The penurious Brecht took her out of the hospital before she was fully recovered, and brought her to recuperate at Mabery Road, where Salka looked after her.[21] Thomas Mann thought of sending his brother to stay with Salka after Heinrich's wife, Nelly, committed suicide in 1944.[22]

It was Viertel's human qualities that drew people to her. Christopher Isherwood, who rented the garage apartment at Mabery Road and found her "the most perfect landlady-hostess imaginable," was in an excellent position to observe the way she ran her salon: "All sorts of celebrities came to the house, not because Salka made the least effort to catch them but because they wanted to see her and to be with their own friends who were also her guests. Actually Salka was a somewhat self-effacing hostess. She greeted newcomers warmly and got them involved in conversation with earlier arrivals, then she disappeared into the kitchen to see how things were going. I remember her most vividly at this moment of greeting; she was strikingly aristocratic and unaffected. Her posture, the line of her spine and neck, was still beautiful; you could believe that she had been a great actress."[23]

Intimates noted her extraordinary warmth—that of "a hearth, a human fireplace."[24] A strong erotic radiation captivated men, despite the fact that she was not conventionally beautiful. Her spunk and optimism never deserted her, even when her circumstances deteriorated after the war. Berthold and many of her friends returned to Europe for good; Gottfried Reinhardt, who had been her live-in lover for ten years, married; and the anti-Communist witch-hunts led to her being graylisted and unemployed. While others described their memories of the salon with inevitable name-dropping, Salka Viertel was the epitome of discretion. Marta Feuchtwanger, widow of Lion, was struck by this quality and Viertel's lack of pretension. After Feuchtwanger read her memoir, *The Kindness of Strangers*, she wrote Viertel that what she admired most was "what she left out. Because her discreetness was so great; the most interesting things she didn't write. . . . If she had written what she knew, she would have made the greatest sensation. And that she didn't do it is even a greater page in her life."[25]

If Salka Viertel's salon had become the substitute for the Prussian Academy, it was because of the inversion of cultural as well as human values that Nazism had represented. Thomas Mann, in his speech for his brother's seventieth birthday, asked: "But . . . what today is the meaning of foreign, the meaning of homeland? . . . When the homeland becomes foreign, the foreign becomes the homeland."[26] With this, the salon had come full circle. Once a compensatory mechanism for institutions that did not yet exist—for example, the Berlin salons before the city's university was established in 1810—the salon now substituted for the

old European institutions that had become poisoned. For a European Jewish woman like Rahel Levin Varnhagen, ostracized and disenfranchised, longing to call the country where she lived her homeland, the salon offered a sense of home. Salka Viertel and her associates, who had repudiated their former homelands, and been rejected by them, demanded to define what German-language culture was; the salon was a place where this "other German" culture could be expressed. Viertel was particularly suited for creating an alternative home—a "zu Hause"—in her salon because early on she had understood that home and estrangement were not geographically determined. In a letter to her husband not long after their arrival in California, she wrote: "I am not one iota more in a foreign land here than I was in Dresden, in Berlin, in Düsseldorf. Had you had any idea how inconsolably alien and lonely I [felt] roaming along the Rhine Bridge—but you never asked me about it. The only kind of home I had was the stage."[27] Berta Zuckerkandl, the Austrian patriot, carried her role as salonière with her into exile, as Jews have ever transported their culture in their wanderings. But for Salka Viertel, the salon was a product of feeling "alien," even before she became an émigré; she needed the salon to create a home, and for her guests, once they had become refugees, it was an instrument of survival. Thomas Viertel remembers his mother often quoting a line of Heinrich Heine: "I had a fatherland, but it was a dream." Salka Viertel's salon took the place of the nonexistent fatherland.

WHITHER THE SALON?

It is an irony inherent in the history of the salon that an institution that served as a catalyst for modern culture and that nurtured innovation and dynamic change was so intimately permeated by the sentiment of nostalgia. Perusing the writings of many of the participants of salon culture after the ancien régime, one is struck by the tone of longing for an idyllic recent past, a moment of perfect sociability. Sabine Lepsius, a guest at the Berlin salon of the Bernsteins, wrote an article in 1913 lamenting the demise of the salons, a phenomenon that she attributed to the "mechanism of daily life," and to a culture that "substitutes sensation for tradition, which it derides."[28] Virginia Woolf commented that salons were thought to be as extinct as dodos.[29]

But the pervasive and recurring theme of the salon's demise was present at its origins. Rahel Levin Varnhagen's letter to Karl Gustav von Brinckmann, who had been one of her most enthusiastic guests and had brought nobles and men of letters to her gatherings, summed up what had distinguished her social experiment—and what had vanished: "The entire constellation of beauty, grace, coquetry, attraction, amorousness, wit, elegance, cordiality, the urge to develop new ideas, honest seriousness, unconstrained exploration and encounter, spirited humor, has *dissipated*."[30] Varnhagen would live another fourteen years and, despite her deteriorating health, would go on receiving guests, among them Heinrich Heine, Ludwig Börne, and other important authors of the younger generation. Should we be surprised that she wrote, in this same letter, of "remnants," that she saw the experience as having "dissipated"?

Yet how could it be otherwise? Salons, by their very nature, are ephemeral. They consist of momentary encounters, of brief impressions received by the senses —of hearing human speech and music, of seeing human gestures and works of art. Speaking, listening, looking, not writing, composing, painting, are the activities of the salon. Its power is anchored in the most fleeting of activities: conversation. We cannot perceive what transpired at the gatherings; we can only measure some aftereffects. The texts describing Varnhagen's salons and published by her husband are suspect, not only because he was so much *parti pris*, but also because the participants themselves were invested in presenting an idyllic image of this shared past. Perhaps only an immediate recollection, such as Alma Schindler's diary entry on the evening she met Gustav Mahler at the Zuckerkandls', can be free of retrospective sentimentality.

In today's world the term *salon* has come to mean a kind of regular entertaining, the type engaged in by socialites featured in the pages of *Vogue*. Recently the *New York Times* celebrated the downtown "salons" of artists young and old, presenting them as heirs to a long tradition that includes Henriette Herz and Gertrude Stein, though contemporary journalists like to replace the old-fashioned "salonière" with the more up-to-date "salonista," a cognate of "fashionista." But surely the salon is more than just the social interaction of a regular group of guests in the orbit of a charming and talented woman, no matter how illustrious the personalities. In considering the nearly two-hundred-year history of Jewish salonières, one understands that their gatherings were not profligate expenditures or merely a question of leisure, but a matter of necessity. For both the woman and her guests, the salon provided opportunity and access otherwise denied. As an institution, the salon was a compensatory mechanism, filling a need, occupying a vacuum. Apart from the pragmatic function of the salon as a performance space, university, and art gallery, its social role as a leveler between classes and as a place of access for women and for Jews diminished in urgency with an ever greater democratization of the public sphere, with true emancipation of both Jews and women. As women entered the workforce in greater numbers and acquired positions of power and influence outside the home, they had less need of the salon, and less time for orchestrating it.

With the resurgence of interest in the subject of salons generally, much has been made of the World Wide Web as a contemporary equivalent. It is considered apt that an Internet magazine is called *Salon*. Closer reflection, though, reveals as many significant discrepancies as affinities between the salon and the chat rooms of the Internet. One of the most attractive— and potentially dangerous—aspects of the Internet is its anonymity. The experience of the salons was diametrically opposed to such anonymity; whatever their dissimilarities or rivalries, however much people from divergent backgrounds did or did not accept one another, they certainly confronted one another. The salon was not a space one entered in order to hide. At its core, it was about face-to-face human encounter. That this encounter rarely lived up to its ideal made the nostalgia for salon sociability all the more poignant. It was a longing for an experience manqué, but an experience that might be appreciated and celebrated as much for its aspirations as for its significant accomplishments.

Bemoaning the lost paradise of a specific social constellation—to use Rahel Varnhagen's memorable word—of people, emotions, and ideas, may in fact be intrinsic to the salon experience. Perhaps the salon must always be somewhat mythical because its very power lies in the utopian ideal of effecting change in such a civilized manner: through conversation and by bringing together people from disparate worlds. In 1819, the same year that Varnhagen wrote to Brinckmann of the unique conviviality that had been her creation, she also wrote to her friend Pauline Wiesel about "recollections of things that were never *there*."[31] Perhaps the salon was always dying out because it never really was all that one wanted it to be; only in the glow of recollection could the ideal be achieved. The power of the salon—the power of conversation—is, and was, in mobilizing that ideal.

Ant. Graff gem.   Alb. Teichel gest.

A Dream of Living Together: Jewish Women in Berlin Around 1800

BARBARA HAHN

A young scholar named August Hennings, visiting Berlin in the 1770s, reported that the city's "Jewish colony . . . has the great advantage that its attractiveness is owed even more to the fame of its scholars than to the beauty of its women." The letter of a friend, he said, "procured me entrance to the house of the famous Mendelssohn. At the home of the banker Itzig, who lives in a palace, I frequently encounter the well-known Friedländer, who is much prized in the cultivated world. . . . [Itzig's] daughters augment the grace of their beauty through their talents, particularly for music, and with a sophisticated spirit."[1] In meeting a philosopher, Berlin's most important banker, and the man who devoted his life to propagating Jewish emancipation and Reform Judaism, this young man obviously found his way into noted and remarkable Jewish houses. Most strikingly, all the women to whom he was introduced remain anonymous.

The letters of Caspar Voght, a Hamburg merchant who visited Berlin in 1803, paint a different picture. Now, almost the only names mentioned are those of Jewish women. In the meantime, their reputation for hospitality has obviously spread far beyond Prussia's capital. As becomes evident from his letters as well as from many others to be considered here, these social activities were understood by their contemporaries to be contested enterprises. The common, idealized image

Fig. 1. Albert Teichel, *Portrait of Henriette Herz*, after the 1792 painting by Anton Graff (Bilski and Braun essay, fig. 20). Teichel's print served as the frontispiece to Joseph Fürst, ed., *Henriette Herz: Ihr Leben und ihre Erinnerungen* (Berlin: Wilhelm Hertz, 1850)

of the "famous Berlin salons" that has come down to us, then, is not at all how these institutions were perceived by those most immediately involved in them. The social circles around Jewish women in the period between the 1780s and 1806 have been adorned with mythology. "Berlin salons"—this topos does not raise questions, but inspires knowing nods. This is because almost all studies and histories depend on a few *printed* sources, and always the same ones. They are so seductive because they cater to the reader's expectations: ready-made stories, with a cast of famous people. The problem is that these texts were written retrospectively and—much more important—were most likely forged.[2] Instead of repeating the tales that show history in too bright a light, this essay raises questions of nuance: How have these salons been handed down historically, and how were they described in writing? Social gatherings leave behind few traces. Conversation and laughter, hushed and booming voices begin to fade the moment they emerge. In a salon, people do not write, but talk. Talk presupposes the presence of others; writing, their absence.

Reporting back to his friends in Hamburg, Caspar Voght sketches a telling image of Jewish conviviality with all its bright and dark sides. In the first days of his visit, he made the acquaintance of Henriette Herz (fig. 1), who had hosted an open house since the 1780s.[3] On February 12, 1803, he lunched with Sara Levy, who had invited a number of scholars for his sake.[4] To judge from his letters, there Voght met the same people with whom he socialized on other days in Christian houses. His next call, however, brought him directly into the center of the conflict that surrounded the conviviality of Jewish women: "After the meal I visited with a very entertaining woman whom I had known earlier in Karlsbad. A Mrs. von Groothusen, formerly Mlle. Meyer, a baptized Jewess, sister of Baroness Eibenberg, who was married for a short time to Prince Reuss [fig. 2]; both fine and cultivated women—but one always notices a trace of their first education."[5] Not only the Meyer sisters were converted. Sooner or later, all the women we will be considering here took the same course, with the exception of the Itzig daughters. It is

readily apparent under which pressure Jewish upper-
middle-class society stood, not merely to acculturate
but also to leave behind their distinctive history, culture,
and faith. The opening of Jewish houses as an attempt
at a common life between Christians and Jews, the rich
social life that these women developed, remains—in
retrospect—an episode.

Voght's letters reveal even more to the modern
reader: beyond Berlin, it was above all the Bohemian
baths where meetings took place. Sara and Mariane
Meyer had spent the summer of 1795 in Karlsbad,
where a friendship with Johann Wolfgang von Goethe
began that was continued for many years in correspon-
dences.[6] At the baths gathered a mixed society similar
to the one that met in the Jewish houses of Berlin:
lower and higher nobility, as well as those actors and
artists who could afford such a stay. Few bourgeois.
A transitional group. No longer the representatives of
the ancien régime and not yet the bourgeoisie of the
nineteenth century.

Caspar Voght, a careful observer of social life, dis-
closes a further social rift. His tone changes perceptibly
when he starts to speak of Rahel Levin,[7] the intellectual
among the "salon ladies": "As of now I know only that
she's ugly—I'll find out the rest later," he writes after

his first meeting with her.[8] He soon tells what "the rest"
is. A few days later he has "drunk tea with Mlle. Levy
[*sic*] and [Friedrich] Schlegel and spent a few pleasant
hours. She is pure nature up to a point and this lends
her entire being a certain slant, except that she is full
of spirit and knowledge; were I to remain here I would
see her often."[9] Rahel Levin, who comes down to us
as very intelligent but physically not very attractive,
disrupts the context of bourgeois femininity. All the
other Jewish hostesses are the daughters or wives of
important men. Yet she remained unmarried until her
early forties; at the high point of Jewish conviviality
she still lived with her widowed mother and four
younger siblings. At the same time, she did not accord
with the clichéd image of the beautiful Jewess; Voght
comments on her looks but on no other woman's. He
is not alone in his negative observations. The French-
born Berlin writer Adelbert von Chamisso calls her
"a strange manifestation of spirit";[10] the book dealer
Johann Daniel Sander writes to his Weimar friend Carl
August Böttiger: "There is a small, 24- or 25-year-old
Jewish girl named Rahel Levi [*sic*]. She is clever, but a
malicious toad, and not with the best reputation, since
she socializes almost entirely with depraved people of
both sexes."[11]

Educated, often well-to-do women whom one was
happy to visit, or "Jewish girls"—the surviving images
of the women who hosted open houses in the brief
period between the mid-1780s and Prussia's defeat by
Napoléon in 1806 oscillate between these poles. We
know of a dozen women who received guests on a more
or less regular schedule. Mostly for tea, sometimes for
lunch, but rarely to evening dinner parties. The last
were for the nobility. Some families set aside a particular day of the week, while most invited guests on an
ad hoc basis.

In retrospect, these gatherings were called "salons"
—a misleading characterization. In contrast to the
French tradition, in which *salon* evokes the Parisian
domiciles of the aristocracy and upper classes, the word
in Germany has echoes of bourgeois Jewish houses in
Berlin around 1800. In Paris, Madame de Tencin or
Madame de Récamier—in Berlin, Henriette Herz and

Rahel Levin. But the very term *salon* in this context is anachronistic. As a designation for social activities, especially in Jewish houses, it was coined only in the 1840s, and thus had from the outset a melancholy tone. One spoke of salons when their flowering had long since faded. The women whose names have entered history in connection with the Berlin salons around 1800 never referred to their socializing this way themselves, even though they certainly used the word in other contexts. Rahel Levin, for instance, called the gatherings staged by the high aristocracy "salons"— for her a distant and inaccessible world. When mentioning the social activities in her own house, she never uses the word but speaks rather of her "society," or "our circle." These terms have no historical or programmatic connotations; they are unburdened and can therefore designate something unprecedented. The social activities that take place evade definition and— for the time being—have not been conceptualized.

What connected the gatherings in so many different Jewish houses, and in what relation did the women who hosted them stand to one another? Our knowledge here is limited. For few of the many billets that moved from house to house in Berlin, few of the many letters written on journeys to Paris, Vienna, or Italy or on summer visits to Bohemian and Brandenburgian spas have survived to our day. Only two participants in this conviviality systematically collected and preserved billets and letters: Rahel Levin, whose papers are archived in Kraków, and a Swedish diplomat, Karl Gustav von Brinckmann (fig. 3), who arrived in Berlin in 1789 and resided there—with substantial interruptions—until 1808. He knew and corresponded with all the Jewish women who hosted open houses at the time, and he saved everything, even the smallest note. Henriette Herz and Dorothea Schlegel (fig. 4), in contrast, in their old age burned everything that they had preserved throughout their lives. Of the papers of other women, nothing, or almost nothing, has survived.[12] What, then, do we know?

The story begins in the 1780s. The first traces of social activities among these women are to be found in letters and billets from and to Sara Meyer. Together with her sister, Mariane, she issued invitations to tea in English, French, and German. A letter to Sara in Yiddish from her brother Heyman from December 14, 1786, demonstrates that the family was transforming itself linguistically at this time as well. Yiddish disappears and German takes over, yet always accompanied by a third language: all of these women also wrote in French. What function this language had can be seen in a letter from Mariane in Vienna to Sara in Berlin dated November 26, 1803: "You have not written to me that you were with madame Levy for *thé* madame Eskeles[13] tells me that she conducts such a pretty house no *maîtresse de la maison* could be more elegant than she is that is more; I hope you see each other often *adio carina*."[14] French is the language of society, the art of conversation, in contrast with which German, from the perspective of these women, tended toward heaviness and inertia.

Sara Levy, about whom the letter was speaking, a recognized harpsichordist, pianist, and music aficionado, was also receiving guests. Written testimony, however, survives only from later years. On September 10, 1803, she writes to Karl Gustav von Brinckmann: "Since we have till now waited in vain for a friendly acceptance of the request we sent you several days ago to join us tomorrow noon, that is on *Sunday,* & now (10 o'clock at night) you will certainly no longer join us for *tea:* we therefore are asking you: whether you have heard us, even if you don't acknowledge us, which . . . we would very much regret. . . . The Levy spouses Saturday the 10th 7br."[15]

The recollections of many of Levy's contemporaries also mention her participation in house concerts.[16] Besides Sara, her sister Hanne and Hanne's husband, Joseph Fliess, had a major role in the musical life of the time.[17] Concerts were held regularly in their house, with many people invited, according to surviving billets.[18] What music was performed and who performed it we do not, unfortunately, know.

In at least one upper-bourgeois house, that of Philippine (fig. 5) and Ephraim Cohen, we know that theatrical productions were hosted.[19] Stephanie de Genlis, who lived in Berlin in 1798, wrote three pieces

Fig. 3. Karl Gustav von Brinckmann. Library of Uppsala University, Sweden

Fig. 4. Dorothea Schlegel. Varnhagen Collection, Biblioteka Jagiellońska, Kraków

for the Cohens' private stage.[20] Her memoirs, however, do not speak of any particularly broad-ranging social life in the family. A different recollection is voiced in the autobiography of Karl August Varnhagen von Ense, who lived with the Cohens as a domestic tutor in 1803. He writes of the "castle-like residence, much larger and more varied than necessary"; a vast, tended garden in the center of the city; and an extensive library with books in German, English, and French. In this house "guests were not seldom invited [to lunch], close friends of the house, men and women, and interesting strangers." In the evening, music was played or guests listened to readings, during which Varnhagen himself read aloud all of Goethe's *Wilhelm Meister*. Even this generous conviviality exhibited a "chaotic fermentation, from which by accident and without purpose and order everything was to be newly shaped."[21]

One house in particular serves as a paradigm for this conflict between old and new, a house in which other types of meetings took place: private lectures, literary circles, tea parties, and somewhat formal debates: "In the evening I visited privy counc[ilor] Herz with whom I had a philosophical discussion for an hour; actually I had intended to make the acquaintance of his pretty, intelligent wife, which I was also able to do. I was invited once and for all to visit every Friday evening."[22] Thus Karl Gustav von Brinckmann wrote in his diary on January 1, 1790. Friday evening—not just any evening. The physician and scientist Markus Herz and his wife, Henriette, invited guests to come on the very evening that Jewish households devote to celebrating the Sabbath. Instead of candles, blessings, and prayers at a family dinner, there were debates with Christian guests. Later in the year, on September 18, Wilhelm von Humboldt (fig. 6) wrote to his future wife, Caroline von Dacheröden, that he must postpone

Fig. 5. Philippine Cohen. Varnhagen Collection, Biblioteka Jagiellońska, Kraków

Fig. 6. Artist unknown, *Wilhelm von Humboldt in His Study in Schloss Tegel*. Oil on canvas, 14 x 11¾ in. (35.5 x 29.8 cm). Freies Deutsches Hochstift, Goethe Museum, Frankfurt

a planned visit to the Herzes' house: "Yesterday the Jews had their long night, when they do not receive guests."[23] Yom Kippur was thus still being celebrated—for how long we do not know—while Sabbath traditions had already loosened.

Nothing could show more clearly how narrow was the space that social activities in Jewish houses opened. For the briefest moment two religions, two cultures, could exist side by side with their own rhythms, their own times. Soon enough it became obvious that the price for such social encounters was the integration of Jews into the dominant Christian culture. Regretfully, almost morosely, Freude Fränkel wrote on October 20, 1792, to the diplomat Brinckmann, "As you know here by me it is Saturday,"[24] thereby informing him that she couldn't fulfill her social duties on that day of the week.

A letter from Rahel Levin to her friend David Veit, who was studying medicine in Göttingen at the time,

shows the painful transition from one world to the other in all its contradictions and tensions: "I also go rather frequently to madame Marchetti's; et, imaginez, yesterday I rode with her in broad daylight on the Sabbath in a royal coach at two-thirty to the opera rehearsal; no one saw me, I would have and would and shall deny it to anyone's face—and even if the person helped me out of the coach! it seems to me that someone in my situation can and must proceed this way."[25] Observant Jews are not, of course, permitted to ride on this day. Rahel Levin apparently can tell no one why or even that she is in a coach with the opera singer Maria Marchetti on a Sabbath. A lie is the only way of dealing with it—in her "situation." It appears that between reality and its perception such a chasm had opened that no rational argument could help someone across it.

As far as we can reconstruct, the Levins did invite guests on the Sabbath, at least for a while. "I see that your letters are often written on Saturdays. Is the assemblee no longer regularly meeting?" David Veit wrote Rahel Levin on March 4, 1794.[26] "Saturday no one visits me, and I have met only two new people, but I cannot write you about them," was her laconic answer.[27] An interesting mix of languages. For "Saturday," *Sonnabend*, a word that in German derives from "eve of Sunday," the Christian holy day, designates a notably different day from "Sabbath." With the Sabbath the Jewish week ends, while the "Sonnabend" shows the shift to the Christian week, which ends on Sunday.

A similar transition takes place around the High Holy Days. We have already mentioned Yom Kippur, whose traces are lost in the 1790s. What gradually emerges in its place is Christmas, one of the most important Christian holidays: "I am at home today only until 3 o'clock, for I have to go out for le caffé le thee et le soupé. Berlin the 24th of Decbr: 1794 Your devoted RL[.] I have to spare you a little trouble for once and write the date myself," we read in a billet from Rahel Levin to Brinckmann.[28] A significant gesture, since the writer almost never cared to mention the date she wrote, which is why Brinckmann often dated her notes upon receipt. This one, though, is dated programmatically. The writer points out that while she is aware of the significance of the day to the Christian world—in Germany, Christmas Eve was and is more important than Christmas Day itself—she is not in the least concerned about it. She pursues her social duties on this day—just as she always does. The shift into French underscores the tradition in which she sees her social activities.

After Prussia's defeat, which brought this form of Jewish sociability to an end, Rahel Levin reflected, not to the Swedish diplomat but to a Jewish woman friend,

> *Wednesday, Christmas Eve 1806 . . . I could tell you much about Christmas! the only celebration in the year that makes a celebratory impression on me—because it is not the anniversary of a celebration that used to be; rather one that persists among us—but how melancholy!—if I wanted—a year ago I still cried bitterly when I saw the Christmas candles lit at the lawyer's house [across the street]; and I imagined the secure and approved peace, that could make someone happy. Now —I remember the year before and feel nothing. I seem like a corpse. And pretensions to happiness, to some substantial, expected happiness, make me smile like a comedy, entirely without bitterness and pain. The candles burn: and I wonder more how it is that human beings can repeat anything. With what passion I gave gifts three and two years ago: now I do not even cry.[29]*

Christmas, a promise of happiness, a promise of peace that was not fulfilled. It was a happiness that remained on the other side of the street, even when one tried to tempt it into one's own house by giving gifts. This failed Christmas story can be read as a parable for what Rahel Levin attempted with her family: to open the house, to practice conviviality. "For me society has always been the half of life," she would later write. Conversations, social gatherings represented a model of human community. In a diary entry from the spring of 1799, we read: "There need be no hierarchy in society; and that of love, the advantage provided by affection to the increase of every sort of pleasure, must be most carefully avoided. The elementary relation within the word society [*Gesellschaft*] ought to alert us already to this: it is an associate-ness [*Gesellenschaft*] for joy or the like. There is no master among it, but entirely equal associates [*Gesellen*]; and it is not appropriate there for anyone to be master."[30]

From the start, many of the surviving billets attest to the fact that this did not, and could not, work. That worlds divided the participants in this social experiment is easily to be detected in the tone of their notes. "We are having a night-thé: please attend, otherwise we shall have no peace and certainly no pleasure. And I promise you as well the most attractive cake," Levin wrote to Brinckmann in the winter of 1794.[31] Around the same time Wilhelm von Humboldt wrote to him:

> *Today is Monday, dear Brinckmann . . . But where shall we meet? I can catch up with you anywhere. Just tell me the place and hour. I know of a bold Rendezvouz, though I think it may be too bold. That would be at the Countess Luise von Voss's. Yesterday she again delighted me greatly,—ach! God! and how*

much I prefer her to all those countesses one must com-
pare with the Jewesses to find at all bearable. After the
Souper though I amused myself greatly. I walked for
two hours altogether with G[entz], and he was in fine
form.—Since the Countess Voss project will certainly
strike you as too bold, I sink down again to Israel and
suggest Levin. If she is not at home, then come here
and await me. All right? H.[32]

This striking billet indicates who besides Jewish women, actresses, and singers gathered at the Levin residence: young intellectuals who at the time were still rather insignificant. No one could have foretold that Friedrich von Gentz would, along with Prince Klemens von Metternich, design the order of a new old Europe, or that Wilhelm von Humboldt would publish innovative linguistic studies and be the architect of the modern European university.

This intercourse ended in great turbulence. Hitzel Fliess divorced her husband in the 1790s and, just like Freude Fränkel and Brendel Mendelssohn Veit (Dorothea Schlegel), married a Christian.[33] These contentious separations, which signified profound ruptures in tradition, were widely discussed in the correspondence of the time. All three women were apparently involved in difficult love affairs with Gentz or Humboldt, during which the young men uttered extremely negative statements on their friends' husbands. The sharp boundary between Jew and Christian is again duplicated: in contrast with Jewish women, Jewish men seemed ultimately unable to integrate into the dominant culture. Thus, Humboldt wrote to Caroline von Dacheröden that Brendel Veit is "indescribably unhappy": "If you knew the husband, there isn't a term for this blandness and vacancy and insensitivity and effeminateness!" Humboldt gladly indulged the love of the unhappy woman, but did not return it: "She loves me in every sense of the word. She feels and knows that she is not as important to me as I am to her, and she is silent sometimes from pride, sometimes from love itself, because she thinks it disturbs me . . . She represents to me the most lively image of gratuitous destruction of a beautiful, majestic bloom whenever I

see her, and so admiration and pity take turns in my heart." A few lines later, another love story in the same constellation: "There is yet another woman here—a Jewess, of course—with whom I had an alliance . . . I noticed for a long time that I was good for her. When I was alone with her and asked her to express her feelings more freely, or when I said that I was well disposed toward her, then she begged me to be silent and wept."[34]

Courtship by the women, rejection by the men. A dichotomy that speaks volumes. Hitzel Fliess and Freude Fränkel both married foreign noblemen and left Berlin and Germany for good. Brendel Veit, who met Friedrich Schlegel at the house of Henriette Herz, accompanied him to Jena and later to Paris. Rahel Levin's billets and letters to Karl Gustav von Brinckmann show that these departures from Berlin disturbed the network of conviviality considerably. For these women had set the intellectual climate of Berlin at the time. They, more than anyone else, were the participants in what would later be called "salons."

When, in the late 1930s, Hannah Arendt wrote her biography of Rahel Levin Varnhagen, she chose to characterize Berlin's social life around 1800 with the same word Karl August Varnhagen had used a century before. She spoke of the "vague, idyllic chaos which the Jewish salon of these days represented."[35] "Chaos" it was, in many respects. The dramatic effects on the lives of some of the women involved have already been noted. During the debates that took place over tea, on walks, or at the baths, anything could be discussed. Or almost anything. On March 8, 1803, Rahel Levin wrote the following quite striking sentence in her diary: "Slave Trade, War, Marriage!—and they scratch their heads and tinker."[36] Letters and other diary entries tell us that the war against France was often debated; as were the remarkable victories of their neighboring country's *armée*, which did not observe the old rules of battle. That something was profoundly wrong in the relation between the sexes, was—as we have seen—not simply a matter for intellectual discussion. Not many people, by contrast, were overly concerned with the slave trade in those days. Rahel Levin's remark provides the signature of the nineteenth and twentieth centuries. In the "vague, idyllic chaos" of this sociability, a new type of thinking was developed that has not really been pursued, even today.

On November 30, 1819, long after the "chaotic" time had passed, Levin attempted to sketch out the prerequisites for that thinking in a letter to Brinckmann, who had meanwhile returned to Sweden:

The entire constellation of beauty, grace, coquetry, attraction, amorousness, wit, elegance, cordiality, the urge to develop ideas, honest seriousness, unconstrained exploration and encounter, spirited humor, has dissipated. All Rez-de-Chaussees are stores, all meetings are dinners or assemblees, all discussions are almost—you see in my dashes the difficulty I have finding a word: I mean a rendez-vous for a more authentic, future [conversation], and a threadbare confusion of concepts. Everyone is smart; he's bought everything he needs for that from some vendor of opinions. There are still a few intelligent people here: and the remnants of a conviviality that is unique in all of Germany.[37]

A constellation—at the time, long before it became a theoretical concept, a word used only in astronomy. A constellation of components, then, that no one had ever put into relation with one another. Levin's series begins with beauty and grace, two notions about which all artists of the time were thinking, as well as anyone who reflected on art. Coquetry, attraction, and amorousness, by contrast, are at home not in theoretical debates but in novels and colloquial speech. In Levin's sentence they prepare a manner of speaking of a knowledge that has no name or site. A knowledge as well for which neither scholars nor artists but an indefinite group of people is responsible. The rhythm of the sentence changes markedly when the discussion turns to what brings these people together: "the urge to develop ideas, honest seriousness." The question remains open as to how this urge and this seriousness are connected to "unconstrained exploration and encounter." This is evident in comparison with the political and theoretical texts being written in this period: there was a love of sentences and chains of sentences that developed pre-

suppositions and conditions. It was the age of the logical conclusion. In Rahel Levin's letter, though, we find something distinct: the even and yet rhythmically disrupted sequence shows that the relations among the factors enumerated have to be rethought, again and again. In what relation does this constellation of words stand to the "difficulty [she has] finding a word"? What is missing, which words do not fit, when Rahel Levin reflects on sociability?

Almost precisely in the middle of the first sentence, which is made up of a chain of similar links, one finds the rhythmically heterogeneous element: "the urge to develop ideas." To think, then. Thinking, not as a lonely activity in front of an empty page, but together with others. Bound together in a constellation of changing factors all of which are essential: No honest seriousness without spirited humor. No amorousness without elegance. No wit without cordiality. In a constellation these moments can forever be reordered in new ways. In the second sentence, though, things have unique designations. "All the Rez-de-Chaussees are stores, all meetings are dinners or assemblees." All sites now have distinct functions, gatherings occur only by invitation. At a table with the rigid seating order of a dinner. Speaking with the predetermined rules of an assembly. At an informal tea, on the contrary, guests could mill about, speaking with this person or that. But then the sentence stumbles, when the subject of "discussions" arises. The writer could not find the suitable word. What are discussions when they are not embedded in a constellation? Two possibilities offer themselves: They could be announcements of "more authentic, future" conversations. Or they could be "a threadbare confusion of concepts." What they are—we only can determine afterward. Conviviality is thus something that will have happened. It is not something that now, at the instant of being together, takes place. Conviviality has a dimension that falls out of simultaneity. Conviviality, one might say, is a task that is never fulfilled. Just for that reason it remains to be done. Not in some utopian form, as the dream of a better time when we will all be equal. It remains to be done in a now of which no one can know whether it is the announcement of a many years, all of Berlin's prominent people frequented us."[38] And Hitzel Fliess, having long since become the Countess von Sparre (fig. 7) and living in Sweden, wrote to Brinckmann after Rahel's death:

> *O how a beloved, so significant past rises in me, and conjures forth the classic garret, the green sofa with its cushions, the piano between the windows, the letters kept or even written by oneself that were hidden under the sofa cushion and then drawn out when they were worthy of the honor of being read: in front of the sofa a small table with a few select books, behind it a door, near the stove, a larger, longer table at which she [Rahel] wrote . . . and then, dear Br[inckmann]: the sacred evenings where you, Gentz, Humboldt and his wife, Prince Louis [Louis Ferdinand of Prussia],[39] and who all else surrounding the wonderful person, and what dear women, yes, even the shadows that appeared there were not without interest.[40]*

In the image of "sacred evenings" the experiment of Berlin conviviality devolves into a cliché. Were Rahel Levin's reflections on society in the spring of 1799 merely a naive fantasy? "There need be no hierarchy in society. There is no master among it, entirely equal associates; and it is not appropriate there for anyone to be master."[41] It was rather the indefatigable gesture of a smart and sad "Jewish girl," whose voice has never been heard quite rightly.

Fig. 7. Wilhelmine von Sparre. Varnhagen Collection, Biblioteka Jagiellońska, Kraków

conversation or mere chatter in a threadbare confusion of concepts.

What survived of the Berlin salons around 1800 was not this task but an idyllic, harmonized image. Here, too, the political restoration proved triumphant. Not only in Germany, but throughout all of Europe in the nineteenth century, politics and society remained stubbornly in their traditional places. In such times, memory tends toward nostalgia. Henriette Herz wrote an autobiographical sketch that rendered the former era of conviviality a golden age. The house of Markus Herz could "with no exaggeration be reckoned among the most respected and fashionable . . . in Berlin. . . . For

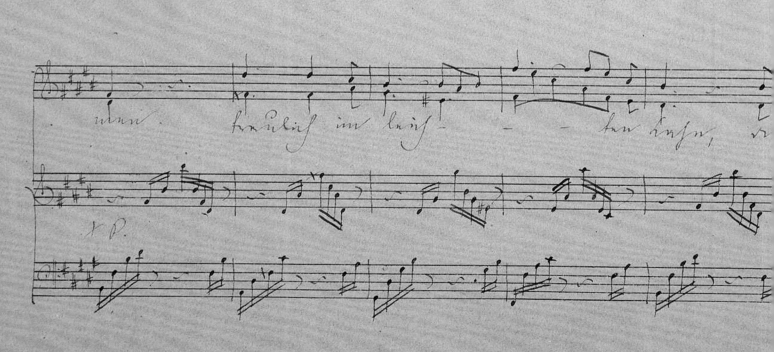

Music, Femininity, and Jewish Identity: The Tradition and Legacy of the Salon

LEON BOTSTEIN

Scrutiny of the role of music in the salons of prominent and wealthy women of Jewish origin in Berlin and Vienna during the long nineteenth century, which extended into the 1920s in the matter of salon culture, necessarily finds itself at the crossroads of three divergent but overlapping contemporary scholarly obsessions. The first involves Jewish emancipation and acculturation during the late eighteenth and nineteenth centuries. The salons that Jews maintained in Berlin, and to a lesser degree in Vienna, have been alternatively idealized as precedents and models or derided as negative object lessons with respect to how Jews, normatively, came to terms with being Jewish in a Gentile world outside a ghetto.[1] From the outset, however, it must be remembered that the world of salons was first and foremost a world of economic privilege. The most constant factor, especially in salons where music played a dominant role, was wealth, and considerable wealth at that.

The legacy of the salon was more symbolic than practical. In its heyday, before 1848, the salon was an extraordinary phenomenon in Berlin and Vienna, considered by some scholars as evidence of an expanding public sphere. Yet its continuation as a significant meeting place for the leading figures of the artistic, intellectual, and political world, particularly for Jews seeking to establish or sustain a salon, became increasingly

Detail of fig. 6

difficult economically and socially as the century wore on. But as a symbol for the Jewish middle class, the retelling of the glamour and greatness of those who created and participated in the pre-1848 salons sufficed as an inspiration regarding the presumed power of culture in the task of integration into Gentile society.

The achievement of a small elite of Jewish women in the setting of the salon helped define musical culture and self-cultivation among German-speaking Jewry for the rest of the nineteenth century. Well beyond the Jewish community, though, the culture of the music salon in the early nineteenth century exerted an important influence on the cultural infrastructure of urban life. In Vienna, salon culture was indispensable to the evolution of the many civic associations dedicated to music, organizations of music education, and the dynamics of a public concert life that endure today even in a city with few Jews.

If the high-society salon per se came to be regarded with ambivalence as a model of the possibility of successful acculturation, integration, and (for some, unfortunately) assimilation, the salon with an emphasis on music has retained a remarkably positive aura. Two of the principal early-nineteenth-century Jewish music salons in Berlin were organized by women who did not convert to Christianity: Sara Levy and Amalie Beer.[2] Fanny Mendelssohn Hensel, in contrast, converted as a child, as did her brother, Felix Mendelssohn. One could argue that for participants in salons concerned primarily with literary and philosophical matters and personalities—the salon of Rahel Levin Varnhagen, for example—remaining Jewish might have been problematic. Even as early as the 1790s, music in its Baroque and classical realizations was understood as part of a Gentile way of life and culture that did not trigger conflict, contradiction, or a sense of inadequacy with respect to one's origin and status as a Jew. Whether construed as abstract, nonrepresentational, sentimental, or even illustrative of emotions and events, music came to be an aesthetic and social arena in which Jews could openly participate in public and in private on an equal footing, without conversion or concession vis-à-vis the daily conduct of Jewish life. Whether justified or not, from

Fig. 1. Johann Gottfried Schadow (German, 1764–1850), *Musical Company*, c. 1820. Pen and ink on paper. Kupferstichkabinett, Staatliche Museen zu Berlin–Preussischer Kulturbesitz

the first decades of emancipation, partly because of the compatibility and prominence of music in the experience of the salons in Berlin and Vienna, secular musical culture and amateur music-making came to occupy a privileged status among German-speaking Jews (fig. 1).

This image of and romance with music among German-speaking Jewry would last beyond 1933. The enthusiasm for music as a cultural medium of Jewish integration persisted in many salonlike contexts long after the most studied and contested era of the salon: the years before 1850, the age of Varnhagen and Beer.[3] One thinks of the Viennese salons of the later nineteenth century, namely those of Caroline Gomperz-Bettelheim's sisters-in-law Josephine and Sophie. Unlike her sisters-in-law and women salon leaders of the early nineteenth century, Gomperz-Bettelheim achieved enormous fame as an artist: she was a professional opera singer. Josephine and Sophie simply married well. Their husbands were, respectively, Baron Leopold Wertheimstein and Baron Eduard Todesco, in whose grand Viennese homes the pre-1848 music salon tradition continued into the mid-1890s, replete with

performances by Gomperz-Bettelheim (accompanied by Brahms's friend Ignaz Brüll, the Jewish composer and pianist), Franz Liszt, and Anton Rubinstein. Hugo von Hofmannsthal read his works in these salons, where one could encounter an ongoing series of melodramas and tableaux vivants.[4] Berta Zuckerkandl's salon in Vienna, which flourished into the twentieth century despite its more political and literary orientation, also included well-known musicians.[5]

These nonprofessional women of culture and their conduct of life became emblematic of an idealized mix of Jewish wealth and cultivation. They were held up, especially to the masses of poor Jews who migrated to Berlin and Vienna after 1848–and to anti-Semites—as counterpoints to the vulgar reduction of wealthy Jews as mere parvenus. The salon women were a Jewish aristocracy within the Gentile world. Precisely because they were deemed, as women, to be powerless, they were insulated from much anti-Semitic criticism. In contrast, the husbands of Caroline's sisters-in-law were thought to take part in the alleged international Jewish financial conspiracy, as was Zuckerkandl's father, Moritz Szeps, who represented Jewish "control" of the world of newspapers.

The intersection of Jewish identity, culture, and anti-Semitism reveals the second scholarly obsession. A good deal of writing on music salons raises questions about gender. Were these salons unusual cases of a brief moment of gender equality, of an assertion of women's power in an otherwise male-dominated world? Or were the salons yet another thinly camouflaged sign of the unjust and damaging subordination of women? What place or importance do salons have for feminists or in any account of the struggle for female equality and independence in modern history, and in the history of music? Were these women, especially those with musical training and ability who were not professionals, true participants or mere hostesses? Was the salon in which music played a major role the only space where women could achieve equal status?[6]

It is crucial to remember that throughout the nineteenth century there were women vocalists on the opera and concert stages, just as there were women actresses

Fig. 2. Wilhelm Hensel (German, 1794–1861), *Clara Schumann, née Wieck*, n.d. Pencil on board, 15⅜ x 11⅜ in. (39.2 x 29 cm). Kupferstichkabinett, Staatliche Museen zu Berlin–Preussischer Kulturbesitz

Fig. 3. Wilhelm Hensel (German, 1794–1861), *Fanny Hensel née Mendelssohn Bartholdy*, 1829. Pencil on board, 8¾ x 6¾ in. (22.3 x 17 cm). Kupferstichkabinett, Staatliche Museen zu Berlin–Preussischer Kulturbesitz

and dancers. But the social status of these women was mixed at best. Not until the second half of the century did women instrumentalists appear as concert stars (consider what a phenomenon Clara Schumann was), and even then they were almost exclusively pianists (fig. 2). It was only in the mid-twentieth century that women began to compete successfully with men as performers and soloists, though with far less success as composers. Because Fanny Mendelssohn Hensel (fig. 3) was an exception and a precursor, her *Sonntagsmusik*, or Sunday musical events, in Berlin can be regarded either as an elaboration of the informal salon tradition before 1815 or as a harbinger of the public professional life that should have been hers as a composer and

performer. The music salon, Hensel's in particular, gains historical significance as illustrative of nineteenth-century barriers to women in public concert life and in the profession of music, especially music composition. Furthermore, within the subject of gender, scholars have raised a question about the influence exerted by women amateurs, patrons, and listeners in the era of the salon. Does the prominence of such patrons as Levy, Beer, and Fanny von Arnstein—or, more particularly, Jewish women—suggest a specific feminine impact on the character and development of music during the nineteenth century?

This question points to the third scholarly obsession, tangentially related to both the first and the second. It concerns the notion that nineteenth-century musical culture was indeed inextricably tied up with gender dynamics and patterns of sexual relations. Music in domestic spaces, whether in middle-class drawing rooms or in grand salons, is a transaction said to have been dominated by gender construction. Musical culture, musical expression, and the nineteenth century's prime musical medium—the piano—are viewed by

Fig. 4. Anton Kolig
(Austrian, 1886–1950),
Portrait of Berta Zuckerkandl,
1915. Oil on canvas, 59 x
31⅞ in. (150 x 81 cm). Wien
Museum

some as veiled emblems of versions of the feminine. Desire, violence, ecstasy, and resentment were at stake as men and women engaged in music, construed as a domestic cultural dynamic dominated by sexual politics.[7]

This notion of music as either gendered or mirroring historical social-sexual interactions forces, in turn, an encounter with the career of anti-Semitism and the Jewish question in German-speaking Europe. From Richard Wagner on, and as late as the era of Otto Weininger (whose ideas and suicide in Beethoven's last apartment were doubtlessly topics at Zuckerkandl's salon), the linking of the feminine (understood as a pejorative) and the Jewish influenced the character of the nineteenth-century aesthetic debate about music.[8] The association of salon culture with visible Jewish women helped render this linkage plausible. By 1900, for many musicians influenced by Wagnerian ideology, even those of Jewish origin such as Gustav Mahler and Arnold Schoenberg, the traditions and repertoire of the salon and nineteenth-century domestic music-making reeked of a repugnant, feminized culture. The term *salon*, when attached to music, therefore immediately suggested something abhorrent.[9] The greatness of Wagner, in the judgment of Friedrich Nietzsche (chiefly in the mid-1870s, but even after his break with Wagner), lay in the composer's attempt to redeem music from the philistine, bourgeois, and superficial, understood as a species of the feminine. In terms of even the eighteenth-century and early Romantic music's embodiment of sexuality, Wagner emancipated music from a deadly notion of the feminine. His view of the feminine is most powerfully represented by Kundry in *Parsifal*. In the post-Wagnerian context, the vision of the corrupting feminine was replaced by the idealized version of the eternal feminine, lifted from the late works of Goethe and set to music in 1910 by Mahler in his Eighth Symphony. This Mahlerian vision was pointedly not an idealization of the Jewish women of the nineteenth century who maintained salons in which music played a primary role. Curiously, Mahler met his wife, Alma Schindler, who had a notoriously anti-Semitic (and famous) artist stepfather, Carl Moll, at Zuckerkandl's home. Likewise, Mahler's former lover, the great oper-

atic soprano Anna Mildenburg (who later married the Austrian writer and ardent Wagnerian Hermann Bahr), was a frequent guest at her dear friend Berta's (fig. 4). But it was those non-Jewish women—not the fin-de-siècle Jewish hostess and her predecessors in Vienna and Berlin—who came to suggest the redemptive eternal-feminine ideal in music.

This mix of gender and racial prejudice in the cultural judgment of music became commonplace even among avowed anti-Wagnerians. The cultivated amateur pianist, usually represented as a woman, who sought to play the sonatas of Beethoven at home was the target of derision and rage on the part of Heinrich Schenker, the great Viennese theorist, pedagogue, and active member of the Jewish community.[10] His extreme German nationalism revealed a Wagner-like glorification of the muscular toughness and rigor in musical forms one finds in Schoenberg's attitudes—and in those of Karl Kraus regarding literature, in particular his critique of Heinrich Heine.[11] A rift developed between the construct of the feminine and the Jewish on one hand and true German culture and musicality on the other. The tastes and habits of the great female salon amateurs and patrons, including Ludwig Wittgenstein's mother, Leopoldine, were suspect. In fact, critics of salon culture, starting with Heine in Paris in the 1830s, pointed to the excessive superficial emphasis placed on music, mostly the work of the hostesses.[12]

Yet we should keep in mind that the nineteenth-century tradition of domestic musical life was far from dominated by women. The Wagnerian critique reflected the fact that from the era of Franz Schubert and the childhood years of Felix and Fanny Mendelssohn to the end of the century, music in the home was linked to specific instrumental and vocal genres and a certain tradition of musical aesthetics for both women and men. After the heyday of the great salons, and after the deaths of central figures in the first generation of musical Romantics—Frédéric Chopin, Felix Mendelssohn, and Robert Schumann, all of whom participated in salon culture—there was a fundamental split in the politics of musical aesthetics and culture. By the end of the 1850s there were two warring camps. On one side were

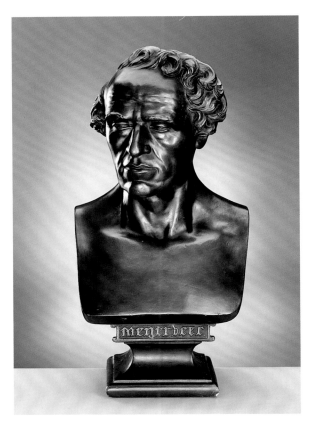

Fig. 5. Jean-Pierre Dantan (Dantan the Younger; French, 1800–1869), *Bust of Giacomo Meyerbeer*, 1864. Bronzed plaster, 27½ x 13 x 10¾ in. (70 x 33 x 27 cm). Stiftung Stadtmuseum Berlin, Hans-und-Luise-Richter-Stiftung

those who propounded a notion of "absolute" music and held on to conservative notions of musical logic and form, including an allegiance to the genres and strategies of eighteenth-century classicism and early nineteenth-century Romanticism. Johannes Brahms, who lived in Vienna after the early 1860s, his ardent champion the critic Eduard Hanslick (also a resident of Vienna), and the composer Max Bruch and the violinist Joseph Joachim (both of whom would reside in Berlin) were principal advocates of this camp.

The opponents dubbed themselves the "New German" school. The chief protagonists were Liszt and Wagner. In their view, music as an expressive medium possessed an emotional and narrative power that necessitated its alliance with language and painting. Instead of absolute music, they argued for music with a poetic and dramatic program and thus for new, not old, genres, notably the tone poem and the music drama. They prized sonic and visual public spectacle and theatricality, not chamber performance. It is no accident that the

so-called conservatives, the absolutists, and the traditionalists featured both Jews and acknowledged philo-Semites such as Bruch and Brahms, whereas the New German camp was closely connected to political and cultural anti-Semitism, in both Vienna and Berlin.[13]

The success of the New German school in concert and opera and, significantly, in Wagner's powerful polemics helped popularize a narrative of music history in German-speaking Europe that explicitly rendered the musical culture of the salon marginal and dated. Wagner successfully argued, commencing with his notorious tract *Das Judentum in der Musik* (*Judaism in Music*, 1850), that Jews were incapable of genuine creativity and exerted a poisonous, deleterious influence on music. Jews epitomized a fashionable urban culture driven by crass materialism whose hegemony needed to be challenged by a rooted, populist, nationalist aesthetics capable of communicating the epic, the tragic, and the heroic. Wagner's primary victims were Felix Mendelssohn, Fanny Hensel's brother, and Giacomo Meyerbeer, Amalie Beer's son (fig. 5). Uppermost in Wagner's mind as an object of destruction was the tradition of music so effectively cultivated in salons of the early nineteenth century. Wagner objected to the construct of music as an aspect of *Bildung*—self-cultivation —as energetically pursued by Sara Levy in Berlin, in Fanny and Felix's parental Berlin home (and later in Fanny's *Sonntagsmusik*), and by Fanny von Arnstein in Vienna.[14] In the second half of the nineteenth century, Wagnerism also helped construct a divide between high art for public consumption and popular music for domestic use, thereby intentionally trivializing the use of musical culture by the Jewish urban elite as a means of integration, acculturation, and assimilation. Paradoxically, this did not deter Jews from becoming ardent admirers of Wagner.

To understand the musical culture of the great salons that women maintained in Berlin and Vienna, especially before 1848, one must grasp the historiographical weight of the Wagnerian account of music history and aesthetics. A critique of the feminine in culture worked hand in glove with anti-Semitism. This admonition helps explain why the music of Felix

Mendelssohn—not to mention his sister's—and of Meyerbeer has been seemingly permanently crippled in terms of reception.[15] In terms of literature and philosophy, the work of personalities who played major roles in the literary and philosophical salons of Rahel Varnhagen, Henriette Herz, and their Viennese counterparts has not suffered as much.

The reasons for this damage transcend the cultural politics of musical aesthetic debates after 1848. The height of salon musical culture preceded a dramatic change and expansion in the character of musical literacy and life in Western Europe. The moment of initial toleration of and emancipation for Jews, the 1780s, coincided with the peak of aristocratic participation and patronage of music in German-speaking Europe. Frederick the Great, Maria Theresa and her children, particularly Joseph II, and the high nobility of the Habsburg Empire were amateur musicians of considerable proficiency. The nonaristocratic elites, from the world of commerce to the professions, as well as the newly ennobled and lower orders of aristocracy, emulated eighteenth-century patterns of sociability and amateurism set by the highest social ranks. Well into the early nineteenth century, the acquisition of musical culture represented an explicit imitation of aristocratic manners.

In this sense, the role of Arnstein and others from privileged Jewish families (the von Heniksteins, Wertheimers, Eskeleses, and Wertheimsteins), in the founding, in 1812, of the Gesellschaft der Musikfreunde, Vienna's leading voluntary music association, was an act of collaboration with the aristocracy that implied acceptance of cultural norms signifying class and status. The music salons of Arnstein, Beer, and two generations of Mendelssohns had antecedents in the domestic musical culture of non-Jewish aristocrats, from the era of the patrons of Mozart (who included several ennobled Jews), Haydn, and Beethoven.[16] Arnstein was, for instance, a subscriber for Beethoven's first publication in Vienna, the Opus 1 trios.[17] The example of Arnstein's daughter, Henrietta von Pereira-Arnstein, suggests that women patrons did participate in early-nineteenth-century salons, just as Haydn's patron Prince Nikolaus

Esterházy played the baryton and Beethoven's patron Archduke Rudolf played the piano. Pereira-Arnstein, after all, had been a pupil of Muzio Clementi and was an accomplished pianist. So, too, was one of Beethoven's admirers, Maria Anna Eskeles, who maintained a salon in Vienna and was described as playing his music well.[18]

As the century advanced, there were distinct shifts in the demographics and character of musical culture. By the 1850s, the aristocracy had turned its attention elsewhere, away from music participation and patronage. The piano, in its nascent modern form, became the widespread and central instrument of music-making, principally in the home. At the same time there was an immense growth in secular choral singing of the sort held in contempt by Mendelssohn, much of it allied to post-Napoleonic nationalism. In addition, by the mid-1850s, music-making that involved the collaboration of amateurs and professionals, a tradition of the late eighteenth century and the salon, had declined. For the layperson, musical culture was increasingly a habit of listening, a more passive and less participatory engagement. Not surprisingly, the locus of musical culture migrated from the home to the public arena of the concert stage. Wagner deftly exploited the presence of a much-expanded audience whose interest was to experience the thrill and power of theatrical spectacle. A new sort of interiority and intimacy, associated with listening with hundreds of other auditors, replaced the exclusive social gatherings for performances characteristic of the salon and the less personalized but equally small and intimate events such as the Schubertiades of the 1820s.

Before this shift, the Jewish embrace of musical culture, perhaps best exemplified by Sara Levy (1761–1854), the oldest and longest-lived of the great women of the salons, was particular in its aesthetic preferences. Perhaps as an indirect result of the writings of Moses Mendelssohn, the conception of music celebrated in Jewish salons derived from the notion that music in a secular arena should connect the ethical and the aesthetic. The philosophical quandary that occupied eighteenth-century thought, vis-à-vis aesthetics, was the capacity, within the sublime, of the ugly to captivate.

If the human being, in Rousseau's sense, was innately empathetic, rational (in an ethical and moral sense), and compassionate, how could art that depicted evil using aesthetic transformation and the criterion of beauty be celebrated?[19] Consequently, as Levy's extensive library of manuscripts and publications suggests, a premium was placed on older repertoire and instrumental music written in Baroque and early classical genres whose qualities were understood as stemming from normative, purely formal qualities of beauty.[20] The music of the Bach family held a favored place, which helps explain the Mendelssohn children's familiarity with and love for it. Levy's tastes extended to quite conservative contemporaries, including Johann Joachim Quantz. A neoclassical approach to the secular tradition of music-making on the part of newcomers is not surprising. Amalie Beer's son Giacomo was sent, as was Mendelssohn, to Goethe's friend and mentor on musical matters, the conservative, anti-romantic Carl Friedrich Zelter. For Levy, the nearly abstract formalism of Baroque and classical music circumvented any plausible conflict with aesthetic pleasure and ethics, much less Jewish religious convictions.[21]

In the early decades of the nineteenth century, the direction that musical romanticism took in Berlin salons sustained the construct of music as nonthreatening to the continuance of Jewish identity and to the reconciliation of the aesthetic and the ethical. Although the Mendelssohns and the Beers embraced the music of Carl Maria von Weber, he, like Felix Mendelssohn, had pursued a path in musical romanticism that revealed close ties to classical practice, primarily in his instrumental works. So did other musicians who played in Amalie Beer's salon: Johann Nepomuk Hummel (Beethoven's pupil), Ignaz Moscheles (a Jew and a friend of Mendelssohn's), Louis Spohr (who would emerge as the most celebrated musician in Germany after Beethoven, and later much admired by the conservatives, Brahms among them), and the virtuosi Friedrich Kalkbrenner (the pianist) and Niccolò Paganini (the violinist). By the 1830s and 1840s, a good deal of vocal and operatic music was performed in salons, alongside readings and dancing. In 1842, Beer held an evening

at which Liszt played excerpts from Meyerbeer's *Les Huguenots*, the opera that had its controversial Berlin premiere that year. Meyerbeer (who never converted) found the Berlin of his youth restrictive and conservative in its musical tastes and left in 1810. He would never reconcile himself to the city's prejudice against his music, which persisted throughout his career.[22]

Despite the rise of a public concert life after 1815, and certainly after 1848, domestic music-making did not disappear in Berlin or Vienna. Quite the contrary. The tradition of the great early-nineteenth-century salons, including that of Hensel's Sunday matinees, continued to the end of the century in home entertainments sponsored by wealthy industrialists and the haute bourgeoisie. Every grand house built during the last quarter of the century had its music room. Between 1862 and 1897, the years Brahms lived in Vienna, he spent many an afternoon and evening in such homes (many of them Jewish) and heard music—sometimes his own—performed. On a more modest scale were the many middle-class parlors, the kind in the United States for which Charles Ives wrote his early songs, where musical entertainment was a matter less of society than of family. Four-hand piano music flourished in these settings, and most of the concert and operatic repertoire became familiar through domestic music-making that involved not only the piano but also amateur quartet ensembles.

Throughout the nineteenth century, a vital aspect of *Bildung* for both men and women was learning to sing or to play an instrument. What was new was the connection between domestic music-making and concert attendance. Until the twentieth century, lieder, sonatas, and all manner of chamber music were staples of German middle-class homes, not concert halls. But participation in the newer pattern of domestic music-making was more contingent on listening to professionals perform a familiar standard repertoire than had been the case in the late eighteenth century. The allure of the solo instrumental concert, the professional quartet, and especially the virtuoso throughout the nineteenth century can be compared to the attraction professional sports and sports stars hold for today's amateur golfers, tennis players, and enthusiasts of hockey, soccer, and football with quite divergent skills.

Just as the Jewish salons of Berlin and Vienna emulated a pattern of home performance and patronage developed by eighteenth-century landed aristocracy, subsequent generations of Jews, eager to anchor themselves in German culture and society, turned to music-making in imitation of the salon era of Felix and Fanny Mendelssohn. With the advent of a large-scale public concert life, the acquisition of musical culture continued to offer a basis on which Jewish identity could be construed as compatible with membership in German society. But central to this extraordinary spread of musical culture was a marked drift in musical literacy and habits away from highly skilled active amateurism on a par with professional standards.

Although anti-Semitism, as expressed in the polemics and politics of musical aesthetics in the early twentieth century, has sought to link Jews and the Jewish influence with modernism, imitative and superficial commercialism, and rootless cosmopolitanism, the conservative aesthetic tastes of domestic music-making in Levy's salon and Arnstein's patronage were carried on by later nineteenth-century Jewish successors. The transformation of a canon into a pantheon—the elevation of Bach, Handel, Mozart, Beethoven, and Schubert—revealed the insecurity of newcomers, defined by class and ethnicity with respect to aesthetic judgment. A pattern that started in the salons—the emulation of aristocratic tastes by nonaristocrats, the preservation of musical tradition—invited a historicizing and standardization of taste. This pattern deepened when the fundamental skills of music-making shifted from a literacy that involved pitch creation (with the voice and instruments like the violin) to a simplified literacy. Fewer amateurs could hear music from the notes on the page. Instead they could reproduce music by rote on the modern piano, an instrument where pitch was fixed.[23] The early-nineteenth-century salon put into place the evolution of a dominant and quite conservative historicized musical taste among German-speaking Jewry, whose adaptability to new music declined dramatically after Wagner's death.

While some early-nineteenth-century salons emphasized the restoration of the past—as demonstrated in the enthusiasm for Bach by the Levys and the Mendelssohns—they also encouraged and supported music by contemporary performer-composers (in the nineteenth century, all instrumentalists composed and all composers performed). As music-making skills shifted to the modern keyboard, the balance between past and present moved toward the use of music in the home to transmit the qualities and virtues of an established canon. The "new" took on a subsidiary role. And when it came to mere entertainment, not high-minded culture, a species of light and popular music, an urban equivalent of folk music, entered the drawing room. Compared with the new works by Beethoven and Mendelssohn first heard in the great salons, this was "easy" music. This music from the middle and late nineteenth century has been branded as salon, or trivial, music.[24] It was partly against the reactionary and self-satisfied cult of classicism in music, underscored at home and accompanied by sentimental genres of piano music and song, that the radical modernists of the early twentieth century rebelled. The response of Jewish composers such as Schoenberg and Mahler was to some extent an intraethnic critique of the conception of musical culture that took shape as their fellow Jews became acculturated to German-speaking Europe.[25]

Of all the great musical salons of the nineteenth century, by far the most interesting and significant was the one that Fanny Hensel maintained in Berlin. She typifies the earlier nineteenth-century absence of a clear boundary between the professional and the accomplished so-called amateur or connoisseur. Indeed, as modern historians have justly argued, of all the leaders of the great salons, Hensel was a professional who under different circumstances would have had a brilliant career as a performer and composer. Only Clara Schumann can be compared with Hensel as a major female compositional talent.

Hensel may have continued the salon tradition of her parents, but she advanced it far beyond their efforts as patrons. Her *Sonntagsmusik* matinees offered strikingly rich large-scale programs, ranging from

Fig. 6. Fanny Mendelssohn Hensel, *Duette: Mein Liebchen, wir sassen beisammen* (*Duet: My Sweetheart, We Sat Together*), 1841. Manuscript. Mendelssohn-Archiv, Staatsbibliothek zu Berlin–Preussischer Kulturbesitz

her brother's music, to compositions by Weber and Heinrich Marschner, to older works by Beethoven and Haydn. The participants included the finest professionals, notably Hensel herself, her brother, the violinist Heinrich Wilhelm Ernst, Liszt, the singer Giuditta Pasta, and Joseph Joachim. Her matinees transformed the salon tradition into private concerts involving choral and instrumental music she composed for tableaux vivants, a particularly favored form of domestic entertainment.[26]

As Marian Wilson Kimber has persuasively argued, it has become ideologically proper (from our political vantage point) to regard Hensel's life and career as a failure.[27] She is taken to be a victim either of her father and her brother or of the uniform prejudice against women as professionals (with the selective exception of star vocalists) and certainly as composers. Hensel's life was, in reality, a mixture of achievement and disappointment. Our contemporary preference for

rigid, normative patterns of professionalism and a public career obscures, well beyond the matter of gender, the difference between the contexts of the first half of the nineteenth century and those of today. No simplified definition of moral and ethical progress regarding gender relations and rights justifies redefining the terms of musicianship and participation in musical life retrospectively so as to distort the criteria Hensel herself applied to the notions of happiness and ambition.

Much has been made of her brother's discouraging Hensel from publication. In fact, Felix congratulated her when she ultimately decided to publish a set of songs in 1846. Hensel, like other composers, continued to write only for performance, without the prospect of publication. It should be remembered that Mendelssohn himself struggled with publication.[28] He chose not to publish much of his greatest music because he was dissatisfied with nearly all of his output, including the famous *Italian* Symphony (1833).[29] Both he and Hensel

were unusually self-critical and more hesitant with respect to public scrutiny than contemporary observers can readily understand from the perspective of a world in which so many, even those with modest talents, crave publicity and fame. Mendelssohn understood the professional "guild" of music to be a harsh world dominated by petty jealousies and less-than-noble commercial interests.

Given his family's prominence and the sort of rage its wealth and talent inspired—Wagner's pathological envy of Mendelssohn is just one example—ambivalence about a public career can be recognized as a form of class, rather than gender, snobbery. No doubt Hensel's world was one in which a woman could not effectively compete with a man in the public arena, but her artistic life was hardly a vacuum. She produced, despite the obstacles she encountered as a woman, a considerable body of work (fig. 6). And not all of it is quite so compelling.[30]

Further, we ought not denigrate, ahistorically, Hensel's role as collaborator with her brother (including her permitting him to publish some of her songs under his name), her drawing room performances, her

leading role in the musical life of Berlin, and her colleagueship with many of the era's greatest artists. She actually managed a life of music and sustained powerful bonds with family—parental and spousal—in a way that, when she is compared with her brother, who has been taken to task for suppressing her career, could easily make her life, personal and professional, the object of envy. Famous as he was, Felix Mendelssohn (fig. 7) may not have been the "winner." His struggles and disappointments—some generated by the extreme expectations placed on him as a result of his precocious and dramatic entrance onto the public musical scene—were well known to Hensel and might have served as a deterrent. Professional status, recognition, and fame defined in contemporary terms are not normative virtues, and were not so more than a century ago.[31]

The world of the salon before 1848 reminds us, not necessarily of a backward or regressive cultural practice, but of an elite world of sociability in which the making of music, the gathering of artists, academicians, and writers, and the participation in performance, discussion, and readings we might elect to view with envy and nostalgia. We cannot measure merit, success, and satisfaction among the privileged in that era by contemporary standards. We might well compare the salon world favorably with today's cultural landscape, where so many, particularly journalists and pundits, complain about the ennui, materialism, and vulgarity of entertainment, the low level of culture and literacy, our collective dependence on consumption, and our passive embrace of mass commercial culture. The nineteenth-century dependence on the piano has been supplanted by our addiction to recorded music transmitted by CD, DVD, and computer. There are, indeed, no modern equivalents to the great musical salons today, and certainly none that could rival Fanny Hensel's. A tradition of patronage and participation in the home leading to a rich, public musical culture pursued by a wealthy nonaristocratic elite has, sadly, no analogue in contemporary life.

Chère Madame Straus

Nous avons trop pensé ensemble
à la guerre pour que nous ne
nous disions pas au soir de la
victoire un tendre mot, Joyeux
à cause d'elle, mélancolique à
cause de ceux que nous aimions
et qui ne la verront pas. Quel
merveilleux allegro presto dans le finale
après les lenteurs infinies du début et de

The Salon and Literary Modernism: Proust, Wilde, Stein

LUCIA RE

Salons—including those of Jewish women such as Geneviève Straus, Ada Leverson, and Gertrude Stein— had a determining influence on literary modernism between the fin-de-siècle and the 1920s. The experience of the salon, with its complex, fluid, multilayered, and, to some, "wasteful" conversations, displaced the nuclear family as a locus of inspiration for some pioneers of the modernist imagination, among them Marcel Proust, Oscar Wilde, and Gertrude Stein herself, and thus undermined the nineteenth-century bourgeois rhetoric of authenticity, normalcy, and productiveness. In and through the conversational discourse and ethos of the salon, with their irony and apparent fatuousness, Victorian norms became fractured and suspended. Categories of narrative time and space, historical continuity and linearity, also lost their legitimacy, as did traditional bourgeois notions about the transparency of the self and the nature of character.

Critics have usually attributed the modernist turn in literature to an increasing prevalence of writing and solitary introspection over voice and sociability. Instead, we might consider how a certain modernism is rooted in the oral, visual, and social experience of the salon. Proust's *À la recherche du temps perdu* is the most eloquent example to be examined here, for the novel's very style and structure were shaped by the author's experience of Geneviève Straus's salon. To be sure, there was no one modernist style fostered by the experience of the salon. Wilde's dialogues and his aphoristic, compressed mode of witty and paradoxical

storytelling differ greatly from the slow unfolding of conversational scenes in Proust's novel. Stein's elliptical, maddeningly repetitive experimental style is in many respects antithetical to Proust's luxuriant writing, and her lax grammar and syntax are removed from Wilde's perfectly finished, elegant sentences. Yet a comparative analysis shows interesting affinities based on the oral foundations of all three, and on their belated embrace of a culture of conversation that the nineteenth century appeared intent on abolishing.

LITERATURE AND THE ART OF CONVERSATION

In the nineteenth century, the ideal of conversation as an artwork, and of the woman-led salon as its privileged, inspired, and inspiring setting, was already an object of nostalgia. Although some late-eighteenth-century salons were devoted to the thought of Enlightenment philosophes (whose ideas eventually led to the collapse of the ancien régime), the decline of conversation, often referred to as worldly (*mondaine*) or polite conversation, was generally perceived as a consequence —regrettable for some, welcome for others—of the French Revolution. "True" conversation was associated with the leisure of the aristocracy. Salons continued to flourish in the post-Napoleonic era in Europe, yet authentic conversation seemed a forgotten art, for the spirit, grace, lightness, and—according to their critics— "frivolousness" that characterized the pre-revolutionary salons were thought to be lost with the rise of the bourgeoisie. One effect of the French Revolution was the promotion of language based on eloquence, oratory, political confrontation, and debate, all of which led away from the art of polite conversation. Under the growing influence of the press, political discussion replaced conversational exchange, eclipsing love, art, and philosophy, the traditional subjects of speculation in aristocratic salons.[1]

The nineteenth-century middle classes had neither the propensity for leisure nor the grace necessary for conversation; the bourgeois seeking to converse found themselves involved in mere discussion instead.[2] The

Detail of fig. 8

Fig. 1. *Abbé Delille Reciting His Poem "La Conversation."* Illustration from Jacques Delille's *La Conversation: Poëme* (Paris: Michaud Frères, 1812)

utilitarian and positivist century, with its insistence on the need to capitalize and to categorize, to fix the principles of economic profit, as well as those of verifiable and objective knowledge, had little use for the vagaries, uncertainties, playfulness, and apparent gratuitousness of such aristocratic arts as salon conversation, based on the exchange of witty aphorisms, paradoxes, and pointed rejoinders. Although conversation naturally evolved and developed throughout the nineteenth century, it did so in ways that were radically opposite to the manner of salons of the previous two centuries. It was put to precise uses—politics, diplomacy, commerce, business, information gathering—in any number of specialized sectors of human activity and knowledge. The disinterested giving of oneself in the arena of conversation, and the practice of a linguistic exchange that had been open-ended, unpredictable, labyrinthine, and eroticized,[3] came to be seen as a waste of time and

energy, and were replaced by purpose. Conversation was thus commodified and inserted into the cycle of production (of wealth, of knowledge, of nationhood, and so on). Rather than an authentic art, it became a technique—or, in so many words, a means to an end.

This decline of conversation was, however, extremely productive in literary terms. Virtually an entire genre developed around the nostalgia generated by the disappearance of the art of conversation. Jacques Delille, for example, in his poem "La Conversation" (1812; fig. 1), evokes in elegant classical verse the world of Madame Geoffrin, one of the most celebrated eighteenth-century salonières.[4] In her "sovereign hands," he writes, she held the reins of conversation, delicately controlling, balancing, encouraging, and setting limits without appearing to do so.[5] For those who, like Delille, celebrated Madame Geoffrin, Madame de Tencin, Madame du Deffand, Mademoiselle de Lespinasse, and other legendary salonières, salon conversation was not only the emblem of a vanished culture but also a political and social symbol. The political and social valence, although tinged with nostalgia, was not necessarily reactionary. In André Morellet's *De la conversation* (*On Conversation*, 1812), conversation under the benevolent aegis of a woman is presented as an ideal of communal sociability for the future, in implicit contrast to the model of political confrontation and aggressive, selfish individualism associated with Napoléon.[6] Honoré de Balzac, one of Marx's and Engels's favorite writers, in his story "Une conversation entre onze heures et minuit" ("A Conversation Between Eleven and Midnight," 1832) imagined an old-fashioned salon, led by three women, where artists, poets, politicians, dandies, and "savants" gather freely to converse and exchange stories in a polite setting removed from the nineteenth century's imperatives to get rich, to capitalize on everything, and to do what is "useful."[7]

The defenders of the "feminine" art of polite conversation were few compared with its detractors. Indeed, it was as a polemical target that conversation was most productive as a literary theme at the end of the eighteenth century and in the nineteenth. The most vehement and influential attack on the art of conversa-

Fig. 2. Jacques-Louis David (French, 1748–1825), *Madame de Récamier*, 1800. Oil on canvas, 68½ x 96 in. (174 x 244 cm). Musée du Louvre, Paris

tion as shallow, vain, and deceptive came from Jean-Jacques Rousseau, who also denounced the excessive power of the "gentle sex" in the salons, where the "natural" inferiority of woman to man was subverted and men were feminized.[8] Romanticism developed as a distinct movement through the gatherings and conversations in the salons of Charles Nodier in Paris, Isabella Teotochi Albrizzi in Venice, and Henriette Herz and Rahel Levin Varnhagen in Berlin, not to mention the cosmopolitan, movable salons of Madame de Staël and Madame de Récamier.[9] In part because of the influence of Rousseau, however, the art of conversation was generally held in low esteem by the Romantics, and often presented as synonymous with emptiness and vacuity. Stendhal's first novel, *Armance, ou quelques scènes d'un salon de Paris en 1827* (*Armance, or Scenes from a Parisian Salon in 1827*), was the last, splendidly ambivalent testimony of the fascination of salon conversation, whose seductiveness is highlighted by the author even as he exposes its alienating and estranging quality. For Stendhal, the salon is a place of perpetual misunderstanding, where it is impossible to bare one's true feelings and where the truth remains, in fact, forever hidden.

European Romanticists, from Alfred de Vigny, François-Auguste-René de Chateaubriand, and Victor Hugo to Ugo Foscolo, Giacomo Leopardi, and Heinrich Heine, eagerly frequented the gatherings of the most gifted salonières of their era and often had passionate erotic or intellectual relationships with them, yet they agreed that "polite," "worldly" conversation was artificial and superficial, incapable of penetrating or revealing the deeper, hidden truths of "man." In *Les Chants du crépuscule* (*Songs of Twilight*, 1835), Hugo decried in particular the sense of perpetual irony and the lack of authentic belief that characterized eighteenth-century salon conversation. It was only through solitary reflection and through writing, rather than conversation, that, according to Chateaubriand, the truth could come to the surface.[10] Ironically, Chateaubriand emerged as a writer and shaped his own identity of "enchanteur" through conversations, exchanges, and contacts in Madame de Récamier's salon (fig. 2), which, after hosting many other guests and readers (including Alphonse de Lamartine, Balzac, Stendhal, and the poet Delphine Gay), became dedicated exclusively to his cult. Chateaubriand never ceased to use Récamier to further his literary career, demanding her undivided devotion even after he moved on to ambassadorships in Berlin and London, while turning to another salonière and lover, Madame de Duras, to promote his political career.[11]

Conversation, and by association the spoken word, were deemed too superficial and "leveling," incapable of expressing the extremes of Romantic sensibility or of fulfilling the Romantic urge for depth, drama, and authenticity. Oral and ephemeral as it was, conversation could not convey what was deep, essential, eternal. This perception would lead to the negative vision of language that Stéphane Mallarmé was to make famous. Conversation for Mallarmé and the Symbolists was only the most blatant manifestation of the inadequacy of language, which nothing but the written poetic word, appearing naked and pure on the white page, surrounded by silence and emptiness, could hope to remedy. True literature had to be independent of, even opposite to, conversation.

As conversation and the spoken word were associated with lack, imperfection, impurity, and even soullessness, they continued to be associated with the feminine, in an increasingly negative sense. Like woman, conversation for the Romantics—and later the Symbolists—was essentially corporeal, superficial, fleeting, frivolous. The many unflattering comments made by Romantic writers about the women in whose salons they congregated reflect this. Chateaubriand, who was often a guest of Madame de Staël's salons, along with Lord Byron, Benjamin Constant, Goethe, Friedrich Schlegel, and other seminal figures of European Romanticism, wrote about the "flaws" of her character, although he conceded that her name should not be forgotten. Goethe, while admitting that she spoke beautifully, also complained that she spoke too much.[12] And even though he became the object of a cult and a symbol of creativity and open-mindedness in a number of late-eighteenth- and early-nineteenth-century salons, such as those of Henriette Herz, Rahel Levin Varnhagen, and other bourgeois Jewish women in Berlin, Goethe was known to make disparaging remarks about both women and Jews.[13]

Despite their disdain, the Romantics developed their own ideal of conversation, which bore little resemblance to that of "feminine," pre-revolutionary polite conversation. The famous *Conversations of Goethe with Eckermann* (*Gespräche mit Goethe in den letzen Jahren seines Lebens*, 1823–32), widely translated and read in Europe and in the United States, purified conversation by reducing it to a dialogue between two men. The goal of the conversation was to reveal the genius of Goethe through his use of words in communication with another man. However, no real reciprocity was involved. Johann Peter Eckermann was present only as an admiring interviewer and as the receptacle of the truth of Goethe's words. Through these one-way conversations, Goethe was to throw the light of his incomparable wisdom on the universe of human knowledge.

This reduced model of conversation was very successful and broadly imitated. Although its function was essentially that of imparting knowledge (philosophical and humanistic rather than technical) and popularizing Goethe's genius, it was part of the process of commodification, and of the transformation of conversation into

a technique and an instrument, that characterized the nineteenth century as a whole. It is not surprising, therefore (Goethe would probably have been dismayed), that the American writer and feminist Margaret Fuller (who translated Goethe's conversations with Eckermann into English) should have discovered a way to capitalize on this model of conversation. Finding herself in need of money, she identified conversation as her best asset. In 1839, for her first, Goethe-inspired class of conversations on Greek mythology, Fuller enlisted twenty-five pupils, at twenty-five dollars each. During the next five years she scheduled regular conversations for women on subjects such as fine arts, ethics, poetry, and philosophy. She encouraged women to be proud of their self-improvement, even though they risked being chided for attending her meetings. Other nineteenth-century salons centered on one personality, and functioned instrumentally as publicity machines. The famous Paris salon of Madame Arman de Caillavet (frequented by Proust as a young man), for example, was, from around 1886, devoted to promoting Anatole France (fig. 3).[14]

As late as midcentury, however, the feminine art of disinterested, polite conversation still had its nostalgic advocates, chief among them the Romantic essayist and critic Charles-Augustin Sainte-Beuve. In a series of portraits (the first published in 1844), Sainte-Beuve evoked seventeenth- and eighteenth-century salonières and literary women in whom he saw the emblems of a world where literature and conversation were still closely and humanely joined.[15] The leisurely and elegant conversational tone with which he portrays these women (a tone his critics dismissed as feminine chatting) conjures the atmosphere of tact, urbanity, and reciprocal generosity of a social milieu where time was not yet compartmentalized and commodified, where men and women participated as equals in the civilized give-and-take of conversation, where writing seemed naturally connected with speaking. Along similar lines, in *La Femme au XVIIIème siècle* (*The Woman of the Eighteenth Century*, 1862), Jules and Edmond de Goncourt configured feminine conversation as an almost utopian, eroticized space. Women, they argued,

Fig. 3. Paul Nadar (French, 1856–1939), *Anatole France*, 1893. Archives Photographiques, Centre des Monuments Nationaux, Paris

impart to conversation an inimitable perfection, making it "without heaviness and without frivolity, knowledgeable without pedantry, gay without tumultuousness, polite without affectation, flirtatious without vulgarity, playful without equivocation. . . . No one dissertates: the words start, the questions come forward, and all that one touches upon is measured. The conversation slides, ascends, descends, goes around and comes back. Swiftness characterizes it, precision makes it elegant."[16] This mythification of the eighteenth-century salonière had no feminist implications. It was, rather, a retrospective idealization of an imaginary femininity.[17]

PROUST: REVERSAL AND THE TRUTH OF CONVERSATION

Marcel Proust's great novel in seven volumes *À la recherche du temps perdu* (*In Search of Lost Time*, 1913–27) was, perhaps more than any other modern and modernist work, imbued with the conversational spirit of the woman-led salons of his age. Yet Proust (fig. 4)

virtually started his literary career with an attack against Sainte-Beuve, the primary advocate of the salon and of "feminine" conversation. This is only one of the paradoxes in Proust's relationship with salonières and the art of conversation. In his influential "Contre Sainte-Beuve" ("Against Sainte-Beuve"), Proust did not directly take issue with his predecessor's characterization of salons. Rather, he disputed his idea that the task of the literary critic is to relate "the man and the work." According to Sainte-Beuve, there is an intimate, natural connection between the writer—his life, his milieu, indeed his *self*—and the work that he writes. The link is provided by language; in reading a man's work, it is as if we hear him speak, and when writing about the work we should first speak to the author, or at least imagine a conversation with him and those who are around him. Here we see the connection between Sainte-Beuve's theory of criticism and his ideal of natural, spontaneous feminine conversation that was devalued and obscured in the nineteenth century.

Proust rejected this argument. Articulating for the first time a theory that anticipates the notion, popularized by Roland Barthes and Michel Foucault in the 1960s and 1970s, of the "death of the author," Proust dared to suggest that there is no necessary connection between the man who writes and the one who speaks in a literary work. "A book," he explained, "is the product of a different self from the one we manifest in our habits, in our social life, in our vices."[18] Applying this viewpoint to Sainte-Beuve's own corpus, Proust concluded that only the critic's poetry was authentic and "true," because finally free of the "salon chatter," the "jeu de l'esprit," the contradictory viewpoints and lies that marred his conversational articles. This strategic attack on Sainte-Beuve has led most interpreters of Proust's works to focus on the text, with little or no consideration for biographical and social background—most conspicuously, contemporary salons and salonières.

In *Recherche*, Proust introduces the reader to several salons led by women, all of which are fundamentally fictional, though they do incorporate elements of actual salons and references to real salonières. A

Fig. 4. Jacques-Émile Blanche (French, 1861–1942), *Portrait of Marcel Proust*, 1892. Oil on canvas, 29 x 23 ⅞ in. (73.5 x 60.5 cm). Musée d'Orsay, Paris

Fig. 5. Paul Nadar (French, 1856–1939), *Madame Lydie Aubernon*, 1883. Archives Photographiques, Centre des Monuments Nationaux, Paris

Fig. 6. Paul Nadar (French, 1856–1939), *Madame Madeleine Lemaire*, 1891. Archives Photographiques, Centre des Monuments Nationaux, Paris

dandy with great charm and conversational skills, Proust was initiated into salon life as a young man, in the early 1890s, when he was still a student. He often visited the middle-class salons (to which many aristocrats also flocked) of Madame Arman de Caillavet, Lydie Aubernon (fig. 5), Madeleine Lemaire (fig. 6), and especially Geneviève Straus, who was a basis for the character of Oriane de Guermantes. Proust drew on Madame Arman de Caillavet for his portrayal of Odette Swann and her salon, which in the novel has as its principal attraction the writer Bergotte (based on Anatole France).[19] Lemaire, a well-known painter of flowers, inspired two characters, Madame de Villeparisis and Madame Verdurin. The latter, however, was based more on Aubernon, who, like Madame Verdurin in the novel, received her guests on Wednesdays and assigned them conversation topics of her choice. But salon life was not just the raw material from which Proust constructed his novel: it played a crucial, structural role in the shaping of the novel and of the vision that subtends it.

The salon is the quintessential site for the study of social stratification in the novel. It is in the salon that Proust stages the conflict between aristocracy and bourgeoisie that, in his view, characterized the period between 1880 and 1920 (the time span covered by the novel). Neither private nor public, but rather somewhere in between, the salons in *Recherche* are ruled by women, whose work is that of inviting, entertaining, cultivating relationships, including and excluding, exhibiting connections, and not least, conversing and shaping opinion. As characters in the novel, women are the most active and influential, and their investment in "symbolic capital" produces results that are momentous for the novel's plot and its respected allegorical account of social and historical mutations in France.[20] The immense and beautifully detailed descriptions of salon scenes and the vicissitudes of individual salonières function in fact as an overarching allegory. Not only do the salons led by women reflect change; they produce it.

Proust presents us with a portrait of two major salons. The first is that of the bourgeois Madame Verdurin and her "little group," introduced in the first volume, *Du côté de chez Swann* (*Swann's Way*, 1913). Madame Verdurin is an upwardly mobile, wealthy middle-class *rentier* filled with bohemian pretensions and resentment toward the aristocracy of the Faubourg Saint-Germain, whose still-considerable power during the Third Republic is an object of secret and perennial envy. At the opposite end of the social spectrum we find the salon of Oriane, the Duchesse de Guermantes, an extraordinarily witty and beautiful woman who rules over the Faubourg and is the object of the adolescent narrator's starstruck admiration and love in *Le Côté de Guermantes* (*The Guermantes Way*, 1920–21).

In Proust's satirical portrait, Madame Verdurin tyrannically presides over a heterogeneous group that, besides her spineless husband, includes such professionals as the neighborhood physician Cottard, little-known or obscure artists (the painter known as Biche; a nameless pianist who plays Wagner; a Polish sculptor), a courtesan with social aspirations (Odette), and a second-rate déclassé aristocrat or two. Madame Verdurin cultivates the group's identity as if it were a cult whose faith lies in the (false) exclusiveness of the salon itself, and in the derision of the aristocracy. Individual worth and intelligence, not class and wealth, are regarded hypocritically as the only values that count, binding together the members of the salon. Precisely because she sees herself as upwardly mobile and intends to use the salon to climb the social ladder, Madame Verdurin cuts all links with her irremediably middle-class family. The little clan, from which she will exclude progressively those who are no longer useful, opening her doors to adepts of higher worth, becomes her family.

Into this salon, in pursuit of Odette, comes Swann, the middle-class Jewish man who is the narrator's alter ego in the first volume. Rich, refined, cultivated, and sensitive, Swann has gained access to the salons of the aristocracy, where, for example, he provides advice on which artworks to buy. He is therefore able to move between salons that are mutually segregated. (The homosexual Charlus, Oriane's brother-in-law and the most snobbish of the Guermantes, takes on a similar role when, in amorous pursuit of the young violinist Morel, he follows him into the Verdurin salon.)

Madame Verdurin is initially suspicious of Swann, for he declines to devote himself completely to the group or sever his links with the aristocracy. Swann is in turn appalled by the crass conversation at the Verdurins', and he is soon expelled. Proust's portrait of Madame Verdurin through Swann's eyes is effectively a caricature. The vulgarity and pretentiousness of her salon is a tragicomic inversion of the qualities that, according to Sainte-Beuve, characterized the woman-led eighteenth-century salon.

In a stunning reversal and revelation for both narrator and reader, by the time of *Sodome et Gomorrhe* (*Sodom and Gomorrah*, 1921), which takes place about twenty years later, Madame Verdurin turns out to have built her salon on a series of shrewd, avant-garde choices and cultural investments. She is revealed to have been the first to introduce the music of Vinteuil (a fictional musician comparable to Claude Debussy), who only later became fashionable in the best aristocratic circles. The obscure and awkward Biche is revealed to be no less than the great Elstir, whose character and art are loosely based on Claude Monet. (By contrast, Elstir's daring Impressionist works were hung in the salon of Oriane de Guermantes, but only on the advice of Swann, and then hardly appreciated by her.) Madame Verdurin has successfully challenged the prestige and power of the aristocracy by investing in and accumulating symbolic capital in the form of art, culture, and intellectual life—the very areas in which the aristocracy was weakest.[21] In the second section of *Sodome et Gomorrhe*, she even capitalizes shrewdly on the Dreyfus Affair, making her salon the center of pro-Dreyfus activism and thus becoming part of a historic moment, the rise of intellectuals as a social group. Émile Zola and Anatole France are among her guests.[22]

In *Le Côté de Guermantes*, Oriane de Guermantes is audacious in her choice of dress, style, and friendships. She daringly innovates the life of the aristocracy, shaking it out of its torpor and bringing it dangerously closer to the bourgeoisie. Swann fascinates her, as does the narrator, who (like Proust himself when he started his assiduous study of salon life) is a promising young man of letters. Her salon is a family bastion, where gentility and the false, narcissistic amiability of the true aristocracy still reign.[23] But in order to show off her enlightened intelligence and discernment, Oriane has opened her doors to a few notable and promising bourgeois artists and professionals, and even to a Jew such as Swann. Although her belief in the natural and exclusive superiority of her class is unshaken, she wishes to show an open mind, and demonstrate to others of her class that the aristocracy can accommodate itself to the new times, by expressing appreciation for excellence and talent (rather than just blood), while remaining dominant. It is this very modernization, especially her friendship with Swann, that later causes her downfall.

The dangers of modernization and democratization for the aristocracy are represented by Madame de Villeparisis and her salon, which, although secondary in *Recherche*, make us see Oriane's salon and the world of the Guermantes more clearly. While she is a Guermantes, Madame de Villeparisis, the mistress of an ex-ambassador, has been marginalized and already lost most of her status when the narrator, in *Le Côté de Guermantes*, is introduced in her salon by her nephew Robert de Saint-Loup, the narrator's intimate friend. True aristocratic snobs no longer frequent her salon, the narrator notes, because they are afraid of meeting doctors' or notaries' wives or other unacceptable characters. He is himself surprised when he runs into his old schoolmate Bloch, a promising playwright, who is painfully self-conscious about his Jewishness and devoid of social and conversational skills. Madame de Villeparisis is treading precariously on the same territory as Madame Verdurin, without, however, the latter's instinct for investment in the up-and-coming. She embodies the old qualities of conversational wit and grace, yet she is frivolous, according to the narrator, and incapable of understanding true art. Madame de Villeparisis, an appreciated painter of delicate flowers and the author of a book of witty but futile memoirs, has opened her salon to artists and writers, men and women (such as Odette, now married to Swann) of different social classes and races, as well as sometimes dubious morality. This has made her salon more interesting to her niece Oriane, who is nonetheless afraid of visiting it too often and who is careful to leave the room whenever Odette enters. Madame de Villeparisis is oblivious of the backlash soon to come from the Dreyfus Affair, which will place Jews (though not the Dreyfusards) on the lowest level of the social scale. In the wake of the affair, during which Oriane maintains a rigorously anti-Dreyfus position, the prestige of Madame de Villeparisis's salon is definitely undone.

Despite the initial awestruck admiration of the young narrator for the Duchesse de Guermantes, and his naive passion for her and her world, when he finally gains entry to Oriane's and other aristocratic salons, he is deeply disillusioned. For Oriane, the newcomers are mere decorations in her exclusive salon. Like Madame Verdurin (for whom artists and intellectuals are but showpieces), she has no real understanding of or appreciation for Vinteuil's music or Elstir's painting. Oriane's conversation, her opinionated pronouncements that pass for manifestations of wit, charm, and intelligence, are vacuous and absurd. Proust's portraits of conversation in the aristocratic salons and of Oriane as salonière are no less satirical than the depiction of Madame Verdurin and her little group. Although in many ways different, the conversation is equally mediocre, pretentious, and false. Oriane and Madame Verdurin each are inverted images of each other in almost every respect. (Madame Verdurin's salon, for example, is openly Dreyfusard, while Oriane's is the opposite.) In his fictional strategy, salon conversations become opposed to the depth, revelatory power, and truthfulness of writing, a writing that can begin only from silence, when all are quiet and the narrator, finally alone with himself, can reconstruct the true design of things.[24]

In the devaluing of conversation in *Recherche*, Proust seems to align himself with the ideology of Romanticism and Symbolism, even though the observations of the narrator find scarce confirmation in the historical evidence. Proust's skewed portrayal of aristocratic conversation contributed considerably to strengthen the (bourgeois) myth that the aristocracy and the ancien régime had no real culture.[25] His comic portrayal of the imbecility of bourgeois conversation in Madame Verdurin's salon was, of course, equally

Fig. 7. William and Daniel Downey (British, active c. 1860–early 1900s), *Sarah Bernhardt in "Francesca de Rimini,"* 1902. Albumen print carte-de-visite, 6½ x 4¼ in. (16.5 x 10.8 cm). The Jewish Museum, New York; Museum Purchase: Fine Arts Acquisitions Committee Fund, 1998–64.10

number of characters in *Recherche* (including Cottard, Charlus, Saint-Loup, Odette, and Swann) are modeled on people whom Proust met at Straus's salon. It was through her that he became acquainted with the work of Monet (Elstir). From what remains of a vast correspondence between Proust and Straus we can ascertain how her character, her salon, and her Jewish identity—distinct from the fictionalized Guermantes—furnished the author with the reality base from which he scrutinized the Faubourg Saint-Germain, both its aristocratic and its bourgeois factions.[27]

Geneviève Straus was an open-minded, liberated, cultivated, and "assimilated" bourgeois Jewish woman.[28] She had neither the vacuous snobbism and cultural shallowness of Oriane de Guermantes nor the narrow-mindedness, vulgarity, thirst for social promotion, and lack of scruples of Madame Verdurin. As the widow of the composer Georges Bizet, she had a somewhat bohemian and romantic, yet culturally distinguished, past, linked to the operatic myth of "Carmen." After a long widowhood, she agreed to marry a wealthy lawyer, Émile Straus, who financed her salon and "let her be." The distinguishing feature of her salon appears to have been its syncretism: a mixture of classes, professions, ethnicities, national origins, and political positions (Socialists and monarchists alike gathered there). Unlike Proust's fictional salonières, she seems not to have been motivated by either the need for social promotion or any other form of snobbish exhibitionism. At Madame Straus's, observed the painter Jacques-Émile Blanche, "la conversation se démonétise"—conversation has its own worth.[29] The composer Charles Gounod wrote in 1896 that the modern artist was increasingly nothing but a product, afraid of being consumed by the audience, "devoured" by the anonymous crowd.[30] In contrast to the world of commodification and depersonalization, Straus's salon had a protective, nourishing and sheltering function. Halfway between the private and the public sphere, it exposed Proust to the multiplicity of "le monde," and to infinitely varied conversation, while still maintaining a sense of intimacy, proximity, communication, and reciprocity between artist and audience.[31]

one-sided. This is all the more ironic in that Proust's own celebrated kaleidoscopic vision was profoundly influenced by his experiences in bourgeois, déclassé, or mixed salons, rather than fully aristocratic ones, which he seems not to have frequented.

The key to Proust's mythical economy lies in the asymmetrical relationship between the fictional Madame de Guermantes and the real-life Geneviève Straus. It has been commonly acknowledged that Straus was in large part the model, although Oriane's blond beauty and fascinating, imperiously avian physical appearance and posture are inspired by two other women, the Countess de Greffulhe and Madame de Chevigné (a descendant of the Marquis de Sade).[26] A

In Madame Straus's salon, the voice and the spoken word reigned supreme in the form of both conversation and recitation (the live reading of texts), without clear borders between the two. Actresses such as Sarah Bernhardt (fig. 7) and Réjane (both featured prominently in *Recherche*), as well as lesser-knowns, interacted socially with the other guests in the Straus drawing room; they were not just "exhibited" and then dismissed, as happened in some more conventional salons. Bernhardt recited poems by Straus's lifelong friend the writer Anna de Noailles, who had her own literary salon. (Her writing was enthusiastically praised on repeated occasions by Proust.)[32] There was singing by Reynaldo Hahn, Proust's intimate friend and lover, and by Straus herself. She liked to perform, and the salon was her stage. According to several witnesses, including her nephew Daniel Halévy, her constant improvisation of intelligent and witty phrases made her fascinating. Proust wrote of her conversation: "On ferait un volume si l'on rapportait tout ce qui a été dit par elle et qui vaut de n'être pas oublié" (One could fill a volume if one related all that has been said by her

that is worth not forgetting).[33] Oriane's conversation in *Recherche*—indeed, all salon conversation in the novel—is instead distinctly unmemorable chatter, for which the narrator shows nothing but contempt.

The flip side of Straus's salon exuberance was her propensity for depression; she often spent weeks, or more, shut away in clinics, taking veronal and morphine.[34] Even this aspect of her character, and her profound melancholy, tied her to Proust, as can be gathered from their extant correspondence. The pointed, witty, and shocking repartee that was apparently a specialty of hers is most often associated with Oriane's style. Yet in *Recherche*, Oriane exhibits a gratuitous cruelty that seems to have been alien to Straus. Unlike Oriane, who invites the narrator into her salon only to show off her ability to spot promising young talent, and who is indifferent to his passion for her, Straus was a sympathetic, generous friend to Proust, at once maternal and erotic, with whom he entertained an intimate correspondence for some thirty years (124 of his letters to her survive, but only 13 of hers to him; fig. 8). The correspondence, one of many maintained by Straus, is a natural continuation of the salon; it expands the flirtatiousness and platonic love of salon conversation. Proust's side is filled with eroticism, even fetishism, and the little we have of hers shows her playing the game, and especially fetishizing the novel that, she says, she cannot stop reading (just as he cannot stop writing it). Only rarely do we get a hint of Straus's resentment in being identified with Oriane, and with Madame Verdurin: in the last analysis, nurturing the larger project of *Recherche* was more important to her. On sending to Straus a special, preview edition of *Le Côté de Guermantes* in October 1920, Proust wrote her that "*everything* that is spiritual in it comes from you."[35] The "it" clearly means the book, yet biographers and critics usually misinterpret this letter and imply that the "it" refers only to the character of Oriane de Guermantes, or to "the Guermantes spirit."[36]

Just how much Geneviève Straus and her salon influenced *Recherche* can be gathered only in light of the Dreyfus Affair. As Chantal Bischoff points out, the fact that Straus was Jewish but also a celebrated and even adored woman of the world helped Proust consider his own Jewishness with less shame.[37] At the time of the Dreyfus Affair, and with the explosion of anti-Semitism in 1895, Madame Straus (who wore black the day Alfred Dreyfus was condemned) turned her salon into the center of pro-Dreyfus forces—unlike the fictionalized Oriane. She astonished those who thought her essentially frivolous, as well as some of her regular guests, whose anti-Semitism provoked them never to return.[38] The real world was suddenly rocked by rancor, deception, suspicion, resentment, disillusionment, betrayal: the Dreyfus Affair overturned the structure of familiar relationships. Everything appeared to be radically different, the opposite even. The social universe, as seen through Madame Straus's salon, underwent a stunning reversal. Yet, Straus herself, like Proust, remained unwavering in her support of Dreyfus.

Proust may have fragmented, reinvented, and transfigured the historical models of his characters, but he depended on shock and disillusionment within actual salon society to generate the structure of his novel. In the letter to Straus mentioned above, Proust pointed out how, in the second part of *Le Côté de Guermantes*, and more so in the last volume, the anti-Dreyfusards have become Dreyfusards "and others that one believed anti-Dreyfusard are madly Dreyfusard." He reassured Straus of his steadfastness; in the end of *Recherche* he told her "you will find me unchanged."[39] The bond between her and Proust, nourished by the uninterrupted conversation of their letters, was never broken. Ironically, then, Straus and her salon seem to have given Proust a model for both the radical reversibility and relativism that characterize the social realm in the novel, and the deep, hidden authenticity associated with the private, namely with the most intimate feelings and recollections that give writing a sense of stability and truth.

The structure of reversal is evident in the plot of *Recherche* and its construction of character. The personalities emerge through conversation, almost never because of what they actually say (for this is often, as has been noted, mere chatter) but because of the respective positions they assume. What matters is how they negotiate and define their social space. Their positions, and hence the nature of character itself, are by rule subject to abrupt and drastic change. Like the social self, character for Proust is but a fictitious, unstable performance within the realm of conversation. It is thus curiously homologous to the capricious, contradictory, and often cruel turns of Oriane's talk in the salon.

The narration of the dinner party at the Verdurins' in *Sodome et Gomorrhe*, organized around the violinist Morel, is the epitome of Proustian irony, and exemplifies how reversal or inversion operates as a structural matrix in the novel. As Roland Barthes observed of *Recherche:* "Inversion as a form invades the entire structure. . . . Sexual inversion is in this regard exemplary. . . . There is an epidemic of inversion, of reversal. Reversal is a law. Every trait is called on to reverse itself, through an implacable movement of rotation."[40] In the course of the dinner for Morel, who has come accompanied by Charlus (who has thus reversed his usual snobbism), it grows obvious that Madame Verdurin, who wants more than anything to mingle with the aristocracy, is ignorant of Charlus's true social status, the very status for which members of his own class view him with awe. For the little group, by contrast, he represents only the incarnation of sexual inversion— an inversion of which his own Faubourg Saint-Germain is unaware. Proust's kaleidoscopic relativism, his sense of the multiplicity and reciprocal incompatibility of points of view, is clear in this sequence. But his reverse specularity is so pervasive that it never stops, perpetually doubling and folding back on itself (much like the conversation described by the Goncourts in *La Femme au XVIIIème siècle*) and producing a sense of vertigo in the reader. In the third volume of *Recherche*, the narrator receives a letter announcing that his dear friend Saint-Loup (through whom he was introduced into Oriane's exclusive salon) is marrying Gilberte, the daughter of Swann and Odette. Earlier, Oriane had publicly defined elegance, and the essence of her salon, as "not knowing Madame Swann." In yet another shocking turnabout, in the final volume (*Le Temps retrouvé*, or *Time Regained*, 1927), Saint-Loup will emerge as a homosexual, the lover of Morel.

The upheaval caused by World War I only accelerated a process of inversion that the Dreyfus Affair had symbolically unleashed in the novel but that was to be endemic to all social reality in France, as Proust sees it. During the war, the Verdurin salon was transformed into a vital information center, with Madame Verdurin replacing Oriane as the dominant personality in the social space, overturning the hierarchy of the first two volumes of the novel. This reversal, together with the ultimate downfall of the Guermantes, is clinched by Madame Verdurin's marriage to the Prince de Guermantes, after he has been financially ruined by the war. Madame Verdurin is the new Princess de Guermantes, while Oriane, by contrast, is *déclassée*, and ends up a sort of double of Madame de Villeparisis, whom she once barely tolerated.

Proust's negative vision of idle conversation was pushed to an extreme later in the twentieth century. The spare dialogues of Samuel Beckett's, Eugene Ionesco's, and Harold Pinter's solitary characters in empty rooms have eclipsed, seemingly forever, the shredded traces of salon sociability whose memory haunts *Recherche*. As we have seen, however, Proust did not so much devalue or "deconstruct" salon conversation as deploy a mythical version of it in order to expose the faltering structure of high society.[41] And while his fictional salon conversations are the object of disparagement throughout *Recherche*, the real-life exchanges over the Dreyfus Affair—with its center at Geneviève Straus's salon—provided the basis for the daring structure of reversibility that informs the novel.

WILDE AND THE DECAY OF CONVERSATION

Oscar Wilde (fig. 9) was effectively brought up in a salon, his mother's. William Butler Yeats wrote of Lady Wilde that "London has few better talkers" and that "when one listens to her . . . one finds it in no way wonderful that Oscar Wilde should be the most finished talker of our time."[42] When Yeats visited Lady Wilde in the late 1880s, both she and her salon had entered a phase of decline, yet he still found her fascinating. Another guest at the time, Catherine Hamilton,

observed that Speranza—as Lady Wilde called herself since the time she started writing and then entertaining in Dublin in the 1840s—despite being now an impoverished widow, had not forgotten the art "de faire un salon."[43]

Lady Wilde, born Jane Francesca Elgee, was the daughter of a Dublin attorney. A gifted linguist, she not only used the English language brilliantly but knew French, German, Italian, Latin, and Greek. Oscar, later dubbed "lord of the language," seems to have inherited from her his linguistic gift (he spoke French fluently, and wrote in it), as well an imposing size and physical appearance, a propensity for posturing, and a decorative, theatrical style of dressing.[44] Before marrying William Wilde, a physician with a scholarly interest in ethnography and Irish folklore, Speranza was famous as a passionate and eloquent patriot, and the author of virulently anti-British articles and poems. With marriage she became less radical, but she continued to write and publish, while conducting, like her husband, extensive research on Irish folklore—a source for many of Oscar's oral stories. William Wilde, who was knighted in 1864 in acknowledgment of his work for the Irish census, had several illegitimate children before marrying her, and was chronically unfaithful; he eventually was involved in a scandalous trial, when Mary Travers, a patient with whom he had had a liaison for several years, brought charges of rape against him and launched a smear campaign against both him and his wife. Lady Wilde, who remained loyal throughout the ordeal, shocked the court by saying that she was "not interested" in the intrigue and found it a nuisance.[45]

Quite emancipated for her time, Lady Wilde was a feminist, and through the salon (which her husband rarely attended) she fashioned within her Dublin home a public space of influence, independence, and creativity.[46] More than a hundred people attended each of her Saturday afternoon receptions, among them writers, professors, barristers, politicians, journalists, students, actors, and musicians. Speranza, it was said, gathered people "whom prudish Dublin had hitherto kept carefully apart."[47] Music was played, stories were told, scenes from plays were enacted, poets read from their

work. Oscar and his brother, William, were allowed to sit at the foot of the dinner table and to play amid the noise, laughter, and often bawdy conversation of the drawing room. They listened to everything that was said.[48] Henriette Corkran, one attendee, recalled that Lady Wilde's "talk was like fireworks—brilliant, whimsical and flashy."[49]

After her husband died, leaving little but debts, and she moved to London, Lady Wilde, then in her mid-fifties, held a successful salon first on Saturdays and later on Wednesdays as well. She also continued to publish essays and poetry, earning little, and edited two important volumes of Irish folktales, many of which her husband had collected. In introducing her London salon to a journalist, she observed that although those who described her as "an Irish Madame Récamier" were perhaps "going a little too far," her project was indeed a salon similar in spirit to that of the famous Frenchwoman, though "on a smaller scale."[50] It is sig-

nificant that she should have been compared to a French *salonière*. Conversation in England since the eighteenth century prevailed in social spaces such as the male-dominated coffeehouse and the club, whereas the salon as an institution—and polite conversation in general—were associated more with France.[51] The well-known Irish propensity for lively conversation was prover-bially considered "Continental" and un-English.[52]

Oscar was a faithful presence in Speranza's London salon, where he brought friends and helped serve tea. He soon became the main attraction of Speranza's crowded drawing room, where photographs of him were prominently on display. Robert Browning, John Ruskin, George Bernard Shaw; Lillie Langtry, the celebrated beauty and actress who was a friend and possibly a lover of Wilde; Marie Corelli, the popular author of romances and gothic novels; Katherine Tynan, the Irish poet, novelist, and memorialist; pro-fessional singers and reciters; and London's cleverest people visited the salon, despite the far from lavish teas; guests apparently knew better than to try actually to drink the tea. In 1887, Speranza, whose feminism deeply influenced her son, helped him, through her salon connections, to assemble the list of contributors for the *Woman's World*, a monthly he edited for more than a year.[53]

Speranza's flamboyance, physical size, outspo-kenness, and penchant for hyperbole, as well as her bohemian reputation and surroundings, made her the object of parodies by those who disliked Oscar and his milieu. He was so indebted to his mother for his con-versational style and passion for epigram and paradox that some scholars have mentioned plagiarism.[54] To view appropriation in this negative way amounts, of course, to an un-Wildean overestimation of originality. For Wilde, plagiarism, or rather the playful appropria-tion and ironic quotation of a phrase, and its slanted relaunching into the arena of discourse, was merely part of the art of conversation.

At the end of the 1880s, Wilde, now more famous, especially for his esprit and witty conversation, drifted away from his mother. He turned himself into a man about town, entering the fashionable world that met in other, ostensibly more modern social spaces such as the coffeehouse and music hall. In the 1890s, at the height of his wealth and fame as novelist and playwright, he offered her a modicum of financial assistance, paying the rent for her dilapidated rooms. He rarely saw her in these years, entering instead the circle of a younger, more fascinatingly modern salonière, Ada Leverson. He returned briefly to his mother's, tragically, after the end of his first trial for "gross indecencies," in May 1895, when he was released on bail and no hotel would take him.[55] Lady Wilde apparently was the one who persuaded Wilde to stay and face a second trial rather than flee the country. Despite his impassioned self-defense speech (yet another demonstration of his oratorical brilliance) and the ovation that followed in the courtroom, he was sentenced to the maximum of two years' imprisonment with hard labor.

Conversation was not simply a fundamental part of Oscar Wilde's art but was, in a sense, its origin and core. This is true as much of the extraordinarily witty dialogues of his plays from the 1890s as it is of the novel *The Picture of Dorian Gray* (1890) and his stories and prose poems. Some of Wilde's essays, too—"The Decay of Lying," for example—are written in the form of conversations. In his preface to a 1908 edition of Wilde's works, Robert Ross, one of Leverson's closest friends and with Wilde a habitué of her dining room and salon in the 1890s, explained that the prose poems were "the kind of story Wilde would tell at the dinner table . . . invented on the spur of the moment, or inspired by a chance observation."[56] As Walter Pater commented in his review of *Dorian Gray* for *The Bookman* (1891): "There is always something of an excellent talker about the writing of Oscar Wilde." Although he disapproved of the character Henry Wotton's immorality and aestheticism, Pater praised the novel for a style that evoked "the ease and fluidity . . . of one telling a story by word of mouth."[57] In his lifetime, and for decades after his death, Wilde was famous chiefly as a conversationalist and raconteur. Contemporaries such as Max Beerbohm, André Gide, Frank Harris, Leverson, Charles Ricketts, Vincent O'Sullivan, and Yeats believed that Wilde's genius was

expressed better in the spoken than in the written word.[58] But others saw in Wilde's oral seductiveness a sign of his depraved effeminacy, and of the essential frivolity of his art. In *Bohemian Literary and Social Life in Paris: Salons, Cafés, Studios* (1928), Sisley Huddleston devoted a chapter to Proust and Wilde and to what he deemed as the morbidity, sensuality, and perversity bred by conversation in certain salons.[59]

Wilde's talent for oral expression has been interpreted even by later critics as a limit of his art, and indication of its shallow and ephemeral nature. In particular, his oral tales, of which various versions were transcribed, reported, and collected by friends and acquaintances, have always been treated in official editions as inferior preliminary sketches, or as apocrypha or questionable texts "without Wilde's authority."[60] But a growing body of scholarship shows not only that conversation and storytelling in a conversational setting underlie many of Wilde's written texts, but also that his oral narratives have a literary dignity of their own that is neither inferior to the written texts nor in fact explicable in terms of the categories of traditional literary criticism (such as "author" and "authority").[61]

In seeking to claim respectability for Wilde's art of talk, several critics have demonstrated its formal and thematic affinities with traditional Irish folktales, which are indeed among Wilde's sources.[62] Yet although Wilde does appropriate Irish motifs and the patterning of Irish folktales, his punning, his aphoristic style, and his constant derailing of discourse through interpolation, slippage, inversion, paradox, and carnivalization, transform his speech acts into something quite different from traditional oral folktales. Rather than construct or confirm identity (ethnic, social, or sexual) and the purposefulness of meaning, Wilde's talk is destabilizing, excessive, and slippery.[63]

Wilde's spoken stories vary widely in theme and form. Some are based on the Irish tales collected by his father and retold and edited by his mother; others are idiosyncratic, often irreverent and subversive retellings of episodes from Shakespeare, Balzac, the Bible, and the saints' lives, as well as fairy tales and comic social stories. In one told to Gide, Wilde adapted the biblical account of the resurrection of Lazarus. In the tale, after Lazarus is brought back to life and freed from his shroud, he fails to come forward to speak to Jesus, remaining sullen and silent. Jesus approaches him and asks what there is beyond the grave. Lazarus replies reproachfully that, contrary to the lies told by Jesus about the marvels of heaven, "there is nothing after death and he who is dead is dead indeed." Jesus puts his finger to his lips and with an imploring look says: "I know. But don't tell anyone."[64] In this and other oral tales, traditional narrative logic is subverted, even inverted; each time the reader tries to pin down the logic of the story, the possibility of a paradoxical inversion presents itself, and the logic slips away. In this case, the ambivalence resides in the heretical paradox of Jesus' lying, and in the allusion to the classic, unresolvable Cretan paradox, also known as the liar's paradox. Gide was reputed by many to be a liar—a trait that Wilde prized and would have taken into account in selecting and telling this story. Wilde reacted to and acted on clues offered to him by the tenor of the conversation and the relationship established with his interlocutors. In Ada Leverson's salon, for instance, he improvised for the very devout Robert Ross a gently satirical story that he called "Saint Robert of Phillimore," which Leverson later transcribed.[65]

According to witnesses, Wilde didn't just improvise and narrate these stories; he also performed them, by giving his voice suggestive intonations and using subtle and seductive mimicry and gestures. Another Leverson regular, Charles Ricketts, recalled a rendition of the oral fable "The Poet," about a young man who tells his incredulous fellow villagers that he has seen mermaids, a centaur, and a faun, during which Wilde conjured the image of the retreating centaur with a barely perceptible turn of the head.[66]

In his reminiscences, Gide shows how Wilde fashioned his storytelling as a progressive seduction. After a telling of "The Poet," Wilde "paused some moments, let the effect of the tale work its way in me, and then resumed: 'I don't like your lips; they're straight, like those of someone who never lied. I want to teach you to lie.'"[67] He then shifted the tone of the conversation

incongruously, moving on to talk abstractly about the nature of the work of art, only to return to a story. Wilde's conversational speech acts (of which the stories are a part) are performative in that, rather than rely on any presumably stable preexisting order, pattern, or structure (social, sexual, narrative, cognitive), they tend to construct, forge, and perform identity (including sexual identity and desire) through the movement of speech.[68] Wilde himself called talk "a sort of spiritualized action."[69]

Gide claims that Wilde "never listened" and that his was a perpetual monologue, rather than a conversation.[70] Doubtless, his kind of conversation and oral narration differed markedly from the seventeenth- and eighteenth-century ideal of a reciprocal, equal, and unselfish exchange. Wilde risked breaking most of the rules nostalgically laid out in 1887 in *The Principles of the Art of Conversation* by John Pentland Mahaffy with the assistance of the Marchioness of Londonderry and Lady Audrey Buller. Mahaffy's requirements of moral worth and truthfulness for the good conversationalist, and his warning against too extravagant an exhibition of humor and wit, run counter to Wilde's habitual practices and his playful praise of immorality and lying. Mahaffy, a Greek scholar who had frequented Lady Wilde's salon in Dublin, was Wilde's teacher at Trinity and, for a time, his friend and fellow traveler. Yet unlike Wilde, he became an incurable snob who persistently and eagerly cultivated the "castle set"; he was a monologist whom no one could talk down.[71] Wilde wrote a negative review of Mahaffy's book, criticizing its inelegant, arid style and the author's lack of charm. Wilde, like Proust, hated snobs and social climbers. As a dandy in dress and conversation, he sought an elegance based not on conformity, imitation, and social promotion but on impertinence, surprise, unpredictability, and beauty.

The eroticized atmosphere of Wildean talk and the pleasure he took in conversation as an art (rather than as productive discussion, debate, or instrument for social promotion) recall the seductiveness of eighteenth-century salon conversation (the ancestor of the dandy is in fact the eighteenth-century libertine), but his ten-

dency to monopolize attention, and especially his spellbinding storytelling, deprived conversation of its communal character. Nonetheless, within the relatively small circle of Ada Leverson's friends and usual guests there existed the atmosphere of a salon. Delighting in frivolous, unproductive, witty, and flippant conversation for its own sake, Leverson's salon was decidedly antibourgeois, while its tolerant morals and flamboyance constituted an implicit affront to the puritanical façade of the British aristocracy.

Among the friends and guests of Ada Leverson were the great dandy Beerbohm (fig. 10), Aubrey Beardsley and his sister, Mabel, Reginald Turner, John Lane, publisher of the scandalous journal *The Yellow Book*, the artists William Rothenstein, Walter Sickert, and John Singer Sargent (fig. 11), and several journalists, actors, and playwrights. Leverson's brilliant parodies of Wilde, published in *Punch*, which surprised and endlessly delighted him,[72] were inspired by salon conversations; these helped disseminate the myth of Wilde and inspired other witty fin-de-siècle talk and writing

by him and others. With her wit, Leverson provoked the wit of others. She was a muse to the entire aesthetic movement called the "Yellow '90s" after Beardsley and Lane's trademark publication, *The Yellow Book*.[73] Wilde used her witty phrases in his plays; she parodied him in her sketches and novels. Like Wilde, she loved the ephemeral quality of fashion and conversation. In her company and in their small group, Wilde felt freer, more relaxed, and less compelled to perform; still, some of his best stories were born in her drawing room.

Because of their oral nature, Wilde's tales lacked a stable or fixed form; several versions of "The Poet," for example, are known, including one in which the poet's disappointed audience stones him to death. The manner of rendering the story also varied according to circumstances. Wilde's golden voice and storytelling were such that he was sometimes referred to as a "merman," after the mythical mermaids whose singing both enticed and threatened. English aristocratic society found him immensely entertaining in the theater, where he often appeared in person, and even in the drawing room,

Fig. 12. Gertrude Stein with her portrait by Picasso. Yale Collection of American Literature, Beinecke Rare Book and Manuscript Library, Yale University, New Haven

heretical modernism, at once carnivalesque and parodic, which, in its playfulness, irreverence, and citational pleasure, was already a kind of postmodernism.

STEIN AND THE SENSE OF SOUND

Unlike Wilde, Gertrude Stein (fig. 12) seems to have been a listener rather than a talker (Proust was both). Yet conversation, and specifically the conversation that went on in her famous salon, played a central, largely overlooked role in her work. Around 1905, all sorts of people began flocking to Gertrude and her brother Leo's apartment at 27 rue de Fleurus in Paris to look at and talk about the strange paintings that the eccentric Americans were buying and hanging in their living room. Friends and acquaintances who visited the Steins included many artists whom they collected (Pablo Picasso and Henri Matisse were regulars), as well as others, along with collectors, art dealers, writers, and expatriates.

The atmosphere on Saturday evenings was decidedly raucous and bohemian; various languages were spoken, and different accents and inflections mingled, intersected, and overlapped. Although after 1913 (and after the interlude of World War I) Alice Toklas imposed a strict ritual that entailed the careful screening and orchestration of guests, the control of conversation (always centered on Gertrude), and the polite serving of tea and cakes (which Toklas made), in the early years the interaction was less polite and much more chaotic. Degrees of conversational eloquence were as varied as the voices. Matisse was articulate and precise. Some people came for the pleasure of sneering and scoffing at the odd paintings. The only consistent ordering principle was Leo's attempt to explain what the paintings were about. His lecturing voice could be heard calling the guests to attention and elaborating "aggressively and proudly" on the technique and significance of specific works and the new Cubist art.[75] Alfred Stieglitz, a frequent visitor, was struck by Gertrude's silence. She seemed to take it all in, with almost stoic acceptance: her brother's didactic tirades, the provocative comments of guests, the ebullience of the artists. Stein

where (like his character Henry Wotton) he would scatter epigrams and fascinate with his stories. Yet his ambivalent sexuality (first bisexual, then homosexual), his Irishness, and his transgressive posing and flaunting of his disregard of conventional principles, beliefs, and morality placed him in a precarious position that eventually led to the disastrous trials and incarceration.

Proust met Wilde in Paris in 1891; he later included some of the Irishman's remarks in *La Prisonnière* (*The Captive*, 1923; attributing them to Charlus), while in *Sodome et Gomorrhe* he alluded to Wilde in a passage about the fate of homosexuals: "Their position unstable, like that of the poet once fêted in all the drawing rooms, and applauded in every theatre in London, and the next day driven out of every lodging house, unable to find a pillow on which to lay his head."[74] In valorizing ephemeral talk, the voice, orality, and the body, and in demystifying the authority of the written word and the aura of the solitary writer who finds the truth only within himself, Wilde inverted the value system that had dominated nineteenth-century literary culture and that influenced a certain kind of Symbolism and modernism, from Mallarmé to Proust, Luigi Pirandello, T. S. Eliot, and Beckett. Wilde ushered in a different,

HENRI MATISSE

ONE was quite certain that for a long part of his being one being living he had been trying to be certain that he was wrong in doing what he was doing and then when he could not come to be certain that he had been wrong in doing what he had been doing, when he had completely convinced himself that he would not come to be certain that he had been wrong in doing what he had been doing he was really certain then that he was a great one and he certainly was a great one. Certainly every one could be certain of this thing that this one is a great one.

Some said of him, when anybody believed in him they did not then believe in any other one. Certainly some said this of him.

He certainly very clearly expressed something. Some said that he did not clearly express anything. Some were certain that he expressed something very clearly and some of such of them said that he would have been a greater one if he had not been one so clearly expressing what he was expressing. Some said he was not clearly expressing what he was expressing and some of such of them said that the greatness of struggling which was not clear expression made of him one being a completely great one.

Some said of him that he was greatly expressing something struggling. Some said of him that he was not greatly expressing something struggling.

He certainly was clearly expressing something, certainly sometime any one might come to know that of him. Very many did come to know it of him that he was clearly expressing what he was expressing. He was a great one. Any one might come to know that of him. Very many did come to know that of him. Some who came to know that of him, that he was a great one, that he was clearly expressing something, came then to be certain that he was not greatly expressing something being struggling. Certainly he was expressing something being struggling. Any one could be certain that he was expressing something being struggling. Some were certain that he was greatly expressing this thing. Some were certain that he was not greatly expressing this thing. Every one could come to be certain that he was a great man. Any one could come to be certain that he was clearly expressing something.

Some certainly were wanting to be needing to be doing what he was doing, that is clearly expressing something. Certainly they were willing to be wanting to be a great one. They were, that is some of them, were not wanting to be needing expressing anything being struggling. And certainly he was one not greatly expressing something being struggling, he was a great one, he was clearly expressing something. Some were wanting to be doing what

23

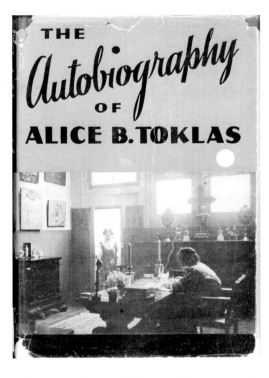

Fig. 13. Gertrude Stein's portrait "Matisse," which appeared in *Camera Work*, August 1912

Fig. 14. Cover of *The Autobiography of Alice B. Toklas*, 1933. Yale Collection of American Literature, Beinecke Rare Book and Manuscript Library, Yale University, New Haven

wrote at night, after she could be sure that no more callers would ring the bell.[76]

Among her writings of that early period of her career were *The Making of Americans*, *Tender Buttons*, and some of the *Portraits* (fig. 13), which defined her style and are still today among the most controversial of her works. The common critical assumption has been that these works were influenced by the new painting and collage techniques. Wendy Steiner, for one, has argued that Stein's portraits are literary versions of paintings and that she used words as geometric forms to produce nonrepresentational abstractions.[77] In adapting Cubist techniques, Stein is purported by some to have radicalized abstraction well beyond Matisse and Picasso,

to the point of unreadability. Stein's language is said to lack any referentiality; it appears to neither reflect nor communicate anything recognizable in the real world. This is all the more contradictory and perverse, it is claimed, because words are naturally communicative and referential.[78]

Echoing the opinion of Stein's brother, who thought her unable to deal effectively with language, and considered her writing an abomination, generations of critics have considered Stein's experimental writing mere nonsense, an arbitrary juxtaposition of words on the page. Only her simpler and more traditional works (especially *Three Lives* and *The Autobiography of Alice B. Toklas*; fig. 14) are consistently admired and taught as part of the modernist canon. The rest is for the most part skeptically relegated to the dubious sphere of avant-garde word game and Dada. But in the poststructuralist era her experimentation with language has begun to gain acceptance and legitimacy.[79] Stein is now reputed to have arrived at an understanding of language similar to that of deconstructionist and feminist thought.[80] Along these same lines, some have argued that Stein's language, which patriarchy can read as nonsense and nothing else, is instead an antilanguage, because Stein created an unprecedented lesbian writing.[81] According to Shari Benstock, "Sexual expression is intimately linked to linguistic expression."[82] The fluidity and openness of Stein's sexual feelings required a novel and experimental language. Though suggestive and useful, these more recent readings of Stein's experimental style may be as narrow in some respects as previous dismissive readings, and they in fact echo (albeit reversing his value judgment) the older, biographical argument by James Mellow and others that the opacity of Stein's writing represents an effort to disguise her lesbianism.[83]

The need to express her sexuality, and at the same time mask or displace it, is certainly a component of Stein's writing, as it was of Wilde's and Proust's. *The Making of Americans*, a work almost as endless as Proust's *Recherche*, chronicles her family's history in an obsessive, infinitely repetitive continuous present that recalls a hypnotic self-analysis. It is like a conversation with herself, through which she finally is able to cut herself off from her brother and, indeed, her family history. Toklas, whom she met in 1907, began to type the manuscript in 1908 as the two were becoming permanent companions, while tensions increased between Gertrude and Leo. The manuscript was completed in October 1911, and she and Leo decided to "disaggregate" sometime thereafter, never to speak again. Yet Stein's work can hardly be limited to this dimension of sexual self-authorization, nor does it seem appropriate to view her experimental work merely as a misguided attempt to do what contemporary painters were doing. Language is Stein's medium, and even when she is talking about painting and painters, it is language primarily that she is exploring.[84]

The eminently social, conversational setting of the salon from which Stein drew her inspiration and where she invested so much of her energy provides a more complex and comprehensive means to grasp the significance of her work. A reading of the *Portraits* in this context suggests that the talk and conversation *about* and *around* painting, rather than just the formal innovation of the paintings themselves or the private

need to express her sexuality or love for Toklas, fascinated and inspired her.

Stein was an extremely good listener (only after her brother left the rue de Fleurus did she begin to enjoy talking more). She has been blamed for trying to imitate painting with language, thus failing in the task of communication. Yet it was precisely a close study of how communication functions in conversation and through the voice that informed her work. Stein listened and paid attention to all functions of language, and to the interaction between interlocutors. She recorded and classified in notebooks the characteristics of speech of her friends and visitors in the salon, and repetition and sound were the keys to her classification. "I take the conversational side of a number of people," she said, "almost everyone sooner or later has a perfectly determined rhythm in everything they do. It is not so much the words they speak, as the sense of the sound that they produce. That impression is what I have tried to set down."[85]

In a historic article, the linguist Roman Jakobson listed six functions of language: referential, emotive, conative, phatic, metalingual, and poetic.[86] The referential function includes the denotative or cognitive aspects of communication (which early critics accused Stein of obfuscating or ignoring). Jakobson's description of the other communicative functions of language evokes Stein's style and understanding of language so strikingly that it is worth quoting at some length. The emotive function expresses and focuses on the speaker's (or addresser's) attitude toward what he or she is speaking about: in other words, emotions. "It tends to produce an impression of a certain emotion, whether true or feigned," and it is carried by certain inflections and emphasized sounds, or prolongation and repetition of sound. Such emphases are significant, Jakobson argues, for the delivery of a message carries emotive information that is no less valuable, coded, and decipherable than referential information. Jakobson relates how, in an experiment, an actor trained in the Stanislavsky method was able to repeat the same elliptical sentence fifty times, each time with a different delivery and expressive content dictated by a different emotional situation, and each was correctly decoded by an audience. The conative function of language focuses on the addressee, as in vocative or imperative sentences whose function is to call on the addressee or a person do something. Such utterances cannot be challenged by such questions as "Is it true or not?"

After these three principal and commonly recognized linguistic functions, Jakobson identifies the other three. The phatic, which involves the maintenance of verbal communication, consists of ritualized, repetitive formulas ranging from pure sound—"uhm, uhm"—to the Shakespearean "Lend me your ears!" to conversations whose sole purpose is to prolong communication: "'Well!' the young man said. 'Well!' she said. 'Well, here we are,' he said. 'Here we are,' she said. 'Aren't we?' 'I should say we were,' he said. 'Eeyop. Here we are.' 'Well!' she said.' 'Well,' he said, 'well.'" The fifth function is the metalingual function, also repetitive, designed to assure that interlocutors speak the same code and understand each other, as in, "Do you know what I mean?" or any other expression verifying the reliability of the language in use, as in the following exasperating dialogue reported by Jakobson: "'The sophomore was plucked.' 'But what is *plucked?*' '*Plucked* means the same as *flunked*.' 'And *flunked?*' 'To be *flunked* is *to fail an exam*.' 'And what is a *sophomore?*' persists the interrogator innocent of school vocabulary." The final function is the poetic, oriented toward the sound of the language and its materiality: effects of rhyme, paronomasia, alliteration, rhythm, and all else that is the usual domain of poetic form belong here. Jakobson stresses that the poetic function is as much a part of everyday conversation as (more self-consciously) of poetry proper.

Stein's early experimental works, including the *Portraits* (among them, "Ada," "Matisse," and "Picasso"), show that while she may have been underplaying the dominant, immediately recognized referential function, her texts deploy with astounding insight and creativity the other functions of linguistic communication in a conversational setting as identified by Jakobson. Her *Portraits* in particular, through redundancy, repetition, circling back, and their spare and emotively nuanced

vocabulary, create a literary style that stands in opposition to the concise, precise clarity and allusive depth of classic modernist style (for example, that of Eliot's *Four Quartets*). Yet once the conversational setting and the predominance of voice (or rather of a "voice effect") over writing are grasped by the reader as the proper interpretative code through which to read her texts, they acquire a clarity and semantic power of their own that are far more exact than deconstructionist critics would suggest. Although Stein subverts the Symbolist and post-Symbolist conventions for producing meaning through writing (her work has little to do with Imagism's visual suggestiveness and metaphoric allusiveness), her style is hardly a Derridean free play of the signifier; nor does it deal exclusively and self-referentially with writing itself, freeing it from the constrictions of patriarchal meaning. In fact, it is misleading to identify Stein as a deconstructionist, for while deconstruction privileges writing or *écriture*, Stein (like Wilde, and unlike Proust) values voice, sound, orality, and the body more than anything else.

Conversation and repetition perform several roles in Stein that vary over time and from text to text. One of these is to express, in a more gradual, less dramatic way than in Proustian inversion, a perceptual and cognitive relativism. The flow of talk circles and circles and apparently yields no definitive single truth, no ultimate disclosure of a stable meaning. It is the process and the movement of conversation that interest Stein, and the multiple, even contradictory perspectives that, like certain Cubist compositions, it generates. At other times, single words and their sounds are highlighted, rather than the conversational flow. Stein treats words as if they were separate individuals participating in a conversation. And still other times, the role of the reader as listener is underscored. The reader is made a part of a conversation in which he or she must pay attention, follow the thread. The words may be common, but the effects are far from ordinary.

In the "Matisse" portrait, for instance, multiple voices and conversations are suggested by the informal tone, the loose grammatical and syntactical structure, the circling repetition (phatic and metalingual) around compositional nuclei of meaning, and the lack of quotation marks in reported speech: "Some said of him, when anybody believed in him they did not believe in any other one. Certainly some said this of him. He certainly very clearly expressed something. Some said that he did not clearly express anything. Some were certain that he expressed something very clearly. And some of such of them said that he would have been a greater one if he had not been one so clearly expressing. Some said he was not clearly expressing what he was expressing and some of such of them said that the greatness of struggling which was not clear expression made of him one being a completely great one."[87] The mention of "clearly expressing something" is an ironic, metalingual (or metalinguistic) reflection on the text's own style, as well as a pointed reference to the key problem of expressiveness in Matisse's brushstrokes and use of color. Even the use of repetition is ironically thematized ("telling this thing again and again"). The repetition in the last two pages of the portrait of the form "this one," which —unlike the more usual "he"—assumes the actual physical presence of the one being talked about and implicitly pointed to, draws the reader into the conversation about Matisse. The artist himself, who was proud of the clarity of his explanations of his work, is reported to have said of Stein's way of listening when he talked in the salon: "When you listen so carefully to me and so attentively and do not hear a word I say then I do say you are very wicked."[88]

Stein's writing is never a transcription of conversational utterances but an attempt to make a new kind of poetry by incorporating conversational aspects of language and communication that are usually deemed hollow, redundant, or excessive within literary discourse. Like Jakobson, Stein felt that repetition is key to verbal communication and conversation. She also believed that linguistic repetition, or circling back to certain verbal themes, constitutes character and what we think of as the individual, with his or her characteristic traits. The word portraits are based on this conclusion, theorized at the same time in *The Making of Americans:* "Always repeating is all of living, everything that is being is always repeating, more and more

listening to repeating gives me completed understanding. Each one then slowly comes to be a whole one to me, each one slowly comes to be a whole one in me, slowly it sounds louder and louder and louder inside me through my ears and eyes and feelings and the talking there is always in me the repeating that is the whole of each one."[89]

Stein was profoundly engaged with the sound of words, and their emotive and phatic functions. In another word portrait, "Two: Gertrude Stein and Her Brother," she speaks almost entirely with emotive utterance: "In sound coming out of her she was expressing all she was feeling and asking all of saying what she was saying."[90] Her vocabulary is mostly spare and simple, but she composes elaborate phonetic patterns to construct meaning and render character. Emotive and phatic communication, as well as repetition of simple words and phrases, were crucial at 27 rue de Fleurus, where so many languages were blended and so many people (including Picasso and Stein herself) spoke a simplified French. When Stein sat for Picasso's famous portrait in the winter of 1905–6, and their legendary friendship began (spurred by her generous patronage), neither was very conversant in French and Picasso— who apparently never read a word of Stein's writing— knew little or no English. Somehow they communicated, and are supposed to have had animated discussions about art,[91] although it seems that much of the time they listened to Picasso's lover Fernande Olivier reading aloud the classic seventeenth-century fables of Jean de La Fontaine, so that they could both improve their French. In a principally French context, it was especially interesting for Stein to hear and explore the sounds of English in comparison with French, and vice versa.

In her own portrait of Picasso, it is the emotional impact of the artist's strong and rough, yet graceful and charismatic, physical presence and the sense that his work is "a thing," a creation born out of his body, that Stein captures. The body becomes the voice through which Picasso is made to speak and is spoken about: "This one was always having something that was coming out of this one that was a solid thing, a charming thing, a lovely thing, a perplexing thing, a disconcerting thing, a complicated thing, an interesting thing, a disturbing thing, a repellant thing, a very pretty thing. This one was one certainly being one having something coming out of him. This one was one whom some were following. This one was one who was working."[92]

The informality of the rue de Fleurus salon and its linguistic multivoicedness differed considerably from the ritualized, highly allusive style of seventeenth- and eighteenth-century salons, where all practiced the art of polite conversation and were well versed in its complex code. Nevertheless, the conversation in the rue de Fleurus was "polite" in its own way, especially after Leo stopped monopolizing it. Here, too, eroticism was very much part of the linguistic exchange, but decorum was always maintained.[93] Stein and Toklas never took part in Paris's lively and flamboyant lesbian scene, which had its own salons. Stein cut her hair short only in 1927, when she was fifty-three and short hair was considered "modern." She and Toklas guarded their privacy even as they opened their house to a more select group of visitors, which in the 1920s included Ernest Hemingway and Sherwood Anderson, whose own conversational styles were influenced by Stein's. No one spoke openly of Stein's lesbianism, and her most explicit texts remained unpublished until after her death, although many knew about it or sensed it. The real nature of the two women's private relationship remains opaque.[94] Certainly, however, Stein's adoption of a "polite" but "natural" conversational writing style that, while often allusively erotic (especially in *Tender Buttons*), both hides and reveals, disguises and exposes, is linked to the compulsion (felt also by Wilde and Proust) to speak publicly, though in a coded way, of a sexuality that was not yet speakable. The salon, replacing the family, provided a venue for this kind of talk, and was thus where their writing could take form.

The rue de Fleurus salon kept by Stein and Toklas continued to be—like those of Geneviève Straus, Lady Wilde, and Ada Leverson—a place that was neither completely public nor completely private, yet was something of both, and that could provide both intellectual and emotional nourishment for them as well as others.[95] Although she became a mythic figure in her own time, Stein was often, like Wilde and Proust, an object of contempt and resentment because of the widespread perception of her sexuality as deviant and of her writing as meaningless and pretentious. She is often described as someone with a disproportionate ego, male-identified, unnatural, unwomanly. Her use of the salon to displace, and even replace, the patriarchal family and her drawing of inspiration from salon conversation in her own ambitious writing conflated in a startling new way the older, apparently separate roles of salonière and artist. Ada Leverson was also salonière and writer, but her stature is not comparable to Stein's, and her work is usually deemed secondary and imitative as a result of its largely parodic nature. Madame de Staël and Anna de Noailles, also salonières and writers, shared a similar fate in being considered minor, inferior artists, Staël for letting excessive verbosity and romantic talk infect her style, Noailles (despite Proust's admiration) for being too mundane. Lady Wilde's writings are all but forgotten. Stein broke that last, unspoken boundary that separated the feminine salonière from the masculine, original artist, and showed—for the first and probably last time—that one could be both at once.

In the unending conversation in the virtual salon that still thrives around her myth, Stein continues to speak, with different voices, and to show herself with different faces. In a lecture at Yale given in 1951 but published only in 1994, the Russian émigré painter and set designer Pavel Tchelitchew remembered Stein in the 1920s as "extremely maternal," "very feminine, very kind," a friend and protector who was always simple, cordial, and jovial.[96] He comically compared the informal yet reassuring style of Gertrude and Alice's teas in the Montparnasse flat with the old-fashioned salon of Anna de Noailles, Proust's poet friend. By the time Tchelitchew was introduced to her in Paris in 1923, she had become a "very tired figure . . . her face covered with powder, [as if] with dust," a relic of a seemingly very remote past. "She was like Madame Récamier . . . she would lie down and speak about love. . . . I [had] to run away [from her] . . . and go up to Montparnasse."[97]

Biographies

SHIRA BRISMAN

AMALIE BEER
(German, 1767–1854)

Born Malka Liepmann Meyer Wulff, Amalie Beer was the older of two daughters of the wealthy Jewish banker Liepmann Meyer Wulff (1745–1812) and his wife, Esther. Amalie's great-grandfather was Jost Liebmann, a court Jew and an elder of the Jewish community who owned the only government-sanctioned synagogue in Berlin; after his death it was managed by his wife, Esther, until the inauguration of the city's first public synagogue, in 1713. Her ancestors' leadership was a heritage that Amalie Beer would continue during her lifetime as one of the most influential Jewish women in Enlightenment Berlin.

Beer's formal education included French and Italian, as well as singing, which she studied with the master Vincenzo Righini. In 1788, she married Jacob (Juda) Herz Beer (1769–1825), the proprietor of a sugar-beet business who would become the richest man of his generation in Berlin. He was a director of the city's stock exchange; a founder of the Luisenstift charity, which awarded stipends to war orphans, and of a major theater; and an elder of the Jewish community. When this munificent philanthropist died, some six thousand people attended his funeral. The Beers had four sons: Jacob Meyer, later known as the composer Giacomo Meyerbeer (1791–1864); Heinrich (1794–1842); Wilhelm (born Wolff, 1797–1850), a banker and astronomer; and Michael (1800–1833), the first Jewish playwright in the German language.

The Beers' wealth enabled them to affect Jewish life in Berlin in the wake of the Edict of Emancipation.

This body of laws, issued in March 1812, did not award Jews absolute and immediate equality but granted partial freedom by abolishing special taxes, allowing them to change residence more easily, and to occupy professional positions they had long been denied. In return, Jews had to assume fixed family surnames, young Jewish men were required to serve in the army, rabbinic courts were abolished, and community records were to be kept in German. The gauntlet had been thrown down for Jews to meet German society. Many responded to the new laws by Germanizing their Hebrew names: in 1812, Malka became Amalie and Juda became Jacob.

Followers of Moses Mendelssohn, the Beers took part in the modernization of Jewish ritual practice. In 1815, Israel Jacobson led the first Reform service in his apartment: worship included Hebrew liturgy, German singing, organ music, and a sermon in German. Jacobson's service was so popular that it was relocated to the Beers' sumptuous residence on the Spandauer Strasse. For eight years, the Beer synagogue attracted considerable numbers of the city's Jewish population. In 1823 the government forced its termination for fear that Jewish adaptation would prevent conversion to the Lutheran Church.

Amalie Beer's involvement in public affairs and philanthropy was not limited to the Jewish community. She was the only Jew invited to participate in a women's-aid society for wounded soldiers, and in 1816 she was recognized with the Luisenorden decoration (the iconic cross was removed from her medal by order of the king). Beer's largesse continued after her death in the form of generous civic grants stipulated in her will.

The Beers' fortune and activities eased their path to friendship with Berlin's most esteemed society. Amalie presided over a prestigious salon that welcomed leading aristocrats, musicians, and scholars, many of them the city's most famous converted Jews: Rahel Levin Varnhagen and her brother, the writer Ludwig Robert; Abraham and Lea Mendelssohn; the pianist Ignaz Moscheles. Salon visitors were distinct from the attendees of the Beer synagogue. Heinrich Heine is the only person recorded to have attended both.

Florine Stettheimer (detail of illustration on page 206)

Johann Karl Kretschmar
(German, 1769–1847),
Amalie Beer, c. 1803. Oil on
canvas, 38¾ x 28 in.
(98.5 x 71 cm). Stiftung
Stadtmuseum Berlin, Hans-
und-Luise-Richter-Stiftung

Perhaps Beer's greatest legacy, however, was in her three accomplished sons. They studied with the best tutors available: Carl Friedrich Zelter and Bernhard Anselm Weber for music, the famous *maskil* Aaron Wolfssohn for Hebrew and Jewish subjects. The boys also studied German, French, history, and geography. Jacob, recognized as a prodigy when he was a child, gave public concerts from an early age, later studied in Venice, then—as Meyerbeer—moved to Paris and composed such masterpieces of grand opera as *Robert le diable* (1831), *Les Huguenots* (1836), and *Le Prophète* (1849). Wilhelm, who served in the military against the Napoleonic invasion before joining his father's banking house, gained fame as an astronomer and published his observations of Mars and a detailed study of the moon. The youngest son, Michael, wrote poetry and, among other tragedies, *Klytemnestra* and *Der Paria* (*The Pariah*). Like their mother, the Beer sons achieved success without converting.

FANNY HENSEL
(German, 1805–1847)

Fanny Cäcilie (Zippora) Mendelssohn was born into a family that played a decisive role in German Jewish history. Her father, Abraham, was the son of the foremost German Jewish Enlightenment philosopher, Moses Mendelssohn, the leading figure in the cultural assimilation of Jews. Fanny's mother, Lea Salomon, was the granddaughter of the banker and court Jew Daniel Itzig. Lea's aunts, Fanny von Arnstein, Cäcilie von Eskeles, and Sara Levy, each hosted an important salon.

Fanny was born on November 14, 1805, in Hamburg, where her father managed the family banking business. She was the oldest of the Mendelssohn children, followed by Felix (1809–1847), Rebecka (1811–1858), and Paul (1812–1874). All four received a highly cultured education, and began studying piano at an early age under their mother's tutelage, but Fanny and Felix were recognized as the family prodigies. In 1811, with the French invasion of the city, the Mendelssohns left Hamburg for Berlin. Fanny and Felix studied piano with Ludwig Berger, and composition under Carl Friedrich Zelter, director of the Singakademie, an organization dedicated to the preservation and performance of eighteenth-century choral music.

In 1816, Abraham and Lea, concerned that their Judaism would thwart their children's full participation in German culture, had them baptized in a Lutheran church. They themselves did not convert until 1822, and in the following year the family added the surname Bartholdy.

Though both Fanny and Felix showed remarkable talent, Abraham Mendelssohn encouraged only his son to pursue a career, reminding his daughter that music could be for her merely an "ornament" to her duties as wife and mother. The two siblings, who were very close, were separated while Felix traveled Europe composing and performing. They maintained their relationship through letters, in which they frequently exchanged scores, correcting and completing each other's compositions. Felix's pursuit of a musical career

Wilhelm Hensel (German, 1794–1861), *Fanny Hensel née Mendelssohn Bartholdy (1805–1847)*, 1829. Pencil on board, 8¾ x 6¾ in. (22.3 x 16.8 cm). Kupferstichkabinett, Staatliche Museen zu Berlin–Preussischer Kulturbesitz

met with great success. In 1829, at the age of twenty, he directed Johann Sebastian Bach's *Saint Matthew Passion* at the Singakademie; this pioneering performance launched a revival of the Baroque composer's work that captivated German audiences. Felix served as a musical director in Düsseldorf (1833–35) before moving to Leipzig, where he conducted and in 1843 founded the city's Conservatory. He protected his sister by publishing her compositions under his name; his lieder Opus 8 and Opus 9, of 1827, for example, included six songs by Fanny. When he met Queen Victoria in 1846 and she asked him to sing "Italien" (Opus 8, No. 3), Felix admitted to the monarch that it was his sister who had composed her favorite song.

In 1821, Fanny met her future husband, the court painter Wilhelm Hensel (1794–1861). They married in 1829 and had a son, Sebastian Ludwig Felix, the next year. Hensel, more supportive of Fanny's musical activities than her father, encouraged her to compose and to organize *Sonntagsmusiken*. These Sunday musicales, initiated in 1823 by the Mendelssohn parents

and led by Fanny beginning in 1831, were held at the Mendelssohns' mansion at 3 Leipziger Strasse. Each concert drew scores of Berlin's celebrated musicians and intellectuals, and attracted visiting performers such as Franz Liszt, Niccolò Paganini, and Clara Schumann. Within this domestic space, Fanny was able to play, conduct, and present her own compositions.

In 1838 she gave the only public performance of her life, presenting Felix's Piano Concerto No. 1 in G Minor at a philanthropic event. Her sojourn in Italy in 1839–40 with her husband and their son inspired her to continue her creative efforts. She met the composers Charles Gounod, Hector Berlioz, and Jules Massenet, all of whom were impressed with her intellect and musical talents. Upon returning to Berlin, she began the composition of *Das Jahr*, a series of piano pieces, one for each month of the year. In 1846, with the encouragement of her friend Robert von Keudell and the consent of Felix, Fanny published Six Songs (Opus 1) under her own name. Four Songs for Piano (Opus 2), Six Songs for Soprano, Alto, Tenor, and Bass (Garden Songs, Opus 3), and Six Melodies for Piano (Opus 4 and Opus 5) were published subsequently, and Fanny was encouraged to compose on a larger scale. Her Trio in D Minor for violin, cello, and piano premiered at her salon. Fanny died of a stroke on May 14, 1847, after rehearsing her brother's *Walpurgisnacht*. Felix's death followed almost seven months later.

HENRIETTE HERZ
(German, 1764–1847)

Henriette Herz was born on September 5, 1764. She was the oldest of the five daughters and two sons of Benjamin de Lemos, a cultured man of Portuguese descent and one of the foremost Jewish doctors in Berlin, and his wife, Esther. The de Lemos household was run according to the laws of Jewish Orthodoxy, with a strong emphasis on secular education. German was spoken in the home, and Henriette was tutored in writing, arithmetic, and geography. She particularly excelled in languages and in the course of her life studied French, English, Spanish, Italian, Greek,

Wilhelm Hensel (German, 1794–1861), *Henriette Herz*, 1823. Pencil on cardboard, 5⅛ x 4⅜ in (12.9 x 11 cm). Kupferstichkabinett, Staatliche Museen zu Berlin–Preussischer Kulturbesitz

Hebrew, Portuguese, Swedish, Turkish, Latin, and Sanskrit. For her linguistic gifts, social charms, charitable heart, and not least her exquisite beauty, Henriette Herz was one of the most renowned Jewish women of Enlightenment Berlin.

In 1779 the fifteen-year-old Henriette married Markus Herz (1747–1803), a physician and philosopher who had studied under Immanuel Kant. Their house became the rendezvous for Berlin's most celebrated artists, writers, scientists, and diplomats, who gathered to hear Markus lecture and to admire Henriette's intelligence, wit, and captivating looks. Under her husband's supervision she continued with languages and studied literature and science. Both Henriette and Markus were members of selective intellectual clubs whose members gathered to dine and discuss recent literature and science. Henriette hosted her own secret club, the Tugendbund, or League of Virtue, founded in 1787, which included Wilhelm von Humboldt and Dorothea Veit (later Schlegel), Moses Mendelssohn's daughter. Members of this exclusive society addressed one another with the informal *du* and made a pact to seek "moral perfection."

In January 1803, Markus Herz died, leaving Henriette to support her sister and mother. Though she received offers to remarry, the proposals stipulated her conversion to Christianity, which Herz refused to do while her mother was alive. She kept close friendships with the men whom she had met through her husband. In 1802 the young Ludwig Börne (then Löb Baruch) had moved to the Herz home to study medicine with Markus. After the doctor's death, Börne found himself in the awkward position of being in love with Herz; she tactfully deflected his passion and sent him to study in Halle. Herz kept up an epistolary relationship with Alexander von Humboldt, who, in 1845, with her finances waning, appealed to Frederick William IV on her behalf. The king doubled the pension that Humboldt had requested for her and visited her home, where he nostalgically recalled the golden age of her salon. Herz's most intimate friendship was with Friedrich Schleiermacher, who had made daily visits to the Herz home since 1794 and whom she encouraged in his writing. After Markus Herz's death, the bond between the theologian and the statuesque beauty aroused the suspicions of Berlin's gossip-hungry society, but the relationship was never other than platonic.

Herz spent most of her life in Berlin, traveling infrequently. In 1810 she went to Dresden and met Goethe, who had been a subject of discussion at her salon. In 1811 she visited Dorothea Schlegel, Fanny von Arnstein, and Cäcilie von Eskeles in Vienna. Her longest journey was to Italy, where she stayed from 1817 to 1819.

In 1817, after her mother died, Henriette converted to Christianity, joining friends who had renounced their Judaism for Protestantism. While she struggled financially in widowhood, she was forever hospitable and charitable. When she died, on October 22, 1847, she left little in the way of a literary legacy. Two works on travel that she translated with Schleiermacher in 1799 and 1800 survive, but she herself destroyed her two novels and most of her extensive correspondence.

ANNA KULISCIOFF

(Russian, c. 1855–1925)

Anna Kuliscioff was born Anja Moiseevna Rozenstein, near Simferopol in the Crimea, between 1854 and 1857. Her father, Moisei, was a wealthy merchant. Although one contemporary source claims that the family converted to Eastern Orthodox Catholicism, there is no proof. As a girl, Kuliscioff studied foreign languages with private tutors. In 1871 she left Russia to study in Zurich, where she fell in with exiled revolutionaries and absorbed the teachings of the anarchist Mikhail Bakunin and the populist Pyotr Lavrov. She married Pyotr Markelovic Macarevich in 1873 and returned with him to Russia. In 1874, Macarevich was sentenced to five years' hard labor for his anarchist activities. To avoid incarceration in Odessa, Kuliscioff fled the city, never to see her husband again. In Kiev, she worked with radicals associated with the Zemlya i Volya (Land and Liberty) party, who fomented peasant uprisings and resorted to terrorist acts against the tsarist authorities. When her colleagues in this armed group were detained,

Kuliscioff again barely escaped arrest. In the summer of 1876 she traveled to Switzerland to retrieve a small press for propaganda printing. Tsarist police kept close watch on her; she lived clandestinely in Kiev and Kharkov, often singing in parks to earn money. In April 1877, using a false passport, she left her native land for the last time. She remained in contact with her father, who, even with her disavowal of family past and religion, continued to send her funds.

Kuliscioff's early exile was spent in Switzerland, England, and France. In late 1877 in Paris, she began an affair with Andrea Costa, an Italian anarchist and follower of Bakunin. During their eight-year romance, they were separated by periods of imprisonment and exile. The year they met, Kuliscioff was arrested in Paris; a revolver was found among her personal belongings. Police records for this arrest are the first documentation of her as "Kuliscioff," an invented surname that identified her with the working class. After her liberation—only by the intercession of the writer Ivan Turgenev—and expulsion from France, where Costa was imprisoned, Kuliscioff went to Switzerland. In September 1879, she was arrested with other radicals in Florence by Italian authorities. After thirteen months in prison, she was acquitted of charges of subversion against the state, in a case that gained her notoriety in the press. During the various periods in prison, Kuliscioff contracted tuberculosis; she later developed a crippling bone disease, either rheumatoid arthritis or tuberculosis of the bone.

Although she was expelled from Italy, Kuliscioff moved between there and Switzerland, aiding Costa, who was based again in his hometown of Imola, in the Socialist cause. In December 1881, she gave birth to their daughter, Andreina; two months later, expelled yet again from Italy, she began medical studies in Bern, against Costa's wishes. In 1884, for health reasons, she went to Naples, where, despite poverty, she pursued her medical studies. Costa, who had been elected the first Socialist deputy to parliament, visited her occasionally from Rome. Kuliscioff received her degree from the University of Naples in 1886; she took courses also in Turin and Pavia to complete her specialization in obstetrics and gynecology. She opened a medical practice in Milan that attended to working women and the poor but left it in 1891 to devote herself to politics and because of her deteriorating health.

What she had failed to attain in her relationship with the patriarchal Costa, Kuliscioff found with Filippo Turati (1857–1932), whom she met in 1885. A Milanese lawyer and published poet, Turati converted to orthodox Socialism under Kuliscioff's influence. In 1889, they established the Milanese Socialist League, which evolved into the Italian Socialist Party (Partito Socialista Italiano, or PSI) three years later. In 1891, they launched *Critica Sociale,* the party's journal, for which they wrote many articles together. Their apartment near the Duomo was home to Italy's most vibrant political salon for some three decades, and until World War I, they led the reformist wing of the PSI. In 1898, they were arrested for abetting a widespread workers' revolt; they were released after serving partial sentences. During their separation they initiated a correspondence of historical importance that would last for more than twenty-five years. After Turati was elected to the Chamber of Deputies in 1906, he spent long periods away from Milan. Kuliscioff's daughter married Luigi Gavazzi, from an established Catholic family, in 1904; they had five children, on whom Kuliscioff doted. She sanguinely viewed Andreina's comfortable bourgeois life as a "historical balance" for her own rebellious youth and suffering.

In Milan, Kuliscioff joined an older generation of Italian feminists led by Anna Maria Mozzoni. Kuliscioff advocated zealously for women working in fields and factories, whose deprivations she had witnessed as a medical doctor and as a union organizer. Her lecture "The Monopoly of Man," delivered at the Circolo Filologico in Milan in 1890, was an influential feminist tract upon its immediate publication. Kuliscioff's lobbying led to labor laws enacted in 1902 to protect women and children; her own articles for *Critica Sociale* linked class struggle and women's emancipation, after the model of August Bebel and Clara Zetkin in Germany. Kuliscioff never hesitated to point out the PSI's hypocritical position on women workers and female suffrage.

In 1912 she founded *La Difesa delle Lavoratrici (The Defense of Women Workers),* the official periodical of the National Organization of Socialist Women. She fought tirelessly for her own party to support the vote for women of all classes; after much internal debate the PSI proposed such an amendment, but it was rejected in 1912 in the Chamber of Deputies.

Soon after, the Revolutionary Socialist Benito Mussolini, whom Kuliscioff came to loathe, assumed control of the PSI and became editor of the party newspaper *Avanti!*. The outbreak of World War I further divided the Socialists between neutralists, including Turati, and interventionists, led by Mussolini. A pragmatist, Kuliscioff realized correctly that dissent over intervention would split the party for good, and in the postwar years she continually urged seizing on workers' revolts and abandoning gradual reforms in favor of decisive political change. She lived long enough to see Mussolini's appointment as prime minister on the wave of parliamentary crises and then his seizure of absolute power in 1925. The PSI was outlawed, along with all opposition, shortly before her death that December. The next year Turati left Italy for Paris, where he would die in exile in 1932.

ADA LEVERSON
(British, 1862–1933)

Ada Esther Beddington was born in London on October 10, 1862, the oldest of eight children in a prosperous Jewish family. Her mother, Zillah, was a pianist who had studied under the celebrated Theodor Leschetizky, and her father, Samuel, was a wool merchant. Ada discovered a passion for literature at an early age; her appetite for novels and poetry in English was supplemented by private tutoring in French, German, Latin, and Greek.

In 1881, Ada married a diamond merchant twelve years her senior, Ernest Leverson, who came from an assimilated Jewish family. Ada was eager to escape parental control; her father disapproved of the marriage. The couple lived at Courtfield Gardens in South Kensington and later on Deanery Street in the fashion-

Ada Leverson. Collection of
Francis Wyndham, London

able Mayfair district. They had two children: George,
born in 1888, who died at five months, of meningitis;
and Violet, born in 1890, who published her mother's
biography, *The Sphinx and Her Circle*, in 1963. The
marriage was strained—Ernest traveled often on business and in his spare time enjoyed gambling. Leverson's
feelings of neglect and her sense of being imprisoned
by the social mores of marriage led her to forge intimate bonds with others. Over the course of her marriage she had liaisons, albeit short-lived, with William
Cuffe, fourth Earl of Desart, and George Moore,
both writers.

Yet it was in her friendships that Leverson found
true intimacy. Endowed with a sharp wit and a gift for
clever conversation, she captivated the great figures
of the aesthetic movement in Britain. Her salon drew
eccentric guests who shared in their criticism of the
parochial tastes, stuffiness, and social prejudices associated with bourgeois Victorian values. Leverson's
coquettish fashions and conversational prowess attracted

dandies, dilettantes, and satirists including Aubrey
Beardsley, Max Beerbohm, Walter Sickert, Charles
Conder, and the causes célèbres Lord Alfred Douglas
and Oscar Wilde.

The satirical social commentary that animated
these private gatherings, especially the dialogue
between Leverson and Wilde, permeated the public
sphere in the artistic output of this circle. Upon meeting
at a party in 1892, the two were immediately friends;
Wilde called her "the wittiest woman in the world"
and gave her the nickname "Sphinx." He encouraged
Leverson to carry their verbal exchanges to print, and
her writings appeared during the 1890s in the journals
Punch and *Black and White*. Several of her contributions
were parodies of Wilde, such as "An Afternoon Party"
(a spoof of *The Picture of Dorian Gray*, in *Punch*, July
15, 1893) and "The Minx" (a spoof of "The Sphinx,"
Punch, July 21, 1894). So deft was she at lampooning
the work of her friend that when Robert Hichens's
satire of Wilde, *The Green Carnation*, appeared anonymously in 1894, it was initially attributed to her.

In May 1895, when he was released on bail after
the first of two criminal trials for "homosexual acts,"
Ada and Ernest welcomed Wilde into their home and
offered financial support when the rest of London
ostracized him. After his death, Leverson devoted
several years to memoirs of him; her reminiscences
were included in the volume *Letters to the Sphinx from
Oscar Wilde*, published in 1930.

In 1902, Ernest Leverson's poor investments
brought the couple into financial distress and they separated permanently. Ernest moved to Canada, where he
lived until his death in 1922, and Ada moved to Radnor
Place, near her parents' home. Though desolate over
the loss of her dearest friends—Beardsley had died in
1898, Wilde two years later—and no longer able to
afford entertaining (or the luxurious dresses she had
once enjoyed), Leverson maintained a keen interest in
the avant-garde literary scene and continued her writing career. She had contacts with T. S. Eliot, Katherine
Mansfield, and Wyndham Lewis through her sister
Violet and brother-in-law Sydney Schiff, whose home
in the early part of the twentieth century became

what Leverson's had been in the "Naughty Nineties." Between 1907 and 1916, Leverson published six novels, including the trilogy *The Little Ottleys*, written with a cleverness that belies a profound understanding of human relationships.

The period after World War I was difficult for Leverson. She grew increasingly hard-of-hearing and forsook her fashionable dress for black garb. She did, however, preserve strong friendships with Edith, Osbert, and Sacheverell Sitwell and other distinctive voices of the literary scene. Leverson died of influenza on August 30, 1933.

MARGHERITA SARFATTI
(Italian, 1880–1961)

Margherita Grassini was born on April 8, 1880, the fourth and last child of Emma Levi and Amedeo Grassini. An acculturated and wealthy Jewish family, the Grassinis lived in a fifteenth-century palazzo on the edge of the Old Ghetto of Venice until 1894, when they moved to the imposing Palazzo Bembo on the Grand Canal. Margherita's grandfather Marco Grassini, a successful banker, was an activist in the unification of Italy after Austrian rule, and served as mayor of the town of Conegliano. Her father, a Sephardi who worshipped at an Ashkenazi synagogue, was a fiscal attorney for the Venetian government; in 1890 he became, as his father had been, a knight of the Crown of Italy. He was also friend and adviser to Giuseppe Sarto, the anti-Socialist cleric who would become Pope Pius X. The British writer Israel Zangwill based his short story "Chad Gadya" (1898)—about the younger generation's estrangement from Judaism—on a seder he had attended with the Grassini family in the mid-1890s. On her mother's side, Margherita was a cousin of the biologist (and later anti-Fascist) Giuseppe Levi, father of the writer Natalia Ginzburg. Margherita's sister Colomba (Lina) killed herself in 1907 after being widowed, and her other sister, Nella, would perish with her husband, Paolo Errera, on the way to Auschwitz in 1944.

Margherita was educated by an impressive trio of private tutors: the historian Pietro Orsi, the Venetian expert Pompeo Molmenti, and Antonio Fradeletto, the founding director of the Venice Biennale, who introduced her to John Ruskin, European writers, and antipositivist philosophers. In 1898, over her father's objections, she married Cesare Sarfatti, an attorney from Padua thirteen years her senior, whom she persuaded to join the Socialist Party (Partito Socialista Italiano, or PSI). During their honeymoon in Paris, they visited the dealer Clovis Sagot, from whom Margherita purchased a set of lithographs and posters by Henri de Toulouse-Lautrec—her first acquisition of Post-Impressionist art. She published her initial art reviews in 1901 and would go on to be among the most prolific critics in Europe between the world wars. The Sarfattis settled in the Brera district in Milan in 1902 to promote Cesare's career in the Socialist Party and further Margherita's entrée into avant-garde groups. They had three children, Roberto, Amedeo, and Fiammetta. Sarfatti came into a large inheritance with the death of her father in 1908; the family moved to a spacious residence at corso Venezia 93, and the next year Sarfatti began her Wednesday-evening salon. She also purchased a country house, Il Soldo (The Penny), in Cavallasca near Lake Como, where she entertained many of the same writers and artists who frequented the Milan salon.

Sarfatti met Benito Mussolini in 1912, and by the next year they were lovers. Their intimate relationship, which lasted almost twenty years, was seemingly tolerated by her husband but not by Mussolini's wife, Rachele, who despised Sarfatti. Together Mussolini and Sarfatti founded and wrote for a number of political journals, through which they articulated his Revolutionary Socialist platform, then his estrangement from the Socialist Party with the outbreak of World War I, and, finally, the founding of Fascism. Sarfatti formulated her own agenda for a stridently nationalist, if modernist, art during the war years, drawing on artists in the Futurist orbit. With the beginning of the war, her son Roberto, who was underage, ran off to join the Italian army. He was ordered home, and at seventeen legally enlisted in the Alpini, elite mountain troops. Killed in 1918 while leading an attack on the Austrian front lines,

he was awarded Italy's highest military honor. His tomb at Col d'Echele was designed by the Rationalist architect Giuseppe Terragni.

Sarfatti's salon became the center of a return to order in art and literature in the postwar years and gave birth to the Novecento (Twentieth Century) movement. During the 1920s, before the implementation of the Fascist fine-art syndicates and centralized exhibition system, she set the agenda for the regime's cultural policies. She never advocated provincialism or retrograde classical revivals, and she maintained professional contacts in France, where she had traveled annually since 1910. In 1925, she served as vice-president of the international jury and in several other capacities at the International Exposition of Modern Decorative and Industrial Arts in Paris; she was awarded the medal of the Legion of Honor for her participation. Her exposure to Constructivist and International Style architecture led her to spearhead the reorganization of the Monza Biennale, an exhibition of regional folkloric crafts, into the Milan Triennale, an industrial and applied-arts

display, by 1930. She was also a staunch defender of Rationalist architecture in Italy.

Cesare Sarfatti died in 1924, and Margherita moved to Rome, where she held her salon on Friday afternoons. In 1925, she published *The Life of Benito Mussolini* (it appeared first in English), a personal memoir and biography of the Duce that was translated into eighteen languages. In 1928, she converted to Catholicism, in the wake of Mussolini's anti-Zionist, anti-Semitic statements, and the year before he signed the Lateran Pact with the Vatican, making Catholicism the national religion of Italy. Until the outbreak of the Ethiopian war in 1935, Sarfatti shaped Mussolini's image in the press in the United States. She fostered relationships with American journalists and published articles for William Randolph Hearst's periodicals under Mussolini's name. She was, however, deeply fearful of the Duce's 1936 alliance with Nazi Germany.

On July 14, 1938, "The Manifesto of the Race" was published in the Roman newspaper *Il giornale d'Italia;* Mussolini was the primary author of the document, which condemned the corruption of the Italian Aryan race through intermarriage with Jews. Recognizing this as a prelude to persecution, Sarfatti fled first to Paris, then to Uruguay and Argentina. In 1947, after almost a decade in exile, she returned to Rome. Over the course of her life, Sarfatti published twenty-four books and hundreds of articles. These include numerous works of art criticism, as well as *I vivi e l'ombra* (1921), a compilation of elegiac poetry commemorating her son Roberto; further reflections on her former lover the dictator, *Mussolini As I Knew Him* (1945); and an unapologetic autobiography, *Acqua passata* (1955).

GERTRUDE STEIN
(American, 1874–1946)

The youngest of Daniel and Amelia Stein's five children, Gertrude was born in Allegheny, Pennsylvania, on February 3, 1874. Both her parents were the offspring of German immigrants who had settled in Baltimore; Daniel Stein was a successful businessman

Alvin Langdon Coburn
(American, 1882–1966),
Gertrude Stein, 1913. Gelatin-
silver print, 3½ x 4¾ in.
(9 x 12 cm). George Eastman
House, Rochester, New York

coterie of artists, critics, and collectors would gather at
their home. Stein's literary experiments with unhinged
syntax and word repetition found complement in the
radical Cubist language of salon habitués Pablo Picasso
and Georges Braque. As Americans, the Steins drew
fellow expatriates in Paris, among them the artists
Marsden Hartley, Maurice Sterne, and Alfred Maurer,
who were intent on absorbing the latest trends in
modernism.

In 1907, Gertrude met Alice B. Toklas, a San
Francisco native who had fled to Paris after her mother's death from cancer. Toklas approved of Gertrude's
writing more than did Leo, who argued with his sister
about Picasso's genius and treated her literary achievements with indifference. By 1909, Toklas had moved
into the rue de Fleurus and begun to transcribe Stein's
Three Lives, a portrait of three working-class women
(published later that year), and her pastiche of artistic
personalities, *The Making of Americans* (published in
1925). Stein's literary portraits of Henri Matisse and
Picasso appeared in 1912 in Alfred Stieglitz's *Camera
Work*, and her experimental novel *Tender Buttons* was
issued in 1914. The American press lambasted her inac-
cessibility, and for the next twenty years Stein would
struggle to find publishers willing to risk the ridicule
that her obscure style often invited. In 1913, Leo left
Paris for Italy, breaking with Gertrude over her self-
proclaimed importance and his changing tastes in art.
They divided their collection, Leo taking the Renoirs
and several Cézannes and leaving Gertrude with most
of the Picassos. Toklas was now Gertrude's companion,
editor, and typist, and co-hostess of what had become
the most famous salon in the French capital.

The two women spent the first year of World
War I in London and Spain. They returned to Paris
in 1916 and joined the American Fund for French
Wounded, delivering supplies to hospitals in a Ford
van. After the war, Stein's salon was the outpost for
the "Lost Generation"—exiles from the American
literary scene, suffering from postwar disillusionment.
Her reputation attracted, among others, Sherwood
Anderson, Ernest Hemingway, F. Scott Fitzgerald,
Carl Van Vechten, and Virgil Thomson. In 1933, she

and banker. Gertrude's early childhood was spent in
Vienna, Paris, and California. In 1891, her father died,
and her oldest brother, Michael, assumed the family
patriarchy. Stein matriculated at Harvard Annex (later
Radcliffe College) in 1893; there she became a favorite
pupil of William James, whose philosophies of pragma-
tism and radical empiricism affected her profoundly.
After graduation in 1897, she enrolled at Johns Hopkins
University medical school, but she left before completing her degree. It was here that Stein became increasingly aware of her lesbianism. Her thinly veiled account
of her frustrated relationships with women was later
transmuted into the novel *Q.E.D.* (written in 1903 and
published posthumously in 1950 as *Things As They Are*).

In 1902, Stein left America to join her brother Leo,
who had moved to Europe to study art and philosophy.
The following year, the two began living together in
Paris at 27 rue de Fleurus. Leo became a passionate
collector of avant-garde painting, buying works by
Édouard Manet, Auguste Renoir, Paul Cézanne, Paul
Gauguin, Pablo Picasso, and Henri Matisse, and inspiring his brother Michael and sister-in-law Sally, as well
as Gertrude, to do likewise. Around 1905, Gertrude
and Leo instituted Saturday as the *jour fixe* on which a

published *The Autobiography of Alice B. Toklas*, in which she assumes the voice of her companion to narrate her own biography. Linear in narrative and accessible in style, this was her most successful work, and the first to bring her significant royalties. In 1934, for the U.S. premiere of the opera *Four Saints in Three Acts* (featuring her words, music by Thomson, and sets and costumes by Florine Stettheimer), Stein returned to her homeland for the first time in some thirty years. A lecture tour, from October 1934 through May 1935, demonstrated how her fame had spread in the United States. Upon her return to Paris, Stein began the second volume of her memoirs, *Everybody's Autobiography*, which was published in 1937.

For most of World War II, Stein and Toklas, both Jews and lesbians, suspended their sociable city life for a quiet period protected by neighbors in Bilignin, in the south of France. While other Jews were rounded up, Stein and Toklas remained untouched by the German army, sheltered by Bernard Faÿ, Stein's friend and translator, who had connections with the Vichy government, and by the mayor and villagers of Culoz, near Bilignin. Stein published two novels in 1941, *Ida* and *Mrs. Reynolds,* the latter an analysis of life under the dictatorships of Hitler and Stalin. She returned with Toklas to Paris in 1944 to find that their paintings had survived unharmed. After the war, Stein issued her reflections on the period in Bilignin, *Wars I Have Seen* (1945), and *Brewsie and Willie* (1946), a light account of the American GIs she and Toklas had entertained and supported after the liberation.

Stein died of stomach cancer on July 27, 1946. Toklas outlived her by twenty-one years, during which she managed her companion's literary estate. When she died in 1967, Toklas was buried in the plot next to Stein's in Père-Lachaise cemetery.

FLORINE STETTHEIMER
(American, 1871–1944)

Born to a wealthy New York German Jewish family on August 29, 1871, Florine Stettheimer was the second youngest of Joseph and Rosetta Stettheimer's five chil-dren. Her mother was the daughter of Jewish immigrants from Germany and Amsterdam, and her father's family had immigrated to Rochester, New York, from Germany in the mid-nineteenth century. Early in Florine's childhood Joseph abandoned the family, leaving his wife to raise Stella, Carrie, Walter, Florine, and Ettie; Rosetta took the children to Europe, where they lived in Munich, Berlin, and Stuttgart with her father's relatives.

In 1890, the family returned to New York. Stella and Walter both married and moved to California. Carrie, Florine, and Ettie remained with their mother and never married. Rosetta's inheritance from her prosperous parents (and support from sisters who had married into the prominent Jewish Weill, Seligman, and Neustadter families) ensured that the daughters could live well without having to work. Carrie, the oldest of the three, who wore stylish skirts and hats and favored the couture of Paul Poiret, organized their salon evenings and menus. From around 1920 on, she assembled an elaborate dollhouse, which is now at the Museum of the City of New York. Ettie, the youngest, received a B.A. and an M.A. from Barnard in 1898, and a Ph.D. in philosophy from the University of Freiburg in 1908, and published two novels, *Philosophy* (1917) and *Love Days* (1923), under the pseudonym Henrie Waste (an acronym of her birth name, *Henrie*tta *Wa*lter *Stet*theimer).

Florine's artistic training began in 1892 at Manhattan's Art Students League. She visited museums and galleries and painted during her European sojourn with her mother and sisters between 1898 and 1914. When they returned to New York on the outbreak of war, they took an apartment on West Seventy-sixth Street. For the next two decades the Stettheimer salon drew an international mix of European émigrés, New York intellectuals, and art world luminaries. In 1926, the weekly gatherings moved with the Stettheimers to their new residence at the Alwyn Court on West Fifty-eighth Street, and in the summers to André Brook, an estate in Tarrytown. Florine also welcomed visitors at her studio in a Beaux Arts building on West Fortieth Street.

Florine's exhibition at the Knoedler gallery in 1916 was the first and last solo show of her life; having sold no paintings and received only tepid reviews, and deeming her private world of friends and family the appropriate audience and subject of her work, Florine largely retreated from public scrutiny beyond her controlled company. The Stettheimer salon and its attendees became both the inspiration for her paintings and the venue for showing her work. Aside from painting, Florine designed decoratively carved frames and furniture, and wrote poetry. Her verse captures intimate moments with family and friends, and critically observes a capitalistic art world: "Art is spelled with a Capital A / And Capital also backs it— / Ignorance also makes it sway / The chief thing is to make it pay."

Stettheimer's most public endeavor was her design of the costumes and sets for the opera *Four Saints in Three Acts* (1934), a collaboration with the composer Virgil Thomson and Gertrude Stein as librettist. Although her coterie of friends encouraged her to exhibit, Stettheimer participated only in select group shows and was known almost exclusively to her intimate circle. Not until after her death was she given

due attention in solo exhibits. The first, in 1946 at the Museum of Modern Art, was arranged by Marcel Duchamp, with a catalogue by Henry McBride; after smaller shows, mostly at university art galleries, Stettheimer was credited with a major retrospective at the Whitney Museum of American Art in 1995.

Rosetta Stettheimer died in 1935, and Florine, craving independence and the opportunity to focus on her painting, broke with her sisters and moved permanently into her studio. When she died, on May 11, 1944, her will stipulated that her works be either burned or sold but not given away. Carrie died six weeks after Florine, and Ettie, who outlived her sisters by eleven years, preserved Florine's legacy by donating her paintings (against her wishes) to major American museums. She also edited her letters and diaries, excising any content she deemed offensive before bequeathing these to Columbia and Yale universities. In 1949 she published a collection of Florine's poems, *Crystal Flowers*. A year earlier, from a boat on the Hudson River, Ettie and Joseph Solomon, the family lawyer, had scattered Florine's ashes to the wind.

GENEVIÈVE STRAUS
(French, 1849–1926)

Geneviève Halévy was born on February 27, 1849, in Paris. Her mother, Léonie Rodrigues-Henriques, was a sculptor and art collector of Portuguese Jewish descent. Her father, Fromental Halévy, was permanent secretary of the Académie des Beaux-Arts and the renowned composer of thirty-two operas, including *La Juive* (1835), a tragedy of religious intolerance between Christians and Jews. His nephew Ludovic Halévy, a novelist and librettist, collaborated with Henri Meilhac on operas of Jacques Offenbach. Geneviève Halévy and her older sister, Esther (born in 1843), studied piano with Charles Gounod. The death of Geneviève's father in 1862 and her sister in 1864 precipitated a chronic melancholy, which was eventually mitigated by the creation of her salon.

Geneviève had met her father's brilliant protégé Georges Bizet at one of her parents' soirées; although her family initially opposed her union to a man of hum-

ble economic origins, the two were married in 1869. Geneviève dismissed the possibility of converting to Bizet's Catholicism, claiming that she had "trop peu de religion pour en changer" (too little religion to change it). They lived at 22 rue de Douai with their son, Jacques (born in 1872), and with Geneviève's cousin Ludovic Halévy; his wife, Valentine; and their two sons, Élie and Daniel. The Bizets' marriage suffered because of their precarious finances, which were exacerbated by the economic chaos of the Franco-Prussian War. Geneviève's fragile nerves and her mother's declining mental health only heightened the tensions.

Mere months after the premiere of his opera *Carmen* in 1875, Georges Bizet died of cardiac arrest; Geneviève was left widowed at the age of twenty-six. Bizet's fame grew posthumously, and Geneviève inherited the fortunes of his success, as well as the rights to her father's oeuvre after her mother's death in 1884. She drew to her home a group of intimate friends whose company staved off her depression, and her salon soon widened in scope and ambition. In 1886, she married Émile Straus, a wealthy lawyer to the Rothschild family and an avid art collector. The couple moved first to 134 boulevard Haussmann, and in 1898 to 104 rue de Miromesnil. In 1893, the construction was finished on their villa, Le Clos des Mûriers, in Trouville, where Geneviève spent many summers.

The Straus drawing room in Paris, decorated with paintings by Jean-Marc Nattier, Georges de La Tour, and Claude Monet, attracted an elegant society of artists, politicians, and nobility that captivated the young Marcel Proust, a schoolmate of Geneviève's son. Over the years of their friendship she served as Proust's muse and literary confidante. In letters to her he ruminated about the shape of his characters and the quality of his prose. In 1908, Geneviève gave Proust a gift of five small notebooks, in which he began to sketch the fragments of his novel *À la recherche du temps perdu* (*In Search of Lost Time*); she provided one of the models for the Duchesse de Guermantes. Her refined elegance and melancholic air were immortalized on canvas by Gustave Moreau, Giovanni Boldini, Auguste Toulemouche, and Jules-Élie Delaunay, and in the pages of Edmond de Goncourt's journals and Guy de Maupassant's *Notre coeur* (*Our Heart*).

In 1894, the French military captain Alfred Dreyfus, a Jew, was charged with espionage against the government. In October 1897, Joseph Reinach, a politician, lawyer, and longtime friend of Geneviève's, announced at her salon that Major Ferdinand Walsin-Esterhazy was the author of the seditious bordereau accusing Dreyfus; upon hearing this defense of Dreyfus, salon habitués Edgar Degas, Jules Lemaître, and Jean-Louis Forain left indignantly, never to return. Geneviève Straus's salon became the center for pro-Dreyfus forces. Émile Zola, a regular attendee, published his "J'Accuse" in the journal *L'Aurore* on January 13, 1898; this fierce call for justice was supported the next day by the "Manifesto of the Intellectuals," signed by Proust, Élie and Daniel Halévy, Jacques Bizet, and others. The Dreyfus Affair, which challenged the status and identity of assimilated Jews, brought politics into Straus's salon, at the cost of broken friendships and turmoil.

After World War I, the salon, well past its heyday, gathered loyal friends of a time past, including the writers Louis Ganderax and Abel Hermant and such promising literary figures as Julien Benda and André

Gide. On November 3, 1922, Jacques Bizet committed suicide; his death was followed fifteen days later by the death of his mother's beloved Proust. Geneviève Straus died on December 22, 1926. Her obituary by Robert de Flers appeared the next day in *Le Figaro:* "With her departs an incomparable woman, unique, with infinite grace and a supreme spirit. . . . Madame Straus's salon gathered five generations of the most celebrated and distinguished artists and men of letters. Here she reigned . . . in the tradition of the *maîtresses de maison* who by their very presence create around them an atmosphere of intelligence, wit, taste, tact, warmth, and trust."

RAHEL LEVIN VARNHAGEN VON ENSE
(German, 1771–1833)

Rahel Levin was born in Berlin on May 12, 1771, the oldest child of Markus Levin and his wife, Chaie. Her father, a wealthy banker and jewelry merchant who ranked with Daniel Itzig and Veitel Ephraim as one of Berlin's privileged Jews, ruled his household in a despotic manner, and when he died in 1790, Rahel assumed responsibility for the education of her siblings and emotional support of the family. Her brother Markus (1772–1826) inherited his father's business and provided for Rahel and their younger siblings, Liepmann (1778–1832), better known as the writer Ludwig Robert; Rose (1781–1840), who married a Dutch lawyer, Carl Asser; and Moritz (b. 1785).

Financially dependent as she was, Rahel Levin felt pressure to marry, yet she found the convention of marriage unsuited to her identity as a freethinker. Before her father's death she had received an education in Hebrew, German, and French, as well as piano, dancing, and sewing. She continued to study languages, philosophy, literature, and music on her own. Her correspondence with David Veit, Rebecca Friedländer, and the actress Pauline Wiesel exemplifies her "dialogical" epistolary style, in which she involved her readers in a dynamic exchange of ideas. Particularly in her letters of 1793–96 to Veit, a young Jewish medical student, she mused on the meaning of Jewishness and on the psychological impact of social discrimination and exclusion from high cultured society.

Levin's intellectual accomplishment and engaging conversational style drew a mixed group of scholars, artists, and nobles to the gatherings she hosted in the Levin residence at Jäger Strasse 54. This first salon, begun in 1790, was attended by Friedrich Schlegel, Friedrich Schleiermacher, Prince Louis Ferdinand of Prussia, Adelbert von Chamisso, and the Humboldt brothers, Alexander and Wilhelm. In 1806 the salon fell victim to external events; Napoléon's entry into Berlin endangered the position of a prominent Jewish woman.

Under the French occupation, the Levin family's wealth was significantly reduced. Disputes caused by these restricted finances culminated in the autumn of 1808, when Rahel's mother moved out of the Jäger Strasse home. Unable to maintain the household on her own, Rahel moved first to Charlotten Strasse and in 1810 to Behrensstrasse 48. Her mother died in October of that year, and Rahel took the family name Robert, which her brother Liepmann had assumed with his baptism in 1800.

Levin had two unsuccessful relationships before her extended courtship with the man who became her husband. In the winter of 1795–96, she met Count Karl Finck von Finckenstein at an opera performance. Their shared interest in music—Finckenstein was a member of the Berlin Singakademie—inspired their love and eventual engagement. But the affair, strained by their difference in social class, ended in 1800. She met the Spanish diplomat Raphael d'Urquijo in 1801; a passionate yet unhappy romance lasted until 1804.

Levin had met Karl August Varnhagen von Ense (1785–1858) on a few occasions since 1803; in 1808 he became infatuated with the woman renowned for her ideas. Fourteen years younger than she, Varnhagen was of the minor nobility. His father was a physician who admired the French Revolution and passed his liberal politics on to his son. After his father's death in 1799, the non-Jewish Varnhagen found employment in the homes of Jewish families. In 1803 he lived as a tutor with the Cohens, middle-class textile manufacturers,

Wilhem Hensel (German, 1794–1861), *Rahel Levin Varnhagen*, 1822. Pencil on paper, 7¼ x 5⅞ in. (18.5 x 14.9 cm). Kupferstich-kabinett, Staatliche Museen zu Berlin–Preussischer Kulturbesitz

and later with the Hertzes, affluent Hamburg bankers who financed his studies at the University of Halle.

A writer, editor, and diplomat, Varnhagen looked to Levin as his intellectual companion, and they maintained an epistolary relationship during their country's unsettling times. In 1813, Prussia declared war on Napoléon, and Levin moved to Prague, where she organized relief efforts in hospitals; this was an opportunity for her to express her patriotism for a fatherland that she loved, but with the bitterness of a rejected daughter.

In 1814, Rahel was baptized as Friederike Antonie Robert Tornow. Days later she married Varnhagen, whose diplomatic duties brought the couple to Vienna, Frankfurt, and Karlsruhe. Varnhagen was suspended from his service in Prussian diplomacy for his overly liberal politics in 1819, and the couple returned to Berlin. This year saw the outbreak of the "Hep! Hep!" riots, a series of attacks on Jewish property that spread throughout Bavaria and demonstrated resistance to Jewish emancipation. Rahel was quick to see the implications; her affront at the violence shows what little success her conversion had in healing the wounds of anti-Semitism. Her second salon, held at Französische

Strasse 20 and from 1827 at Mauer Strasse 36, was pervaded by liberal political sentiment. The salon attracted many of the same illustrious visitors as the first salon had, as well as a younger crowd of writers. Rahel became an important confidante for both Heinrich Heine and Ludwig Börne.

Rahel Varnhagen was among the foremost promoters of the "Goethe cult"—the veneration of the poet not only for his literary merits but also for his profound insights into the human psychological condition. She had met Goethe in Karlsbad in 1795, and he visited her in Frankfurt in 1815. Her writings on him, excerpts from correspondence with Varnhagen, appeared as her first publication, in the journal *Morgenblatt für gebildete Stände*, in 1812. These and other scattered pieces were published under the pseudonym G or Friederike, or under her brother Ludwig Robert's name. She knew that her letters constituted a literary achievement; four months after she died on March 7, 1833, her husband issued her collected letters and diaries as *Rahel: Ein Buch des Andenkens für ihre Freunde*. This was more than, as the subtitle suggests, a book of reminiscences for her friends; it is a literary legacy that has captured the fascination, imagination, and sympathies of generations.

SALKA VIERTEL
(Austro-Hungarian/American, 1889–1978)

Salka Viertel was born Salomea Sara Steuermann on June 15, 1889, in Galicia (then part of Austria-Hungary, now Poland/Ukraine). Her father, Auguste Steuermann, was the first Jewish mayor of Sambor. He and his wife, Clara, had three other children: Rose, Eduard, and Siegmund.

Salka studied Latin, Greek, and German at school, learned French from her governess, and spoke Polish and Ukrainian at home. At an early age she discovered a passion for theater. She worked as an actress in Pressburg (Pozsony), Teplitz-Schönau (Teplice), and Zurich before moving to Berlin to join Max Reinhardt's Deutsches Theater. It was here that she met Ernst Lubitsch and F. W. Murnau, then actors in Reinhardt's ensemble. Her brother Eduard studied with Arnold

Schoenberg; as a solo pianist he premiered the composer's *Pierrot lunaire*.

In 1908, Salka joined the Viennese company Neue Wiener Bühne as a principal actress. While playing Vassilisa in a 1916 production of Maxim Gorky's *Lower Depths,* she met the Viennese writer and director Berthold Viertel (1885–1953), who left his wife to marry her in 1918. After World War I, Berthold was an influential theater and film director in Dresden, Düsseldorf, and Berlin. In 1923, the Viertels founded Die Truppe, an Expressionist theater company and innovative school that produced plays by Shakespeare, Friedrich von Schiller, and Henrik Ibsen, and employed Georg Grosz, Friedrich Kiesler, and Friedl Dicker as set designers. During Salka's years in the avant-garde theater, the Viertels had three sons, Hans (b. 1918), Peter (b. 1920), and Thomas (b. 1925). Peter went on to write screenplays, dramas, and novels, notably *White Hunter, Black Heart.*

In 1928, Berthold was invited to write the screenplay for Murnau's second American film, *4 Devils* (1928). Bankrupted by the artistically successful yet financially challenged Die Truppe, the Viertels left Berlin for Hollywood, where Berthold would work for Fox, Paramount, and Warner Bros. In addition to writing the script for Murnau's *4 Devils* and *City Girl* (1930), he directed such Hollywood films as *Seven Faces* and *The One Woman Idea* (both 1929) and *The Man from Yesterday* (1932). Salka had minor roles in *Seven Faces* and in three German-language films: *Die heilige Flamme* (*The Sacred Flame,* 1931), which Berthold co-directed with William Dieterle; Dieterle's *Die Maske fällt* (1930); and a version of *Anna Christie* starring Greta Garbo (1931). Salka had met Garbo at a party at Ernst Lubitsch's in 1929, and the two were instant friends; after their first meeting, it was said, the path to a Hollywood production with Garbo was through collaboration with Salka Viertel. A brilliant teacher of elocution, she helped Garbo feel comfortable speaking English—acquaintances claimed that Garbo's accent was identical to her friend's. Garbo encouraged Salka, who was now over forty, to shift her focus from acting to writing. Viertel co-wrote the screenplays for Garbo's films *Queen Christina* (1933), *The Painted Veil* (1934), *Anna Karenina* (1935), *Conquest* (1937), and *Two-Faced Woman* (1941), as well as the Jean Negulesco film *Deep Valley* (1947).

While Salka remained in Santa Monica with their sons, Berthold, less at home and now less successful in California than his wife, traveled often to New York and abroad for work in film and theater. Disinclined to return to the United States, he remained in Berlin until the burning of the Reichstag in 1933; he then joined the already sizable German émigré community in London, and met with success directing the film *Little Friend* (1934), a thriller written with his friend and disciple Christopher Isherwood. Berthold returned to Hollywood in 1938.

The Viertels had gone to California intending to stay only a few years, but with the onset of war in Europe, Santa Monica began to seem like home. As she recounted in her memoir *The Kindness of Strangers* (1969), Salka Viertel readily adapted to the climate and the culture. On Sunday afternoons her home at 165 Mabery Road welcomed such émigrés as Thomas and Heinrich Mann, Bertolt Brecht, Fred Zinnemann, Schoenberg, Reinhardt, Dieterle, and Murnau. An outpost of Mitteleuropa, with its conversational tone and home-cooked meals, Viertel's salon attracted refugees with similar backgrounds. Its hostess's reputation for hospitality reached talented individuals desperate to flee Europe. In response to letters of appeal, she encouraged colleagues at MGM to sign affidavits for writers and artists stranded in Europe, among them Leonhard Frank, Walter Mehring, and Alfred Döblin. Her efforts led to the establishment of the European Film Fund, a Hollywood endeavor to rescue Jews and others in danger.

In 1942, Salka Viertel was put on an FBI "Watch List," and in 1951 she was given an entry in the "Communist Index." Members of the Free Germany Committee, including Thomas Mann and Brecht, met at her house in 1943 to compose a statement that the German people be considered not the architects of Nazism but its first victims. This nostalgia for German culture, blended with horror at what was happening in Europe, characterized the ambivalence felt by Viertel and her circle.

Salka's brother Siegmund (known as Dusko) had died under the German occupation, but her mother was able to leave in 1941 for the United States. Her sister, Rose, who had had a successful stage career, narrowly escaped the war, fleeing to South America with her husband, the theater director Joseph Gielen, and their son, Michael, who would become a conductor. In 1943, Viertel lost her screenwriting job at MGM. Garbo, who was growing more reclusive, had turned down leading roles in scripts coauthored by Viertel. The Viertels' marriage, strained by each partner's extramarital affairs and Berthold's travels, ended in 1944. He returned to Europe for good in 1949, and worked in Vienna and Berlin, and for the Salzburg Festival; he died in Zurich in 1953.

Salka's salon dissolved under the inquisition of the Hollywood film industry. The country that had been a safe haven was now a place of persecution, and many of her friends left their adopted homeland for Europe. Her application for a passport in order to visit the dying Berthold was denied by the State Department in 1953, on the grounds that she had been a Communist sympathizer. Salka Viertel did eventually leave her beloved Pacific Ocean. She died in Switzerland in 1978.

BERTA ZUCKERKANDL
(Austrian, 1864–1945)

Berta Szeps Zuckerkandl was born in Vienna on April 13, 1864, the second of five children of Amalie Schlesinger and Moritz Szeps. Szeps was editor in chief of the *Neues Wiener Tagblatt*, a progressive Viennese newspaper; the well-to-do Jewish family traveled frequently and entertained distinguished guests. Berta's private tutors included the art historian Albert Ilg. Her older sister, Sophie, would marry Paul Clemenceau, brother of the French prime minister. Her brother Julius, a political journalist, was editor of the liberal newspaper *Fremdenblatt* and of the *Wiener allgemeine Zeitung*. Two other siblings, Leo and Ella, died young.

Moritz Szeps, who was concerned over Franco-Austrian relations, met Crown Prince Rudolf in 1881. The two shared a liberal outlook and a pro-French stance that was critical of the politics of Rudolf's father, Franz Joseph. As a teenager, Berta served as her father's secretary and was privy to the confidential correspondence between him and Rudolf, which lasted until the prince's suicide in 1889. Szeps's distrust of the Germans and hope for an alliance between Austria and France often endangered his career. In order to avoid dependence on private financiers, he left the *Neues Wiener Tagblatt* in 1886 to establish his own paper, the *Wiener Tagblatt*. Three years later he founded *Wissen für Alle*, a magazine dedicated to intellectual developments and written for the working class.

In 1883, Berta was introduced to Emil Zuckerkandl (1849–1910), a surgeon and anatomist from a Jewish family. They married in April 1886 and after a honeymoon in Paris settled in Graz; later they moved to Vienna. Their only son, Fritz, was born in 1895. Emil lectured at the internationally renowned medical school of the University of Vienna. His research contributed greatly to the study of topographical and comparative anatomy, and to knowledge of the chromaffin system, important in maintaining blood pressure; he is remembered with various anatomical terms named for him.

In 1883, the same year Berta met Emil, her father met Georges Clemenceau, leader of the radical

republicans in the French senate. When Szeps traveled to Zurich in March 1885 to confer with the French politician on the dangerous consequences of Germany's encroaching on the Belgian border, Berta went with him. Her sister's marriage to Paul Clemenceau the next year strengthened Berta's cultural and political connections with France, while exposure to the Parisian art world inspired her activity in Viennese artistic circles. She was a successful art critic for the *Wiener allgemeine Zeitung,* and later wrote columns for the *Neue Wiener Journal;* she also contributed to the German periodicals *Deutsche Kunst und Dekoration* and *Die Kunst für Alle.* A collection of her articles on contemporary art and design, *Zeitkunst Wien,* was published in 1908.

Berta Zuckerkandl's Viennese salon was an outpost for the avant-garde—and more. It was here that Gustav Klimt, Otto Wagner, and Josef Hoffmann nurtured ideas for the Vienna Secession, an independent association of artists, architects, and designers founded in 1897—and here that the composer Gustav Mahler met

his future wife, Alma Schindler, in 1901. Zuckerkandl staunchly supported the Secession and its members. When a scandal erupted surrounding Klimt's paintings for the university, she defended the artist; she later published an important interview with him in 1905. It was also through her connections that Hoffmann and the Wiener Werkstätte received the architectural commission for the Purkersdorf Sanatorium, which was financed by her brother-in-law Viktor Zuckerkandl.

In 1916, six years after her husband's death, Zuckerkandl moved to an apartment at Oppolzergasse 6. Later that year, she went to Switzerland on a publicity tour for Austrian art. Upon reading newspapers in Bern, she realized how much of the world was opposed to Germany's wartime actions. Like her father, Zuckerkandl believed in the power of an alliance between Austria and France. Using contacts she had made through her sister's Paris salon and through Georges Clemenceau, she secretly attempted to negotiate between Austria and the Allies. Count Czernin, the Austrian foreign minister, sent her to Switzerland to meet her sister and discuss France's possible partnership with Austria. Though the exact details are unknown, it is clear that Georges Clemenceau felt betrayed by his sister-in-law, and his relations with his brother and Sophie were never the same. Paul Clemenceau did not even visit his brother on his deathbed.

After the war, with Austria in desperate need of food, Zuckerkandl and several internationally connected men appealed to the Hoover Commission, which was coordinating aid in Switzerland. The commission agreed to make a special visit to Austria. Despite her profound dejection with the political circumstances in her homeland, Zuckerkandl never lost hope in its cultural fertility or in the potential for cultural, if not political, diplomacy linking Austria and France. Between the wars she translated French plays for the German-speaking Viennese audience. The first of these, a drama by Paul Géraldy, was performed at the Burgtheater, not far from her home; she also translated works by Henri Lenormand, Jean Anouilh, and Marcel Achard. For her efforts in promoting French culture, she was awarded the Order of the Legion of Honor. In 1919, Hugo von Hofmannsthal approached Zuckerkandl with an idea for the Salzburg Festival. The first Festival paper bore an introduction by her.

During the 1930s, Zuckerkandl witnessed attacks against her friends by the Nazis; she was also aware of deportations. With the help of Paul Clemenceau and Géraldy, she escaped to Paris in 1938; her son, a chemist, had moved to France in 1934. In the French capital she hosted a salon, where she welcomed fellow refugees, among them Alma Mahler, now married to the writer Franz Werfel. While in Paris, Zuckerkandl published her memoirs, in English, French, and German. She was visiting her son, who had been mobilized in Bourges, when France fell to the Germans. Fritz put his mother on a bus, but was not able to accompany her; while separated from him, she had several run-ins with German officers. In one instance, as she spent the night hiding with others in a movie theater, Zuckerkandl hurriedly destroyed her papers before they could be confiscated—better to have no evidence of nationality than to be found out as an Austrian Jew. She was eventually reunited with Fritz in Montpellier, and the two joined Fritz's wife and son in Algiers.

After the liberation of North Africa by the American army, Zuckerkandl worked for an Allied radio station. When she fell ill in September 1945, she flew for the first time, to Paris. She died there on October 16, 1945, and was buried in Père-Lachaise cemetery.

Notes

The Power of Conversation

Translations are by the authors unless otherwise noted.

INTRODUCTION

1. See Jürgen Habermas, *The Structural Transformation of the Public Sphere: An Inquiry into a Category of Bourgeois Society* (1962), trans. Thomas Burger with Frederick Lawrence (Cambridge, Mass.: MIT Press, 1991), esp. chap. 5, "The Social-Structural Transformation of the Public Sphere," 141–80, which assesses the disintegration of liberal dialogue and critical reflection by the mass media.

2. On the general customs of the eighteenth-century French salon, see Benedetta Craveri, *Madame du Deffand and Her World*, trans. Teresa Waugh (Boston: David R. Godine, 1994), 64–65.

3. Ibid., 89. See also Dena Goodman, *The Republic of Letters: A Cultural History of the French Enlightenment* (Ithaca, N.Y.: Cornell University Press, 1994), chap. 3, "Governing the Republic of Letters: *Salonnières* and the Rule(s) of Polite Conversation," 90–135.

4. Stephen Kale assesses the erroneous notion that salon culture ended after 1789 in "Women, the Public Sphere, and the Persistence of Salons," *French Historical Studies* 25 (Winter 2002): 114–48. Attention to salons resumes in earnest in English-language studies on early-twentieth-century literary modernism. See Robert M. Crunden, *American Salons: Encounters with European Modernism, 1885–1917* (New York: Oxford University Press, 1993); Shari Benstock, *Women of the Left Bank: Paris, 1900–1940* (Austin: University of Texas Press, 1986); and Steven Watson, *Strange Bedfellows: The First American Avant-Garde* (New York: Abbeville, 1991).

5. Jewish women who hosted salons include those individuals featured in this book, most of whom were professional writers, artists, musicians, or politicians. Other women are mentioned in passing in the catalogue texts. Space and time did not permit inclusion of such figures as Betty de Rothschild in Paris, Berta Fante in Prague, the Cone sisters in Baltimore, Misia Sert in Paris (who, though not Jewish, hosted her salon of arguably Jewish identity with her husband, Thadée Nathanson), and Lily Brik in Moscow. We also distinguished those who held salons proper, with regular hours and a circle of habitués, from occasional if important hostesses (such as Peggy Guggenheim). To narrow the field further, we concentrated on those who were Jewish on both parental sides. Our selection is by no means exhaustive but is representative of the salon as a singular platform for accomplished women.

6. Habermas, *Structural Transformation*, chap. 2, "Social Structures of the Public Sphere," 27–56.

7. Ibid., 35. Since its publication in 1962, Habermas's book has been at the center of debate on the public and private spheres. Although some feminists have critiqued his analysis as "gender

blind" (see Joan B. Landes, *Women and the Public Sphere in the Age of the French Revolution* [Ithaca, N.Y.: Cornell University Press, 1988]), Habermas does identify the exclusion of women from political representation as one of many contradictions embodied by the bourgeois public sphere. It remains to be explored whether Habermas's view of salons was influenced by Hannah Arendt's study of salon culture in *Rahel Varnhagen: The Life of a Jewess*, published in German in 1958, or in her even earlier *The Origins of Totalitarianism*, pt. 1, *Anti-Semitism* (New York: Harcourt Brace Jovanovich, 1951). Together the writings of Habermas and Arendt have prompted revisionist considerations of women's relationships to the public domain in ideology and practice; see most notably Joan B. Landes, ed., *Feminism, the Public and the Private* (Oxford: Oxford University Press, 1998). Their writings have also provided the theoretical framework for this study.

8. The English version of the French salon and the origins of the bluestocking are discussed in Evelyn Gordon Bodek, "Salonières and Bluestockings: Educated Obsolescence and Germinating Feminism," *Feminist Studies* 3 (Spring–Summer 1976): 185–99.

9. Peter Thornton, *Seventeenth-Century Interior Decoration in England, France and Holland* (New Haven and London: Yale University Press, 1978), 7–10. The term *salon* for seventeenth- and eighteenth-century gatherings is an anachronism: only in the nineteenth century did the word come to refer to the social activity inside the home, as opposed to an interior space in private aristocratic residences. See Dena Goodman, "Enlightenment Salons: The Convergence of Female and Philosophic Ambitions," *Eighteenth-Century Studies* 22 (Spring 1989): 330, n. 2.

10. Benedetta Craveri, *La civiltà della conversazione* (Milan: Adelphi, 2001), esp. chap. 2, "Le figlie di Eva," 32–54.

11. See Elizabeth C. Goldsmith's fundamental study of salon politesse, *Exclusive Conversations: The Art of Interaction in Seventeenth-Century France* (Philadelphia: University of Pennsylvania Press, 1988).

12. Immanuel Kant, *Anthropology from a Pragmatic Point of View*, trans. Victor Lyle Dowdell (Carbondale: Southern Illinois University Press, 1978), 185–89, 228. See also the claim of Charles-Louis de Secondat Montesquieu: "Man, they say, is a social animal. In this matter a Frenchman appears to me . . . more of a man than any other; he is the man par excellence, for he seems to be intended solely for society." Letter 88, *Persian Letters*, trans. John Davidson, 2 vols. (London: Chiswick Press, 1892), 2:27.

13. This analysis of the "woman question" and the *précieuses* is indebted to Carolyn Lougee's study *Le Paradis des Femmes* (Princeton, N.J.: Princeton University Press, 1976).

14. Goodman, *Republic of Letters*.

15. Habermas, *Structural Transformation*, 31.

16. Marie-Thérèse Rodet Geoffrin (1699–1777) apprenticed at the salon of Madame Claudine-Alexandrine de Tencin (1682–1749), who also mentored Mademoiselle Jeanne-Antoinette Poisson (Madame de Pompadour, mistress of Louis XV). Daughter of a valet to the Dauphine, and orphaned young, Geoffrin married the wealthy director of the royal glass works at Saint-Gobain. She was fourteen, he some thirty-five years her senior. Renowned for her generosity, this bourgeois woman financially supported the Encyclopédistes and the numerous artists who frequented her forty-year-long salon. Julie-Jeanne de Lespinasse (1732–1776) was the product of an adulterous union. After her mother's death, and being without dowry, she was taken in by the aristocratic salonière Madame du Deffand. A falling-out in 1764 drove Lespinasse to the protection of Deffand's rival Madame Geoffrin; she eventually began her own nightly gatherings, though her role was of hostess rather than participant in the discussions of the philosophes who attended. Protestant and Swiss-born Suzanne Curchod (1739–1794), who had come to Paris as a governess, married her compatriot Jacques Necker, minister of finance under Louis XVI, in 1765. In 1790 they retreated to the Necker family estate, Château de Coppet, on Lake Geneva. Her husband published her writings posthumously; their daughter was Germaine de Staël. For biographical sketches of these and other salon women and their habitués, see Amelia Gere Mason, *The Women of the French Salons* (New York: Century, 1891); Goodman, *Republic of Letters*, 305–11; and Craveri, *Madame du Deffand*, 395–432.

17. Daniel Gordon, *Citizens Without Sovereignty: Equality and Sociability in French Thought, 1670–1789* (Princeton, N.J.: Princeton University Press, 1994), 193.

18. Madeleine de Scudéry, *"De l'air gallant" et autres conversations*, ed. Delphine Denis (Paris: Honoré Champion, 1998), 67–75.

19. Gordon, *Citizens Without Sovereignty*, 108–9.

20. See ibid., 192, and chap. 1, "Ideal Types of Sociability," esp. 33–69. For a dissenting view of women's actual power in the salons, by comparison with men in the academy, see Erica Harth, *Cartesian Women: Versions and Subversions of Rational Discourse in the Old Regime* (Ithaca, N.Y.: Cornell University Press, 1992), esp. 22–33.

21. Germaine de Staël-Holstein, *Germany* (New York: Hurd and Houghton, 1871), 70.

22. Habermas, *Structural Transformation*, 46–51.

23. Craveri, *Civiltà*, 207–8, 222–28.

24. In Paris, for example, the Bavarian Friedrich Melchior Grimm edited the *Correspondance littéraire*, which was privy to information gleaned from salon circles. See Goodman, *Republic of Letters*, esp. chap. 4, "Into Writing: Epistolary Commerce in the Republic of Letters," 136–82.

25. Habermas, *Structural Transformation*, 37–43.

26. Montesquieu, Letter 108, *Persian Letters*, 2:69.

27. Mario Praz, *Conversation Pieces: A Survey of the Informal Group Portrait in Europe and America* (University Park: Pennsylvania State University Press, 1971). One passage in Praz's book (pp. 128–29), a standard in the field, is worth reading for his anti-Semitic observations on Jewish artists of high society as parvenus and on their over-refined, "feminine pliancy" (Johan Zoffany and Proust are his examples). Praz goes on to note that the first serious exhibition of British conversation pieces was organized by Sir Philip Sassoon and held in his home, in 1930.

28. Goodman, *Republic of Letters*, 86; Michael Fried, *Absorption and Theatricality: Painting and Beholder in the Age of Diderot* (Chicago: University of Chicago Press, 1980), 7–70.

29. Barbara Scott, "Madame Geoffrin: A Patron and Friend of Artists," *Apollo* 85 (January–March 1967): 98–103. In 1772, Geoffrin sold two paintings she had commissioned from Vanloo —*La Conversation espagnole* and *La Lecture*—to Catherine the Great, with whom she maintained a long correspondence. As Scott notes (p. 99), artists brought their works to Geoffrin's Monday evenings to be viewed by collectors and connoisseurs— testimony to the marketing role of the salon.

30. Abbé Galiani to Madame d'Épinay, April 13, 1771, cited in Goodman, "Enlightenment Salons," 337.

31. Elise Goodman, *The Portraits of Madame de Pompadour: Celebrating the Femme Savante* (Berkeley: University of California Press, 2000), 65–79.

32. Ibid., 93–95. See also chap. 5, "Styling the *Salonnière* and the Philosophe," 118–37.

33. De Staël was first active as a salonière during the revolution, but her liberal and feminist politics led to exile by Napoléon in 1803. She continued her salon, with its international guests, in the family château on Lake Geneva.

34. Janis Bergman-Carton, *The Woman of Ideas in French Art, 1830–1848* (New Haven and London: Yale University Press, 1995), 172–76; Mary D. Sheriff, *The Exceptional Woman: Elisabeth Vigée-Lebrun and the Cultural Politics of Art* (Chicago: University of Chicago Press, 1996), 243–61; Joan DeJean, "Portrait of the Artist as Sappho," in Madelyn Gutwirth et al., eds., *Germaine de Staël: Crossing the Borders* (New Brunswick, N.J.: Rutgers University Press, 1991), 122–37.

35. Bergman-Carton, *Woman of Ideas*, 161–121. The author differentiates between the overwhelming negative depictions of women writers in public caricatures by Paul Gavarni and Honoré Daumier, and the "reverential" type in paintings of literary women by Eugène Delacroix and Henri Lehmann. George Sand served as the main model for masculinizing or interiorizing the *femme auteur*.

36. See Landes, *Women and the Public Sphere*.

37. Jean-Jacques Rousseau, *Politics and the Arts: Letter to M. d'Alembert on the Theatre* (1758), trans. Allan Bloom (Ithaca, N.Y.: Cornell University Press, 1960), 103, 104–5, cited in Landes, *Women and the Public Sphere*, 88.

38. Kale, "Women, Public Sphere, and Persistence of Salons." Kale (p. 135) argues that a new internal structure characterized the salons of the nineteenth century: they were run by couples, or leadership "was in the hands of a *maître de maison* or a male guest with a woman acting as hostess." The salons of Jewish women (see below) prove an exception to this development.

39. Nicole Arnaud-Duc, "The Law's Contradictions," in Geneviève Fraisse and Michelle Perrot, eds., *Emerging Feminism from Revolution to World War*, vol. 4 of *A History of Women* (Cambridge, Mass.: Belknap Press of Harvard University Press, 1993). On the increasing number of public roles for women, see Leonore Davidoff, "Regarding Some 'Old Husbands' Tales': Public and Private in Feminist History," in Landes, *Feminism*, 164–94.

40. The salon's potential to combine the two forms of political action—agonistic and associational—and thus to transcend gender binaries is debated in essays collected in Landes, *Feminism*: Seyla Benhabib, "Models of Public Space: Hannah Arendt, the Liberal Tradition, and Jürgen Habermas," 65–99; Bonnie Honig, "Toward an Agonistic Feminism," 100–132; and Landes, "The Public and the Private Sphere: A Feminist Reconsideration," 135–63.

41. Honig, "Toward an Agonistic Feminism," 120–25.

42. Arnaud-Duc, "Law's Contradictions," 80–113.

43. Margherita Sarfatti, *Acqua passata* (Rocca San Casciano, Italy: Cappelli, 1955), 75. As a salon rival and later a political opponent, Sarfatti is quick to point out the chinks in Kuliscioff's armor: "Through discipline and sheer will she conquered the material and moral virtues of domestic order and polish, and so her house gleamed. With her shrunken hands she spent twenty-five minutes each morning wiping and scrubbing the toilet and tub herself, refuting the notion that her 'maids'—two sisters who adored her like God and the holiest—would do a job so 'humiliating.' And so, to the usual objection 'In an egalitarian society who cleans the toilets?' she was able to respond triumphantly, 'The most worthy.'"

44. Craveri, *Civiltà*, 51, 319–22.

45. Gordon, *Citizens Without Sovereignty*, 33.

46. Rainer Schmitz, ed., *Henriette Herz in Erinnerungen, Briefen und Zeugnissen* (Frankfurt: Insel, 1984), 67.

47. Ettinger, "Ideological Changes in Jewish Society," in H. H. Ben-Sasson, ed., *A History of the Jewish People* (Cambridge, Mass.: Harvard University Press), 845.

48. See Deborah Hertz's *Jewish High Society in Old Regime Berlin* (New Haven and London: Yale University Press, 1988), which includes a detailed analysis of the social and intellectual gaps in Prussian society that were filled by the first Jewish salons. Ulrike

Weckel, "A Lost Paradise of a Female Culture? Some Critical Questions Regarding the Scholarship on Late Eighteenth- and Early Nineteenth-Century German Salons," *German History* 18 (2000): 310–36, challenges the "alleged uniqueness" of these salons as centers of sociability, as well as the application of the term "salon." On similar revisionist lines, see also Barbara Hahn, "Die Salons der Rahel Levin Varnhagen," in Hannelore Gärtner and Annette Purfürst, eds., *Berliner Romantik: Orte, Spuren und Begegnungen* (Berlin: Trescher, 1992).

49. In her travelogue, *Germany*, 77–90, Germaine De Staël proclaimed that the spirit of conversation reigned in Paris, whereas sociability in Germany was inhibited by the strict upholding of rank, the lack of "amalgamation between men and women," and the distasteful, smoke-filled rooms. See also Deborah Hertz, "Madame de Staël Pays a Visit to the Berlin Salons of the Lucky Jewish Dilettantes," in Sander L. Gilman and Jack Zipes, eds., *Yale Companion to Jewish Writing and Thought in German Culture, 1096–1996* (New Haven and London: Yale University Press, 1997), 116–23.

50. Hertz, *Jewish High Society;* Amos Elon, *The Pity of It All: A History of Jews in Germany, 1743–1933* (New York: Metropolitan Books, 2002), esp. chap. 3, "Miniature Utopias," 65–100.

51. Stephen Beller, *Vienna and the Jews, 1867–1938: A Cultural History* (Cambridge: Cambridge University Press, 1989), 99.

52. George Mosse, "Jewish Emancipation: Between *Bildung* and Respectability," in Jehuda Reinharz and Walter Schatzberg, eds., *The Jewish Response to German Culture: From the Enlightenment to the Second World War* (Hanover, N.H.: University Press of New England, 1985), 1–16.

53. Peter Gay, *Freud, Jews, and Other Germans: Masters and Victims in Modernist Culture* (Oxford: Oxford University Press, 1978), 98.

54. A counterargument, that Jews moved toward the mainstream and figure more among cultural reactionaries than among cultural revolutionaries, can be found in ibid., chap. 2, "Encounter with Modernism: German Jews in Wilhelminian Culture," 93–168.

55. Francine du Plessix Gray, "Mayakovsky's Last Loves," *New Yorker*, January 7, 2002, 38–55; Bengt Jangfeldt, ed., *Love Is the Heart of Everything: Correspondence Between Vladimir Mayakovsky and Lili Brik, 1915–1930*, trans. Julian Graffy (New York: Grove, 1987).

56. Goodman, *Republic of Letters*, 220.

57. Leora Auslander, *Taste and Power: Furnishing Modern France* (Berkeley: University of California Press, 1996).

58. Bertha [*sic*] Zuckerkandl, *Österreich intim: Erinnerungen, 1892–1942*, ed. Reinhard Federmann (Frankfurt: Propyläen, 1970), 186.

59. Henry McBride, *Florine Stettheimer* (New York: Museum of Modern Art, 1946), 13.

60. Mosse, "Jewish Emancipation," 8–9.

61. Marriage was the only means for social mobility and cutting across estates, and since no civil marriage existed in Prussia until 1846, Jewish women had to convert to marry Christians. For most it was a painful experience, even if it led to personal emancipation as women and as writers. For the statistics on intermarriage among the early salonières, see Hertz, *Jewish High Society*, 206, 244.

62. Wilhelm von Humboldt, cited in Hannah Arendt, *Rahel Varnhagen: The Life of a Jewess*, ed. Liliane Weissberg, trans. Richard and Clara Winston (1958; reprint, Baltimore: Johns Hopkins University Press, 1997), 238.

63. Julius Carlebach, "The Forgotten Connection: Women and Jews in the Conflict Between Enlightenment and Romanticism," *Leo Baeck Institute Yearbook* 24 (1979): 109.

64. On modern stereotypes of the Jew, see Sander Gilman, *Difference and Pathology: Stereotypes of Sexuality, Race, and Madness* (Ithaca, N.Y.: Cornell University Press, 1985); and Gilman, *The Jew's Body* (New York: Routledge, 1991). The history of the Jews in Italy requires a qualification of pan-European anti-Semitism and its stereotypes, as argued in Emily Braun, "The Faces of Modigliani: Identity Politics Under Fascism," in Mason Klein, ed., *Modigliani: Beyond the Myth* (New York: The Jewish Museum, and New Haven and London: Yale University Press, 2004), 25–41.

65. Kurt Fervers, *Berliner Salons: Die Geschichte einer grossen Verschwörung* (Munich: Deutscher Volksverlag, 1940). Gesa von Essen, "'Hier ist noch Europa!' Berta Zuckerkandls Wiener Salon," in Roberto Simanowski, Horst Turk, and Thomas Schmidt, eds., *Europa—Ein Salon? Beiträge zur Internationalität des literarischen Salons* (Göttingen: Wallstein, 1999), 200.

66. Arendt, *Origins of Totalitarianism*, pt. 1, *Anti-Semitism*, chap. 3, "The Jews and Society," 54–88; Hannah Arendt, *The Jew as Pariah: Jewish Identity and Politics in the Modern Age*, ed. Ron H. Feldman (New York: Grove, 1978).

67. Arendt, *Origins of Totalitarianism*, 79–88. See also Morris B. Kaplan, "Refiguring the Jewish Question: Arendt, Proust, and the Politics of Sexuality," in Bonnie Honig, ed., *Feminist Interpretations of Hannah Arendt* (University Park: Pennsylvania State University Press, 1995), 106–33.

68. Arendt, *Rahel Varnhagen*. Arendt began the project in 1929 after writing her dissertation on the concept of love in Augustine's *Confessions*, under Karl Jaspers at the University of Heidelberg. The biography was not published until 1957, first in English. For excellent analyses of the relationship between Arendt and her subject, see Liliane Weissberg, "Introduction: Hannah Arendt, Rahel Varnhargen and the Writing of (Auto)biography," in Arendt, *Rahel Varnhagen*, 3–65; Dagmar Barnouw, chap. 2, "The Life Story of a German Jewess," in her *Visible Spaces: Hannah Arendt and the German-Jewish Experience* (Baltimore:

Johns Hopkins University Press, 1990), 30–71; and Seyla Benhabib, "The Pariah and Her Shadow: Hannah Arendt's Biography of Rahel Varnhagen," in Honig, *Feminist Interpretations of Arendt*, 83–104.

69. Arendt, *Rahel Varnhagen*, 257.

70. Heinrich Heine, cited in ibid., 259.

71. Barnouw, in "Life Story of a German Jewess," 38–41, accounts for the influence of Bernard Lazare, the French Jewish journalist and Dreyfusard, on Arendt's concepts of the parvenu and the pariah. In criticizing the Jewish community for its lack of political action, Arendt, following Lazare, positioned herself as an outsider (a conscious pariah), critical of her own group.

72. Arendt, *Rahel Varnhagen*, 258. As Weissberg writes in the same volume (p. 15), Arendt redeems Levin at the end of her book, since she acknowledged her Jewishness on her deathbed: "With the stroke of a pen, she [Arendt] cut a quotation in which Rahel, shortly before her death, admitted to her Jewish origins, but embraced her Christian faith. Despite her conversion, Rahel was allowed, in Arendt's account, to die as a Jew." Arendt also rectified the censorial editing of Levin's letters, posthumously, by her husband, who disguised the names of certain Jewish correspondents and emphasized her full assimilation. As Weissberg points out, however, Arendt chose to overlook Levin's editorial marks, and it is unclear how many changes were made without her approval.

73. See Hannah Arendt, *The Human Condition* (1958; reprint, Chicago: University of Chicago Press, 1998), 175–81, where she argues (p. 180) that political action is "human performance," like theater, and is inseparable from speech, which "begins" and "leads." Arendt continues: "This revelatory quality of speech and action comes to the fore where people are *with* others and neither for or against them—that is, in sheer human togetherness." For a revisionist interpretation of Arendt's positive evaluation of salon sociability, see Benhabib, "Pariah and Her Shadow," 95–101.

74. Arendt, *Human Condition*, 167–68.

75. Suzanne Curchod Necker, *Nouveaux mélanges extraits des manuscrits de Mme Necker*, ed. Jacques Necker (Paris: C. Pougens, 1801), cited in Goodman, *Republic of Letters*, 105.

THE ROMANCE OF EMANCIPATION

1. At the time of their marriage, Henriette de Lemos was fifteen and Markus Herz thirty-two; see Deborah Hertz, *Jewish High Society in Old Regime Berlin* (New Haven and London: Yale University Press, 1988), 200, who notes that such an age difference was unusual among the couples whose women members hosted regular gatherings.

2. Later in life, Herz was to comment on her former beauty, evoking exactly these features: "I am now 65 years old . . . and therefore I am well permitted to speak of my recognized beauty at that time, of which not even the smallest trace remains visible. The dark, shining eyes have become paler and duller, the raven-black hair has become white, the white, pearl-like teeth have grown black and decayed, the lovely oval of the face has become gaunt and long." Rainer Schmitz, ed., *Henriette Herz in Erinnerungen, Briefen und Zeugnissen* (Frankfurt: Insel, 1984), 45. Therbusch's portrait, a reminder of the beauty of her youth, held pride of place in the aging Herz's rather dingy and unadorned home. See the recollection of Fanny Lewald, *Meine Lebensgeschichte* (1871), cited in ibid., 429–30.

3. Schmitz, *Henriette Herz*, 9–10. See also Hertz, *Jewish High Society*, 99.

4. Amateur theatrical productions were staged in the homes of a number of wealthy Jewish families in Berlin. In her memoirs, Herz recounts that as a child she was to play a country girl in one such production, which the elders of the Jewish community then decided to forbid; she went alone to plead with them and persuaded them to reverse their decision. See Schmitz, *Henriette Herz*, 12–13.

5. For Nattier's allegorical portraits of women as Hebe, see Xavier Salmon, *Jean-Marc Nattier, 1685–1766*, exh. cat. Musée National des Châteaux de Versailles et de Trianon (Paris: Réunion des Musées Nationaux, 1999), cat. nos. 21, 39, 70.

6. Benjamin West, Francis Cotes, and George Romney also created allegorical portraits of women as Hebe in the 1770s. See Nicholas Penny, ed., *Reynolds*, exh. cat. (London: Royal Academy of Arts and Weidenfeld and Nicolson, 1986), 50–51, 81–82.

7. Liliane Weissberg observes that most allegorical portraits of women as Hebe include an eagle partaking of the nectar, an element absent in Therbusch's rendition: "In Christian symbolism, the eagle is a sign of rebirth by baptism. In Berlin of 1778 . . . the eagle, as Prussia's heraldic symbol, held a different, political, meaning. Was a Jewish woman allowed to serve this eagle?" Weissberg, *Life as a Goddess: Henriette Herz Writes Her Autobiography*, Braun Lectures in the History of the Jews of Prussia, no. 6 (Ramat-Gan, Israel: Bar-Ilan University Press, 2001), 12. Another explanation for the absence of the eagle relates more to the limits of acculturation than to matters of politics. The eagle, after all, is an incarnation of Zeus; without it, Henriette can be seen as playing a part in one of the theatrical productions in which she excelled as a child. Had an eagle appeared in the painting, either the strongly Christian associations or the pagan elements would have come to the fore.

8. The term *salon* is problematic in describing these early gatherings. As Barbara Hahn discusses in her essay in this volume, the women involved never used this term, referring instead to a "circle" or "society."

9. Petra Wilhelmy-Dollinger, *Die Berliner Salons mit kulturhistorischen Spaziergängen* (Berlin: Walter de Gruyter, 2000), 60.

While Herz is generally considered the first Jewish woman to host a salon, there is still too little information to determine this definitively. Billets exist from the Meyer sisters from the 1780s, and we do not know when Sara Levy first hosted her "open house."

10. Herz was born in Berlin, the son of a poor Torah scribe. He came into contact with Kant in Königsberg. Herz earned a good living as a physician but never achieved the wealth of some other husbands of Jewish women who opened their homes, as in the Beer, Arnstein, Eskeles, or Mendelssohn families. Herz was awarded the title of Hofrat, or privy councillor.

11. Mirabeau wrote an essay in support of Jewish rights entitled *Sur Moses Mendelssohn, sur la réforme politique des juifs: et en particulier sur la révolution tentée en leur faveur en 1753 dans la Grande-Bretagne* (London, 1787).

12. Language was crucial, both in maintaining the separation of the Jews from the surrounding society—and thus preventing assimilation—and as an agent of acculturation. In his ethical will, Moses Sofer (known as Hatam Sofer; 1762–1839), rabbi of Pressburg (Bratislava) and a leading exponent of traditional Judaism, warned: "The daughters may read German books, but only those . . . written in our own way, according to the interpretations of our teachers . . . and absolutely no others! Be warned not to change your Jewish names, speech and clothing." Cited in Paul Mendes-Flohr and Jehuda Reinharz, eds., *The Jew in the Modern World: A Documentary History*, 2nd ed. (New York: Oxford University Press, 1995), 172. The accusation that Jews were incapable of speaking proper German, and the derision of their attempts to speak it as "mauscheln" (to speak Yiddish-inflected German), continued well into the twentieth century.

13. See Steven M. Lowenstein, *The Berlin Jewish Community: Enlightenment, Family, and Crisis, 1770–1830* (New York: Oxford University Press, 1994), esp. 25–54.

14. See Dohm's *Über die bürgerliche Verbesserung der Juden* (Berlin, 1781), cited in Mendes-Flohr and Reinharz, *Jew in the Modern World*, 32. Dohm was hardly without anti-Jewish prejudice. His text referred to the "fanatic hatred with which the ancestors of the Jews persecuted the founder of Christianity," and to the "lack of fairness and honesty in the one field in which they [the Jews] were allowed to make a living—commerce."

15. Ibid., 31.

16. The "Oriental" flavor of the turban is striking, especially as this drawing is generally accepted as a preparatory study for Schadow's neoclassical portrait bust of Herz as a herm. In 1871, when Schadow and Herz were both seventeen, the artist modeled a clay version—considered to be the first sculptural work by the artist—which broke during firing. A second version was created in 1783, of which Schadow sold casts to members of the Herz circle. See Bernhard Maaz, ed., *Johann Gottfried Schadow und die Kunst seiner Zeit*, exh. cat. (Düsseldorf: Kunsthalle, Nuremberg: Germanisches Nationalmuseum, and Berlin: Nationalgalerie, 1994), 202, cat. no. 5. Schadow, an exact contemporary and close

friend of Henriette Herz, would become the most important German sculptor of his time. His wife, Marianne Devidel, was a Jewish convert and also a friend of Henriette's. On his relationship to Herz, see Angelika Wesenberg, "Zwischen Aufklärung und Frühromantik: Jugendjahre in Berlin," ibid., 41–47.

17. Schmitz, *Henriette Herz*, 26, 35. Herz worked on her memoirs for some years after 1823 but stopped after describing her childhood and the early years of her marriage. What has survived is a combination of her writings and descriptions of her social circle that she recounted to Joseph Fürst, who published it all in 1850. Because Fürst edited and augmented the material, the accuracy of the text is not certain. After its publication, a number of Herz's acquaintances claimed that there were distortions in it. See Rainer Schmitz's afterword, ibid., 435ff.

18. Dorothea Veit eventually divorced her Jewish husband and converted to Christianity to marry the writer and philosopher Friedrich von Schlegel, whom she had met at Herz's salon. Caroline von Humboldt became increasingly anti-Semitic and most likely influenced her husband in this regard. Though the Humboldts broke off their friendship with Rahel Levin Varnhagen and Wilhelm expressed disdain for her on several occasions, he remained loyal to Herz. Alexander von Humboldt arranged for the impoverished widow to receive a modest pension from King Frederick William IV in her old age. Publicly, Wilhelm von Humboldt supported Jewish rights, both in regard to the Edict of Emancipation of 1812 and later at the Congress of Vienna. In 1810 he wrote his wife that he was working with all his might "to give Jews civil rights so that it would no longer be necessary, out of generosity, to go to Jewish houses." Cited in Hertz, *Jewish High Society*, 280. On Caroline von Humboldt's termination of her friendship with Rahel Levin Varnhagen, see Hannah Arendt, *Rahel Varnhagen: The Life of a Jewess*, ed. Liliane Weissberg, trans. Richard and Clara Winston (1958; reprint, Baltimore: Johns Hopkins University Press, 1997), 245–46. Henriette Herz converted to Protestantism in 1817, after her mother's death.

19. On the intellectual clubs, reading societies, and other forms of social discourse in which enlightened Berlin Jews engaged, see Hertz, *Jewish High Society*, 86–95.

20. Johann Gottfried Schadow acquired the Graff portrait from Herz's estate after her death.

21. See Markus Herz to Anton Graff, May 5, 1792, cited in Schmitz, *Henriette Herz*, 251–52.

22. This detail is visible only in Graff's painting. In a print made after the painting, the white fabric covering her upper torso is opaque, revealing little.

23. Karl August Böttiger noted in his travel diary during a visit to Berlin in 1797: "There is a saying: Whoever has not seen the Gendarmenmarkt and Mad[ame] Herz, has not seen Berlin. On account of her *colossal perfection*, she is one of the proud Junoesque beauties." *Literarische Zustände und Zeitgenossen* (1838), cited in Schmitz, *Henriette Herz*, 413. Ludwig Börne, who lived

in the Herz home as a student and was smitten with Henriette, recalled: "A Juno! That was what everyone was calling her then." Ludwig Börne to Jeanette Wohl, February 18, 1828; *Sämtliche Schriften*, 4:860, cited in Weissberg, *Life as a Goddess*, 30. Juno is the Roman counterpart to the Greek goddess Hera.

24. As Herz aged, she went to great lengths to preserve her youthful appearance. For this, as well as an analysis of her relationship to the image of her body as reflected in her writing, see Weissberg, *Life as a Goddess*, 19ff.

25. Schmitz, *Henriette Herz*, 28. Dorothea Veit complained in 1798 that women were not allowed to speak at Herz's gatherings, lest they "profane" the philosophical discussions; see Hertz, *Jewish High Society*, 114, 158. It is interesting to note Ulrike Weckel's discovery that Herz was one of the subscribers in 1783–84 to the women's journal *Pomona*, which "demanded of women a certain measure of self-denial in social settings." This included the following advice published in 1783: "Allow your intellect to show only in the modest silence that reveals your pleasure at hearing rational and useful conversation." Ulrike Weckel, "A Lost Paradise of a Female Culture? Some Critical Questions Regarding the Scholarship on Late Eighteenth- and Early Nineteenth-Century German Salons," *German History* 18, no. 3 (2000): 328.

26. Wilhelm von Humboldt to Charlotte Diede, March 1832, cited in Schmitz, *Henriette Herz*, 427.

27. Schmitz, *Henriette Herz*, 29.

28. Over the years, Markus Herz's guests included Jewish and non-Jewish intellectuals active in Enlightenment circles, among them Johann Erich Biester, editor of the journal *Berlinische Monatsschrift;* Karl Philipp Moritz, a novelist, professor, and journalist; Friedrich Nicolai, Moses Mendelssohn's friend and one of Germany's preeminent publishers and booksellers; the Protestant philosopher Wilhelm Abraham Teller; Dohm; and David Friedländer, Mendelssohn's follower, founder of the first Jewish Free School, and a leader in the movement for religious reform and political emancipation.

29. The Humboldts used Hebrew script in a number of letters to Henriette Herz—a development, perhaps, of the coded communications of the Tugendbund. See Schmitz, *Henriette Herz*, 67.

30. Johann Gottfried Schadow, *Kunst-Werke und Kunst-Ansichten* (1849), cited in ibid., 411.

31. Friedrich Schleiermacher to Charlotte Schleiermacher, July 1798, cited in Schmitz, *Henriette Herz*, 269.

32. Reprinted in Rahel Varnhagen, *Gesammelte Werke*, ed. Konrad Feilchenfeldt, Uwe Schweikert, and Rahel E. Steiner, 10 vols. (Munich: Matthes und Seitz, 1983), 10:253–79. For a discussion of how Schleiermacher's ideal diverged from that of the Jewish hostesses, see Heidi Thomann Tewarson, *Rahel Levin Varnhagen: The Life and Work of a German Jewish Intellectual* (Lincoln: University of Nebraska Press, 1998), 41ff.

33. Schmitz, *Henriette Herz*, 67.

34. Birgit Verwiebe, ed., *"Classizismus und Romantizismus": Kunst der Goethe Zeit*, exh. cat. (Berlin: Nationalgalerie, 1999), 76.

35. The neoclassical style and the treatment of dress and of curls held in place by a simple ribbon closely resemble the work of Johann Gottfried Schadow, with whom Tieck had studied and in whose studio he had worked since 1794.

36. Other sculptural portraits by Tieck either bear no inscribed name or have the sitter's full name, as with portraits of the poet Clemens Brentano (1803) and the painter and architect Karl Friedrich Schinkel (1819); see Verwiebe, *"Classizismus und Romantizismus,"* cat. nos. 496, 498.

37. In the 1790s, she used the family name Robert during her travels; she officially changed her name in 1810 to Friederike Robert Tornow. In 1814 she converted to Christianity and was baptized Friederike Antonie Robert Tornow; upon her marriage a few days later, her family name became Varnhagen von Ense. In a letter to a friend about to convert, Rahel observed: "I consider this changing of names important. You thereby become to some extent outwardly a different person; and this is especially necessary." [Letter to Ernestine Goldstücker], May 16, 1818, in Varnhagen, *Gesammelte Werke*, 2:536, translation from Tewarson, *Rahel Levin Varnhagen*, 219.

38. Bernhard Maaz, *Christian Friedrich Tieck, 1776–1851: Leben und Werk unter besonderer Berücksichtigung seines Bildnisschaffens, mit einem Werkverzeichnis* (Berlin: Gebr. Mann, 1995), cat. no. 11, 257. See also Barbara Hahn's analysis of a text that Rahel gave Varnhagen before their marriage, where she discusses Tieck's portrait and the "flaws" of her chin, as a prelude to reflecting on her "excess of gratitude and . . . consideration for the human countenance." Barbara Hahn, *Die Jüdin Pallas Athene: Auch eine Theorie der Moderne* (Berlin: Berlin Verlag, 2002), 73–74. In 1835, after his wife's death, Varnhagen ordered sixty plaster versions of the portrait and six bronze casts from Tieck as a memorial to her; he distributed them widely. It is possible that the inscription "Rahel" dates from this later casting, and that the artist's name and date inscribed along the lower left edge of the roundel date from 1796.

39. "Rahel: Brief an Varnhagen von Ense, nach dem Tode seiner Gattin, von Gustav Freiherrn von Brinckmann," in Karl August Varnhagen von Ense, *Vermischte Schriften*, vol. 19 (Leipzig, 1876), 225f, cited in Barbara Hahn, "Der Mythos vom Salon: 'Rahels Dachstube' als historisches Fiktion," in Hartwig Schultz, ed., *Salons der Romantik: Beiträge eines Wiepersdorfer Kolloquiums zu Theorie und Geschichte des Salons* (Berlin: Walter de Gruyter, 1997), 228.

40. Hans Wahl, ed., *Karl von Nostitz, der Adjutant des Prinzen Louis Ferdinand: Ein Lebensbild aus den Befreiungskriegen* (Weimar, 1916), 101, cited in Günter de Bruyn, ed., *Rahels erste Liebe: Rahel Levin und Karl Graf von Finckenstein in ihren Briefen* (Frankfurt: Fischer, 1986), 64–65.

41. Marion Kaplan notes Rahel Levin's particular admiration for Goethe's bildungsroman *Wilhelm Meisters Lehrjahre* (*Wilhelm Meister's Apprenticeship*, 1796) and claims that her "embrace of Goethe, who came to represent the symbol of *Bildung* for Jews and other Germans alike, serves as a starting point for the German-Jewish romance with *Bildung*." Marion Kaplan, "1812: The German romance with *Bildung* begins, with the publication of Rahel Levin's correspondence about Goethe," in Sander L. Gilman and Jack Zipes, eds., *Yale Companion to Jewish Writing and Thought in German Culture, 1096–1996* (New Haven and London: Yale University Press, 1997), 124. For the description of the décor in Rahel's home, see the letter of September 1835 from Countess von Sparre (formerly Hitzel Fliess and Baroness Wilhelmine von Boye) to Karl Gustav von Brinckmann (Archive Trolle Ljungby), cited in Barbara Hahn's essay in this volume. Lessing, the leading author of the Berlin Enlightenment, was much admired by Rahel Levin Varnhagen. His drama *Nathan der Weise* (*Nathan the Wise*, 1779) presented the first noble Jewish protagonist in German literature, modeled on Lessing's friend Moses Mendelssohn.

42. "Rahel Levin und ihre Gesellschaft: Gegen Ende des Jahres 1801 (Aus den Papieren des Grafen S****)," in K. A. Varnhagen von Ense, *Denkwürdigkeiten und Vermischte Schriften*, vol. 8 (Leipzig: F. A. Brockhaus, 1859), 563–94, citation on 574, translation from Tewarson, *Rahel Levin Varnhagen*, 36. August Wilhelm Schlegel was Friedrich's brother.

43. Weckel, "Lost Paradise of Female Culture?" 332.

44. Hahn, "Der Mythos vom Salon," 223–28.

45. Clemens Brentano to Sophie Mereau, November 24, 1804, cited in Tewarson, *Rahel Levin Varnhagen*, 37.

46. Karl Gustav von Brinckmann, "Rahel: Brief an Varnhagen von Ense," in Varnhagen von Ense, *Denkwürdigkeiten und vermischte Schriften*, 653, cited in Tewarson, *Rahel Levin Varnhagen*, 38.

47. Karl Gustav von Brinckmann to Luise von Voss, October 10, 1802, Goethe and Schiller Archives, Weimar. We thank Barbara Hahn for providing us with a transcription of this passage.

48. Varnhagen, *Gesammelte Werke*, 7/2:79–80, cited in Arendt, *Rahel Varnhagen*, 88.

49. Varnhagen, *Gesammelte Werke*, 7/1:56, cited in Tewarson, *Rahel Levin Varnhagen*, 63. Even after her conversion, Rahel expressed respect for her Jewish origins, and solidarity with Jews. She wrote a friend who was planning to convert: "You will not be ashamed of your Jewish descent and abandon the nation whose misfortune *and* deficiencies you know too well, in order that one may not say, there is still something Jewish about her!" [Letter to Ernestine Goldstücker], May 16, 1818, in Varnhagen, *Gesammelte Werke*, 2:537, translation from Tewarson, *Rahel Levin Varnhagen*, 219.

50. In recent years, Rahel Levin Varnhagen's correspondence has been the subject of prolific scholarship and analysis. See, e.g., Barbara Hahn and Ursula Isselstein, eds., *Rahel Levin Varnhagen: Die Wiederentdeckung einer Schriftstellerin* (Göttingen: Vandenhoeck und Ruprecht, 1987); Deborah Hertz, ed., *Briefe an eine Freundin: Rahel Varnhagen an Rebecca Friedländer* (Cologne: Kiepenhauer und Witsch, 1988); Barbara Hahn, *"Antworten Sie mir!": Rahel Levin Varnhagens Briefwechsel* (Basel: Roter Stern, 1990); Ursula Isselstein, *"Der Text aus meinem beleidigten Herzen": Studien zu Rahel Levin Varnhagen* (Turin: Tirrenia, 1993); Barbara Hahn, with Birgit Bosold, eds., *Rahel Levin Varnhagen: Briefwechsel mit Pauline Wiesel* (Munich: C. H. Beck, 1997); and Rahel Levin Varnhagen, *Briefwechsel mit Ludwig Robert*, ed. Consolina Vigliero (Munich: C. H. Beck, 2001).

51. "Rahels u. a. Bemerkungen in A. W. Schlegels Vorlesungen zu Berlin 1802," box 203, Varnhagen Collection, Biblioteka Jagiellońska, Kraków. Varnhagen made notations in brackets on the document to identify the hand of each participant. For an analysis of it, see Renata Buzzo Màrgari, "Schriftliche Konversation im Hörsaal," in Hahn and Isselstein, *Rahel Levin Varnhagen*, 104–27.

52. Rahel Varnhagen to Friedrich Gentz, October 26, 1830, in Friedhelm Kemp, ed., *Rahel Varnhagen: Briefwechsel*, 4 vols. (Munich: Winkler, 1979), 3:183–84.

53. Rahel Levin to Wilhelm Bokelmann, July 2, 1801, in ibid., 1:337. Bokelmann was a Hamburg merchant with whom Rahel shared a romantic interlude in Paris after the end of her engagement with Count von Finckenstein.

54. Rahel Levin to Friedrich de la Motte Fouqué, December 31, 1811, cited in Uwe Schweikert, "'Am Jüngsten Tag Hab Ich Recht': Rahel Varnhagen als Briefschreiberin," in Varnhagen, *Gesammelte Werke*, 10:20.

55. F. Meusel, ed., *Friedrich August v. d. Marwitz: Ein märkischer Edelmann im Zeitalter der Befreiungskriege*, vol. 2/2 (Berlin, 1913), 20f., cited in Helmut Berding, *Moderner Antisemitismus in Deutschland* (Frankfurt: Suhrkamp, 1988), 46.

56. Varnhagen, *Gesammelte Werke*, 1:328–29, cited in Tewarson, *Rahel Levin Varnhagen*, 92–93. The cavalry officer Otto Friedrich Ludwig von Schack also appears in Count von Salm's account of an evening at Rahel's.

57. Rahel Levin to Friedrich de la Motte Fouqué, in Varnhagen, *Gesammelte Werke*, 1:436, cited in Tewarson, *Rahel Levin Varnhagen*, 97.

58. Varnhagen, *Gesammelte Werke*, 2:609–10. See also Barbara Hahn's essay in this volume.

59. Heinrich Heine, *Säkularausgabe*, vol. 20 (Berlin: Akademie-Verlag, and Paris: Centre Nationale de la Recherche Scientifique, 1970), 254, cited in Tewarson, *Rahel Levin Varnhagen*, 194. Rahel Varnhagen, in turn, saw Heine as an heir to her struggles; in a letter she outlined all that offended her—beginning with the expression *hep*, which was linked to persistent anti-Jewish prejudice—and charged him with addressing these matters in his

writing, in his own style: "I have greeted you with everything I can [now] say about the present. You will say all this in wonderful, elegiac, fantastic, incisive, always witty, melodic, stimulating, often thrilling ways; say it soon. But the text from my own offended heart will always have to be your own." Varnhagen, *Gesammelte Werke*, 9:813, cited in ibid., 199.

60. Eduard Devrient, *My Recollections of Felix Mendelssohn-Bartholdy, and His Letters to Me,* trans. Natalia MacFarren (London: Richard Bentley, 1869), 36–37.

61. The text continues: "There are born warriors and born gardeners, I must go into battle!—and as a private—silently confront the cannonballs. Whom I obey, I do not know; but I am ready to be pushed but not to be commanded. . . . Like Posa, I have *lost*. And yet [I] do not want to belong to those people who do *not* put *themselves* at risk. *Everyone* that I loved here has mistreated me. They know nothing of it: I will not tell them; therefore I am going. . . . The comedy will begin anew; I *must* love. Only I may no longer remain with *these* troops. Adieu!" *Rahel: Ein Buch des Andenkens für ihre Freunde*, 1:207–8, cited in Bruyn, *Rahels erste Liebe*, 301–2. Posa is the Marquis Posa in Friedrich von Schiller's *Don Carlos*.

62. Cited in Bruyn, *Rahels erste Liebe*, 302.

63. *Zeitung für die elegante Welt*, July 31, 1834, cited in Hahn, *Jüdin Pallas Athene*, 17. As distinct from the allegorical portrait of Henriette de Lemos, the allusion here to a pagan goddess is not a sign of the subject's acculturation, of the possibility of Jews adopting Western culture as they saw fit. Instead a direct link is drawn between Rahel Varnhagen's wisdom and her Jewish origins, although these origins do not prevent her from being German—and Protestant—to the core: "She was a Jewess and so blessed by this birth with all that a higher education could grant such a being. The natural sensitivity of her fellow tribesmen and unprejudiced skeptical nature multiplied her gifts to infinity. She stands there as the veritable child of the north, as Protestant in the highest sense, as a true German woman with a German soul and every German characteristic."

64. See Steven M. Lowenstein, "Jewish Upper Crust and Berlin Jewish Enlightenment: The Family of Daniel Itzig," in Frances Malino and David Sorkin, eds., *From East and West: Jews in a Changing Europe, 1750–1870* (London: Basil Blackwell, 1990), 182–201.

65. See Leon Botstein's essay in this volume; and Peter Wollny, "Sara Levy and the Making of Musical Taste in Berlin," *Musical Quarterly* 77, no. 4 (1993): 651–88. Sara Levy was Wilhelm Friedemann Bach's only Berlin student. Another of the Itzig sisters, Babette Salomon, was the mother of Lea Salomon, who married Abraham Mendelssohn, son of Moses Mendelssohn and brother of Dorothea Mendelssohn Veit Schlegel. Babette gave her grandson Felix Mendelssohn a copy of the score of J. S. Bach's *Saint Matthew Passion*, which he conducted to acclaim in Berlin in 1829.

66. Leon Botstein has described the process whereby music served "as a cultural medium of Jewish integration" through the nineteenth century and well into the twentieth. See his "Social History and the Politics of Aesthetics: Jews and Music in Vienna, 1870–1938," in Leon Botstein and Werner Hanak, eds., *Vienna: Jews and the City of Music, 1870–1938*, exh. cat. Jüdisches Museum der Stadt Wien and Center for Jewish History, New York (Annandale-on-Hudson, N.Y.: Bard College, and Hofheim: Wolke Verlag, 2004), 43–63.

67. Hilde Spiel, "Jewish Women in Austrian Culture," in Josef Frankel, ed., *The Jews of Austria: Essays on Their Life, History and Destruction* (London: Vallentine-Mitchell, 1967), 99. When Fanny von Arnstein arrived in Vienna, the Empress Maria Theresa, Joseph II's mother, who despised Jews, was still on the throne. The following year she forbade them to live in the city without her express permission (p. 98).

68. In her lifetime, stories circulated about her access to the emperor and his admiration of her. The most reliable report is in a letter of April 1819 from the Prussian state councilor Stägemann, a guest at the Arnstein salon during the Congress of Vienna: "When Frau von Arnstein . . . like Esther before Ahasuerus begged the Emperor Joseph for benevolence toward her people, he answered her: 'I will do everything for them that I can; but I cannot like them; just look at them! Can you like them?'" See Hilde Spiel, *Fanny von Arnstein oder die Emanzipation: Ein Frauenleben an der Zeitwende, 1758–1818* (Frankfurt: Fischer, 1962), 106.

69. Kininger was best known for his portraits of the Viennese aristocracy, especially women. In Thieme-Becker's catalogue of his works, no. 113 is described as a mezzotint, "Franziska Freiin v. Arnstein, after J. Guérin, 1804." Ulrich Thieme and Felix Becker, *Allgemeines Lexikon der bildenden Künstler*, vol. 20 (Leipzig: E. A. Seeman, 1927), 332. Jean-Urbain Guérin, an Alsatian artist, was a student and friend of David's.

70. The position of her torso, with the right arm crossing the chest and the head turned to face the viewer, recalls David's portrait of another famous salonière, Madame Récamier (1800; Musée du Louvre, Paris); see Re essay, fig. 2.

71. The importance that Fanny von Arnstein attached to the jewels is evident in her will drafted in 1793: "My pearls, as my favorite pieces of jewelry, I ask to be divided into necklaces for each of my sisters . . . so that these pearls, as a cherished present from my husband, should never pass out of my family." Cited in Spiel, *Fanny von Arnstein*, 200.

72. Cited in Spiel, "Jewish Women in Austrian Culture," 100.

73. Cited in Spiel, *Fanny von Arnstein*, 276.

74. Cited in ibid., 175.

75. *Bemerkungen oder Briefe über Wien eines jungen Bayern auf einer Reise durch Deutschland an eine Dame vom Stande* (Leipzig: Baumgärtnersche Buchhandlung, 1804), 112–13, cited in Alice

Hanson, *Musical Life in Biedermeier Vienna* (Cambridge: Cambridge University Press, 1985), 114–15.

76. Cited in Spiel, *Fanny von Arnstein*, 282. Shortly after writing this letter, Gentz fell out with the Arnsteins, ostensibly over comments Fanny had made about Pauline Wiesel, the nonconformist, controversial beauty who counted among her lovers Prince Louis Ferdinand, Brinckmann, and Gentz himself, and who was a close friend and correspondent of Rahel Levin Varnhagen. On the demise of the friendship between Gentz and the Arnsteins, see ibid., 275ff. Earlier, Gentz had written that the gatherings at the Arnsteins' "counterbalance the disagreeableness of Vienna—the Arnstein house is the greatest, and in a sense the only resource of all foreigners arriving here" (277–78). During the Congress of Vienna, the heyday of Fanny's salon, years after their falling-out, Gentz made a point of retiring early, on the evening of her soirées.

77. When they first married, Fanny and Nathan lived at his parents' on the Graben, and Fanny had the freedom to entertain as she pleased only after his father died. The couple moved to the Palais Wilczek on the Herrengasse around 1799. During the Congress of Vienna, they rented elegant quarters on the Hoher Markt. See Spiel, *Fanny von Arnstein*, 54f., 151–52, 236, 423f.

78. [Johann Ferdinand von Schönfeld], *Jahrbuch der Tonkunst für Wien und Prag* (Vienna, 1796), 5, cited in Otto Biba, "Jewish Families, Composers, and Musicians in Vienna in the First Half of the Nineteenth Century," in Botstein and Hanak, *Vienna*, 66.

79. Johann Friedrich Reichardt, *Vertraute Briefe geschrieben auf einer Reise nach Wien und den österreichischen Staaten zu Ende des Jahres 1808 und zu Anfang 1809*, ed. Gustav Gugitz, vol. 1 (Munich: Georg Müller, 1915), 104–5. Henriette, who had studied with Muzio Clementi, like many daughters of salonières continued the tradition of her mother and aunts, as did Marianne von Eskeles, later Countess von Wimpffen, the daughter of Cäcilie and Bernhard von Eskeles. Their son, Daniel (Denis), was an accomplished cellist; his wife also hosted a salon. See Biba, "Jewish Families, Composers, and Musicians," 67, 70.

80. *Dix variations sur l'air favori de l'Opéra: "Der Dorfbarbier" pour le pianoforte composées et dediées à Madame la Baronne Fanny d'Arnstein par Ignace Moscheles agé de quatorze ans.* See Biba, "Jewish Families, Composers, and Musicians," 68–69. Biba notes that Moscheles was actually sixteen in 1810, when this piece was published.

81. See Spiel, *Fanny von Arnstein*, 119–20. Beethoven benefited from the advice and services of the firm Arnstein & Eskeles and played in the more intimate setting of the salon of Fanny's daughter, Henrietta. See Spiel, "Jewish Women in Austrian Culture," 102.

82. Autograph album leaf, January 20, 1823. See *Das Werk Beethovens: Thematisch-bibliographisches Verzeichnis seiner sämtlichen vollendeten Kompositionen* (Munich: G. Henle, 1955),

622f (WoO 151). We thank Andreas Sperlich for this reference. Cäcilie von Eskeles first met Goethe in 1808.

83. For a list of original manuscripts in their collections and published music to which they subscribed, see the appendix in Wollny, "Sara Levy and Making of Musical Taste," 670, 677. Wollny notes that many of the scores owned by the Itzig sisters were works for two keyboards; as gifted pianists and harpsichordists, they may have played the pieces together (658 and 683, n. 35).

84. Cited in Spiel, *Fanny von Arnstein*, 326, 328.

85. Three objects that are today in the collection of the Jüdisches Museum der Stadt Wien bear inscriptions relating to the Arnstein and Eskeles families. A large Torah ark curtain has an inscription indicating that Fanny von Arnstein had intended to dedicate it before her death but that her husband and daughter were now donating it in 1818–19; see Sotheby's Tel Aviv, *Sale of Important Judaica: Books, Manuscripts, Works of Art, and Paintings*, April 6, 1994, lot 146. A Torah mantle was donated by Cäcilie von Eskeles in honor of Nathan von Arnstein in 1819. A silver Torah shield is said to have belonged to Nathan von Arnstein. (We thank Felicitas Heimann-Jelinek for bringing these objects to our attention.) Fanny von Arnstein's will stipulated donations to Jewish and non-Jewish charities.

86. Cited in Spiel, *Fanny von Arnstein*, 435.

87. Cited in Hilde Spiel, ed., *Der Wiener Kongress in Augenzeugenberichten* (Düsseldorf: Karl Rauch, 1965), 339.

88. Cited in ibid., 338.

89. For some of Gentz's reactions to Grattenauer, see Spiel, *Fanny von Arnstein*, 280ff.

90. Karl Wilhelm Grattenauer, *Wider die Juden: Ein Wort der Warnung an alle unsere christlichen Mitbürger* (Berlin: J. W. Schmidt, 1803).

THE MUSIC SALON

1. For a discussion of the role of music salons in Jewish acculturation, see Leon Botstein's essay in this volume; Barbara Hahn, "Häuser für die Musik," in Beatrix Borchard and Monika Schwarz-Danuser, eds., *Fanny Hensel geb. Mendelssohn Bartholdy: Komponieren zwischen Geselligkeitsideal und romantischer Musikästhetik*, 2nd ed. (Kassel: Furore, 2002), 3–26; and Botstein, "Social History and the Politics of the Aesthetic: Jews and Music in Vienna, 1870–1938," in Botstein and Werner Hanak, eds., *Vienna: Jews and the City of Music, 1870–1938*, exh. cat. Jüdisches Museum der Stadt Wien and Center for Jewish History, New York (Annandale-on-Hudson, N.Y.: Bard College, and Hofheim: Wolke Verlag, 2004), 43–63.

2. Called the "Berlin Croesus," Liebmann Meyer Wulff (also spelled Liepmann; 1745–1812) was the richest man in Berlin at

the time of his death. He was descended from a Viennese family who had come to Berlin in the 1670s, and he built his fortune by supplying the Prussian army with grain, and the postal system with horses, and as the owner of the Prussian lottery concession. Though a traditional Jew, he did not oppose the Enlightenment. After the death of Daniel Itzig in 1799, Wulff became chief elder of the community and represented it before Prussian authorities in the quest for civic rights. See Steven M. Lowenstein, *The Berlin Jewish Community: Enlightenment, Family, Crisis, 1770–1830* (New York: Oxford University Press, 1994), 90; and Gerd Heinemann, "Liepmann Meyer Wulff: Ein Geschäftsmann im Dienste dreier preussischer Könige," in Sven Kuhrau and Kurt Winkler, with Alice Uebe, eds., *Juden, Bürger, Berliner: Das Gedächtnis der Familie Beer-Meyerbeer-Richter*, exh. cat. (Berlin: Stiftung Stadtmuseum Berlin and Henschel, 2004), 33–48.

3. For details on her charitable work and philanthropy, see Sven Kuhrau, "Amalie Beer, Salondame, Wohltäterin und Patriotin: Das Programm einer individuellen Akkulturation," in Kuhrau and Winkler with Uebe, *Juden, Bürger, Berliner*, 58–60.

4. On the Beer family, see the various essays and the extensive bibliography in Kuhrau and Winkler with Uebe, *Juden, Bürger, Berliner*.

5. Heinrich's marriage to Rebecka Meier, whose mother, Recha, was a daughter of Moses Mendelssohn and sister of Abraham Mendelssohn, linked the Beer and Mendelssohn families. Heinrich and Rebecka also entertained visiting celebrities: Fanny Mendelssohn recorded in her diary an evening spent at their home: "Saturday [May 2] . . . at Heinr[ich] Beer with Paganini, who played a sonata, his Glöckchen rondo, and 'nel cor più non mi sento' in a divine manner." Diary entry, May 5, 1829, in Fanny Hensel, *Tagebücher*, ed. Hans-Günter Klein and Rudolf Elvers (Wiesbaden: Breitkopf und Härtel, 2002), 16.

6. Petra Wilhelmy-Dollinger, *Die Berliner Salons mit kulturhistorischen Spaziergängen* (Berlin: Walter de Gruyter, 2000), 149.

7. Kretschmar could have known a first-century marble statue in the Vatican collection from engravings, and he most likely would have seen the original during his sojourn in Rome in 1803. Kuhrau suggests a different source for Beer's pose, the Aphrodite of Fréjus. See Kuhrau, "Amalie Beer," 52 and 65, nn. 13 and 15. On Kretschmar, see Helmut Börsch-Supan, "Johann Karl Heinrich Kretschmar," *Der Baer von Berlin: Jahrbuch des Vereins für die Geschichte Berlins* 27 (1978): 97–122, esp. 109–10.

8. Heinz and Gudrun Becker, *Giacomo Meyerbeer—Weltbürger der Musik*, exh. cat., Staatsbibliothek Preussischer Kulturbesitz (Wiesbaden: Ludwig Reichert, 1991), 54–55.

9. See Jacob Herz Beer to Giacomo Meyerbeer, May 31, 1811, in ibid., 46f.

10. For Jacob Beer's involvement with Berlin theater, see Sebastian Panwitz, "Jacob Herz Beer: Unternehmer und Religionsreformer in der Umbruchzeit," in Kuhrau and Winkler with Uebe, *Juden, Bürger, Berliner*, 79f.

11. Friedrich Wilhelm Gubitz, *Nach Erinnerungen und Aufzeichnungen*, vol. 2 (Berlin, 1868), 140, cited in Kuhrau, "Amalie Beer," 52–53.

12. Cited in Werner Mosse, *The German-Jewish Economic Elite, 1820–1935: A Socio-cultural Profile* (Oxford: Clarendon Press, 1989), 305.

13. Michael Beer, *Der Paria: Trauerspiel in einem Aufzuge* (Stuttgart: J. G. Cotta, 1829), 12. For the play's reception, see Jürgen Stenzel, "Assimilation durch Klassik: Michael Beers 'Der Paria,' Heine, Goethe," *Jahrbuch des Freien Deutschen Hochstifts* (1987): 314–35. For an alternative interpretation, stressing universal themes as opposed to the Jewish context, see Lothar Schirmer, "Michael Beer: 'Die reine Absicht gleicht der guten That,'" in Kuhrau and Winkler with Uebe, *Juden, Bürger, Berliner*, 115ff.

14. Heinrich Heine, a guest at the Beer salon, admired *Der Paria* but saw it as counterproductive; he claimed that in creating the character of Gadhi, a "disguised Jew," Beer established a facile equivalency between pariahs and Jews. See Heine's letter to Moses Moser, January 21, 1824, in Friedrich Hirth, ed., *Heinrich Heine Briefe*, vol. 1 (Mainz: Florian Kupferberg, 1950), 137. Although Heine was a friend of both Giacomo and Michael, he had ambivalent relations with them, in large part because he resented their wealth.

15. See Eduard Fuchs, *Die Juden in der Karikatur: Ein Beitrag zur Kulturgeschichte* (Munich: Albert Langen, 1921), 220 and figs. 85, 87, 98.

16. See Kuhrau, "Amalie Beer," 60–63.

17. See Michael A. Meyer, "The Religious Reform Controversy in the Berlin Jewish Community, 1814–1823," *Leo Baeck Institute Yearbook* 24 (1979): 139–51. On the history of the Reform movement, see Michael A. Meyer, *Response to Modernity: A History of the Reform Movement in Judaism* (Oxford: Oxford University Press, 1988).

18. Nahum N. Glatzer, "On an Unpublished Letter of Isaak Markus Jost," *Leo Baeck Institute Yearbook* 22 (1977): 135.

19. Deborah Hertz, "Ihr offenes Haus—Amalia Beer und die Berliner Reform," in *Kalonymos: Beiträge zur deutsch-jüdischen Geschichte aus dem Salomon Ludwig Steinheim Institut* 2, vol. 1 (1999): 4. On the history and design of the Beer/Meyerbeer Torah curtain, see Emily D. Bilski, "Der Toravorhang der Hans-und-Luise-Richter-Stiftung," in Kuhrau and Winkler with Uebe, *Juden, Bürger, Berliner*, 195–97.

20. On the villa, see Heinz Becker, "Die Beer'sche Villa im Tiergarten: Porträt eines Berliner Wohnhauses," *Berlin in Geschichte und Gegenwart: Jahrbuch des Landesarchivs Berlin* (1990): 61–86.

21. Felix Eberty, *Jugenderinnerungen eines alten Berliners* (Berlin: Verlag für Kulturpolitik, 1925), 103.

22. Ibid., 10.

23. Friederike Liman to Rahel Levin Varnhagen, in Birgit Anna Bosold, "Friederike Liman, Briefwechsel mit Rahel Levin Varnhagen und Karl Gustav von Brinckmann sowie Aufzeichnungen von Rahel Levin Varnhagen und Karl August Varnhagen: Eine historisch-kritische Edition mit Nachwort" (diss., University of Hamburg, 1996), 208, cited in Kuhrau, "Amalie Beer," 54.

24. Ludwig Börne, *Berliner Briefe 1828*, ed. Ludwig Geiger (Berlin, 1905), 23, cited in Becker, "Beer'sche Villa im Tiergarten," 78.

25. Wilhelmy-Dollinger, *Berliner Salons*, 150.

26. Adolf von Wilke, "Berliner Hof und Gesellschaft ums Jahr 1840: Aus den Erinnerungen einer Diplomatenfrau," in *Erforschtes und erlebtes aus dem alten Berlin: Festschrift zum 50 Jährigen Jubiläum des Vereins für die Geschichte Berlins* (Berlin: Die Verein, 1917), 463.

27. Marianne Spohr, diary entry, July 24, 1845, cited in Walter Ederer, "Louis Spohrs Besuche in Berlin: Ein Beitrag zur preussischen Musikgeschichte," in Hartmut Becker and Rainer Krempien, eds., *Louis Spohr: Festschrift und Ausstellungskatalog zum 200. Geburtstag* (Kassel: Georg Wenderoth, 1984), 84.

28. Eberty mentions her "lack of true *Bildung*" in *Jugenderinnerungen eines alten Berliners*, 102.

29. Gustav Friedrich Manz, "Michael Beers Jugend und dichterische Entwicklung bis zum *Paria*" (diss., University of Freiburg im Breisgau, 1891), 10–11, cited in Lothar Kahn, "Michael Beer (1800–1833)," *Leo Baeck Institute Yearbook* 12 (1967): 150.

30. Felix Mendelssohn-Bartholdy to Fanny Hensel, February 22, 1831, cited in Françoise Tillard, *Fanny Mendelssohn*, trans. Camille Naish (Portland, Oreg.: Amadeus, 1996), 202.

31. See, e.g., the diary entry of February 15, 1824, of Fanny and Felix's composition teacher, Zelter: "Music at the Mendelssohns'. Felix played his new Trio in C Minor with viola for the first time." Cited in Hans Günter Klein, ed., *"Das verborgene Band": Felix Mendelssohn Bartholdy und seine Schwester Fanny Hensel: Ausstellung der Musikabteilung der Staatsbibliothek zu Berlin-Preussischer Kulturbesitz zum 150. Todestag der beiden Geschwister*, exh. cat. (Wiesbaden: Ludwig Reichert, 1997), 72. As with the gatherings of Herz and Levin Varnhagen, the use of the term *salon* to describe the music-making at the Mendelssohn home, whether organized by the Mendelssohn parents or by Fanny Hensel, has been called into question. See Beatrix Borchard, "Opferaltäre der Musik," in Borchard and Schwarz-Danuser, *Fanny Hensel geb. Mendelssohn Bartholdy*, 27ff.

32. Hensel, *Tagebücher*, 35.

33. For the literature on the limits on Fanny's musical career and a balanced assessment of the interlocking topics of gender, class, and religion, see Leon Botstein's essay in this volume. See also Nancy Reich, "The Power of Class: Fanny Hensel," in R.

Larry Todd, ed., *Mendelssohn and His World* (Princeton, N.J.: Princeton University Press, 1991), 86–99; and Marcia Citron, "The Lieder of Fanny Mendelssohn Hensel," in *Musical Quarterly* 69, no. 4 (1983): 570–93.

34. Abraham Mendelssohn to Fanny Mendelssohn, July 16, 1820, in Sebastian Hensel, ed., *Die Familie Mendelssohn, 1729–1847: Nach Briefen und Tagebüchern* (Frankfurt: Insel, 1995), 124.

35. Ibid., 126.

36. See Lowenstein, *Berlin Jewish Community*, 120–33.

37. Sebastian Hensel, ed., *The Mendelssohn Family (1729–1847) from Letters and Journals . . .*, 2nd ed., trans. C. Klingemann, vol. 1 (New York, 1882), 79–80, cited in Paul Mendes-Flohr and Judah Reinharz, *The Jew in the Modern World: A Documentary History*, 2nd ed. (New York: Oxford University Press, 1995), 258.

38. "I, as a soul of Jewish descent, have projected a spiritual and operatic homeland between the poet and the composer." Fanny Hensel to Felix Mendelssohn, May 18, 1830, in Marcia J. Citron, ed. and trans., *The Letters of Fanny Hensel to Felix Mendelssohn* (New York: Pendragon, 1987), 97.

39. Eva Weissweiler, *Fanny Mendelssohn: Ein Portrait in Briefen* (Frankfurt: Ullstein, 1991), 80–83, cited in Tillard, *Fanny Mendelssohn*, 158–59. Felix's reply to his father makes it clear that he had not intended this and that it was the idea of the concert organizers, because of the fame of his grandfather; see letter from Felix Mendelssohn-Bartholdy to Abraham Mendelssohn-Bartholdy, July 16, 1829, transcript in the Mendelssohn Family Archives, Collection Leo Baeck Institute, New York.

40. Carl Fiedrich Zelter to Goethe, October 26, 1821, in Friedrich Wilhelm Riemer, ed., *Briefwechsel zwischen Goethe und Zelter in den Jahren 1796 bis 1832*, 6 vols. (Berlin: Duncker und Humblot, 1833–34). The published version of this letter was amended to eliminate Zelter's reference to circumcision, but the offensive phrase *Judensohn* remained. For both texts, see Klein, *"Das verborgene Band,"* 76–78.

41. See Julius H. Schoeps, "Christliches Bekenntnis oder Marranentum?" in Borchard and Schwarz-Danuser, *Fanny Hensel geb. Mendelssohn Bartholdy*, 267. Fanny's letter to Felix is from December 1, 1833. In a letter of November 24, 1834, she bemoans the fact that in a country without freedom of the press, it is nevertheless permitted to malign innocent private people in print. See Klein, *"Das verborgene Band,"* 68.

42. Anti-Jewish sentiment played a decisive role in denying Mendelssohn the directorship of the Berlin Singakademie after Zelter's death in 1832. See Eduard Devrient, *My Recollections of Felix Mendelssohn-Bartholdy, and His Letters to Me*, trans. Natalia MacFarren (London: Richard Bentley, 1869), 150.

43. Fanny Hensel to Felix Mendelssohn, undated [c. early November 1829], in Citron, *Letters of Hensel to Mendelssohn*, 96. The Hensels were married on October 3, 1829.

44. "Umweht von Maiduft, / Unter des Blütenbaums Helldunkel . . . In holdem Tiefsinn sass das Mägdlein, / Flüsterte wollen wir gehen, und ging nicht." The translation by Bettina Reinke-Welsh is taken from the liner notes to the recording *Fanny Mendelssohn, Lieder* (Hyperion, 2000).

45. See Cécile Lowenthal-Hensel, *Preussische Bildnisse des 19. Jahrhunderts: Zeichnungen von Wilhelm Hensel*, exh. cat. (Berlin: Staatliche Museen-Preussischer Kulturbesitz, 1981).

46. "Ah, quite, this man 'tis I!" Fanny set several of Heine's poems to music.

47. Hensel, *Tagebücher*, 86. The singers Auguste von Fassmann, Pauline Decker, and Rosa Curschmann were leading performers in Berlin; Clara Novello, an English soprano, visited the city in 1838. "Titus" refers to Mozart's opera *La clemenza di Tito*, which was performed on January 21, 1838. For the benefit concert on February 19, 1838–Fanny's only public performance as a pianist—she played Felix's Piano Concerto No. 1 in G Minor, Opus 25.

48. Cited in Klein, *"Das verborgene Band,"* 193. Kinkel studied music in Berlin in the 1830s and often attended the *Sonntagsmusiken*.

49. On Leipziger Strasse 3 and the varying experience of playing and listening to music there, see Borchard, "Opferaltäre der Musik," 27–44. On the building itself, see Michael Cullen, "Leipziger Strasse Drei—Eine Baubiographie," in *Mendelssohn-Studien* 5 (1982): 9–77; and Cécile Lowenthal-Hensel, "Neues zur Leipziger Strasse Drei," in *Mendelssohn-Studien* 7 (1990): 141–51.

50. Hensel, *Tagebücher*, 88.

51. Borchard, "Opferaltäre der Musik," 43.

52. Leon Botstein notes that Felix "transformed Goethe's Druids and pagans into Jews who refused to convert." Botstein, "The Aesthetics of Assimilation," in Todd, *Mendelssohn and His World*, 22.

53. *Die preussische Zeitung*, cited in Reich, "Power of Class," 97.

THE LITERARY SALONS OF THE BELLE ÉPOQUE

1. Ada Leverson, "Afterwards," in *Letters to the Sphinx from Oscar Wilde, with Reminiscences of the Author by Ada Leverson* (London: Duckworth, 1930), reprinted in Violet Wyndham, *The Sphinx and Her Circle: A Biographical Sketch of Ada Leverson, 1862–1933* (London: Andre Deutsch, 1963), 121.

2. In a letter to the writer (and her lover), George Moore, Leverson wrote: "I am not afraid of death but I am of scandal, of which I have a special horror." Wyndham, *Sphinx and Her Circle*, 22.

3. Grant Richards, *Memories of a Misspent Youth, 1872–1896* (London: William Heinemann, 1932), cited in Julie Speedie,

Wonderful Sphinx: The Biography of Ada Leverson (London: Virago, 1993), 45.

4. Wyndham, *Sphinx and Her Circle*, 18.

5. Ibid., 13–14.

6. Ibid., 24, 26.

7. Max Beerbohm to Robert Ross, [November 14, 1894], in Rupert Hart-Davis, ed., *Letters of Max Beerbohm, 1892–1956* (London: John Murray, 1988), 6. Ross, who wrote art criticism and ran a gallery in London, most likely introduced Wilde to homosexual practice; he was Wilde's literary executor and most devoted friend, and his ashes were transferred to Wilde's tomb at Père-Lachaise cemetery in Paris in 1950.

8. Wyndham, *Sphinx and Her Circle*, 113.

9. William Rothenstein, *Men and Memories: Recollections, 1872–1900* (London: Faber and Faber, 1931), reprinted in E. H. Mikhail, ed., *Oscar Wilde: Interviews and Recollections*, 2 vols. (London: Macmillan, 1979), 1:159.

10. See also Stanley Weintraub, *Aubrey Beardsley: A Biography* (New York: George Braziller, 1967), 60.

11. An exchange from Wilde's *A Woman of No Importance* is attributed to Leverson: "*Lord Illingworth:* 'Nothing spoils a romance so much as a sense of humor in the woman.' *Mrs. Allonby:* 'Or the want of it in the man.'" Oscar Wilde, *The Complete Illustrated Stories, Plays and Poems of Oscar Wilde* (London: Chancellor, 1991), 380.

12. Oscar Wilde to Ada Leverson, [c. July 15, 1893], in Merlin Holland and Rupert Hart-Davis, eds., *The Complete Letters of Oscar Wilde* (New York: Henry Holt, 2000), 569. In a telegram of November 18, 1893, Wilde compared her dialogue to that of Gyp in France (ibid., 577). For a bibliography of Leverson's sketches, see Julie Speedie, "'Wonderful, Witty, Delightful Sketches': Ada Leverson's Periodical Contributions to 1900, a Checklist and an Introduction," *Turn of the Century Women* 4, no. 2 (1987): 11–22.

13. Oscar Wilde to Ada Leverson, [c. July 15, 1893], in Holland and Hart-Davis, *Complete Letters of Wilde*, 569. On Leverson's parodies, see Margaret Debelius, "Countering a Counterpoetics: Ada Leverson and Oscar Wilde," in Talia Schaffer and Kathy Alexis Psomiades, eds., *Women and British Aestheticism* (Charlottesville: University Press of Virginia, 1999), 192–210. See also Charles Burkhart, *Ada Leverson* (New York: Twayne, 1973); William M. Harrison, "Ada Leverson's Wild(e) *Yellow Book* Stories," *Victorian Newsletter* 96 (Fall 1999): 21–28; and Dennis Denisoff, *Aestheticism and Sexual Parody, 1840–1940* (Cambridge: Cambridge University Press, 2001), 104–9.

14. Telegram from Oscar Wilde to Ada Leverson, January 8, 1895, in Holland and Hart-Davis, *Complete Letters of Wilde*, 627.

15. Robert Hichens, *The Green Carnation* (London: William Heinemann, 1894). Wilde wrote to Leverson, [September 23,

1894?]: "Of course you have been deeply wronged. But there are many bits not unworthy of your brilliant pen." Holland and Hart-Davis, *Complete Letters of Wilde*, 615.

16. Ada Leverson, "The Importance of Being Oscar," in Wyndham, *Sphinx and Her Circle*, 106.

17. See Jeffrey Weeks, *Coming Out: Homosexual Politics in Britain from the Nineteenth Century to the Present* (London: Quartet, 1977), 1–44; Richard Dellamora, *Masculine Desire: The Sexual Politics of Victorian Aestheticism* (Chapel Hill: University of North Carolina Press, 1990); and Alan Sinfield, *The Wilde Century: Effeminacy, Oscar Wilde and the Queer Moment* (New York: Columbia University Press, 1994).

18. N. John Hall, *Max Beerbohm: A Kind of Life* (New Haven and London: Yale University Press, 2002), 52.

19. See Richard Dellamora, *Friendship's Bonds: Democracy and the Novel in Victorian England* (Philadelphia: University of Pennsylvania Press, 2004). We thank the author for sharing his manuscript with us before its publication. One of the most popular novels of the period, *Trilby* by George Du Maurier, features the diabolical Jewish musician Svengali. In his cartoons for *Punch*, Du Maurier attacked Wilde and the dandy aesthetes. According to Dennis Denisoff, "the late-Victorian dandy-aesthete and the Jew" were "virtually interchangeable stereotypes signifying cultural degeneracy." Denisoff, *Aestheticism and Sexual Parody*, 84.

20. Speedie, *Wonderful Sphinx*, 91.

21. Leverson, "Importance of Being Oscar," 105.

22. In the essay "The Critic as Artist: II," Wilde wrote: "Close to your hand lies a little volume, bound in some Nile-green skin that has been powdered with gilded nenuphars and smoothed with hard ivory. It is the book that Gautier loved, it is Baudelaire's masterpiece." Oscar Wilde, *Intentions* (London: Unicorn, 1945), 129–30. The similarity between the texts is too striking to be coincidental.

23. William Rothenstein, *The Life and Death of Conder* (London: Dent, 1938), xiv.

24. Verlaine's volume of poems inspired by Watteau's *fête galante* paintings, *Choix des poesies* was published in 1869 and influenced Conder. See Ann Galbally, *Charles Conder: The Last Bohemian* (Melbourne: Melbourne University Press, 2002), 171.

25. We thank Linda Gertner Zatlin for information on the drawing's provenance.

26. Holland and Hart-Davis, *Complete Letters of Wilde*, 578, n. 3.

27. Matthew Sturgis, *Aubrey Beardsley: A Biography* (London: Flamingo, 1999), 129–32. The sequence of events is presented somewhat differently in Tomoko Sato, "Salomé: The Legacy of Oscar Wilde," in *The Wilde Years: Oscar Wilde and the Art of His Time*, exh. cat. (London: Barbican Art Galleries with Philip Wilson, 2000), 68. See also Weintraub, *Aubrey Beardsley*, 55ff.

28. In a letter to Ada Leverson of April or May 1895, during the period of Wilde's legal troubles, Beardsley assumed a nasty tone: "I look forward eagerly to the first act of Oscar's new Tragedy. But surely the title *Douglas* has been used before." Henry Maas, J. L. Duncan, and W. G. Good, eds., *The Letters of Aubrey Beardsley* (London: Cassell, 1970), 82. See also Sturgis, *Aubrey Beardsley*, 157ff.

29. Leverson, "Importance of Being Oscar," 107.

30. Ada Leverson, "The Last First Night," reprinted in Wyndham, *Sphinx and Her Circle*, 110–11.

31. Philippe Jullian, *Esthètes et magiciens: L'art fin de siècle* (Paris: Perrin, 1969), 132. For artistic interpretations of Salome over the centuries, see Eleonora Bairati, *Salomè: Immagini di un mito* (Nuoro, Italy: Ilisso, 1998). For Salome as a symbol of dangerous female depravity in the fin-de-siècle, and its relationship to racial anti-Semitism, see Bram Dijkstra, *Idols of Perversity: Fantasies of Feminine Evil in Fin-de-Siècle Culture* (Oxford: Oxford University Press, 1986), 385–401.

32. Oscar Wilde, *Salome*, in *Complete Illustrated Stories, Plays and Poems*, 564.

33. Sato, "Salomé," 67. For Wilde's relationship to modern women, see Margaret Diane Stetz, "The Bi-Social Oscar Wilde and 'Modern' Women," *Nineteenth-Century Literature* 55, no. 4 (2001): 515–37.

34. Salome declares: "Thy body was a column of ivory set upon feet of silver. It was a garden full of doves and lilies of silver. It was a tower of silver decked with shields of ivory. There was nothing in the world so white as thy body. There was nothing in the world so black as thy hair . . . nothing so red as thy mouth. Thy voice was a censer that scattered strange perfumes" (Wilde, *Salome*, 566). In the Song of Songs the lover is described as having hair "black as a raven," lips like lilies, his belly "a tablet of ivory. . . . His legs are like marble pillars set in sockets of fine gold" (Song of Songs 5:11, 13–15). The imagery of doves, lilies, the tower, and silver recurs throughout the biblical text to describe the body of the beloved.

35. Jean Pierrot, *The Decadent Imagination, 1880–1900*, trans. Derek Coltman (Chicago: University of Chicago Press, 1981), 201. Both Salome and the Sphinx were subjects in the works of the French Symbolist painter Gustave Moreau, which influenced Wilde. The transmission of influence took place via Joris-Karl Huysmans's descriptions of Moreau's Salomé paintings in his influential novel *À rebours (Against Nature)*; see Sato, "Salomé," 62. On contemporary interpretations of the sphinx theme, see Robert Goldwater, *Symbolism* (New York: Harper and Row, 1979), 53–56; and Dijkstra, *Idols of Perversity*, 327–35.

36. Oscar Wilde, "The Sphinx," in *Complete Illustrated Stories, Plays and Poems*, 826.

37. "The Minx: A Poem in Prose," *Punch*, July 21, 1894, 33.

38. Wilde's poem reads: "But you can read the Hieroglyphs on the great sand-stone obelisks, / And you have talked with Basilisks, and you have looked on Hippogriffs." "The Sphinx," in *Complete Illustrated Stories, Plays and Poems*, 828.

39. Oscar Wilde to Ada Leverson, [July 20, 1894], in Holland and Hart-Davis, *Complete Letters of Wilde*, 593.

40. In a letter to Reginald Turner in May 1897, Wilde wrote: "Remember me to the Sphinx, and all those who do not know her secret. I know it of course. The open secret of the Sphinx is Ernest." Ibid., 855.

41. Ada Leverson, "An Afternoon Party," *Punch*, July 15, 1893, 13.

42. Speedie, *Wonderful Sphinx*, 40.

43. Hall, *Max Beerbohm*, 101–3. Kathleen Graham argues that Leverson proved detrimental to Beerbohm; see "The Good Dandy," *Humanities Association Review* 29, no. 1 (1978): 37–60.

44. *Punch* 108, February 2, 1895, 58. Leverson's use of the word *queer* is ambivalent; it meant strange, odd, and eccentric but also signified sexually perverse; see Richard Dellamora, "Pure Oliver," in John Schad, ed., *Dickens Refigured: Bodies, Desires, and Other Histories* (Manchester: Manchester University Press, 1996), 75. According to Kathleen Graham, the title of the sketch did not come from Leverson but was changed by *Punch*'s editor Francis Burnand, whose intent was malicious. See Graham, "Good Dandy," 55.

45. Leverson, "Afterwards," 119.

46. Oscar Wilde, "The Decay of Lying," in *Intentions*, 18, 28.

47. Edmond and Jules de Goncourt, *The Woman of the Eighteenth Century*, trans. Jacques Le Clercq and Ralph Roeder (New York: Minton, Balch, 1927), 262–63, 266.

48. Edmond and Jules de Goncourt, *Pages from the Goncourt Journal*, ed. and trans. Robert Baldick (London: The Folio Society, 1980), October 13, 1855, 39.

49. Edmond et Jules de Goncourt, *Journal: Mémoires de la vie littéraire*, vol. 3, *1879–1890* (Paris: Fasquelle and Flammarion, 1956), April 17, 1889, 961; see also vol. 4, *1891–1896* (1956), May 20, 1892, 255, and March 4, 1896, 941.

50. Ibid., vol. 3, *1879–1890*, May 28, 1887, 680. Goncourt goes on to mock the women as unworthy of distinction, for they are merely chic in a common bourgeois way.

51. Ibid., November 26, 1885, 507.

52. Michael R. Marrus, *The Politics of Assimilation: The French Jewish Community at the Time of the Dreyfus Affair* (Oxford: Clarendon Press, 1971), 40.

53. Jacques-Émile Blanche, *La Pêche aux souvenirs* (Paris: Flammarion, 1949), 171.

54. Léon Blum, *Souvenirs sur l'affaire* (Paris: Gallimard, 1935), 62–63.

55. Pierre Birnbaum, "Anti-Semitism and Anti-Capitalism in Modern France," in Frances Malino and Bernard Wasserstein, eds., *The Jews in Modern France* (Hanover, N.H.: University Press of New England, 1985), 214–23.

56. Élisabeth de Gramont, *Pomp and Circumstance*, trans. Brian Downs (New York: Jonathan Cape and Harrison Smith, 1929), 26.

57. The sisters Warchawska, Marie Kann and Lulia (wife of composer Albert Cahen), were aunts of the actress and dancer Ida Rubenstein. Marie Kann counted among her guests Guy de Maupassant, Paul Bourget, Edmond de Goncourt, Anatole France, the painter Léon Bonnat, and Joseph Reinach. See Michael Lerner, *Maupassant* (New York: George Braziller, 1975), 196–99. In describing the two, Jacques-Émile Blanche took from the Song of Songs (1:5): Marie "was white like a calla lily and the snowdrop," Lulia "dark, but comely, like the tents of Kedar, like the pavilions of Solomon,'" in *Pêche aux souvenirs*, 173.

58. Marcel Proust, *The Guermantes Way*, vol. 3 of *In Search of Lost Time*, trans. C. K. Scott Moncrieff and Terence Kilmartin, rev. D. J. Enright (New York: Modern Library, 1998), 253.

59. Ibid., 792.

60. Robert F. Byrnes, *Antisemitism in Modern France* (New Brunswick, N.J.: Rutgers University Press, 1950), 110. See also the contrasting figures of Rachel and her father, Eléazar, in *La Juive* (1835), the opera by Fromental Halévy (father of the salonière Geneviève Straus).

61. Gramont, *Pomp and Circumstance*, 30.

62. See Jacques-Émile Blanche's critical remarks in *Mes modèles: Souvenirs littéraires* (Paris: Stock, 1984), 115.

63. Proust, *The Guermantes Way*, 69–85.

64. George D. Painter, *Marcel Proust: A Biography*, 2nd ed., 2 vols. (New York: Random House, 1989), 1:161.

65. Edith Wharton, *A Backward Glance: An Autobiography* (orig. publ. 1933; New York: Touchstone, 1998), 265.

66. Painter, *Marcel Proust*, 2:5. In regard to a chapter entitled "How to Choose a Lover," Montesquiou wrote: "This is absurd, as everyone knows she never bothers to choose." Montesquiou was lucky to emerge unscathed from this encounter, as Stern's son was a skilled swordsman.

67. André de Fouquières, *Mon Paris et ses parisiens*, vol. 4 (Paris: Horay, 1953), 50–52, cited in Jean-Yves Tadié, *Marcel Proust: A Life*, trans. Euan Cameron (New York: Viking, 2000), 201.

68. Tadié, *Marcel Proust*, 201, notes that "it was at Mme Stern's home that Marcel panicked at not finding Reynaldo there, just as Swann does with Odette."

69. On the Goldschmidt family, see Werner E. Mosse, *The German-Jewish Economic Elite, 1820–1935: A Socio-cultural Profile* (Oxford: Clarendon Press, 1989), 167–71.

70. Isabella married Paul Errera, a son of the founder of the Errera-Oppenheim bank, who taught law and was a liberal mayor of Uccle in Belgium (1911–21). She amassed an impressive collection of paintings, drawings, books, and textiles, most of which were bequeathed at her death to Belgian public institutions. Her salon reflected her husband's professional activities and her passion for art and philanthropy. Among her guests was the artist Fernand Khnopff, who painted her portrait. On Errera, see Daniel Dratwa, "Portraits de quelques femmes laïques et juives," in Yolanda Mendes da Costa and Anne Moretti, eds., *Femmes—Libertés—Laïcité* (Brussels: Éditions de l'Université de Bruxelles, 1988), 140–41. Errera's erudition is also evidenced by the encyclopedic studies she published on the fine and decorative arts. See also Milantia Errera-Bourla, *Les Errera: une histoire Juive; parcours d'une assimilation* (Brussels: Racine, 2000), 159. We thank Luisa Levi D'Ancona for this reference. For information on the Franchetti family, we thank Marina Arbiv.

71. *Le Figaro*, April 20, 1896, 2:2 (Kolb-Proust Archives, Library of the University of Illinois at Urbana-Champaign). The program for this evening, which was attended by Proust, included the recitation of a poem by Robert de Montesquiou.

72. *Le Gaulois*, April 20, 1896, 2:3; see also *Le Figaro*, April 20, 1896, 2:2 (Kolb-Proust Archives).

73. Charles Marie René Leconte de Lisle, "La rose de Louveciennes," in *Oeuvres de Leconte de Lisle: derniers poèmes* (Paris: Alphonse Lemerre, 1952), 84. In April 1895, Madame Beer hosted an evening in memory of the poet and in honor of Robert de Montesquiou, during which works by both were read. See *Le Gaulois*, April 20, 1895, 2:2; and *Le Figaro*, April 21, 1895, 2:2–3 (Kolb-Proust Archives).

74. "Portrait de Madame ***," in *Le Banquet*, November 1, 1892, in Marcel Proust, *Textes retrouvés*, ed. Philip Kolb (Paris: Gallimard, 1971), 59–60.

75. La Gandara employed a similar pose—a standing woman seen from the back and almost in profile—in portraits of Sarah Bernhardt (1892) and Madame Pierre Gautreau (1898), John Singer Sargent's famous "Madame X." We are grateful to Gabriel Badea-Päun, who is preparing a catalogue raisonné of La Gandara's work. Typically, Edmond de Goncourt could not resist a slight: "Then there is the question of the portrait of La Gandara, representing Mme Beer, the Jewess, at whose home Leconte de Lisle died. She has very beautiful skin and an opulent neck, but the rest of her is rather ordinary and she has no eyes to speak of." *Journal*, vol. 4, *1891–1896*, May 3, 1896, 975.

76. Dornis's first works of literary analysis concerned Leconte de Lisle, but she soon expanded her range. Her publications include *Leconte de Lisle intime* (1896), *La Poésie italienne contemporaine* (1898), *Le Théâtre italien contemporain* (1904), *La Sensibilité dans la poésie française contemporaine (1885–1912)* (1912), and *Hommes d'action et de rêve* (1921), as well as the novels *La Voie Douloureuse* (1894), *Les Frères d'élection* (1896), and *La Force de vivre* (1901).

77. See Ernest Tissot, *Princesses de lettres* (Paris: Fontemoing, 1909), with a section devoted to Jean Dornis, 141–85.

78. Gramont, *Pomp and Circumstance*, 287, which goes on to say that like a true Parisian, Straus was "only able to breathe where there was no air and catching cold if she drove to the Bois. But as soon as the electric lights went on she began to revive and make ready for holding her own with the familiars of her drawing-room."

79. On the relationship of the work of the Halévys to Jewish concerns, see Diana Hallman, *Opera, Liberalism and Antisemitism in Nineteenth-Century France: The Politics of Halévy's "La Juive"* (Cambridge: Cambridge University Press, 2002). According to Hallman (pp. 85–88), strong evidence shows that before his marriage to Léonie Rodrigues-Henriques in 1842, Fromental was romantically involved with a chorister at the Opéra, Aimée Clothilde Proche. It was well known in Opéra circles that they had three children together—all baptized. Léon had a child in 1829 with the Comédie-Française actress Lucinde Paradol (whose religious identity is unknown). Anatole Prévost-Paradol was raised in Léon's household, with Fromental's financial support, after his mother died in 1843. Léon may have converted; his son Ludovic, Geneviève's cousin, was baptized two years after his birth. See Henri Loyrette, ed., *Entre le théâtre et l'histoire: La famille Halévy, 1760–1960* (Paris: Réunion des Musées Nationaux, 1996).

80. George Sand to Pauline Viardot, October 1851, cited in Hallman, *Opera, Liberalism and Antisemitism*, 273.

81. Chantal Bischoff, *Geneviève Straus: Trilogie d'une égérie* (Paris: Balland, 1992), 55.

82. Léonie's collection, the mother-daughter relationship, and the history of family illness are all discussed in detail in ibid., 18–41, 67–81.

83. Goncourt, *Journal*, vol. 3, *1879–1890*, November 21, 1883, 285.

84. Bischoff, *Geneviève Straus*, 114. Françoise Balard, *Geneviève Straus: Biographie et correspondance avec Ludovic Halévy, 1855–1908* (Paris: Centre Nationale de la Recherche Scientifique, 2002), 160, writes that Émile and Geneviève were married in an official civic ceremony and then, later the same day, held a religious ceremony at home, with the chief rabbi Zadoc-Kahn presiding.

85. Sylvia Kahan, *Music's Modern Muse: A Life of Winnaretta Singer, Princesse de Polignac, 1865–1943* (Rochester, N.Y.: University of Rochester Press, 2003).

86. Blanche's memoirs as an international society portrait painter document the mingling of Straus's and Ada Leverson's guests in Dieppe, although the two salonières themselves never met. Leverson's sister, Violet, and her husband, Sydney Schiff, were close to Proust, but after the heyday of the Straus salon. See Jacques-Émile Blanche, *Portraits of a Lifetime: The Late Victorian Era, The Edwardian Pageant, 1870–1914*, trans. Walter Clement (New York: Coward-McCann, 1938).

87. Tadié, *Marcel Proust*, 73. We thank Lucia Re for her collaboration in this section on the salon of Geneviève Straus; see also her essay in this volume.

88. Jean-Yves Tadié, ed., *Marcel Proust: L'écriture et les arts* (Paris: Gallimard, Bibliothèque Nationale de France and Réunion des Musées Nationaux, 1999), 264–65.

89. William C. Carter, *Marcel Proust: A Life* (New Haven and London: Yale University Press, 2000), 741, 753.

90. Ibid., 386; Carter (p. 624) believes that spring 1916 was their last meeting.

91. Céleste Albaret, *Monsieur Proust*, trans. Barbara Bray (New York: McGraw-Hill, 1976), 82, 153, 155, 224. Aside from constant literary encouragement, Straus advised Proust what medications to take on the basis of her own experience of anxiety and depression.

92. Philip Kolb, ed., *Correspondance de Marcel Proust*, 21 vols. (Paris: Plon, 1970–93), 21:657.

93. Carter, *Marcel Proust*, 584.

94. Giuseppe (Joseph) Primoli, *Notes intimes*, July 25, 1888, cited in Lamberto Vitali, *Un fotografo fin de siècle: Il Conte Primoli* (Turin: Einaudi, 1968), 60.

95. Cited by Daniel Halévy, "Deux portraits de Madame Straus," in Marcel Proust, *Correspondance avec Daniel Halévy* (Paris: Fallois, 1992), 179. Halévy, it should be noted, did not speak altogether favorably of Émile Straus. For another version of this remark, see Fernand Gregh, *L'Âge d'or* (Paris: Grasset, 1947), 169.

96. Cited in Bischoff, *Geneviève Straus*, 140.

97. Gramont, *Pomp and Circumstance*, 289. The author notes that her own mother, who entertained the upper crust, "envied Mme Émile Straus, her entresol, and her clever friends" (p. 198). She observes: "The *gratin* (upper crust) is a product of the nineteenth century, in absolute opposition to the eighteenth, whose liberty of thought it has banished altogether with its free and easy manner, its love of actuality, its artistic discernment, and immediate contact with life" (p. 167).

98. Painter, *Marcel Proust*, 1:99, writes that the subjects for Madame Aubernon's evening receptions were communicated in advance. "The guests did not always take the custom as seriously as she wished. 'What is your opinion of adultery?' she asked Mme Straus one week, when that happened to be the theme, and Mme Straus replied: 'I'm so sorry, I prepared incest by mistake.'"

99. Bischoff, *Geneviève Straus*, 136.

100. Gramont, *Pomp and Circumstance*, 291–92.

101. Vitali, *Fotografo fin de siècle*, 60. When Madame Straus asked him why he dutifully came with her, Degas replied, "Because of the red hands of the young girl who holds the pins."

102. Painter, *Marcel Proust*, 1:90–91; Carter, *Marcel Proust*, 751–52; Proust, *The Guermantes Way*, 800–819.

103. Cited in Painter, *Marcel Proust*, 1:91. Giuseppe Primoli remarked on the facial tics that made her suddenly appear like a "madwoman. . . . So out of politeness I avoided looking at her." *Notes intimes*, July 7, 1884, cited in Vitali, *Fotografo fin de siècle*, 60.

104. See the works and furniture listed in the estate auction catalogue, *Catalogue des tableaux modernes, aquarelles, pastels, dessins . . . terres cuites du XVIIIe siècle . . . meubles et sieges anciens . . . composant la Collection Émile Straus*, sale cat., June 3–4, 1929 (Paris: Galerie Georges Petit, 1929).

105. Jean Sutherland Boggs, *Portraits by Degas* (Berkeley: University of California Press, 1962). See the unidentified portrait of a woman, no. 117, which appears to be of the same sitter, posed on a couch, as in no. 116. The image bears more than a passing resemblance to a youthful Geneviève Bizet (in the period of her widowhood, 1875–86) not only in the hairstyle but also the soulful eyes and in the slight discrepancy in the one on the left. Since Degas was a regular at 22 rue de Douai and frequently sketched the Halévy family, he would have inevitably captured Geneviève. For this information, I am indebted to the expertise of George T. M. Shackelford, Chair, Art of Europe, Museum of Fine Arts, Boston. Lerner, *Maupassant*, reproduces a Boldini (pl. 11), which he identifies as Madame Straus, without documentation.

106. Proust, *The Guermantes Way*, 620.

107. Goncourt, *Journal*, vol. 3, *1879–1890*, March 28, 1887, 659–60.

108. Ibid., November 21, 1883, 285, and August 14, 1886, 588 (both remarks translated by Carter, *Marcel Proust*, 92). See also Goncourt's comments about the Straus marriage, January 18, 1887, 636, and March 28, 1887, 660.

109. Painter, *Marcel Proust*, 1:228. On the Dreyfus Affair and Proust's circles, see ibid., 223–55; Carter, *Marcel Proust*, 247–54; and Tadié, *Marcel Proust*, 299–303.

110. The photographs, which were once in a Halévy family album, have been attributed to Degas and dated to c. 1888, on the basis of subject, style, and technique, by Eugenia Parry Janis, "Degas' Photographic Theatre," in *Degas: Form and Space* (Paris: Guillaud, 1984), 60–64. On the split between the artist and the Halévy family, see Linda Nochlin, "Degas and the Dreyfus Affair: A Portrait of the Artist as an Anti-Semite," in Norman L. Kleeblatt, ed., *The Dreyfus Affair: Art, Truth, and Justice* (Berkeley: University of California Press, 1987), 96–116.

111. See Gregh, *Âge d'or*, 291; and Gramont, *Pomp and Circumstance*, 26: "I do not for a moment believe that France took Dreyfus's side because of Madame de Caillavet [who was Jewish]. Madame de Caillavet would, at a pinch, have become a Nationalist."

112. Norman L. Kleeblatt, "The Dreyfus Affair: A Visual Record," and Susan Rubin Suleiman, "The Literary Significance of the Dreyfus Affair," both in Kleeblatt, *Dreyfus Affair*, 6–7 and 120–21.

113. Robert Dreyfus in *La Revue de Paris*, October 15, 1936, cited in Balard, *Geneviève Straus*, 226.

114. Straus to Ludovic Halévy, August 14, 1898, in ibid., 253.

115. Proust overheard the comments at a salon and recounted them to Madame Straus in a letter of May 7, 1905; Kolb, ed., *Correspondance de Proust*, 6:33.

116. Proust, *The Guermantes Way*, 252–53.

117. Blanche, *Mes modèles*, 60.

118. Halévy, "Deux portraits de Madame Straus," 179. As Halévy writes (p. 176), Straus really had three salons, each with a different tone: first at 22 rue de Douai; from 1886 at 134 boulevard Haussmann; and after 1898 in rue de Miromesnil. One habitué of the last salon, Abel Hermant, describes it in *Souvenirs de la vie mondaine* (Paris: Plon, 1935), 230–48.

119. Blum, *Souvenirs sur l'affaire*, 24–27.

120. Letter from Proust to Reynaldo Hahn, November 15, 1895, in Philip Kolb, ed., *Marcel Proust: Selected Letters, 1880–1903*, trans. Ralph Manheim (Garden City, N.Y.: Doubleday, 1983), 105.

121. Bischoff, *Geneviève Straus*, 280.

122. Proust, *The Guermantes Way*, 796.

123. On Élie Halévy and on Fromental Halévy's synagogal music, see Hallman, *Opera, Liberalism and Antisemitism*, 75–77, 92–95.

124. Proust, *The Guermantes Way*, 620.

125. Abel Hermant, cited in Bischoff, *Geneviève Straus*, 160.

THE POLITICAL SALON

1. "Anna Kuliscioff," report prepared May 11, 1899, Prefettura di Milano. Reprinted in pamphlet form by the Fondazione Anna Kuliscioff, Milan.

2. Cesare Lombroso and Guglielmo Ferrero, *La donna delinquente, la prostituta e la donna normale* (Turin: Roux, 1893). Criminal behavior, according to Lombroso, produced quick physiognomic degeneration in women, since the female sex was already lower on the evolutionary ladder.

3. A witness to Kuliscioff's 1879 trial in Florence (for conspiracy against the Italian state) described her as having "the face of a Madonna . . . she reminded one of the gracious figures of the Pre-Raphaelites." Recounted in Filippo Turati, ed., *Anna Kuliscioff in memoria* (1926; reprint, Milan: Enrico Lazzari, 1989), 25. See also her obituary that appeared in *La Stampa*, December 30, 1925, reprinted as "Mente magnifica," in ibid., 151. An account of Kuliscioff's early revolutionary activities is found in

Franco Venturi, "Anna Kuliscioff e la sua attività rivoluzionaria in Russia," *Movimento Operaio* 4 (January–February 1952): 277–86.

4. Mary Gibson, *Born to Crime: Cesare Lombroso and the Origins of Biological Criminology* (Westport, Conn.: Praeger, 2002), 82–85. On the influence of Kuliscioff on Gina and Paola Lombroso, see Delfina Dolza, *Essere figlie di Lombroso: Due donne intellettuali tra '800 e '900* (Milan: Franco Angeli, 1990), 60–70. According to Gustavo Sacerdote, "Ricordi e impressioni," in *Anna Kuliscioff in memoria*, 74, Lombroso called her "the most beautiful woman in Europe."

5. Details of Kuliscioff's early biography derive from Lev Deich (who knew her), "Anna Rozenstein Macarevich," in *Rol yevreev v russkom revoliutsionnom dvizhenii* (The role of Jews in Russian revolutionary history; Berlin: Idisher literarisher farlag, 1923). Drawing on Deich, Naomi Shepherd, *A Price Below Rubies: Jewish Women as Rebels and Radicals* (Cambridge, Mass.: Harvard University Press, 1993), 69, writes: "Her father was a Jewish merchant 'of the first guild' entitled from 1859 to live anywhere in the Russian Empire. This made him one of only five hundred Jewish merchants who enjoyed such a privilege." Kuliscioff's birth date appears variously as 1853, 1854, 1855, and 1857. She may well have adopted the last date to make herself closer to Turati's age; see Marina Addis Saba, *Anna Kuliscioff: Vita privata e passione politica* (Milan: Mondadori, 1993), 4–5. Kuliscioff's university career was interrupted in 1873, when the tsar ordered all Russians studying abroad to return home. Kuliscioff's early Russian years are also documented in Paolo Pillitteri, *Anna Kuliscioff: Una biografia politica* (Venice: Marsilio Editori, 1986), 25–35.

6. Shepherd, *Price Below Rubies*, 1–15, 58–64, 70–77.

7. Franco Venturi, *Roots of Revolution: A History of the Populist and Socialist Movements in Nineteenth Century Russia*, trans. Francis Haskell (New York: Grosset and Dunlap, 1966), 570–71.

8. Venturi, "Anna Kuliscioff," 277, reports that Moisei Rozenstein had converted his family to the Russian Orthodox Church, but there is no evidence for that. Paolo Treves writes that his father, the salon habitué and renowned Socialist Claudio Treves, was particularly close to Kuliscioff because of their shared Jewish ancestry; see "Portici Galleria 23," in *Esperienze e studi socialisti in onore di Ugo Guido Mondolfo* (Florence: La Nuova Italia, 1957), 335. On the Balfour Declaration and a state for Jews, see Kuliscioff to Filippo Turati, December 13, 1917, in Filippo Turati and Anna Kuliscioff, *Carteggio Filippo Turati e Anna Kuliscioff*, ed. Alessandro Schiavi and Franco Pedrone, 6 vols. (hereafter *CTK*; Turin: Einaudi, 1949–77), 4:778. According to Luciano Forlani, "Spigolature letterarie nel carteggio Costa-Kuliscioff (1880–1885)," in *Anna Kuliscioff e l'età del riformismo* (Milan: Avanti! 1977), 373–74, she adored Heine's writings for their anticlerical, antifeudal spirit and for his championing the emancipation of the Jews and the other oppressed.

9. As documented by Shepherd, *Price Below Rubies*, 71–84, Kuliscioff's female comrades in the Russian anarchist underground suffered from severe depression. Many killed themselves after long imprisonments, and at least one was executed.

10. From 1886 to 1890, Kuliscioff worked among the poor and in a private clinic, where she treated women from the working and lower-middle classes. She gave it up for health reasons (the onset of rheumatoid arthritis made it difficult for her to walk up flights of stairs) and turned exclusively to politics.

11. Giuseppe Del Bo, ed., *La corrispondenza di Marx e Engels con italiani (1848–1895)* (Milan: Feltrinelli, 1964), 489. In the previous sentence Labriola disparaged the other Milanese Socialists as worthless.

12. Giuseppina Rossi, *Salotti letterari in Toscana* (Florence: Le Lettere, 1992); Daniela Pizzagalli, *L'amica: Clara Maffei e il suo salotto nel Risorgimento italiano* (Milan: Mondadori, 1997); Goffredo Capone, *Tre circoli milanesi: Clara Maffei, Anna Kuliscioff, Margherita Sarfatti* (Milan: Privately printed, n.d.); Maria Teresa Mori, *Salotti: La sociabilità delle élite nell'Italia dell'Ottocento* (Rome: Carocci, 2000).

13. Margherita Sarfatti, "Il salotto che comandava all'Italia," in Sarfatti, *Acqua passata* (Rocca San Casciano, Italy: F. Cappelli, 1955), 74; Sarfatti, *Dux* (Milan: Mondadori, 1926), 129–30.

14. Personal memoirs of the salon include Virgilio Brocchi, *Luce di grandi anime* (Verona: Mondadori, 1956), 143–91; Antonio Graziadei, *Memorie di trent'anni* (Rome: Edizioni Rinascita, 1950), 41; Treves, "Portici Galleria 23," 332–36; Filippo Tommaso Marinetti, *La grande Milano tradizionale e futurista* (Milan: Mondadori, 1969), 3–4; and Ivanoe Bonomi, "Quel che essa fu," 84, and Giovanni Ansaldo, "La vocazione," 126–28, along with other recollections in *Anna Kuliscioff in memoria*. See also Spencer Di Scala, *Dilemmas of Italian Socialism: The Politics of Filippo Turati* (Amherst: University of Massachusetts Press, 1980), 9.

15. Addis Saba, *Anna Kuliscioff*, 111.

16. Vera Modigliani, *Esilio* (Milan: Garzanti, 1946), 123.

17. Addis Saba, *Anna Kuliscioff*, 104. As Sarfatti recounts in *Acqua passata*, 76–77, in line with her "austere mind," Kuliscioff preferred "a tasteful, rational cut in clothes. So much so, that I always dressed with great care in the expectation that she would scrutinize my appearance for any signs of frivolity."

18. Anna Kuliscioff, "Il monopolio dell'uomo," lecture given April 27, 1890, at the Circolo Filologico Milanese, reprinted in *Anna Kuliscioff in memoria*, 246.

19. See, for example, the testaments in *Anna Kuliscioff in memoria* by Alessandro Levi and Rodolfo Mondolfo, both under the title "Un cervello maschile, un cuore materno," 85–86; Giuseppe Canepa, "Anima pura," 89; Giovanni Zibordi, "Femminismo e femminilità," 141–42; and from a feminist perspective, Simona Martini, "Apostolato di donna," 148.

20. Giovanni Ansaldo, "La signora Anna," in Willy Farnese [Giovanni Ansaldo], *Il vero signore: Guida di belle maniere* (Milan: Longanesi, 1947), excerpted in Alessandro Schiavi, *Anna Kuliscioff* (Rome: Opere Nuove, 1955), 77; Mario Borsa, "La sua bontà," in *Anna Kuliscioff in memoria*, 58–62.

21. Treves, "Portici Galleria 23," 333; Ugo Guido Mondolfo and Fausto Pagliari, "Anna Kuliscioff: La vita e l'azione," in *Anna Kuliscioff in memoria*, 36.

22. Treves, "Portici Galleria 23," 336.

23. Some seventy-six percent of women were illiterate at the time of Italian unification in 1870; after 1901, the majority was not: see Martin Clark, *Modern Italy, 1871–1995* (New York: Longman, 1996), 169. Kuliscioff's most important writings were collected in *Anna Kuliscioff in memoria*, 213–340. See also Maricla Boggio and Annabella Cerlani, eds., *Anna Kuliscioff: Con gli scritti di Anna Kuliscioff sulla condizione della donna* (Venice: Marsilio, 1977).

24. Addis Saba, *Anna Kuliscioff*, 113.

25. Mondolfo and Pagliari, "Anna Kuliscioff," 36.

26. Kuliscioff to Engels, January 19, 1894, in Del Bo, *Corrispondenza di Marx e Engels*, 516.

27. For "an almost interminable list of visitors" see Maria Casalini, *La signora del socialismo italiano* (Rome: Editori Riuniti, 1987), 173. Among the regulars were the journalists Luigi Salvatorelli, Giovanni Amendola, and Mario Missiroli, the historian Gaetano Salvemini, the Socialist leaders Enrico Ferri, Camillo Prampolini, and Costantino Lazzari, and the younger group of Pietro Nenni, Giovanni Ansaldo, Ugo Guido Mondolfo, and Alessandro Schiavi. Numerous references to droppers-by and heated discussions are found in *CTK*, vol. 2.

28. Ansaldo, "La signora Anna," 76, 78, and Alessandro Schiavi, "La signora Anna," in *Anna Kuliscioff in memoria*, 50.

29. For comments on her conversation style, see ibid. (both Ansaldo and Schiavi), and Mondolfo, "Un cervello maschile, un cuore materno," 88; Zibordi, "Femminismo e femminilità," 139; and Pietro Nenni, "Una consolatrice," in *Anna Kuliscioff in memoria*, 95.

30. Kuliscioff to Turati, March 28, 1906, *CTK*, 2:398.

31. Addis Saba, *Anna Kuliscioff*, 302–5.

32. Kuliscioff to Turati, May 27, 1907, *CTK*, 2:552. See also Nino Valeri, *Turati e la Kuliscioff* (Florence: Felice Le Monnier, 1974); and Claudia dall'Osso, ed., *Amore e socialismo: Un carteggio inedito/Filippo Turati, Anna Kuliscioff* (Florence: La Nuova Italia, 2001).

33. Angiolo Cabrini, "Ricordando," in *Anna Kuliscioff in memoria*, 70–71. Despite Kuliscioff's ferocious sense of independence, she was overjoyed when her daughter married into a solid Catholic family (a development that Sarfatti, *Acqua passata*, 79, found most ironic). As Kuliscioff wrote to Turati on March 24,

1904: "I only want one thing: for Ninetta [Andreina] to be happy. Besides, there has to be a law of equilibrium in the universe: I rebelled against everyone and everything; I suffered greatly, I sacrificed the best years of my youth, and now my daughter in compensation will respect all laws and advantages." *CTK*, 2:174.

34. Anna Kuliscioff, "Suffragio universale?" *Critica Sociale*, March 16–April 1, 1910. She also advocated maternity leave and pay for housewives, and considered motherhood the finest (though not necessarily an exclusive) occupation. See Addis Saba, *Anna Kuliscioff*, 174–241; Casalini, *Signora del socialismo italiano*, 223–41; Franca Pieroni Bortolotti, "Anna Kuliscioff e la questione femminile," in *Anna Kuliscioff e l'età del riformismo*, 104–39; and Claire LaVigna, "The Marxist Ambivalence Toward Women: Between Socialism and Feminism in the Italian Socialist Party," in Marilyn J. Boxer and Jean H. Quataert, eds., *Socialist Women: European Socialist Feminism in the Nineteenth and Early Twentieth Centuries* (New York: Elsevier North-Holland, 1978), 146–81.

35. Addis Saba, *Anna Kuliscioff*, 35.

36. Casalini, *Signora del socialismo italiano*, 227.

37. Altobelli, Balabanoff, Margherita Sarfatti, Linda Malnati, and Carlotta Clerici served on the board. The journal was modeled after *Gleichheit*, founded by the German Socialist Clara Zetkin, with whom Kuliscioff was in regular correspondence. Kuliscioff was editor for the first two years and for reasons of health passed the position on to Balabanoff. Within the first year, the nationally distributed paper reached a circulation of fourteen thousand. It became a weekly in 1921 and ceased publication in 1925. See Fiorenza Taricone, "La Difesa delle Lavoratrici: Socialismo e movimento femminile," in Giulio Polotti, ed., *La Difesa delle Lavoratrici (1912–25)* (reprint, Milan: Istituto Europeo Studi Sociali, 1992), 3–20.

38. Ravizza was involved in the Società Umanitaria, whose various programs provided assistance to workers, while Maino founded the Asilo Mariuccia, a shelter for unwed mothers and children (especially those of prostitutes). Both women headed the Milan suffragists through the Pro Suffragio organization. See Annarita Buttafuoco, *Le Mariuccine: Storia di un'istituzione laica, l'Asilo Mariuccia* (Milan: Franco Angeli, 1984).

39. Mario Borsa, "La sua bontà," 61: "No woman, from any social class, could resist Kuliscioff's charm"; see also Zibordi, "Femminismo e femminilità," 139, and the impressions of Paola and Gina Lombroso in Dolza, *Essere figlie di Lombroso*, 60–63, 74–75. A more nuanced appraisal of Kuliscioff is given by her rival Sarfatti in *Acqua passata*, 79, 81, who also makes a point of stressing Kuliscioff's "Slavic" disposition. For Kuliscioff's ambivalent relationships with bourgeois and upper-class women, see Addis Saba, *Anna Kuliscioff*, 174–241; and Casalini, *Signora del socialismo italiano*, 223–41.

40. Addis Saba, *Anna Kuliscioff*, 323.

41. Philip V. Cannistraro and Brian R. Sullivan, *Il Duce's Other Woman* (New York: William Morrow, 1993), 94. According to Brocchi, *Luce di grandi anime*, 175, Mussolini once said that "Kuliscioff is the sole political brain of Italian Socialism," a remark he undoubtedly lifted from Labriola, see note 10, above.

42. Sarfatti, *Dux*, 138.

43. Luigi Salvatorelli and Giovanni Mira, *Storia d'Italia nel periodo fascista* (Turin: Einaudi, 1956), 561–62.

THE SALONS OF MODERNISM

1. A number of the salon guests contributed to a privately published volume in memory of the Bernsteins: Georg Treu, ed., *Carl und Felicie Bernstein: Erinnerungen ihrer Freunde* (Dresden, 1914). See also Emily D. Bilski, ed., *Berlin Metropolis: Jews and the New Culture, 1890–1918*, exh. cat. (Berkeley: University of California Press, and New York: The Jewish Museum, 1999), 3, 5–6, and, in that volume, Barbara Hahn, "Encounter at the Margins: Jewish Salons Around 1900," 198–200.

2. Sabine Lepsius, "Ueber das Aussterben der 'Salons,'" *März* 7 (1913): 226–27.

3. See Emily Bilski's forthcoming article in a special issue of *Jewish Studies Quarterly*, January 2005.

4. For Laforgue's essay, see Linda Nochlin, ed., *Impressionism and Post-Impressionism, 1874–1904: Sources and Documents* (Englewood Cliffs, N.J.: Prentice-Hall, 1966), 14–20. In 1883, Laforgue went with Carl Bernstein to see the exhibition of the Bernsteins' paintings at the Gurlitt gallery; this was the occasion for the essay, originally intended for a German publication in a translation by Carl Bernstein, which seems never to have appeared.

5. Georg Brandes, "Japanische und impressionistische Kunst," in Erik M. Christensen and Hans-Dietrich Loock, eds., *Berlin als deutsche Reichshauptstadt: Erinnerungen aus den Jahren 1877–1883*, trans. Peter Urban-Halle (Berlin: Colloquium, 1989), 557–58.

6. See Barbara Paul, "Drei Sammlungen französischer impressionistischer Kunst im kaiserlichen Berlin: Bernstein, Liebermann, Arnhold," *Zeitschrift des Deutschen Vereins für Kunstwissenschaft* 42, no. 3 (1988): 11–20.

7. See Johann Georg Prinz von Hohenzollern and Peter-Klaus Schuster, eds., *Manet bis van Gogh: Hugo von Tschudi und der Kampf um die Moderne*, exh. cat. (Berlin: Nationalgalerie, and Munich: Neue Pinakothek, 1996).

8. Bertha [*sic*] Zuckerkandl, *Österreich intim: Erinnerungen, 1892–1942*, ed. Reinhard Federmann (Frankfurt: Propyläen, 1970), 100.

9. Emil Zuckerkandl is considered the father of modern rhinology. The Nazis removed his statue from the University in Vienna. Felicitas Heimann-Jelinek, ed., *Zu Gast bei Beer-Hofmann*, exh.

cat. (Vienna: Jüdisches Museum der Stadt Wien, and Amsterdam: Joods Historisch Museum, 1998), 96.

10. Frau [Berta] Szeps-Zuckerkandl, *My Life and History, by Berta Szeps*, trans. John Sommerfield (London: Cassell, 1938), 130.

11. Ibid., 131.

12. Ludwig Hevesi, "Zum Geleit," in B[erta] Zuckerkandl, *Zeitkunst Wien, 1901–1907* (Vienna: Hugo Heller, 1908), ix.

13. Szeps-Zuckerkandl, *My Life and History*, 143.

14. William M. Johnston, *The Austrian Mind: An Intellectual and Social History, 1848–1938* (Berkeley: University of California Press, 1983), 121.

15. Berta Zuckerkandl, "Wiener Geschmacklosigkeiten," *Ver sacrum* 1, no. 2 (1898): 4.

16. Ibid., 5.

17. Ibid., 6.

18. *Deutsches Volksblatt*, May 1900, cited in Tobias Natter and Gerbert Frodl, eds., *Klimt's Women* (Cologne: Dumont, and New Haven and London: Yale University Press, 2000), 68.

19. Zuckerkandl, *Österreich intim*, 62–66. On the "Klimt Affair," see Peter Vergo, *Art in Vienna, 1898–1918: Klimt, Kokoschka and Their Contemporaries* (London: Phaidon, 1975), 49–62; and Carl E. Schorske, *Fin-de-Siècle Vienna: Politics and Culture* (New York: Vintage, 1981), 225–54.

20. *Die Fackel*, no. 59 (mid-November 1900), 19, cited in Alma Mahler-Werfel, *Diaries, 1898–1902*, selected and trans. Antony Beaumont (Ithaca, N.Y.: Cornell University Press, 1998), 348, n. 8.

21. Michael Huey, "The Aestheticized Individual: Subjects and Their Objects in Turn-of-the-Century Vienna," in *Viennese Silver: Modern Design, 1780–1918* (New York: Neue Galerie, and Vienna: Kunsthistorisches Museum, 2003), 344. For Loos's critique of attempts to create an Austrian modern style, see Janet Stewart, *Fashioning Vienna: Adolf Loos's Cultural Criticism* (London: Routledge, 2000).

22. Szeps-Zuckerkandl, *My Life and History*, 142–43.

23. Professor Emile Zuckerkandl, Berta's grandson, recalls that Sophie Clemenceau was always beautifully dressed.

24. Szeps-Zuckerkandl, *My Life and History*, 147.

25. For Poiret in Vienna, see Wolfgang Georg Fischer, "Paul Poiret à Vienne, Emilie Flöge à Paris," in Jean Clair, ed., *Vienne, 1880–1938: L'apocalypse joyeuse*, exh. cat. (Paris: Centre Pompidou, 1986), 556ff.; and Berta Zuckerkandl, "Paul Poiret und die Klimt Gruppe," *Neue Wiener Journal*, November 25, 1923, 5.

26. For a description of this meeting, see Szeps-Zuckerkandl, *My Life and History*, 144–45; and Zuckerkandl, *Österreich intim*, 56–61.

27. Szeps-Zuckerkandl, *My Life and History*, 150.

28. Alma Schindler [Mahler], diary entry, November 7, 1901, in Mahler-Werfel, *Diaries, 1898–1902*, 442; supplemented with information from Henry-Louis de La Grange and Günther Weiss, eds., *Ein Glück ohne Ruh': Die Briefe Gustav Mahlers an Alma* (Berlin: Siedler, 1995), 51–52.

29. See Lucian O. Meysels, *In meinem Salon ist Österreich: Berta Zuckerkandl und ihre Zeit* (Vienna: Herold, 1984), 204–13.

30. Hugo von Hofmannsthal to Arthur Schnitzler, January 28, 1922, in *Hugo von Hofmannsthal-Arthur Schnitzler: Briefwechsel*, ed. Therese Nickl and Heinrich Schnitzler (Frankfurt: Fischer, 1964), 295. For Berta Zuckerkandl's recollection of the evening, see her *Österreich intim*, 145–46.

31. Zuckerkandl, *Österreich intim*, 186. The walls of her bedroom were hung with "Gobelins [tapestries] that functioned like paintings." Hoffmann used the same foliage-and-blossom pattern that was in the fashion department of the Wiener Werkstätte for the curtains and lampshades and on the walls and ceilings of Zuckerkandl's dining room. See Eduard F. Sekler, *Josef Hoffmann, The Architectural Work: Monograph and Catalogue of Works* (Princeton, N.J.: Princeton University Press, 1985), cat. no. 196, 376. For information on the décor, including the Peche curtains in the living room, we thank Prof. Emile Zuckerkandl.

32. Renée Price, with Pamela Kort and Leslie Topp, eds., *New Worlds: German and Austrian Art, 1890–1940*, exh. cat. (New York: Neue Galerie, and New Haven and London: Yale University Press, 2002), 467.

33. Zuckerkandl, *Österreich intim*, 186.

34. See Milan Dubrovic, *Veruntreute Geschichte: Die Wiener Salons und Literatencafés* (Berlin: Aufbau, 2001), 154ff.

35. On October 21, 1917, after one of his frequent visits to Zuckerkandl, Schnitzler noted in his diary: "She spent four months in Switzerland. Diplomatic negotiations . . . President v. L. correctly says that it is good to employ her for diplomatic missions, because one can always disavow her." Arthur Schnitzler, *Tagebuch, 1917–1919*, ed. Werner Welzig (Vienna: Verlag der Österreichischen Akademie der Wissenschaften, 1985), 84.

36. See Zuckerkandl, *Österreich intim*, 180–84; and Meysels, *In meinem Salon ist Österreich*, 255–60.

37. Personal communication from Prof. Emile Zuckerkandl.

38. Schorske, *Fin-de-Siècle Vienna*, 8–9. See also Jacques Le Rider, *Modernity and the Crisis of Identity*, trans. Rosemary Morris (New York: Continuum, 1993).

39. See Tag Gronberg, "The Inner Man: Interiors and Masculinity in Early Twentieth-Century Vienna," *Oxford Art Journal*, January 24, 2001, 67–88.

40. Russell A. Berman, "Introduction" to Arthur Schnitzler, *The Road into the Open*, trans. Roger Byers (Berkeley: University of California Press, 1992), ix.

41. Ludwig Hevesi, *Acht Jahre Secession* (Vienna: Carl Koneger, 1906), 394.

42. Helene von Nostitz, *Aus dem alten Europa: Menschen und Städte* (Reinbeck bei Hamburg: Rowohlt, 1964), 88.

43. Sarfatti was a prodigious critic—one of the most influential in Europe between the wars; her first reviews were of the Venice Biennale of 1901, for *Il Secolo Nuovo*. In addition to her monographic studies on various artists, she wrote *Segni colori e luci: Note d'arte* (Bologna: Nicola Zanichelli, 1925) and *Storia della pittura moderna* (Rome: Cremonese, 1930). For a comprehensive bibliography of her art writings only (more than five hundred), see Lorella Giudici, "Regesto degli scritti d'arte di Margherita Sarfatti (1901–38)," in Elena Pontiggia, *Da Boccioni a Sironi: Il mondo di Margherita Sarfatti* (Milan: Skira, 1997), 209–14.

44. The influence of Picasso's primitivism on Boccioni is discussed in Emily Braun, "Vulgarians at the Gate," in *Boccioni's Materia: A Futurist Masterpiece and the Avant-garde in Milan and Paris* (New York: Solomon R. Guggenheim Foundation, 2004), 6–7.

45. Richard Sennett, *The Fall of Public Man* (New York: W. W. Norton, 1974), 15, 60–63.

46. For an argument that Stein's lesbianism led to Picasso's use of the mask, see Robert Lubar, "Unmasking Pablo's Gertrude: Queer Desire and the Subject of Portraiture," *Art Bulletin* 79, no. 1 (1997): 56–84. Catharine Stimpson, "The Somograms of Gertrude Stein," in Susan Rubin Suleiman, ed., *The Female Body in Western Culture: Contemporary Perspectives* (Cambridge, Mass.: Harvard University Press, 1985), 30–43, analyzes the reactions of Stein's contemporaries to her triple "monstrosities" of fat woman, Jew, and lesbian. According to Philip V. Cannistraro and Brian R. Sullivan, *Il Duce's Other Woman: The Untold Story of Margherita Sarfatti* (New York: William Morrow, 1993), 59, Sarfatti "endorsed the libertarian mores that governed love affairs in her Bohemian world." They also governed traditions among aristocratic feminists. She is presumed (by contemporaries and her biographers) to have had extramarital liaisons with Boccioni and Corrado Alvaro; rumors among her peers spoke of homosexual dalliances with Valentine de St. Point and Colette.

47. As recounted by Fiammetta Sarfatti Gaetani, Sarfatti's daughter, in interviews with Emily Braun, Rome, autumn 1986. Boccioni painted Sarfatti in his earlier Divisionist style in 1911 at her country house Il Soldo (The Penny) near Lake Como, where she invited many of her salon habitués. Sarfatti salvaged and kept the portrait; it is unclear whether she subsequently paid him for it. It is reproduced in Pontiggia, *Da Boccioni a Sironi*, no. 28, 107.

48. Cannistraro and Sullivan, *Il Duce's Other Woman*, 335. Stein and Sarfatti never met.

49. Bernard Berenson, diary entry, November 11, 1952, in *Sunset and Twilight: From the Diaries of 1947–1958* (London: Hamish Hamilton, 1963), 283.

50. Margherita Sarfatti, *Acqua passata* (Rocca San Casciano, Italy: F. Capelli, 1955), 39.

51. See the essential biography by Cannistraro and Sullivan, *Il Duce's Other Woman*.

52. Guests books of Margherita Grassini Sarfatti, Rome, March 15, 1926–November 1933, and November 1933–July 14, 1938. We thank Margherita Gaetani, Rome, for access to this material. These are the only two extant guest books; it is unclear whether Sarfatti maintained any earlier.

53. Alma Mahler-Werfel, diary entry, April 2, 1928, in *Mein Leben* (Frankfurt: Fischer, 1965), 162.

54. Virgilio Brocchi, *Luce di grandi anime* (Milan: Mondadori, 1956), 168.

55. In 1938, shortly after the publication of the "The Manifesto of the Race," the Fascist minister Giuseppe Bottai recorded in his diary that Mussolini had made a point of telling him in private: "Even I have had a Jewish lover: Sarfatti. Intelligent, Fascist, the mother of a real hero. But, five years ago, foreseeing that the Jewish problem would become a major concern, I took steps to free myself from her. I had her dismissed from *Il Popolo d'Italia* and from her editorship at *Gerarchia* . . . with regular severance pay, you understand." Cannistraro and Sullivan, *Il Duce's Other Woman*, 515.

56. See Renzo De Felice, *Gli ebrei italiani sotto il fascismo* (Turin: Einaudi, 1988); Vivian B. Mann, ed., *Gardens and Ghettos: The Art of Jewish Life in Italy*, exh. cat. (New York: The Jewish Museum, and Berkeley: University of California Press, 1989), 136–89; and Alexander Stille, *Benevolence and Betrayal: Five Italian Jewish Families Under Fascism* (New York: Summit Books, 1991).

57. Cannistraro and Sullivan, *Il Duce's Other Woman*, 98, 343.

58. On Sarfatti's early years, see ibid., 19–36.

59. The influence of Sarfatti's Jewish background on her formulation of Fascism is hypothesized by Simona Urso in *Margherita Sarfatti: Dal mito del Dux al mito americano* (Venice: Marsilio, 2003), 47–48, 231–32.

60. Sarfatti grew closer to Marinetti after her husband successfully defended him against charges of obscenity for his novel *Mafarka il futurista* (1909). They were also connected through the publisher Umberto Notari, a supporter of Futurism, who attended both their salons and hired Sarfatti to write for the journal *Gli Avvenimenti*. On the Futurist avant-garde and cultural marketing, see Braun, "Vulgarians at the Gate," 1–5, 13–16.

61. Unpublished memoir by Amedeo Sarfatti, c. 1969, 2. We are grateful to the late Pierangela Sarfatti, wife of Amedeo, and to Philip Cannistraro for access to this document.

62. Works in Sarfatti's collection bearing personal dedications to her include unpublished drawings by Luigi Russolo, Adolfo

Wildt, and Giorgio de Chirico, and the Medardo Rosso sculpture *Il bambino ebreo* (*The Jewish Boy*), which he inscribed to her in the wax surface.

63. Margherita Grassini Sarfatti, "I pittori delle 'Nuove tendenze' alla Famiglia Artistica di Milano," *Avanti!* June 17, 1914. Her wartime essays were published in the anthology *La fiaccola accesa* (Milan: Istituto Editoriale Italiano, 1919).

64. Urso, *Margherita Sarfatti*, 90–91, 109–10, 132–34. Sarfatti's abnegation of a role for women in public affairs (herself excluded) and her view of woman as "custodian of the species" and maternal guardian of the nation-state fed directly into Fascist antifeminist policies. See also Victoria de Grazia, "Il fascino del priapo: Margherita Sarfatti biografa del Duce," *Memoria*, no. 4 (June 1982): 149–54; and de Grazia, *How Fascism Ruled Women: Italy, 1922–45* (Berkeley: University of California Press, 1992).

65. "Contro tutti i ritorni in pittura—Manifesto futurista" was signed in January 1920 and published in *Roma futurista*, April 25–May 2, 1920. The core group of Sarfatti's salon contributed short stories and illustrations for *Ardita* (from *ardito*, the storm trooper), co-founded by Sarfatti and Mussolini in 1919 as a monthly literary supplement to *Il Popolo d'Italia*.

66. The incident is described in Cannistraro and Sullivan, *Il Duce's Other Woman*, 220, according to the eyewitness accounts of guests present that evening.

67. The original seven artists were Dudreville, Sironi, Funi, Anselmo Bucci, Piero Marussig, Gian Emilio Malerba, and Ubaldo Oppi. Dudreville, cited in Rossana Bossaglia, *Il Novecento italiano*, 2nd ed. (Milan: Charta, 1995), 73. On Sarfatti and the Novecento, which had its first show in March 1923, see ibid., 19–24; Anna Nozzoli, "Margherita Sarfatti, organizzatrice di cultura: *Il Popolo d'Italia*," in Marina Addis Saba, ed., *La corporazione delle donne: Ricerche e studi sui modelli femminili nel ventennio fascista* (Florence: Vallecchi, 1988), 227–72; and Emily Braun, *Mario Sironi and Italian Modernism: Art and Politics Under Fascism* (New York: Cambridge University Press, 2000), 90–112.

68. Cannistraro and Sullivan, *Il Duce's Other Woman*, 389.

69. We thank Dr. Piero Foà for information and documents pertaining to his parents, the journalists Carlo and Eloisa Foà. Eloisa was the niece of Sarfatti's brother-in-law Paolo Errera, who with his wife, Nella, Sarfatti's sister, died on a train to Auschwitz. The Foàs escaped to Brazil.

70. Ugo Ojetti, diary entry, November 4, 1925, in *I taccuini, 1914–1943* (Florence: Sansoni, 1954), 204.

71. For speculation on the Sarfatti marriage and Mussolini, see Cannistraro and Sullivan, *Il Duce's Other Woman*, 180, 202. Cesare Sarfatti died in January 1924 and was buried in the Jewish section of the Cimitero Monumentale in Milan. Adolfo Wildt designed his marble tombstone, surmounted by a bronze menorah. See Giovanni Ginex and Ornella Selvafolta, *Il Cimitero Monumentale di Milano: Guida storico-artistica* (Cinisello

Balsamo, Italy: Silvana, 1996), 196. Sarfatti converted to Catholicism in 1928, on the eve of the Lateran Pact, not only to please her lover, but also in light of Mussolini's objections to Zionist sentiment among Italian Jews and his increasing political use of anti-Semitism. Upon her death in 1961, Sarfatti was buried in a small cemetery in Cavallasca, near her country house. Her simple marble plinth was designed by the sculptor Emilio Greco: it bears a cast of Adolfo Wildt's head of Victory and her name carved in large script in the signature style of Mario Sironi.

72. Corrado Alvaro, *Quasi una vita: Giornale di uno scrittore* (Milan: Bompiani, 1950), 58.

73. Ibid.; Cannistraro and Sullivan, *Il Duce's Other Woman*, chap. 22, "Dictator of Culture," 326–49.

74. Sarfatti, *The Life of Benito Mussolini*, trans. Frederic Whyte (London: Thorton Butterworth, 1925), 346.

75. Sarfatti's relationship with Americans in Rome and her trip to the United States in 1934 are detailed in Cannistraro and Sullivan, *Il Duce's Other Woman*, chap. 25 ("New Deal and New Order"), 396–417.

76. Already in the early 1920s, Mussolini objected to many of her guests who held anti-Fascist sentiments, and complained of Cesare's clients who were not affiliated with the party. Sarfatti responded that she would never be swayed by the opinions of any anti-Fascists she might invite to the salon. (Cannistraro and Sullivan, *Il Duce's Other Woman*, 272–73.)

77. Sarfatti's guest books include the names of many artists later associated with the Scuola Romana—Roberto Melli, Mario Mafai, Scipione, Afro and Mirko Basaldella, and Corrado Cagli. Although the style of these artists' works tended toward the lyrical and antimonumental—in contrast to the Novecento—theirs was never an official movement, and in the postwar years its role as a cultural frond was exaggerated. "Mimì" Pecci-Blunt began the Galleria della Cometa in 1935 to promote these artists and in 1937 opened a branch in New York. Moravia wrote for a few of the catalogues. The Cometa was accused of promoting "Jewish art" during the period of the racial laws (Melli and Cagli were Jews), and closed in 1938.

78. Giuseppe Prezzolini, diary entry, January 12, 1939, in *Diario, 1900–1941*, vol. 1 (Milan: Rusconi, 1978), 616.

EXPATRIATES AND AVANT-GARDES

1. Gertrude Stein, *The Autobiography of Alice B. Toklas* (hereafter *AABT;* 1933; reprint, New York: Vintage, 1990), 89.

2. Marcel Proust, *The Guermantes Way*, vol. 3 of *In Search of Lost Time*, trans. C. K. Scott Moncrieff and Terence Kilmartin, rev. D. J. Enright (New York: Modern Library, 1998), 252–53. Stein claimed that the three most important novels of her generation were her own *The Making of Americans*, Proust's *À la recherche du temps perdu*, and James Joyce's *Ulysses*. See James R. Mellow,

Charmed Circle: Gertrude Stein and Company (New York: Praeger, 1974), 122.

3. Jacques-Émile Blanche, *Portraits of a Lifetime: The Late Victorian Era, the Edwardian Pageant, 1870–1914*, trans. Walter Clement (New York: Coward-McCann, 1938), 276.

4. Stein, *AABT*, 41.

5. See Mellow, *Charmed Circle;* Bruce Kellner, ed., *A Gertrude Stein Companion: Content with the Example* (New York: Greenwood, 1988); Shari Benstock, *Women of the Left Bank: Paris, 1900–1940* (Austin: University of Texas Press, 1986); Steven Watson, *Strange Bedfellows: The First American Avant-Garde* (New York: Abbeville, 1991); and Robert M. Crunden, *American Salons: Encounters with European Modernism, 1885–1917* (New York: Oxford University Press, 1993). In her own time, several of Stein's former guests took umbrage at the inaccuracies of many of her recollections and at her self-aggrandizement. In reaction to *The Autobiography of Alice B. Toklas*, a group of notables—Georges Braque, Eugene and Maria Jolas, and Henri Matisse, André Salmon, and Tristan Tzara—published their own *Testimony Against Gertrude Stein* (The Hague: Servire, 1935) as a supplement to the magazine *Transition*.

6. Gertrude arrived at 27 rue de Fleurus in the fall of 1903, following Leo, who had already secured the studio. He began collecting in earnest that year. Toklas arrived in Paris in 1907 and moved into 27 rue de Fleurus permanently in autumn 1910. By 1912, Leo rarely attended the Saturday evenings.

7. Gertrude Stein, "'Have They Attacked Mary. He Giggled.' An Utterance from the High Priestess of Cubist Literature," *Vanity Fair*, June 1917, 55.

8. Ibid.

9. Fernande Olivier, journal entry, February–March 1906, in *Loving Picasso: The Private Journal of Fernande Olivier*, trans. Christine Baler and Michael Raeburn (New York: Harry N. Abrams, 2001), 178.

10. Brenda Wineapple, *Sister Brother: Gertrude and Leo Stein* (New York: G. P. Putnam's Sons, 1996), 212.

11. Stein, *AABT*, 49.

12. See Jerrold Seigel, *Bohemian Paris: Culture, Politics, and the Boundaries of Bourgeois Life, 1830–1930* (New York: Viking, 1986); and Elizabeth Wilson, *Bohemians: The Glamorous Outcasts* (New Brunswick, N.J.: Rutgers University Press, 2000).

13. Leo Stein to Gertrude Stein in London, February 1913, on the occasion of her thirty-ninth birthday, cited in Mellow, *Charmed Circle*, 200.

14. Stein, *AABT*, 13.

15. Ibid.

16. Gertrude Stein, *Paris France* (New York: Charles Scribner's Sons, 1940).

17. Gertrude Stein, *Everybody's Autobiography* (New York: Random House, 1937), 76.

18. Claudia Roth Pierpont, "The Mother of Confusion: Gertrude Stein," in *Passionate Minds: Women Rewriting the World* (New York: Vintage, 2000), 41. Mary Smith Costelloe's husband, Bernard Berenson, was a Lithuanian-born Jew raised in Boston. As Wineapple, *Sister Brother*, 257, notes, Berenson took to calling her an "Angry Saxon."

19. Benstock, *Women of the Left Bank*, 269–307. On Barney's lesbian circle, see also Whitney Chadwick, *Amazons in the Drawing Room: The Art of Romaine Brooks* (Berkeley: University of California Press, 2000).

20. Benstock, *Women of the Left Bank*, 8–21.

21. Stein, *AABT*, 12.

22. Leo Stein, *Appreciation: Painting, Poetry and Prose* (New York: Crown, 1947; reprint, Lincoln: University of Nebraska Press, 1956), 195.

23. Leon Katz, "Matisse, Picasso and Gertrude Stein," in *Four Americans in Paris: The Collections of Gertrude Stein and Her Family*, exh. cat. (New York: Museum of Modern Art, 1970), 51; Stein, *AABT*, 114.

24. Wendy Steiner, *Exact Resemblance to Exact Resemblance: The Literary Portraiture of Gertrude Stein* (New Haven and London: Yale University Press, 1978), esp. chap. 2, "The Steinian Portrait: The History of a Theory," 27–63. Steiner's text is the standard on Stein's portraits, though she does not consider their relationship to Stein's salon.

25. Ibid., 40. As Steiner writes (pp. 29–40), Stein's theory and practice of portraiture were grounded in her psychology studies with her mentor William James at Radcliffe College.

26. Wineapple, *Sister Brother*, 335, notes that Macdonald-Wright heard Gertrude Stein reciting the portraits of "Matisse" and "Picasso."

27. Marsden Hartley to Gertrude Stein, cited in Donald Gallup, "The Weaving of a Pattern: Marsden Hartley and Gertrude Stein," *Magazine of Art* 41 (November 1948), 257.

28. Stein's portrait of Hartley, entitled "M___NH___," from the play *IIIIIIIII*, was printed in a brochure for the artist's exhibition in January 1914 at Stieglitz's 291 gallery. On Hartley, see Barbara Haskell, *Marsden Hartley* (New York: Whitney Museum of American Art and New York University Press, 1980). Hartley used the mandorla form in other works of the period, where it sometimes veers more toward a mountain shape; only in *One Portrait of One Woman* does it take on a vaginal configuration.

29. Stein, *AABT*, 138.

30. Steiner, *Exact Resemblance to Exact Resemblance*, 81–82, 98.

31. The history and holdings of the Stein collection are described in the exhibition catalogue *Four Americans in Paris*.

32. Henry McBride, "Pictures for a Picture of Gertrude," *ART News* 49 (February 1951): 18. On the Americans influenced by the art and company of the Stein salon, see Gail Stavitsky, *Gertrude Stein: The American Connection* (New York: Sid Deutsch Gallery, 1990).

33. Marsden Hartley to Alfred Stieglitz, July 12, 1912; Alfred Stieglitz/Georgia O'Keeffe Archive, Yale Collection of American Literature, Beinecke Rare Book and Manuscript Library, Yale University, New Haven. Reprinted in James Timothy Voorhies, ed., *My Dear Stieglitz: Letters of Marsden Hartley and Alfred Stieglitz, 1912–1915* (Columbia: University of South Carolina Press, 2002), 20. The sketch, done from memory, is likely a compilation of *The Architect's Table* and other works by Picasso of the same time, since certain features (the vivid blue and ornate frame described in the letter) do not correspond to the Stein canvas.

34. Gino Severini, *The Life of a Painter*, trans. Jennifer Franchina (Princeton, N.J.: Princeton University Press, 1995), 92.

35. Mellow, *Charmed Circle*, 86; Stein, *AABT*, 44–45. The foremost introducer was the writer and man-about-town Henri-Pierre Roché.

36. See James Mellow, "Gertrude Stein and the Dadaists," *Arts Magazine* 51 (May 1977): 124–26; and Beth Venn, "New York Dada Portraiture: Rendering Modern Identity," in Francis Naumann, *Making Mischief: Dada Invades New York*, exh. cat. (New York: Whitney Museum of American Art and Harry N. Abrams, 1996), 272–79.

37. Mellow, *Charmed Circle*, 169–72. Dodge's article, "Speculations, or Post-Impressionism in Prose," appeared in the March 1913 *Arts and Decoration*, a special number devoted to the Armory Show.

38. Stein, *AABT*, 140; Alvin Langdon Coburn, *Men of Mark* (London: Duckworth, 1913).

39. Ibid., 15.

40. Gertrude Stein, *G.M.P. (Matisse Picasso and Gertrude Stein)* (1912; reprint, Mineola, N.Y.: Dover, 2000), 203.

41. Stein, *AABT*, 123–24.

42. Ibid., 88.

43. Robert Hughes, "The Rise of Andy Warhol," *New York Review of Books*, February 18, 1982, reprinted in Steven Henry Madoff, ed., *Pop Art: A Critical History* (Berkeley: University of California Press, 1997), 378.

44. Marsden Hartley, "The Paintings of Florine Stettheimer," *Creative Art* 9 (July 1931): 19.

45. Several of the 1929 and 1934 menus (with guest lists) devised by Carrie Stettheimer are in the Stettheimer papers, Yale Collection of American Literature, Beinecke Rare Book and Manuscript Library, Yale University, New Haven, ser. 4, box 10, folder 173.

46. Barbara Bloemink, *The Life and Art of Florine Stettheimer* (New Haven and London: Yale University Press, 1995), 96 and 264, n. 22.

47. Florine Stettheimer, *Crystal Flowers* (New York: Ettie Stettheimer, 1949), 82. Stettheimer's contemporaries—Charles Demuth, Marsden Hartley, Carl Van Vechten, and Henry McBride, all homosexuals—were the first to write of the French allusion (they identified it as eighteenth-century) in her work. The theme was developed in full in the first monograph on the artist, Parker Tyler's *Florine Stettheimer: A Life in Art* (New York: Farrar, Straus, 1963).

48. Naumann, *Making Mischief*. On the origins of "Yankee Doodle Dandy," see Ellen Moers, *The Dandy: Brummell to Beerbohm* (New York: Viking, 1960).

49. Duchamp, Buenos Aires, November 12, 1918, to the Stettheimer sisters, reprinted in Francis Naumann and Hector Obalk, eds., *Affectionately, Marcel: The Selected Correspondence of Marcel Duchamp* (Ghent: Ludion, 2000),69.

50. On *Four Saints in Three Acts*, see Bloemink, *Life and Art of Florine Stettheimer*, 187–99. Their first documented meeting occurred in California early in 1935.

51. H. L. Mencken to the Stettheimer sisters; November 27, 1929. Stettheimer papers, ser. 1, box 3, folder 50.

52. Henry McBride, "Artists in the Drawing Room," *Town and Country*, December 1946, 77.

53. Stettheimer, *Crystal Flowers*, 42.

54. Carl Van Vechten "Prelude," in Tyler, *Florine Stettheimer*, xiii.

55. Ibid., 59.

56. See Elisabeth Sussman, "Florine Stettheimer: A 1990s Perspective," in Elisabeth Sussman and Barbara Bloemink, *Florine Stettheimer: Manhattan Fantastica*, exh. cat. (New York: Whitney Museum of American Art, 1995), 54–66.

57. Stephen Birmingham, *"Our Crowd": The Great Jewish Families of New York* (1967; reprint, Syracuse, N.Y.: Syracuse University Press, 1996).

58. Ibid., 91–92. Max Stettheimer, Joseph's father, a "colorless man, moody and uncommunicative," had earlier formed an unhappy union with Babette Seligman. As Birmingham writes (p. 351), Adele Walter, Rosetta's sister, married David Seligman, the son of scion Joseph Seligman, and then, upon his death, David's first cousin Henry Seligman. A celebrated party-giver in the 1920s, she lived on East Fifty-sixth Street and had a home in Palm Beach. Bloemink, *Life and Art of Florine Stettheimer*, 1, documents that the Stettheimers were related to the Jewish "One Hundred" families Seligman, Goodhart, Bernheimer, Beer, Neustadter, Walter, and Guggenheim. The sisters' aunt Josephine Walter, who never married, received a diploma from Mount Sinai Hospital and was the first woman intern in America. She finished her medical studies in Europe and eventually opened a

practice in New York specializing in women's health. Bloemink also notes (p. 284, n. 25) that the sisters were apparently distantly related to Natalie Barney.

59. Florine Stettheimer, diary entry, April 26, 1910, Stettheimer papers, ser. 2, box 6, folder 112. Ettie, in her diary entry of March 31, 1919 (Stettheimer papers, ser. 2, box 7, folder 131), wrote that Florine refused an offer to exhibit in "Dr. Stickney Grant's Church; her grounds being that she did not respect the church that baptized fashionable Jews." After Florine's death, out of jealousy or typical family propriety, Ettie removed anything she considered too personal from her sister's sketchbooks and diaries, thus eradicating key elements of Florine's legacy.

60. On the Stettheimer circle and uptown New York "civic intellectuals," see Thomas Bender, *New York Intellect: A History of Intellectual Life in New York City, from 1750 to the Beginnings of Our Own Time* (New York: Alfred A. Knopf, 1987), 327–28.

61. Stettheimer, *Crystal Flowers*, 60.

62. Florine Stettheimer to Carrie and Ettie Stettheimer, April 11, 1934, Stettheimer papers, ser. 1, box 5, folder 91.

63. Hartley, "Paintings of Florine Stettheimer," 21. On "unexpected turns" in salon conversation, see McBride, "Artists in the Drawing Room." On Stettheimer and Proust, see Carl Van Vechten's preface to Tyler, *Florine Stettheimer*, xiii.

64. One of Duchamp's four luggage tags for Rrose Sélavy (see below in text) bears the handwritten inscription "Ettie qu'êtès." Stettheimer papers, ser. 1, box 1, folder 20.

65. On October 2, 1923, Florine wrote in her diary: "I have not yet finished the two portraits. Ettie has a Xmas tree burning bush combination—I have decided the Xmas tree is an outcome of the burning bush of Moses." Stettheimer papers, ser. 2, box 6, folder 114.

66. Elizabeth Goldsmith, *Exclusive Conversations: The Art of Interaction in Seventeenth-Century France* (Philadelphia: University of Pennsylvania Press, 1988), 10–11, 31. In the summer of 1922, Ettie wrote this note to Duchamp (on pink paper), alluding to their sexually incompatible relationship. It is unclear if she ever sent it: "Pensée-cadeau / Vers a Un Ami/ Je voudrais être faite sur mesure / Pout toi, pour toi— / Mais je suis ready-made par la nature, / Pour quoi, pour quoi / Comme je ne le sais pas j'ai fait des rectifications / Pour moi—." Stettheimer papers, ser. 1, box 1, folder 19.

67. Duchamp, Rouen, January 3, 1922, to Ettie Stettheimer, reprinted in Naumann and Obalk, eds., *Affectionately, Marcel*, 105.

68. Birmingham, *"Our Crowd,"* 350.

69. Stettheimer, *Crystal Flowers*, 42.

70. Ibid., 5.

71. On Duchamp's ambiguous sexuality and its relation to his lifelong artistic themes of the Bride and the Bachelor, see Jerrold Seigel, *The Private World of Marcel Duchamp: Desire, Liberation,*

and the Self in Modern Culture (Berkeley: University of California Press, 1995), esp. chap. 7, "Working and Loving," 184–213.

72. Ibid., 145.

73. Barbara Bloemink, "Florine Stettheimer: Hiding in Plain Sight," in Naomi Sawelson-Gorse, ed., *Women in Dada: Essays on Sex, Gender, and Identity* (Cambridge, Mass.: MIT Press, 1998), 501. Bloemink was the first to speculate that Duchamp may have used Florine as a model for Rrose Sélavy.

74. See Duchamp's letters to the sisters cited in Naumann and Obalk, eds., *Affectionately, Marcel*, 101, 122, 133. See also unpublished correspondence from Duchamp dating from 1919 to 1925, signed "Rrose," in the Stettheimer papers, ser. 1, box 1, folders 19, 20. In his letters, Duchamp also turns the greeting "Chère Ettie" into "Cherry Tree," and calls the sisters the "Cherry Orchard," as in Anton Chekhov's play with three sisters. Florine penned her own inside and subversive take on Duchamp's *Bride Stripped Bare by Her Bachelors, Even:* "The happy bride dropped all / her clothes / Then powdered her broad / but delightful nose / 'An dis is what for is / my bridal veil / Covering me all up / I look quite pale'/ Chuckled blissfully dusky / black Rose." *Crystal Flowers*, 38.

75. George Chauncey, *Gay New York: Gender, Urban Culture and the Making of the Gay Male World, 1890–1940* (New York: Basic Books, 1994), 132–36.

76. On the history and role of salon portraiture in the second half of the seventeenth century, see Bendetta Craveri, *La civiltà della conversazione* (Milan: Adelphi, 2001), 222–36.

77. Stettheimer, *Crystal Flowers*, 79.

78. See Cécile Whiting, "Decorating with Stettheimer and the Boys," *American Art* 13 (Spring 2000): 34; Susan Fillin-Yeh, "Dandies, Marginality, and Modernism: Georgia O'Keeffe, Marcel Duchamp, and Other Cross-Dressers," in Sawelson-Gorse, *Women in Dada*, 174–203; and Linda Nochlin, "Florine Stettheimer: Rococo Subversive," *Art in America* 68 (September 1980): 64–83.

79. Bloemink, *Life and Art of Florine Stettheimer*, 106; on Stettheimer's sympathy for black causes and her appreciation of racial uniqueness, see Nochlin, "Florine Stettheimer," 70–73.

80. Birmingham, *"Our Crowd,"* 312.

81. Paul Rosenfeld, "Art: The World of Florine Stettheimer," *Nation*, May 4, 1922, 522. In a letter of 1939 to Fania Marinoff, Van Vechten's wife, Ettie revealed the family's ambivalence toward Christmas: "I myself have a very *unpleasant* conscience about celebrating Xmas at all, which I only do—after reducing the celebration to its smallest dimension—because our family, brought up in Germany, got the Xmas habit." Bloemink, *Life and Art of Florine Stettheimer*, 271, n. 37.

82. Paul Rosenfeld, "Florine Stettheimer," *Accent* 5 (Winter 1945): 99–102.

83. Henry McBride, *Florine Stettheimer*, exh. cat. (New York: Museum of Modern Art, 1946), 10. McBride writes that Florine Stettheimer "seemed often a furtive guest rather than one of the genji loci which she undoubtedly was, for her demure presence invariably counted."

84. Bender, *New York Intellect*, 324–28.

85. Bloemink, *Life and Art of Florine Stettheimer*, 191.

86. As Bloemink, ibid., 223–27, writes, Barr had been removed from his post as director of the Modern in 1939, and demoted to curator, while Francis Taylor was negotiating over Barr's head for a possible merger of the Metropolitan and the Modern. The Whitney could not settle on a permanent site to hold Gertrude Vanderbilt Whitney's growing collection of living American artists, and when she died in 1943, Taylor opened secret discussions with a trustee to incorporate the collection into the Metropolitan. (Whitney and Force had offered it to the Metropolitan in 1929, but the director, Edward Robinson, had refused it.) Among Stettheimer's habitués represented in the painting are the artists Demuth, Elie Nadelman (as one of his own portrait busts), Robert Locher (the *compère*), Pavel Tchelitchew, McBride (with the "Stop" and "Go" flags); and Austin, Wheeler, Askew, and his wife, Constance.

THE SALON IN EXILE

1. Samuel N. Behrman to Salka Viertel, November 24, 1965, Nachlass Viertel, 80.1.60/7, Handschriftenabteilung, Deutsches Literaturarchiv, Schiller-Nationalmuseum, Marbach am Neckar, Germany.

2. Christopher Isherwood, *Prater Violet* (New York: Random House, 1945), 23.

3. Berthold Viertel to Salka Viertel, [c. August 1928], Nachlass Viertel, 78.856/12.

4. Salka Viertel, *The Kindness of Strangers: A Theatrical Life, Vienna, Berlin, Hollywood* (New York: Holt, Rinehart and Winston, 1969), 139.

5. Ibid., 143.

6. Berthold Viertel to Salka Viertel, cited in ibid., 190.

7. Viertel, *Kindness of Strangers*, 142.

8. Ibid., 134–35.

9. Ibid., 140.

10. Tallulah Bankhead, *Tallulah: My Autobiography* (New York: Harper and Brothers, 1952), 198.

11. Viertel, *Kindness of Strangers*, 144.

12. Gottfried Reinhardt, *The Genius: A Memoir of Max Reinhardt* (New York: Alfred A. Knopf, 1979), 303.

13. John Houseman, *Unfinished Business: A Memoir* (London: Chatto and Windus, 1986), 266.

14. Werner Mittenzwei, *Das Leben des Bertolt Brecht, oder, Der Umgang mit den Welträtseln*, 2 vols. (Frankfurt: Suhrkamp, 1987), 2:181.

15. Bertolt Brecht to Karl Korsch, [August 1941], in Bertolt Brecht, *Letters*, ed. John Willet, trans. Ralph Manheim (London: Methuen, 1990), 339.

16. For Brecht's journal entries with the text of the declaration, and an exchange of letters between Brecht and Thomas Mann over this incident, see Michael Winkler, ed., *Deutsche Literatur in Exil, 1933–1945: Texte und Dokumente* (Stuttgart: Reclam, 1977), 256–62.

17. Thomas Mann, *Tagebücher, 1940–1943*, ed. Peter de Mendelssohn (Frankfurt: Fischer, 1982), 152–53; Mann, *Tagebücher, 1944–1946*, ed. Inge Jens (Frankfurt: Fischer, 1986), 13, 129.

18. Alfred Döblin to Hermann Kesten, July 24, 1941, in Hans Wysling, ed., *Letters of Heinrich and Thomas Mann, 1900–1949*, trans. Don Reneau and Richard and Clara Winston (Berkeley: University of California Press, 1998), 414–15.

19. Viertel, *Kindness of Strangers*, 250.

20. Mittenzwei, *Leben des Bertolt Brecht*, 2:17.

21. Ruth Berlau, *Brechts Lai-Tu: Erinnerungen und Notate*, ed. Hans Bunge (Darmstadt: Luchterhand, 1985), 199–201.

22. Thomas Mann, diary entry, December 17, 1944, in Mann, *Tagebücher, 1944–1946*, 135.

23. Christopher Isherwood, *Lost Years: A Memoir, 1945–1951*, ed. Katherine Bucknell (New York: HarperCollins, 2002), 70–71.

24. Elizabeth Frank, personal communication to Emily Bilski, June 10, 2003.

25. Marta Feuchtwanger, oral history interview conducted by Lawrence Weschler, August 1975, transcript 1188–89. Specialized Libraries and Archival Collections, Feuchtwanger Memorial Library, University of Southern California, Los Angeles.

26. Thomas Mann, "Address on Heinrich Mann's Seventieth Birthday: Delivered on May 2, 1941, During a Gathering at Frau Salka Viertel's," in Wysling, *Letters of Mann, 1900–1949*, 292.

27. Salka Viertel to Berthold Viertel, September 14, 1928, Nachlass Viertel, 78.907/4.

28. Sabine Lepsius, "Ueber das Aussterben der 'Salons,'" *März* 7 (1913): 228–29. Consider also the title of the book by Jeanne Maurice Pouquet about her mother, Madame Arman de Caillavet, *The Last Salon: Anatole France and His Muse*, trans. Lewis Galantière (New York: Harcourt, Brace, 1927), and see the passage from Edith Wharton's *Backward Glance* at the beginning of our essay.

29. Virginia Woolf, "A Modern Salon," in Woolf, *Carlyle's House and Other Sketches*, ed. David Bradshaw (London: Hesperus, 2003), 12.

30. Rahel Varnhagen, *Gesammelte Werke*, ed. Konrad Feilchenfeldt, Uwe Schweikert, and Rahel E. Steiner, 10 vols. (Munich: Matthes und Seitz, 1983), 2:609–10.

31. Rahel Varnhagen to Pauline Wiesel, April 30, 1819, cited in Barbara Hahn, "Der Mythos vom Salon: 'Rahels Dachstube' als historische Fiktion," in Hartwig Schultz, ed., *Salons der Romantik: Beiträge eines Wiepersdorfer Kolloquiums zu Theorie und Geschichte des Salons* (Berlin: Walter de Gruyter, 1997), 234.

A Dream of Living Together

Translated by James McFarland.

1. August Hennings, writing in 1772, quoted in Ludwig Geiger, *Berlin, 1688–1840: Geschichte des geistigen Lebens der preussischen Hauptstadt*, vol. 1 (Berlin: Paetel, 1895), 383–84. He mentions Moses Mendelssohn (1729–1786), Daniel Itzig (1723–1799), and David Friedländer (1750–1834), who was married to Blümche, one of the nine Itzig daughters.

2. See the chapter "The Myth of the Salon" in Barbara Hahn, *The Jewess Pallas Athena* (Princeton, N.J.: Princeton University Press, forthcoming 2005).

3. Henriette Herz, daughter of Esther and Benjamin de Lemos, was born in 1764 in Berlin. She married the physician and philosopher Markus Herz (1747–1803) in 1779 and in 1817 converted to Protestantism. She died in Berlin in 1847.

4. A daughter of Miriam (1727–1788) and Daniel Itzig, Sara Levy was born in Berlin in 1761. She married the banker Samuel Salomon Levy (1760–1806) in 1783 and died in Berlin in 1854.

5. Sophie von Grotthuss, born in Berlin in 1763 as Sara Meyer, was the daughter of Rösl and Aron Meyer. She married the merchant Lipman Wulff in 1778 and divorced him ten years later. That same year she converted to Protestantism but returned to Judaism after a few weeks. In 1797 she married Baron Ferdinand Dietrich von Grotthuss. She died in 1828 in Oranienburg. Her sister Mariane (b. 1770) converted with her to Protestantism and in 1797 married Prince Heinrich XIV Reuss (1749–1799), the Austrian ambassador to Prussia. After Reuss's death, the family refused to grant Mariane Meyer the family's name; the Austrian emperor bestowed her the name von Eybenberg. She died in Vienna in 1812.

6. Only Goethe's letters to the sisters have been published. The complete correspondence with Sophie von Grotthuss and Mariane von Eybenberg will be published in 2006.

7. Rahel Levin, daughter of Chaie and Markus Levin, was born in Berlin in 1771; she changed her last name to Robert around 1800. In 1814 she converted to Protestantism a few days before her marriage to the Prussian diplomat Karl August Varnhagen von Ense (1785–1858). Her Christian name was Friederike Antonie. She died in Berlin in 1833.

8. *Caspar Voght und sein Freundeskreis: Briefe aus dem tätigen Leben*, vol. 2 (Hamburg: Veröffentlichungen des Vereins für Hamburgische Geschichte, 1964), 130–31.

9. Ibid., 142. The poet Friedrich Schlegel was a friend of Rahel Levin Varnhagen's.

10. *Aus Chamissos Frühzeit: Ungedruckte Briefe nebst Studien*, ed. Ludwig Geiger (Berlin: Paetel, 1905), 74.

11. Letter dated January 14, 1797, *Die Briefe Johann Daniel Sanders an Carl August Böttiger*, ed. Bernd Maurach, vol. 1 (Bern: Peter Lang, 1990), 83–88, here 85.

12. The papers of Sophie von Grotthuss and Mariane von Eybenberg, however, run to some nine hundred pages.

13. A daughter of Miriam and Daniel Itzig, Zippora (later Cäcilie) was born in Berlin in 1760. She married Benjamin Isaak Wulff in 1777, then divorced him and married the banker Baron Bernhard von Eskeles (1753–1839), with whom she lived in Vienna untill her death in 1836.

14. Varnhagen Collection, Biblioteka Jagiellońska, Kraków, box 57. The translation tries to keep as much as possible from the original letters with their lack of punctuation and distinction of foreign words, etc. Underlined words, however, are rendered in italics.

15. Brinckmann papers, Archive Trolle Ljungby (hereafter ATL).

16. In his memoirs, Ludwig Rellstab describes private concerts, but only after 1806. His father, together with Count Lehndorf, "who blew the recorder quite skillfully," and Sara Levy, the "accomplished pianist," organized these: "Both of them had the frequent desire to play with an orchestra, and so they came together with my father in order to divide the costs of this. These concerts took place in the evening between 6 and 9 o'clock in our residence, which was furnished for them, where two respectable chambers, each with four front windows, joined together." Sara Levy used the opportunity to play only "Sebastian and Philipp Emanuel Bach." Ludwig Rellstab, *Aus meinem Leben*, vol. 1 (Berlin: Guttentag, 1861), 117. See also Peter Wollny, "Sara Levy and the Making of Musical Taste in Berlin," *Musical Quarterly* 77, no. 4 (1993): 651–88.

17. Hanne Itzig was born in Berlin in 1748 and married Joseph Fliess in 1766. She died in Berlin in 1801.

18. One such concert was held on April 11, 1793; see a billet from Rahel Levin to Brinckmann; ATL.

19. Pessel—her Christian name was Philippine—was the daughter of Vögelchen and Moses Zülz, who later took on the name Bernhard. Her parents owned the silk factory for which Moses Mendelssohn once worked. She was born in Berlin in 1776 and married Ephraim Cohen in 1794; the couple had six children. In 1800 the family converted and joined the French Reformed Church.

20. Stephanie de Genlis, *Mémoires inédits*, vol. 5 (Paris: Ladvocat, 1825), 60–65.

21. Karl August Varnhagen, *Denkwürdigkeiten des eigenen Lebens*, ed. Konrad Feilchenfeldt, vol. 1 (Frankfurt: Klassiker Verlag, 1987), 239–51.

22. Brinckmann papers, ATL.

23. *Wilhelm und Caroline von Humboldt in ihren Briefen*, ed. Anna von Sydow, vol. 1 (Berlin: Ernst Siegfried Mittler und Sohn, 1910), 216.

24. Brinckmann papers, ATL.

25. Rahel Varnhagen, *Gesammelte Werke*, ed. Konrad Feilchenfeldt, Uwe Schweikert, and Rahel E. Steiner, 10 vols. (Munich: Matthes und Seitz, 1983), 7/1:76.

26. Ibid., 188.

27. Ibid., 204.

28. Brinckmann papers, ATL.

29. Varnhagen, *Gesammelte Werke*, 1:306–7.

30. Diary A, Varnhagen Collection, box 204.

31. Brinckmann papers, ATL.

32. Ibid.

33. Hitzel Zülz, sister of Philippine Cohen, married the physician Isaac Fliess (1770–c. 1829) in 1791. Her second marriage was to the Swedish major Baron von Boye in 1798, whom she also divorced. Her third marriage was to the Swedish general Count Bengt Erland von Sparre (1774–1837). She died in Sweden in 1839. Freude Meyer was born in Neustrelitz in 1767 and married Michael Joseph Fränkel (1746–1813) in 1787. After her divorce in 1798, she changed her first name to Sophie and married the Austrian merchant Simon von Pobeheim. Brendel, the oldest daughter of Fromet and Moses Mendelssohn, was born in Berlin in 1763. She married the banker and merchant Simon Veit in 1783 and had two sons, the painters Johannes and Philipp Veit. In 1797, she met Friedrich Schlegel. After divorcing her husband in 1799, she converted to Protestantism and married Schlegel in 1804. Four years later, the couple converted to Catholicism. She died in Frankfurt in 1839.

34. *Wilhelm und Caroline von Humboldt*, 178–80.

35. Hannah Arendt, *Rahel Varnhagen: The Life of a Jewess*, ed. Liliane Weissberg, trans. Richard and Clara Winston (1958; Baltimore: Johns Hopkins University Press, 1997), 127.

36. Varnhagen, *Gesammelte Werke*, 1:259.

37. Varnhagen, *Gesammelte Werke*, 1:609–10.

38. Rainer Schmitz, ed., *Henriette Herz in Erinnerungen, Briefen und Zeugnissen* (Leipzig: Gustav Kiepenheuer, 1984), 51.

39. Prince Louis Ferdinand of Prussia (1772–1806), a friend of Rahel Levin's.

40. Written in September 1835; Brinckmann papers, ATL.

41. Diary A, Varnhagen Collection, box 204.

Music, Femininity, and Jewish Identity

1. See, e.g., Petra Wilhelmy-Dollinger's "Emanzipation durch Gesellligkeit: Die Salons jüdischer Frauen in Berlin zwischen 1780 und 1830," in Marianne Awerbuch and Stefi Jersch-Wenzel, eds., *Bild und Selbstbild der Juden Berlins zwischen Aufklärung und Romantik: Beiträge zu einer Tagung* (Berlin: Colloquium, 1992), 121–38.

2. On Beer, see Steven M. Lowenstein, *The Berlin Jewish Community: Enlightenment, Family, Crisis, 1770–1830* (New York: Oxford University Press, 1994), 107; and Petra Wilhelmy-Dollinger, *Der Berliner Salon im 19. Jahrhundert (1780–1914)* (Berlin: Walter de Gruyter, 1989), 144–46.

3. See Leon Botstein, "Introduction: The Tragedy and Irony of Success; Locating Jews in the Musical Life of Vienna," and "Social History and the Politics of the Aesthetic: Jews and Music in Vienna, 1870–1938," in Botstein and Werner Hanak, eds., *Vienna: Jews and the City of Music, 1870–1938*, exh. cat. Jüdisches Museum der Stadt Wien and Center for Jewish History, New York (Annandale-on-Hudson, N.Y.: Bard College, and Hofheim: Wolke Verlag, 2004), 13–22, 43–63; originally published in German as *Quasi una fantasia: Juden und die Musikstadt Wien* (Vienna: Wolke, 2003).

4. See Elisabeth Derow-Turnauer, "Women and the Musical Aesthetics of the Bourgeoisie," in Botstein and Hanak, *Vienna*, 123–29.

5. See Lucian O. Meysels, *In meinem Salon ist Österreich: Berta Zuckerkandl und ihre Zeit* (Vienna: Herold, 1984).

6. The role of music in the education of women during the nineteenth century is a well-documented, albeit complicated, subject. Consider, for example, the ambivalent attitude toward musical skills that Jane Austen and George Eliot reveal in their novelistic protagonists. In the case of *Middlemarch*, Rosamond Vincy is quite gifted and skilled, inspiring the envy of her own brother. But her musical skills, acknowledged qualities, and their capacity to forge a connection with the romantic (and, in ethnic terms, exotic) hero Will Ladislaw remain, in the end, on the borderline of the activities of the mind that have some genuine connection to spiritual depth and profundity. The real heroine, Dorothea Brooke, is utterly unmusical even though the man she loves is the opposite. Likewise, Jane Austen's novels describe marginal skill in singing and playing. Its uses in the procuring of a suitor trivialize the romantic conceit concerning the special spiritual power of music. This socially limited appropriation of active amateurism on behalf of a stylized definition of femininity flourishes side by side with the heady discussion among male philosophers and poets about the unique status of music as a vehicle for human experience. Consider, for example, Schopenhauer and Novalis in the German-speaking context. There is clearly more than one set of historical trajectories at work regarding the role of women and music. In the salons, women and men alike seem to have revealed a considerable range of musical skills, and the socially useful flourished side by side with the discourse concerning the philosophical significance of music. For a somewhat different take, which suggests a reconciliation of a deeper musicality in Dorothea, see Phyllis Weliver, *Women Musicians in Victorian Fiction, 1860–1900: Representations of Music, Science, and Gender in the Leisured Home* (Aldershot: Ashgate, 2000), esp. chaps. 5 and 7. For a wider-ranging discussion, see Lucy Green, *Music, Gender, Education* (Cambridge: Cambridge University Press, 1997).

7. See Richard Leppert, "Sexual Identity, Death, and the Family Piano," *Nineteenth-Century Music* 16, no. 2 (1992): 105–28; and Peter J. Rabinowitz, "'With Our Own Dominant Passions': Gottschalk, Gender and the Power of Listening," *Nineteenth-Century Music* 16, no. 3 (1993): 242–52.

8. See Otto Weininger, *Sex and Character* (1906; reprint, New York: Fertig, 2003); on Weininger, see Chandak Sengoopta, *Otto Weininger: Sex, Science, and Self in Imperial Vienna* (Chicago: University of Chicago Press, 2000).

9. In this context it may be useful to consider Mahler's relationship with his wife, Alma. Alma was not Jewish and was, in fact, despite her many Jewish husbands and lovers, quite anti-Semitic. But she was remarkably gifted and skilled as a musician. Her talents never exceeded the forms and requirements of the late-nineteenth-century salon. Nonetheless, perhaps inspired by her teacher Alexander Zemlinsky, she developed higher ambitions. In part motivated by his own egotism, but I believe also by Wagnerian ideology, Mahler extracted from his soon-to-be wife a promise that essentially put an end to her ambitions as a composer and required her to play the role of dutiful wife capable by her education of acting as a copyist and helpmate. By analogy to George Eliot's *Middlemarch*, Alma can be compared to Dorothea and Mahler to Causabon. One has to concede that both men—one fictional, one real—were crudely intolerant of their wives' talents and aspirations. Alma's otherwise unenviable human characteristics should not obscure this fact. See Henry-Louis de La Grange, *Gustav Mahler*, vol. 2, *Vienna: The Years of Challenge, 1887–1904* (Oxford: Oxford University Press, 1995), 418–89.

10. This image of the female amateur as representative of musical superficiality is reflected in the dedication of a tract by Carl Reinecke of 1895 about how to play the Beethoven piano sonatas. The little volume was written in an epistolary style and addressed to "a female friend." Reinecke, a composer in his own right, was perhaps nineteenth-century Germany's most prominent musical pedagogue. Carl Czerny published his own *Letters to a Young Lady* about piano playing in the 1830s. See Carl Reinecke, *Die Beethoven'schen Clavier-Sonaten: Briefe an eine Freundin* (Leipzig: Reinecke, 1895; Eng. trans., 1898).

11. See Schenker's opening essay, "The Mission of German Genius," in *Der Tonwille: Pamphlets in Witness of the Immutable Laws of Music*, ed. William Drabkin, trans. Ian Bent et al., vol. 1 (Oxford: Oxford University Press, 2004); see also Leon Botstein, "Gedanken zu Heinrich Schenkers jüdischer Identität," in Evelyn Fink, ed., *Rebell und Visionär: Heinrich Schenker in Wien* (Vienna:

Lafite, 2003), 11–17. On Kraus and Heine, see Edward Timms, *Karl Kraus, Apocalyptic Satirist: Culture and Catastrophe in Habsburg Vienna* (New Haven and London: Yale University Press, 1986).

12. Heine is quoted in Ernst Siebel, *Der grossbürgerliche Salon, 1850–1918: Geselligkeit und Wohnkultur* (Berlin: Reimer, 1999), 33–34.

13. In this great divide, the case of Anton Bruckner is interesting. Bruckner's compositions, particularly his symphonies, were not strictly programmatic despite their evident religious subtext. At the same time, Bruckner was deeply influenced by Wagner and closely associated in his own lifetime with reactionary Germano-centric and anti-Semitic politics in Vienna. The tension in Viennese musical politics, both in the salons and in public, was more pointedly between the followers of Brahms and those of Bruckner's with the Wagnerians as a backdrop, even though the focal point of the controversy was Bruckner's symphonic output, which was definitely not Lisztian. See Leon Botstein, "Brahms and His Audience: The Later Viennese Years, 1875–1897," in Michael Musgrave, ed., *The Cambridge Companion to Brahms* (Cambridge: Cambridge University Press, 1999), 51–75.

14. See Hilde Spiel, *Fanny von Arnstein: A Daughter of the Enlightenment, 1758–1818*, trans. Christine Shuttleworth (New York: Berg, 1991).

15. On the reception of Mendelssohn, see the essays in Peter Mercer-Taylor, ed., *The Cambridge Companion to Mendelssohn* (New York: Cambridge University Press, 2004). On the reception of Meyerbeer, see Martin Cooper, "Giacomo Meyerbeer, 1791–1864," in *Proceedings of the Royal Musical Association*, 90th sess. (1963–64): 97–129; and Reiner Zimmermann, *Giacomo Meyerbeer: Eine Biographie nach Dokumenten* (Berlin: Parthas, 1998), 7.

16. See Paul Nettl, "Jewish Connections of Some Classical Composers," *Music and Letters* 45, no. 4 (1964): 337–44.

17. See Peter Wollny, "Sara Levy and the Making of Musical Taste in Berlin," *Musical Quarterly* 77, no. 4 (1993): 651–88.

18. See Otto Biba, "Jewish Families, Composers, and Musicians in Vienna in the First Half of the Nineteenth Century," in Botstein and Hanak, *Vienna*, 65–75.

19. See Anselm Gerhard, ed., *Musik und Ästhetik im Berlin Moses Mendelssohns* (Tübingen: Niemeyer, 1999).

20. See Wollny, "Sara Levy," 656–60.

21. See Leon Botstein, "Neoclassicism, Romanticism, and Emancipation: The Origins of Felix Mendelssohn's Aesthetic Outlook," in Douglass Seaton, ed., *The Mendelssohn Companion* (Westport, Conn.: Greenwood, 2001), 1–27.

22. See Heinz Becker, "Giacomo Meyerbeer und seine Vaterstadt Berlin," in Carl Dahlhaus, ed., *Studien zur Musikgeschichte Berlins im frühen 19. Jahrhundert* (Regensburg: Gustav Bosse, 1980), 429–50.

23. See Leon Botstein, "Listening Through Reading: Musical Literacy and the Concert Audience," *Nineteenth-Century Music* 16, no. 2 (1992): 129–45.

24. See the essays in Carl Dahlhaus, ed., *Studien zur Trivialmusik des 19. Jahrhunderts* (Regensburg: Gustav Bosse, 1967).

25. See Leon Botstein, "Arnold Schoenberg: Language, Modernism, and Jewish Identity," in Robert S. Wistrich, ed., *Austrians and the Jews in the Twentieth Century: From Franz Joseph to Waldheim* (New York: St. Martin's, 1992), 162–83; Botstein, "Music and the Critique of Culture: Arnold Schoenberg, Heinrich Schenker, and the Emergence of Modernism in fin de siècle Vienna," in Juliane Brand and Christopher Hailey, eds., *Constructive Dissonance: Arnold Schoenberg and the Transformations of Twentieth-Century Culture* (Berkeley: University of California Press, 1997), 3–22; and Botstein, *Judentum und Modernität: Essays zur Rolle der Juden in der deutschen und österreichischen Kultur, 1848 bis 1938* (Vienna: Böhlau, 1991).

26. See Françoise Tillard, *Fanny Mendelssohn*, trans. Camille Naish (Portland, Oreg.: Amadeus, 1996).

27. See Marian Wilson Kimber, "The 'Suppression' of Fanny Mendelssohn: Rethinking Feminist Biography," *Nineteenth-Century Music* 26, no. 2 (2002): 113–29.

28. See the balanced account of the Fanny-Felix relationship in R. Larry Todd, *Mendelssohn: A Life in Music* (Oxford: Oxford University Press, 2003).

29. See John Michael Cooper, *Mendelssohn's "Italian" Symphony* (New York: Oxford University Press, 2003).

30. See Sarah Rothenberg, "'Thus Far, but No Farther': Fanny Mendelssohn-Hensel's Unfinished Journey," *Musical Quarterly* 77, no. 4 (1993): 689–708. Despite the recent enthusiasm for Fanny's music, even the finest works, such as the cycle *Das Jahr*, can be subject to criticism as being weaker than its most ardent admirers might like to hear.

31. It is ironic that the denigration of Mendelssohn's music continues to this day. Charles Rosen's review of R. Larry Todd's recent biography repeats the standard view that Mendelssohn's music, except for the early work and such notable exceptions as the violin concerto, is essentially empty and thin. I believe this to be a problematic and wrong-headed view that predates even Wagner and echoes the attitudes of Mendelssohn's contemporary detractors. This opinion certainly mirrors Mendelssohn's own anxieties about confronting the public world of music criticism and explains the tortured, self-critical sensibility of his later years. Despite Todd's analysis, Rosen continues to uphold the notion that Mendelssohn was excessively facile and privileged as a mature composer and lacking in profundity. See Charles Rosen, "Prodigy Without Peer: A Composer Who Fell from Grace by Sticking to the World of Ease," *Times Literary Supplement*, March 19, 2004, 3–4. It is truly amazing how recalcitrant the Wagnerian pattern of reception has been.

The Salon and Literary Modernism

Translations are by the author unless otherwise noted.

1. The widespread perception of the decline of conversation may be gathered, for example, from the entry "Conversation" in the third volume of the *Nouveau Larousse* dictionary (7 vols., 1898–1904), ed. Claude Augé. See Emmanuel Godo, *Histoire de la conversation* (Paris: Presses Universitaires de France, 2003), 202. On the tradition of the woman-led salon in the seventeenth and eighteenth centuries, see esp. Benedetta Craveri, *La civiltà della conversazione* (Milan: Adelphi, 2001).

2. See Marc Fumaroli, *Trois institutions littéraires* (Paris: Gallimard, 1994), 175.

3. This is how Madame de Staël describes conversation in "De l'esprit de la conversation," in *De l'Allemagne* (*On Germany*, 1810).

4. Alone among the most celebrated French salonières, Madame Marie-Thérèse Geoffrin (1699–1777) was of bourgeois origins. See Verena von der Heyden-Rynsch, *Europäische Salons: Höhepunkte einer versunkenen weiblichen Kultur* (Munich: Artemis und Winkler, 1992), 73–77.

5. Quoted in Godo, *Histoire de la conversation*, 206.

6. Morellet's political and social idealism is discussed in ibid., 206–12. See also Craveri, *Civiltà*, 480.

7. Godo, *Histoire de la conversation*, 232–34.

8. See Jean-Jacques Rousseau, *Julie, ou La Nouvelle Héloïse* (1761), in *Oeuvres complètes*, ed. Bernard Gagnebin and Marcel Raymond, 5 vols. to date (Paris: Gallimard/Pléiade, 1959–95), 2:232–35, and "Lettre à d'Alembert sur les spectacles" (1756), ibid., 5:93.

9. Madame Récamier's salon was held in Paris from 1819 to 1822, then in Rome and in Florence, and then again in Paris.

10. On Hugo's, Vigny's, and Chateaubriand's views of conversation, see Godo, *Histoire de la conversation*, 215–16. On Heine, see Heyden-Rynsch, *Europäische Salons*, 151.

11. Heyden-Rynsch, *Europäische Salons*, 131.

12. Ibid., 124–26. The same mix of praise and criticism may be found in contemporary readers of Madame de Staël. Fumaroli, *Trois institutions littéraires*, 197, claims that although she restored the link between literature and conversation, she was excessively enamored of tempestuous eloquence and exhibited a distinctly "un-French" lack of refined esprit and elegance.

13. Heyden-Rynsch, *Europäische Salons*, 137.

14. Madame Arman de Caillavet was often referred to as Anatole France's muse, yet she in effect produced his image, giving him the necessary self-confidence to write with authority and to become a public figure. She apparently wrote several of the articles that he signed. More than a hundred people attended her salon each Sunday, including members of parliament and lawyers as well as artists and writers.

15. Among the women Sainte-Beuve portrayed were Madame du Deffand, Madame Geoffrin, Mademoiselle Lespinasse, and Madame de Caylus. See Fumaroli, *Trois institutions littéraires*, 182; and Godo, *Histoire de la conversation*, 218–19.

16. Quoted in Godo, *Histoire de la conversation*, 219.

17. The flip side of this idealization was the Goncourts' misogynistic appraisal of the women of their century, whom they portrayed in their novels as animalistic and inferior.

18. Marcel Proust, *Contre Sainte-Beuve, précedé de Pastiches et mélanges et suivi de Essais et articles*, ed. Pierre Clarac and Yves Sandre (Paris: Gallimard, 1971), 221–22. The essay "Contre Sainte-Beuve," which remained unfinished, was not published until 1954. See Marc Fumaroli, "Littérature et conversation: La querelle Proust-Sainte-Beuve," in Gérald Cahen, ed., *La Conversation: Une Art de l'instant* (Paris: Autrement, 1999), 102–21.

19. In Proust's *Recherche*, the character of the great writer Bergotte, the star of Odette Swann's salon, is much admired by the narrator, just as in real life Proust admired Anatole France. But the relationship between France and his muse is suppressed in the novel. For Madame Swann, whose pretentious salon resembles Madame Verdurin's, Bergotte is merely a celebrity whom she exhibits to gain further social acceptance and erase her past as a demimondaine.

20. For the notion of "symbolic capital," see Pierre Bourdieu, *Language and Symbolic Power*, ed. John B. Thompson, trans. Gino Raymond and Matthew Adamson (Cambridge: Polity, 1991). Catherine Bidou-Zachariasen's sociological study, *Proust sociologue: De la maison aristocratique au salon bourgeois* (Paris: Descartes, 1997), is based on Bourdieu.

21. This instrumental, aggressive use of art and culture leads Bidou-Zachariasen to give a rather heroicized account of Madame Verdurin, who strangely emerges as the real protagonist of the novel. The narrator's tone, however, does not bear this out, for Madame Verdurin always appears in a grotesque, satirical light even when at the peak of her social success.

22. The idea that the Dreyfus Affair signaled the birth of intellectuals as a group has been traced back to Julien Benda's famous pamphlet *La Trahison des clercs* (*The Treason of the Intellectuals*, 1927). Among the works on this topic, see Susan Rubin Suleiman, "The Literary Significance of the Dreyfus Affair," in Norman L. Kleeblatt, ed., *The Dreyfus Affair: Art, Truth, and Justice* (Berkeley: University of California Press, 1987), 117–39.

23. Bidou-Zachariasen argues that, because of the preeminence of the family, Oriane's is not a salon at all, but just a *maison* in the old tradition of the aristocracy.

24. See *Le Temps retrouvé*, vol. 4 of *À la recherche du temps perdu* (Paris: Gallimard/Pléiade, 1987–89), 292. Compare *Time*

Regained, vol. 6 of *In Search of Lost Time*, trans. C. K. Scott Moncrieff and Terence Kilmartin, rev. D. J. Enright (New York: Modern Library, 1992–93), 302. On the devaluing of conversation in Proust, see Godo, *Histoire de la conversation*, 268–76; and Fumaroli, *Trois institutions littéraires*, 208.

25. See Jean-François Revel, *Sur Proust* (Paris: Grasset, 1964).

26. Laure Rièse, *Les Salons littéraires parisiens du Second Empire à nos jours* (Toulouse: Privately printed, 1962), 146; Chantal Bischoff, *Geneviève Straus: Trilogie d'une égérie* (Paris: Balland, 1992), 271.

27. The decline of the prestige of conversation and of salons led by women in the nineteenth century resulted in the dispersal of letters, diaries, and notes that document their history. Thus, fictional renderings such as Proust's are often the only known accounts. Most of Madame Straus's immense correspondence has been lost, including most of her letters to Proust, as have most of Ada Leverson's letters to Oscar Wilde. Nonetheless, enough material has survived to enable historians to attempt biographies of some of these women. Chantal Bischoff's and Andrée Jacob's (see note 34, below) biographies of Geneviève Straus offer a portrait strikingly different from the fictionalized one in *Recherche*, and even from the more realistic but tiny sketch in the *Pastiches et mélanges* of *Contre Sainte-Beuve*.

28. For more on Madame Straus, see the entry on her in this volume.

29. Jacques-Émile Blanche, *La Pêche aux souvenirs* (1949), quoted in Bischoff, *Geneviève Straus*, 295.

30. Charles Gounod, "De l'artiste dans la société moderne," in *Mémoires d'un artiste* (Paris: Calmann-Lévi, 1896), 275–93.

31. On the salon as an institution of the public (as opposed to the private, family sphere), see Jürgen Habermas's classic study, *The Structural Transformation of the Public Sphere: An Inquiry into a Category of Bourgeois Society* (1962), trans. Thomas Burger with Frederick Lawrence (Cambridge, Mass.: MIT Press, 1991), esp. 45–46. For a feminist critique of this dichotomy and of Habermas's tendency to overlook gender, see Joan B. Landes, "The Public and the Private Sphere: A Feminist Reconsideration," in Johanna Meehan, ed., *Feminists Read Habermas: Gendering the Subject of Discourse* (New York: Routledge, 1995), 91–116.

32. See, e.g., his review, which appeared in 1907 in *Le Figaro*: "Les éblouissements par la Comtesse de Noailles," in *Essais et articles*, in *Contre Sainte-Beuve*, 533–45. On her work as a source of inspiration for Proust, see William C. Carter, *Marcel Proust: A Life* (New Haven and London: Yale University Press, 2000), 369.

33. Proust, *Pastiches et mélanges*, in *Contre Sainte-Beuve*, 53. This phrase is quoted approvingly by Proust's friend Robert Dreyfus in his memoir, "Madame Straus et Marcel Proust," in *De Monsieur Thiers à Marcel Proust* (Paris: Plon, 1939).

34. Andrée Jacob, *Il y a un siècle—Quand les dames tenaient salon: Geneviève Straus* (Paris: Arnaud Seydoux, 1991), 190; Bischoff, *Geneviève Straus*, 132.

35. Marcel Proust, *Correspondance avec Madame Straus* (Paris: Union Générale d'Éditions, 1994), 271.

36. See, e.g., Jean-Yves Tadié, *Marcel Proust: A Life*, trans. Euan Cameron (New York: Viking, 2000), 75; and Antoine Compagnon, *Connaissez-vous Brunetière? Enquête sur un antidreyfusard et ses amis* (Paris: Seuil, 1997), 75.

37. Bischoff, *Geneviève Straus*, 280.

38. Ibid., 160.

39. Proust, *Correspondance avec Madame Straus*, 271–72.

40. Roland Barthes, "An Idea of Research," in *The Rustle of Language*, trans. Richard Howard (New York: Hill and Wang, 1986), 274.

41. Although in his "Littérature et conversation" Fumaroli acknowledges that Proust's rendering of salon conversation is but a pastiche and a caricature, he makes no reference to Madame Straus or to any of the actual salonières known to Proust, reducing the question to a debate between Sainte-Beuve and Proust alone.

42. W. B. Yeats, *Letters to the New Island* (September 1889), quoted in Horace Wyndham, *Speranza* (London: Boardman, 1951), 181. For Yeats's impressions of Wilde as a talker, see also his *Autobiographies* (London: Macmillan, 1955), 134–39.

43. Wyndham, *Speranza*, 172. See also Victoria Glendinning, "Speranza," in Peter Quennell, ed., *Genius in the Drawing-Room* (London: Weidenfeld and Nicolson, 1980), 109.

44. Critics often charge Lady Wilde with smothering her son's masculinity because she supposedly dressed him as a girl. Richard Ellmann disputes this in *Oscar Wilde* (New York: Alfred A. Knopf, 1988), 17–18.

45. Glendinning, "Speranza," 105. Travers was awarded a farthing in damages by the court.

46. Lady Wilde's feminist essays, among them "The Bondage of Woman" and "Venus Victrix," are collected in *Social Studies* (London: Ward and Downey, 1893).

47. *Atheneum*, quoted in Glendinning, "Speranza," 103. See also Wyndham, *Speranza*, 75.

48. Ellmann, *Oscar Wilde*, 21; Wyndham, *Speranza*, 70; Glendinning, "Speranza," 103. The boys' sister, Isola, died of a fever when she was nine.

49. Henriette Corkran, *Celebrities and I* (1902), quoted in Davis Coakley, *Oscar Wilde: The Importance of Being Irish* (Dublin: Town House, 1994), 74.

50. Glendinning, "Speranza," 106.

51. Exceptions included Lady Elizabeth Montagu's salonlike "Bluestocking Circle," which cultivated intellectual conversation

and influenced the Bloomsbury circle, which also resembled a salon. David Hume and Anthony Ashley Cooper, third Earl of Shaftesbury, among others, sang the praises of polite conversation, which for Hume gave shape to an ethicopolitical ideal, whereas Shaftesbury associated it with aesthetic perfection and taste. For Hume (who had visited French salons), gallantry, not eroticism, marked the relationship between men and women in conversation, gallantry being in his view a gracious way to gloss over woman's natural inferiority. See Hume's "Of Essay Writing," in *Essays Moral, Political and Literary* (London: Oxford University Press, 1963), 258.

52. In his play *An Ideal Husband* (1895), Wilde has the worldly, seductive, and Machiavellian Mrs. Cheveley, just back to London after a long period on the Continent, say: "I am tired of living abroad. I want to come back to London. I want to have a charming house here. I want to have a salon. If one could only teach the English how to talk, and the Irish how to listen, society here would be quite civilised." *The Importance of Being Earnest and Other Plays*, ed. Peter Raby (Oxford: Clarendon Press, 1995).

53. Olive Schreiner, Arthur Symons, Katherine Tynan, and Marie Corelli were among the contributors. Along with fashion, the journal addressed suffragism and other feminist concerns, such as new professions for women. Lady Wilde contributed a feminist poem to one issue, "Historic Women."

54. C. Robert Holloway, "Seduced by the Wildes," in Giovanna Franci and Giovanna Silvani, eds., *The Importance of Being Misunderstood: Homage to Oscar Wilde* (Bologna: Patron, 2003), 39–48. Holloway quotes words often attributed to Wilde— "When you are as old as I, young man, you will know there is only one thing worth living for, and that is sin"—and he shows that this smirky taunt, along with much other material assumed to be original, was actually taken from Lady Wilde. Holloway used his scholarly findings (from the Wilde collection at the Clark Library, University of California, Los Angeles) to write a play, *Oscar and Speranza*, which he produced and directed. Others, such as the biographer Richard Ellmann, tend to downplay the value of her teachings and her importance in Oscar's life. Even Ellmann, however, admits that she was "warm and humorous" (*Oscar Wilde*, 125). Glendinning contends instead that "Oscar would not have been Oscar without the qualities that he inherited from her" ("Speranza," 112).

55. He later moved in with Ada Leverson and her husband, who, in defiance of the wave of opprobrium against him, took care of Wilde while he awaited his second trial. For more on Ada Leverson, see the essay on her in this volume.

56. *Second Collected Edition of Oscar Wilde's Works: Essays and Lectures*, vol. 11 (London: Methuen, 1908), xi–xii.

57. Quoted in Karl Beckson, ed., *Oscar Wilde: The Critical Heritage* (London: Routledge and Kegan Paul, 1970), 86.

58. See, e.g., Leverson's affectionate memoir, "The Importance

of Being Oscar," published by her daughter, Violet Wyndham, in *The Sphinx and Her Circle: A Biographical Sketch of Ada Leverson, 1862–1933* (New York: Vanguard, 1963), where Wilde is described as "a spectacular genius, greater, perhaps, as an improviser in conversation than as a writer" (p. 113). Leverson notes that even in the gloomy days between his trials, when he was staying with her, he talked "in the most enchanting way about everything except his trouble" and would often "improvise prose poems, like those published in his works" (p. 117).

59. Sisley Huddleston, *Bohemian Literary and Social Life in Paris: Salons, Cafés, Studios* (London, George G. Harrap, 1928), 326–40.

60. *The Complete Works of Oscar Wilde*, vol. 1, *Poems and Poems in Prose*, ed. Bobby Fong and Karl Beckson (Oxford: Oxford University Press, 2000), 217–18.

61. See Deirdre Toomey, "The Story-Teller at Fault: Oscar Wilde and Irish Orality," in Jerusha McCormack, ed., *Wilde the Irishman* (New Haven and London: Yale University Press, 1998); and Thomas Wright, "The Talker as Artist: The Spoken Stories of Oscar Wilde," in Franci and Silvani, *Importance of Being Misunderstood*, 351–65. Drawing from previous collections and accounts (including two in French edited by Guillot de Saix), Wright has collected a number of Wilde's oral stories in *Table Talk* (London: Cassell, 1988).

62. Besides Toomey and Wright (see previous note), see Richard Pine, *The Thief of Reason: Oscar Wilde and Modern Ireland* (Dublin: Gill and Macmillan, 1995), 161–98.

63. The fascination, fear, and sexual draw held by this use of talk are evident in the character of Gabriel Nash—based on Wilde himself—in Henry James's novel *The Tragic Muse*. See Shelley Salamensky, "Henry James, Oscar Wilde, and 'Fin-de-Siècle Talk,'" *Henry James Review* 20, no. 3 (1999): 275–81.

64. Wilde, *Table Talk*, 95.

65. Wyndham, *Sphinx and Her Circle*, 123. See also Wilde, *Table Talk*, 117.

66. Wilde, *Table Talk*, 64.

67. André Gide, "Oscar Wilde: In Memoriam," in E. H. Mikhail, ed., *Oscar Wilde: Reviews and Recollections*, 2 vols. (London: Macmillan, 1979), 292.

68. On the notion of performative identity, see Judith Butler, "Performative Acts and Gender Constitution: An Essay in Phenomenology and Feminist Theory," in Sue-Ellen Case, ed., *Performing Feminisms: Feminist Critical Theory and Theatre* (Baltimore: Johns Hopkins University Press, 1990).

69. Ellmann, *Oscar Wilde*, 281.

70. Gide, "Oscar Wilde," 291.

71. By the late 1880s, Mahaffy had become a Tory, and contemptuous of Irish home rule. When Lady Wilde received a gift copy of the conversation manual from him and was asked for her

opinion, she answered: "I think that you should have written it in Greek. Scholars would then understand it. My son Oscar tells me you are familiar with the language." See Wyndham, *Speranza*, 69.

72. Wilde called Leverson "Sphinx" in honor of her witty parody of his poem "The Sphinx," after the parody appeared in *Punch*.

73. Julie Speedie, *Wonderful Sphinx: The Biography of Ada Leverson* (London: Virago, 1993), 45.

74. *Sodome et Gomorre*, vol. 3 of *À la recherche du temps perdu*, 17. See also *Sodom and Gomorrah*, vol. 5 of *In Search of Lost Time*, 20.

75. See John Malcom Brinnin, *The Third Rose: Gertrude Stein and Her World* (Reading, Mass.: Addison-Wesley, 1987; orig. publ. London: Weidenfeld and Nicolson, 1959), 51.

76. For accounts of this period of Stein's life and her interaction with her brother and their guests, see Brinnin, *Third Rose*, 51–55, as well as Janet Hobhouse, *Everybody Who Was Anybody: A Biography of Gertrude Stein* (New York: G. Putnam's Sons, 1975); Shari Benstock, *Women of the Left Bank: Paris, 1900–1940* (Austin: University of Texas Press, 1986), 143–93; and Brenda Wineapple, *Sister Brother: Gertrude and Leo Stein* (New York: G. Putnam's Sons, 1996).

77. Wendy Steiner, *Exact Resemblance to Exact Resemblance: The Literary Portraiture of Gertrude Stein* (New Haven and London: Yale University Press, 1978), 135.

78. See, among others, Brinnin, *Third Rose*, 139–41; and Michael J. Hoffman, *The Development of Abstractionism in the Writings of Gertrude Stein* (Philadelphia: University of Pennsylvania Press, 1966). Brinnin states that her attraction to painting led Stein "to wish for the same plastic freedom for literature" (p. 139). As a result, her works are "impossible to read," for the materials of literary language—namely, words (with their sound, rhythm, and verbal density)—are unlike the materials of painting and music (p. 140). Painting and music can work in and of themselves without reference to external meaning, Brinnin argues, whereas words always "communicate something beyond themselves" (p. 141). If that something is not taken into account and given a precise order, and words are treated only as formal elements, the result is difficult to interpret. Hoffman concurs; according to him, *Tender Buttons* marks the beginning of Stein's tendency to use words as "plastic elements in creations that have no iconic relationship to anything conceptually recognizable in the external world" (153). Abstract writing is "an impossibility" and Stein's art a failure, he concludes, because language is inherently communicative, and all communication is referential (176–78).

79. See especially the thoughtful discussion of Stein's experimentalism in Richard Kostelanetz's introduction to *The Yale Gertrude Stein* (New Haven and London: Yale University Press, 1980).

80. The poststructuralist feminist critic Marianne DeKoven, in particular, has provided interesting readings of Stein, inspired by Jacques Derrida and Julia Kristeva, in which such texts as *Tender Buttons* are seen as transgressing the limits of patriarchal language and exhibiting a presymbolic play of the signifier. See Marianne DeKoven, *A Different Language: Gertrude Stein's Experimental Writing* (Madison: University of Wisconsin Press, 1983). See also the essays collected in Shirley Neuman and Ira B. Nadel, eds., *Gertrude Stein and the Making of Literature* (Boston: Northeastern University Press, 1988).

81. See Benstock, *Women of the Left Bank*, 163–73; and Catharine Stimpson, "The Somograms of Gertrude Stein," in Henry Abelove, Michèle Aina Barale, and David M. Halperin, eds., *The Lesbian and Gay Studies Reader* (New York: Routledge, 1993), 642–52.

82. Benstock, *Women of the Left Bank*, 163.

83. See James R. Mellow, *Charmed Circle: Gertrude Stein and Company* (New York: Praeger, 1974). For a more nuanced reading of Stein's allusions to lesbianism, especially in *Tender Buttons*, see Elisabeth A. Frost, "'Replacing the Noun': Fetishism, Parody, and Gertrude Stein's *Tender Buttons*," in *The Feminist Avant-Garde in American Poetry* (Iowa City: University of Iowa Press, 2003).

84. On the primacy of language in Stein, see Nancy Gray, "The Language of Gertrude Stein," in *Language Unbound: On Experimental Writing by Women* (Urbana: University of Illinois Press, 1992), 38–80. Although Gray persuasively argues the centrality of language in Stein's work, she overlooks the importance of actual salon conversation.

85. Quoted in Brinnin, *Third Rose*, 148.

86. Roman Jakobson, "Closing Statement: Linguistics and Poetics," in T. Sebeok, ed., *Style in Language* (Cambridge, Mass.: MIT Press, 1960), 350–77. The discussion and examples of the emotive, metalingual, and phatic functions are on pp. 354–56.

87. Gertrude Stein, *Writings, 1903–1932*, ed. Catharine Stimpson and Harriet Chessman (New York: Library of America, 1998), 279–81.

88. Hobhouse, *Everybody Who Was Anybody*, 50.

89. Gertrude Stein, *The Making of Americans: Being a History of a Family's Progress* (New York: Something Else, 1966), 300.

90. *Two: Gertrude Stein and Her Brother and Other Early Portraits* [1908–12], vol. 1 of *Unpublished Works of Gertrude Stein*, ed. Janet Flanner (New Haven: Yale University Press, 1951), 9.

91. Benstock, *Women of the Left Bank*, 153.

92. Stein, *Writings, 1903–1932*, 283.

93. Benstock, *Women of the Left Bank*, 175. For Stein's sexual magnetism with men as well as women, see the testimony of Donald Sutherland quoted on p. 171, where Hemingway is reported to have been sexually attracted to Stein.

94. Some, including Benstock, argue that Toklas was subservient to Stein, almost a traditional wife and even servant. Bravig Imbs, who knew the couple in the 1920s, and others maintain that Toklas, who was a brilliant conversationalist and carefully orchestrated the salon and the couple's life, was really in control. See Linda Simon, ed., *Gertrude Stein Remembered* (Lincoln: University of Nebraska Press, 1994), 121; and Diana Souhami, *Gertrude and Alice* (London: Pandora, 1991).

95. Benstock, *Women of the Left Bank*, says that the salon ended in 1913, when Toklas moved in and theirs become a stable, very private, and intimate relationship.

96. Simon, *Gertrude Stein Remembered*, 97.

97. Ibid., 94.

Selected Bibliography

The first section is devoted to discussions of salons in general. Following that are sections on individual salonières, with major works and archives listed.

Salons

Agulhon, Maurice. *Le Cercle dans la France bourgeoise, 1810–1848: Étude d'une mutation de sociabilité.* Paris: A. Colin and École des Hautes Études en Sciences Sociales, 1977.

Aprile, Sylvie. "La République au salon: Vie et mort d'une forme de sociabilité (1865–1885)." *Revue d'Histoire Moderne et Contemporaine* 38 (1991): 473–87.

Arendt, Hannah. *The Jew as Pariah: Jewish Identity and Politics in the Modern Age.* Edited by Ronald Feldman. New York: Grove, 1978.

———. *The Origins of Totalitarianism.* Part 1, *Anti-Semitism.* New York: Harcourt Brace Jovanovich, 1951.

Barbiera, Raffaello. *Il salotto della contessa Maffei e la società milanese, 1834–1886.* Milan: Fratelli Treves, 1895.

Beaumont-Vassy, Édouard Ferdinand de la Bonninière. *Les Salons de Paris, et la société parisienne sous Napoléon III.* Paris: Ferdinand Sartorius, 1868.

Bender, Thomas. *New York Intellect: A History of Intellectual Life in New York City, from 1750 to the Beginnings of Our Own Time.* Baltimore: Johns Hopkins University Press, 1987.

Benstock, Shari. *Women of the Left Bank: Paris, 1900–1940.* Austin: University of Texas Press, 1986.

Bergman-Carton, Janis. *The Woman of Ideas in French Art, 1830–1848.* New Haven and London: Yale University Press, 1999.

Bodek, Evelyn Gordon. "Salonières and Bluestockings: Educated Obsolescence and Germinating Feminism." *Feminist Studies* 3 (Spring–Summer 1976): 185–99.

Botstein, Leon, and Werner Hanak, eds. *Vienna: Jews and the City of Music, 1870–1938.* Exh. cat. Jüdisches Museum der Stadt Wien and Center for Jewish History, New York. Annandale-on-Hudson, N.Y.: Bard College; Hofheim: Wolke Verlag, 2004.

Calhoun, Craig, ed. *Habermas and the Public Sphere.* Cambridge, Mass.: MIT Press, 1992.

Craveri, Benedetta. *La civiltà della conversazione.* Milan: Adelphi, 2001.

———. *Madame du Deffand and Her World.* Translated by Teresa Waugh. Boston: David R. Godine, 1994.

Crunden, Robert. *American Salons: Encounters with European Modernism, 1885–1917.* New York: Oxford University Press, 1993.

Dubrovic, Milan. *Veruntreute Geschichte: Die Wiener Salons und Literatencafés.* Vienna: Paul Zsolnay, 1985. Reprint, Berlin: Aufbau, 2001.

Dulong, Claude. "From Conversation to Creation." In Natalie Davis and Arlette Farge, eds., *Renaissance and Enlightenment Paradoxes*, 396–98. Vol. 3 of *A History of Women.* Cambridge, Mass.: Harvard University Press, 1993.

Fiette, Suzanne. *La Noblesse française des lumières à la Belle Époque: Psychologie d'une adaptation.* Paris: Perrin, 1997.

Fraisse, Geneviève. *Reason's Muse: Sexual Difference and the Birth of Democracy.* Translated by Jane Marie Todd. Chicago: University of Chicago Press, 1994.

Françoise, Étienne, ed. *Sociabilité et société bourgeoise en France, en Allemagne et en Suisse, 1750–1850.* Paris: Éditions Recherche sur les Civilisations, 1986.

Goldsmith, Elizabeth. *Exclusive Conversations: The Art of Interaction in Seventeenth-Century France.* Philadelphia: University of Pennsylvania Press, 1988.

Goldsmith, Elizabeth, and Dena Goodman. *Going Public: Women and Publishing in Early Modern France.* Ithaca, N.Y.: Cornell University Press, 1995.

Goncourt de, Edmond, and Jules de Goncourt. *The Woman of the Eighteenth Century.* London: Allen and Unwin, 1928.

Goodman, Dena. "Enlightenment Salons: The Convergence of Female and Philosophic Ambitions." *Eighteenth Century Studies* 22 (1989): 329–50.

———. *The Republic of Letters: A Cultural History of the French Enlightenment.* Ithaca, N.Y.: Cornell University Press, 1994.

Goodman, Elise. *The Portraits of Madame de Pompadour: Celebrating the Femme Savante.* Berkeley: University of California Press, 2000.

Gordon, Daniel. *Citizens Without Sovereignty: Equality and Sociability in French Thought, 1670–1789.* Princeton, N.J.: Princeton University Press, 1994.

Graf, Hansjörg. *Der kleine Salon: Szenen und Prosa des Wiener Fin de Siècle.* Stuttgart: Goverts, 1970.

Green, Lucy. *Music, Gender, Education.* Cambridge: Cambridge University Press, 1997.

Gutwirth, Madelyn. *Madame de Staël, Novelist: The Emergence of the Artist as Woman.* Urbana: University of Illinois Press, 1978.

————. *Twilight of the Goddesses: Women and Representation in the French Revolutionary Era*. New Brunswick, N.J.: Rutgers University Press, 1992.

Habermas, Jürgen. *The Structural Transformation of the Public Sphere: An Inquiry into a Category of Bourgeois Society*. Translated by Thomas Burger. Cambridge: Polity, 1989.

Hahn, Barbara. "Conversations at the Margins: Jewish Salons Around 1900." In *Berlin Metropolis: Jews and the New Culture, 1890–1918*, edited by Emily D. Bilski, 188–207. Exh. cat. Berkeley: University of California Press; New York: The Jewish Museum, 1999.

————. *Die Jüdin Pallas Athene: Auch eine Theorie der Moderne*. Berlin: Berlin Verlag, 2002.

Hall, Evelyn. *The Women of the Salons and Other French Portraits*. Freeport, N.Y.: Books for Libraries, 1969.

Hargrave, Mary. *Some German Women and Their Salons*. New York: Brentano's, 1912.

Harth, Erica. *Cartesian Women: Versions and Subversions of Rational Discourse in Old Regime France*. Ithaca, N.Y.: Cornell University Press, 1992.

Hertz, Deborah. *Jewish High Society in Old Regime Berlin*. New Haven and London: Yale University Press, 1988.

Heyden-Rynsch, Verena von der. *Europäische Salons: Höhepunkte einer versunkenen weiblichen Kultur*. Munich: Artemis und Winkler, 1992.

Honig, Bonnie, ed. *Feminist Interpretations of Hannah Arendt*. University Park: Pennsylvania State University Press, 1995.

Hundt, Irina. *Vom Salon zur Barrikade: Frauen der Heinezeit*. Stuttgart: J. B. Metzler, 2002.

Kale, Steven. "Women, the Public Sphere, and the Persistence of Salons." *French Historical Studies* 25 (Winter 2002): 115–48.

Landes, Joan. *Women and the Public Sphere in the Age of the French Revolution*. Ithaca, N.Y.: Cornell University Press, 1988.

————, ed. *Feminism, the Public and the Private*. Oxford: Oxford University Press, 1988.

Lepsius, Sabine. "Ueber das Aussterbens der 'Salons.'" *März* 7 (1913): 222–34.

Lougee, Carolyn C. *Le Paradis des Femmes: Women, Salons, and Social Stratification in Seventeenth-Century France*. Princeton, N.J.: Princeton University Press, 1976.

Maertz, Gregory, ed. *Cultural Interaction in the Romantic Age: Critical Essays in Comparative Literature*. Albany: State University of New York Press, 1998.

Mason, Amelia. *The Women of the French Salons*. New York: Century, 1891.

Meehan, Johanna, ed. *Feminists Read Habermas: Gendering the Subject of Discourse*. New York: Routledge, 1995.

Meyer, Bertha. *Salon Sketches: Biographical Studies of Berlin Salons of the Emancipation*. New York: Bloch, 1938.

Myers, Sylvia Harcstark. *The Bluestocking Circle: Women, Friendship, and the Life of the Mind in Eighteenth Century England*. Oxford: Clarendon Press, 1990.

Pekacz, Jolanta. *Conservative Tradition in Pre-Revolutionary France: Parisian Salon Women*. New York: P. Lang, 1999.

Petersen, Nadya. "Women on the Verge of a New Language: Russian Salon Hostesses in the First Half of the Nineteenth Century." In *Russia, Women, Culture*, edited by Helena Goscilo, 209–24. Bloomington: Indiana University Press, 1996.

Picard, Roger. *Les Salons littéraires et la société française, 1610–1789*. New York: Brentano's, 1943.

Quennell, Peter, ed. *Affairs of the Mind: The Salon in Europe and America from the Eighteenth to the Twentieth Century*. Washington, D.C.: New Republic Books, 1980.

Rièse, Laure. *Les Salons littéraires parisiens du Second Empire à nos jours*. Toulouse: Privately printed, 1962.

Schultz, Hartwig, ed. *Salons der Romantik: Beiträge eines Wiepersdorfer Kolloquiums zu Theorie und Geschichte des Salons*. Berlin: Walter de Gruyter, 1997.

Seibert, Peter. *Der literarische Salon: Literatur und Geselligkeit zwischen Aufklärung und Vormärz*. Stuttgart: J. B. Metzler, 1993.

Sennett, Richard. *The Fall of Public Man*. New York: W. W. Norton, 1974.

Severit, Frauke, ed. *Das alles war ich: Politikerinnen, Künstlerinnen, Exzentrikerinnen der Wiener Moderne*. Vienna: Böhlau, 1998.

Siebel, Ernst. *Der grossbürgerliche Salon, 1850–1918: Geselligkeit und Wohnkultur*. Berlin: Reimer, 1999.

Simanowski, Roberto, Horst Turk, and Thomas Schmidt, eds. *Europa—Ein Salon? Beiträge zur Internationalität des literarischen Salons*. Göttingen: Wallstein, 1999.

Thornton, Peter. *Seventeenth-Century Interior Decoration in England, France and Holland*. New Haven and London: Yale University Press, 1978.

Tunley, David. *Music in the Nineteenth Century Parisian Salon*. Armidale, Australia: University of New England Press, 1997.

Von Arnstein bis Zuckerkandl: Jüdischer Stifter und Mäzene zwischen Tradition und Avantgarde. Exh. cat. Österreichischen Zinnfigurenmuseum, Schloss Pottenbrunn. Pottenbrunn, Austria: Museumsverein, 1993.

Watson, Steven. *Strange Bedfellows: The First American Avant-Garde*. New York: Abbeville, 1991.

Weckel, Ulrike. "A Lost Paradise of a Female Culture? Some Critical Questions Regarding the Scholarship on Late Eighteenth- and Early Nineteenth-Century German Salons." *German History* 18, no. 3 (2000): 310–35.

Whalen, Meg Freeman. "A Little Republic Filled with Grace: The Nineteenth-Century Music Salon." *Women of Note Quarterly* 3 (November 1995): 16–26.

Wilhelmy-Dollinger, Petra. *Der Berliner Salon im 19. Jahrhundert (1780–1914)*. Berlin: Walter de Gruyter, 1989.

Wollny, Peter. "Sara Levy and the Making of Musical Taste in Berlin." *Musical Quarterly* 77, no. 4 (1993): 651–88.

Fanny von Arnstein and Cäcilie von Eskeles

Eshkolot, Zeev, ed. *The Eskeles Genealogy*. Haifa: Z. Eshkolot, 1995.

Spiel, Hilde. *Fanny von Arnstein: A Daughter of the Enlightenment, 1758–1818*. Translated by Christine Shuttleworth. New York: Berg, 1991.

Amalie Beer

Becker, Heinz. "Die Beer'sche Villa im Tiergarten: Porträt eines Berliner Wohnhauses." In *Berlin in Geschichte und Gegenwart: Jahrbuch des Landesarchivs Berlin*, 209–24. Berlin: Landesarchivs Berlin, 1990.

Becker, Heinz and Gudrun. *Giacomo Meyerbeer: Weltbürger der Musik*. Wiesbaden: Ludwig Reichert, 1991.

Glatzer, Nahum N. "On an Unpublished Letter of Isaak Markus Jost." *Leo Baeck Institute Yearbook* 22 (1977): 129–37.

Jacobson, Egon, and Leo Hirsch. *Jüdische Mütter*. Berlin: Vortrupp, 1936.

Kuhrau, Sven, and Kurt Winkler with Alice Uebe, eds., *Juden, Bürger, Berliner: Das Gedächtnes der Familie Beer-Meyerbeer-Richter*. Berlin: Henschel, 2004.

Meyerbeer, Giacomo. *The Diaries of Giacomo Meyerbeer*, 4 vols. Translated by Robert Ignatius Letellier. Madison, N.J.: Fairleigh Dickinson University Press, 1999–2004.

Wilhelm Beer: Genius der Astronomie und Ökonomie, 1797–1850. Berlin: Staatsbibliothek zu Berlin, Preussischer Kulturbesitz, 1997.

Zimmerman, Reiner. *Giacomo Meyerbeer: Eine Biographie nach Dokumenten*. Berlin: Henschel, 1991.

MAJOR ARCHIVES

Leo Baeck Institute, New York

Stiftung Stadtmuseum Berlin. Beer and Meyerbeer collections in Hans-und-Luise-Richter-Stiftung

Fanny Mendelssohn Hensel

Borchard, Beatrix, and Monika Schwarz-Danuser, eds. *Fanny Hensel geb. Mendelssohn Bartholdy: Komponieren zwischen Geselligkeitsideal und romantischer Musikästhetik*. Stuttgart: J. B. Metzler, 1999.

Botstein, Leon. "The Aesthetics of Assimilation: Reconstructing the Career of Felix Mendelssohn." In *Mendelssohn and His World*, edited by R. Larry Todd, 5–42. Princeton, N.J.: Princeton University Press, 1991.

Brown, Clive. *A Portrait of Mendelssohn*. New Haven and London: Yale University Press, 2003.

Büchter-Römer, Ute. *Fanny Mendelssohn-Hensel*. Rheinbeck bei Hamburg: Rowohlt, 2001.

Citron, Marcia J., ed. and trans. *The Letters of Fanny Hensel to Felix Mendelssohn*. New York: Pendragon, 1987.

Cullen, Michael. "Leipziger Strasse Drei—Eine Baubiographie." *Mendelssohn-Studien* 7 (1990): 9–77.

Hellwig-Unruh, Renate. *Fanny Hensel geb. Mendelssohn Bartholdy: Thematisches Verzeichnis der Kompositionen*. Adliswil, Switzerland: Kunzelmann, 2000.

———. "'. . . so bin ich mit meiner Musik ziemlich allein': Die Komponistin und Musikerin Fanny Hensel, geb. Mendelssohn." In *Stadtbild und Frauenleben: Berlin im Spiegel von 16 Frauenporträts*, edited by Henrike Hülsbergen. Berlin: Historisches Kommission zu Berlin and Stapp, 1997.

Hensel, Fanny. *Tagebücher*. Edited by Hans-Günter Klein and Rudolf Elvers. Wiesbaden: Breitkopf und Härtel, 2002.

Hensel, Sebastian. *The Mendelssohn Family (1729–1847) from Letters and Journals*. New York: Harper and Brothers, 1881.

Klein, Hans-Günter. *"Das verborgene Band": Felix Mendelssohn Bartholdy und seine Schwester Fanny Hensel: Ausstellung der Musikabteilung der Staatsbibliothek zu Berlin-Preussischer Kulturbesitz zum 150. Todestag der beiden Geschwister*. Exh. cat. Wiesbaden: Ludwig Reichert, 1997.

Lowenthal-Hensel, Cécile. "Neues zur Leipzigerstrasse Drei." *Mendelssohn-Studien* 7 (1990): 141–51.

———. *Preussische Bildnisse des 19. Jahrhunderts: Zeichnungen von Wilhelm Hensel*. Exh. cat. Berlin: Staatliche Museen-Preussischer Kulturbesitz, 1981.

Maurer, Annette. "'. . . ein Verdienst um die Kunstzustände unserer Vaterstadt'—Fanny Hensels 'Sonntagsmusiken.'" *Viva voce* 42 (May 1997): 11–13.

Reich, Nancy B. "The Power of Class: Fanny Hensel." In *Mendelssohn and His World*, edited by R. Larry Todd, 86–99. Princeton, N.J.: Princeton University Press, 1991.

Tillard, Françoise. *Fanny Mendelssohn*. Translated by Camille Naish. Portland, Oreg.: Amadeus, 1996.

Todd, R. Larry. *Mendelssohn: A Life in Music*. Oxford: Oxford University Press, 2003.

Weissweiler, Eva. *Fanny Mendelssohn: Ein Portrait in Briefen*. Frankfurt: Ullstein, 1991.

Wilson Kimber, Marian. "The 'Suppression' of Fanny Mendelssohn: Rethinking Feminist Biography." *Nineteenth-Century Music* 26 (Fall 2002): 113–29.

MAJOR ARCHIVE

Staatsbibliothek zu Berlin. Mendelssohn-Archiv

Henriette Herz

Fürst, J. *Henriette Herz, ihr Leben und ihre Erinnerungen*. Leipzig: Zentralantiquariat der Deutschen Demokratischen Republik, 1977.

Landsberg, Hans. *Henriette Herz: Ihr Leben und ihre Zeit*. Weimar: G. Kiepenheuer, 1913.

Schmitz, Rainer, ed. *Henriette Herz in Erinnerungen, Briefen und Zeugnissen*. Frankfurt: Insel, 1984.

Weissberg, Liliane. *Life as a Goddess: Henriette Herz Writes Her Autobiography*. Braun Lectures in the History of the Jews in Prussia, no. 6. Ramat-Gan, Israel: Bar-Ilan University Press, 2001.

Anna Kuliscioff

Addis Saba, Marina. *Anna Kuliscioff: Vita privata e passione politica*. Milan: Mondadori, 1993.

Anna Kuliscioff in memoria. Edited by Filippo Turati. Milan: Privately printed, 1926. Reprint, Milan: Enrico Lazzari, 1989.

Boggio, Maricla, and Annabella Cerlani, eds. *Anna Kuliscioff: Con gli scritti di Anna Kuliscioff sulla condizione della donna*. Venice: Marsilio, 1977.

Casalini, Maria. *La signora del socialismo italiano*. Rome: Editori Riuniti, 1987.

Pillitteri, Paolo. *Anna Kuliscioff: Una biografia politica*. Venice: Marsilio, 1986.

Sarfatti, Margherita. *Acqua passata*. Rocca San Casciano, Italy: F. Cappelli, 1955.

Shepherd, Naomi. *A Price Below Rubies: Jewish Women as Rebels and Radicals*. Cambridge, Mass.: Harvard University Press, 1993.

Treves, Paolo. "Portici Galleria 23." In *Esperienze e studi socialisti in onore di Ugo Guido Mondolfo*. Florence: La Nuova Italia, 1957.

Turati, Filippo, and Anna Kuliscioff. *Carteggio Filippo Turati e Anna Kuliscioff*. Edited by Alessandro Schiavi and Franco Pedrone. 7 vols. Turin: Einaudi, 1949–77.

Valeri, Nino. *Turati e la Kuliscioff*. Florence: Felice Le Monnier, 1974.

MAJOR ARCHIVES

Fondazione Anna Kuliscioff, Milan

Biblioteca Comunale, Imola. Andrea Costa papers

Ada Leverson

Burkhart, Charles. *Ada Leverson*. New York: Twayne, 1973.

Ellmann, Richard. *Oscar Wilde*. New York: Vintage, 1988.

Hall, John N. *Max Beerbohm Caricatures*. New Haven and London: Yale University Press, 1997.

Hichens, Robert. *The Green Carnation*. London: William Heinemann, 1894.

Holland, Merlin. *The Real Trial of Oscar Wilde: The First Uncensored Transcript of the Trial of Oscar Wilde vs. John Douglas (Marquess of Queensberry)*. New York: Fourth Estate, 2003.

Holland, Merlin, and Rupert Hart-Davis, eds. *The Complete Letters of Oscar Wilde*. New York: Henry Holt, 2000.

Leverson, Ada. "Overheard Fragment of a Dialogue." *Punch*, January 12, 1895, 24.

Speedie, Julie. *Wonderful Sphinx: The Biography of Ada Leverson*. London: Virago, 1993.

Sturgis, Matthew. *Aubrey Beardsley: A Biography*. London: Flamingo, 1999.

Wilde, Oscar. *Letters to the Sphinx from Oscar Wilde, with Reminiscences of the Author by Ada Leverson*. London: Duckworth, 1930.

Wyndham, Violet. *The Sphinx and Her Circle: A Biographical Sketch of Ada Leverson, 1862–1933*. New York: Vanguard; London: Andre Deutsch, 1963.

MAJOR ARCHIVES

William Andrews Clark University Memorial Library, University of California, Los Angeles. Oscar Wilde and the 1890s collection

Houghton Library, Rare Books and Manuscripts, Harvard University, Cambridge, Massachusetts

Mark Samuels Lasner, private collection, Washington, D.C.

Pierpont Morgan Library, New York. Literary and Historical Manuscripts, Gordon N. Ray collection

Princeton University Library, New Jersey. Aubrey Beardsley collection

Margherita Sarfatti

Bossaglia, Rossana. *Il Novecento italiano*. 2nd ed. Milan: Charta, 1995.

Braun, Emily. *Mario Sironi and Italian Modernism: Art and Politics Under Fascism*. New York: Cambridge University Press, 2000.

Cannistraro, Philip V., and Brian R. Sullivan. *Il Duce's Other Woman: The Untold Story of Margherita Sarfatti*. New York: William Morrow, 1993.

Franchi, Enrico. "Mercoledì sera: Casa Sarfatti." *Corriere Adriatico*, July 8, 1926.

Grazia, Victoria de. "Il fascino del priapo: Margherita Sarfatti, biografa del Duce." *Memoria* 4 (June 1982): 149–54.

Nozzoli, Anna. "Margherita Sarfatti, organizzatrice di cultura: *Il popolo d'Italia*." In *La corporazione delle donne: Ricerche e studi sui modelli femminili nel ventennio fascista*, edited by Marina Addis Saba, 227–72. Florence: Vallecchi, 1988.

Pontiggia, Elena. *Da Boccioni a Sironi: Il mondo di Margherita Sarfatti*. Milan: Skira, 1997.

Sarfatti, Margherita. *Acqua passata*. Rocca San Casciano, Italy: F. Cappelli, 1955.

———. *The Life of Benito Mussolini*. Translated by Frederic Whyte. London: Thorton Butterworth, 1925.

Urso, Simonetta. *Margherita Sarfatti: Dal mito del Dux al mito americano*. Venice: Marsilio, 2003.

MAJOR ARCHIVES

Archivio Centrale dello Stato, Rome

Piero Foà papers, Detroit

Sarfatti family papers, Rome and Philadelphia

Gertrude Stein

Brinnin, John Malcolm. *The Third Rose: Gertrude Stein and Her World*. Reading, Mass.: Addison-Wesley, 1987.

Four Americans in Paris: The Collections of Gertrude Stein and Her Family. New York: The Museum of Modern Art, 1970.

Mellow, James R. *Charmed Circle: Gertrude Stein and Company*. New York: Praeger, 1974.

Shattuck, Roger. *The Banquet Years: The Origins of the Avant-Garde in France, 1885 to World War I: Alfred Jarry, Henri Rousseau, Erik Satie and Guillaume Apollinaire*. New York: Vintage, 1968.

Stavitsky, Gail. *Gertrude Stein: The American Connection*. Exh. cat. New York: Sid Deutsch Gallery, 1990.

Stein, Gertrude. *The Autobiography of Alice B. Toklas*. New York: Harcourt Brace, 1933. Reprint, New York: Vintage, 1990.

———. *Paris France*. New York: Charles Scribner's Sons, 1940. Reprinted as *Paris France: Personal Recollections*, London: Peter Owen, 1971.

Steiner, Wendy. *Exact Resemblance to Exact Resemblance: The Literary Portraiture of Gertrude Stein*. New Haven and London: Yale University Press, 1978.

Wineapple, Brenda. *Sister Brother: Gertrude and Leo Stein*. New York: G. P. Putnam's Sons, 1994.

MAJOR ARCHIVES

Beinecke Rare Book and Manuscript Library, Yale University, New Haven. Yale Collection of American Literature. Mabel Dodge Luhan papers; Henry McBride papers; Gertrude Stein and Alice B. Toklas papers; Alfred Stieglitz/Georgia O'Keeffe archive; Carl Van Vechten papers

Florine Stettheimer

Birmingham, Stephen. *"Our Crowd": The Great Jewish Families of New York*. New York: Harper and Row, 1967.

Bloemink, Barbara. *The Art and Life of Florine Stettheimer*. New Haven and London: Yale University Press, 1995.

———. *Friends and Family: Portraiture in the World of Florine Stettheimer*. Exh. cat. Katonah, N.Y.: Katonah Museum of Art, 1993.

McBride, Henry. *Florine Stettheimer*. Exh. cat. New York: The Museum of Modern Art, 1946.

Nochlin, Linda. "Florine Stettheimer: Rococo Subversive." *Art in America* 68 (September 1980): 64–83.

Sussman, Elisabeth, and Barbara Bloemink. *Florine Stettheimer. Manhattan Fantastica*. Exh. cat. New York: Whitney Museum of American Art, 1995.

Tyler, Parker. *Florine Stettheimer: A Life in Art*. New York: Farrar, Straus, 1963.

Whiting, Cecil. "Decorating with Stettheimer and the Boys." *American Art* 13 (Spring 2000): 25–49.

MAJOR ARCHIVES

Beinecke Rare Book and Manuscript Library, Yale University, New Haven. Yale Collection of American Literature. Henry McBride papers; Florine and Ettie Stettheimer collection; Alfred Stieglitz/Georgia O'Keeffe archive; Carl Van Vechten papers

Rare Book and Manuscript Library, Columbia University, New York. Florine Stettheimer collection

Geneviève Straus

Balard, Françoise. *Geneviève Straus: Biographie et correspondance avec Ludovic Halévy, 1855–1908*. Paris: Centre National de la Recherche Scientifique, 2002.

Bischoff, Chantal. *Geneviève Straus: Trilogie d'une égérie*. Paris: Balland, 1992.

Carter, William. *Marcel Proust: A Life*. New Haven and London: Yale University Press, 2000.

Catalogue des tableaux modernes, aquarelles, pastels, dessins . . . terres cuites du XVIIIe siècle . . . meubles et sieges anciens . . . composant la Collection Émile Straus. Sale cat. (June 3–4, 1929). Paris: Galerie Georges Petit, 1929.

Gramont, Élisabeth de. *Pomp and Circumstance*. Translated by Brian Downs. New York: Jonathan Cape and Harrison Smith, 1929.

Jacob, Andrée. *Il y a un siècle—Quand les dames tenaient salon*. Paris: Arnaud Seydoux, 1991.

Kleeblatt, Norman, ed. *The Dreyfus Affair: Art, Truth, and Justice*. Exh. cat. Berkeley: University of California Press, 1987.

Loyrette, Henri. *Entre le théâtre et l'histoire: La famille Halévy (1760–1960)*. Paris: Arthème Fayard and Réunion des Musées Nationaux, 1996.

Painter, Georges D. *Marcel Proust: A Biography*. 2 vols. 2nd ed. New York: Random House, 1989.

Proust, Marcel. *Chroniques*. Paris: Gallimard, 1927.

———. *Correspondance avec Madame Straus*. Paris: Union Générale d'Éditions, 1994.

Tadie, Jean-Yves. *Marcel Proust: A Life*. Translated by Evan Cameron. New York: Penguin Books, 2000.

MAJOR ARCHIVES

Bibliothèque Nationale de France, Paris. Département des Manuscrits, Geneviève Halévy, Robert de Montesquiou, and Marcel Proust collections

Fondazione Giuseppe Primoli, Rome

Madame Henriette Guy-Loé, private collection, Paris

Rahel Levin Varnhagen

Arendt, Hannah. *Rahel Varnhagen: The Life of a Jewess*. Edited by Liliane Weissberg and translated by Richard and Clara Winston. 1957. Reprint, Baltimore: Johns Hopkins University Press, 1997.

Benhabib, Seyla. "The Pariah and Her Shadow: Hannah Arendt's Biography of Rahel Varnhagen." In Bonnie Honig, ed., *Feminist Interpretations of Hannah Arendt*, 83–104. University Park: Pennsylvania State University Press, 1995.

Bruyn, Günter de. *Rahels erste Liebe: Rahel Levin und Karl Graf von Finckenstein in ihren Briefen*. Berlin: Der Morgen, 1985. Reprint, Frankfurt: Fischer, 1986.

Hahn, Barbara. *"Antworten Sie mir!": Rahel Levin Varnhagens Briefwechsel*. Basel: Stroemfeld/Roter Stern, 1990.

———. "Der Mythos vom Salon: 'Rahels Dachstube' als historische Fiktion." In *Salons der Romantik: Beiträge eines Wiepersdorfer Kolloquiums zu Theorie und Geschichte des Salons*, edited by Hartwig Schultz, 213–34. Berlin: Walter de Gruyter, 1997.

Hahn, Barbara, and Ursula Isselstein, eds. *Rahel Levin Varnhagen: Die Wiederentdeckung einer Schriftstellerin*. Göttingen: Vandenhoeck und Ruprecht, 1987.

Isselstein, Ursula. *Studien zu Rahel Levin Varnhagen*. Turin: Tirrenia, 1993.

Tewarson, Heidi Thomann. *Rahel Levin Varnhagen: The Life and Work of a German Jewish Intellectual*. Lincoln: University of Nebraska Press, 1998.

MAJOR ARCHIVES

Biblioteka Jagiellońska, Kraków. Varnhagen collection

Staatsbibliothek zu Berlin. Handschriften Abteilung, Varnhagen collection

Salka Viertel

Barron, Stephanie. *Exiles + Emigrés: The Flight of European Artists from Hitler*. Exh. cat. Los Angeles: Los Angeles County Museum of Art; New York: Harry N. Abrams, 1997.

Brecht, Bertolt. *Letters*. Edited by John Willet and translated by Ralph Manheim. London: Methuen, 1990.

Heilbut, Anthony. *Exiled in Paradise*. Boston: Beacon, 1983.

Isherwood, Christopher. *Lost Years: A Memoir, 1945–1951*. Edited by Katherine Bucknell. New York: HarperCollins, 2002.

Jansen, Irene. *Berthold Viertel: Leben und künstlerische Arbeit im Exil*. New York: Peter Lang, 1992.

Naficy, Hamid, ed. *Home, Exile, Homeland*. New York: Routledge, 1999.

Paris, Barry. *Garbo: A Biography*. New York: Alfred A. Knopf, 1995.

Viertel, Salka. *The Kindness of Strangers: A Theatrical Life, Vienna, Berlin, Hollywood*. New York: Holt, Rinehart and Winston, 1969.

Wysling, Hans, ed. *Letters of Heinrich and Thomas Mann, 1900–1949*. Translated by Don Reneau and Richard and Clara Winston. Berkeley: University of California Press, 1998.

Feuchtwanger Memorial Library, University of Southern
California, Los Angeles. Specialized Libraries and Archival
Collections, German exiles collection (Berthold and Salka
Viertel)

Schiller-Nationalmuseum, Marbach am Neckar, Germany.
Deutsches Literaturarchiv, Handschriftenabteilung, Nachlass
Viertel (Salka Viertel and Berthold Viertel collection)

Berta Zuckerkandl

Essen, Gesa von. "'Hier ist noch Europa!'—Berta Zuckerkandls
Wiener Salon." In *Europa—Ein Salon? Beiträge zur International-
ität des literarischen Salons*, edited by Roberto Simanowski, Horst
Turk, and Thomas Schmidt, 191–213. Göttingen: Wallstein, 1999.

Herling, Olaf. "Berta Zuckerkandl (1864–1945), oder Die Kunst
weiblicher Diplomatie." In *Das alles war ich: Politikerinnen,
Künstlerinnen, Exzentrikerinnen der Wiener Moderne,* edited by
Frauke Severit, 53–74. Vienna: Böhlau, 1998.

Meysels, Lucian. *In meinem Salon ist Österreich: Berta
Zuckerkandl und ihre Zeit*. Vienna: Herold, 1984.

Nebehay, Christian M. *Gustav Klimt: Sein Leben nach zeit-
genössischen Berichten und Quellen*. Vienna: Galerie Christian M.
Nebehay, 1969. Reprint, Munich: Deutsche Taschenbuch, 1976.

Wagener, Mary Louise. "Pioneer Journalistinnen. Two Early
Twentieth-Century Viennese Cases: Berta Zuckerkandl and
Alice Shalek." Ph.D. diss., Ohio State University, 1976.

Zuckerkandl, Berta Szeps. *Clemenceau tel que je l'ai connu*.
Algiers: Éditions de la Revue Fontaine, 1944.

———. *My Life and History*. Translated by John Sommerfield.
New York: Alfred A. Knopf, 1939. Published in England as Berta
Szeps, *My Life and History*. London: Cassell, 1938.

———. *Österreich intim: Erinnerungen, 1892–1942*. Edited by
Reinhard Federmann. Frankfurt: Propyläen, 1970.

———. *Zeitkunst Wien, 1901–1907*. Vienna: H. Heller, 1908.

MAJOR ARCHIVES

Hochschule für Angewandte Kunst, Vienna

MAK–Austrian Museum of Applied Arts, Vienna. Wiener
Werkstätte collection

Österreichische Nationalbibliothek, Vienna. Handschriften-
sammlung; Porträtsammlung/Bildarchiv, Dora Kallmus/
Madame D'Ora collection

Van Pelt Library, University of Pennsylvania, Philadelphia.
Special Collections, Mahler-Werfel collection

Berta Zuckerkandl papers, Palo Alto, California

Contributors

EMILY D. BILSKI is an independent scholar and curator specializing in nineteenth- and twentieth-century art and cultural history. Her publications include *Berlin Metropolis: Jews and the New Culture, 1890–1918* (1999), winner of the National Jewish Book Award; *Golem! Danger, Deliverance, and Art* (1988); and *Art and Exile: Felix Nussbaum (1904–1944)* (1985). She has served as curator of numerous exhibitions at The Jewish Museum, New York, including its first permanent exhibition, *Culture and Continuity: The Jewish Journey* (1993). She is currently editing the volume on art for the scholarly edition of Martin Buber's complete works and is consulting curator at the new Jewish Museum in Munich.

EMILY BRAUN is Professor of Art History at Hunter College and the Graduate Center at the City University of New York. In 2002–3 she was a Fellow at the Dorothy and Lewis B. Cullman Center for Scholars and Writers at the New York Public Library. Her numerous publications on modern Italian art include *Mario Sironi and Italian Modernism: Art and Politics Under Fascism* (2000) and an essay in *Modigliani: Beyond the Myth* (2004). As a contributing author, she has twice received the annual Henry Allen Moe Prize for Catalogues of Distinction in the Arts for her essays in *Northern Light: Realism and Symbolism in Scandinavian Painting* (1982) and *Gardens and Ghettos: The Art of Jewish Life in Italy* (1990).

LEON BOTSTEIN has been President of Bard College, where he is the Leon Levy Professor in the Arts and Humanities, since 1975. He is also music director of the American Symphony Orchestra; music director of the Jerusalem Symphony Orchestra/Israel Broadcast Authority; co-artistic director of the Bard Music Festival; and editor of the *Musical Quarterly*. His book *Judentum und Modernität: Essays zur Rolle der Juden in der deutschen und österreichischen Kultur, 1848–1938* (1991) is forthcoming in an English translation. He is the coeditor of *Vienna: Jews and the City of Music, 1870–1938* (2004) and editor of *The Compleat Brahms* (1999). He is also the author of *Jefferson's Children: Education and the Promise of American Culture* (1997).

SHIRA BRISMAN is Curatorial Assistant at The Jewish Museum. She worked on the exhibitions *The Russian Avant-Garde Book, 1910–1934* (2002) and *Collaborations with Parkett: 1984 to Now* (2001) at The Museum of Modern Art, and on the exhibition *Edward Lear and the Art of Travel* (2000) as the Duncan Robinson Fellow at the Yale Center for British Art. She received a bachelor of arts degree in art history from Yale University in 2001.

BARBARA HAHN recently joined Vanderbilt University as Distinguished Professor of German and was formerly a faculty member at Princeton University; she has also taught at the University of Michigan, the University of Frankfurt/Oder, and other institutions. Among her many publications are *Die Jüdin Pallas Athene: Auch eine Theorie der Moderne* (2002), forthcoming in English translation; *Unter falschem Namen: Von der schwierigen Autorschaft der Frauen* (1991); and *"Antworten Sie mir": Rahel Levin Varnhagens Briefwechsel* (1990). Together with Ursula Isselstein she is co-editing Rahel Levin Varnhagen's correspondence and diaries.

LUCIA RE is Professor of Italian at the University of California, Los Angeles. She recently completed a book entitled *Women and the Avant-Garde: From Futurism to Fascism*. Her translation into English (with Paul Vangelisti) of Amelia Rosselli's first book of avant-garde poems, *War Variations* (1964), is forthcoming in a bilingual edition with a critical introduction. Her book *Calvino and the Age of Neorealism: Fables of Estrangement* (1990) won the MLA Marraro Prize, and her translation into Italian of *Borges: A Literary Biography* by Emir Rodríguez Monegal received the 1982 Comisso Prize.

Index

Page numbers in italics refer
to illustrations.

Illustration Credits

Italic numerals refer to page numbers.

Bilski and Braun Essay: *Frontispiece* RMN. *3* VCBJ. *4* APS, p. 27. *5–6* BNF, Département des Estampes. *8* © The J. Paul Getty Museum (top), © 1994 Christie's Images Inc. (bottom). *9* Scala/ARNY. *10* RMN. *11* Foto Marburg/ARNY. *12–13* © Musée d'Art et d'Histoire, Ville de Genève. *16* BPK. *17* YCAL. *18* YCAL (top), Fondazione Anna Kuliscioff, Milan (bottom). *19* BPK (top), The Bancroft Library, University of California, Berkeley (bottom). *23* BPK. *24* RMN. *25* BPK. *27* BPK. *30* VCBJ. *32* VCBJ. *34* Jewish Museum, Vienna (top), © 1996 MMA (bottom). *36* Germanisches Nationalmuseum, Nuremberg. *38–39* SMB. *40* RMN (left), BPK (right). *41* BPK. *42* From Eduard Fuchs, *Die Juden in der Karikatur: Ein Beitrag zur Kulturgeschichte* (Munich: Albert Langen, 1921), p. 70 (top), LBI (bottom). *43* SMB. *44* LBI. *45* Collection of Daniel M. Friedenberg, New York. *47–48* BPK. *49* BPK (top). *51* CML (left). *58* Princeton University Library. *61* AFFP (top), BNF, Département des Estampes (bottom). *62* APS, p. 73. *63* APS, p. 28 (left), BNF, Département des Estampes (right). *64* APS, p. 76 (left), APS, p. 65 (right).

65 APS, p. 42. *66* From Raymond Bouyer et al., *A. de la Gandara et son oeuvre* (Paris: Éditions de "La Plume," 1902), p. 13. *67* RMN. *68* From *Entre le théâtre et l'histoire: La Famille Halévy, 1760–1960* (Paris: Fayard and Editions de la Réunion des musées nationaux, 1996). *69* Museum of Art, Rhode Island School of Design, photograph by Eric Gould. *70* BNF, Département des Estampes. *71* APS, p. 63. *72* AFFP. *73* The Museum of Fine Arts, Houston (left), APS, p. 35 (right). *74* From Norman L. Kleeblatt, *The Dreyfus Affair: Art, Truth, and Justice* (Berkeley: University of California Press, 1987), p. 7. *77–79* ICCD. *83* From *Anna Kuliscioff in Memoria* (Milan: Enrico Lazzari, 1926), p. 173. *85* Harvard University Fine Arts Library, Cambridge, Massachusetts (top), BPK (bottom). *86* BONB. *87* BONB (right). *88* The Robert Gore Rifkind Collection, Beverly Hills, California. *90* MAK–Austrian Museum of Applied Arts/Contemporary Art, Vienna (top), Cooper-Hewitt, National Design Museum, Smithsonian Institution (bottom). *91* Wien Museum (top left), from *Ver Sacrum* 4, no. 9 (1901): 159 (bottom). *92* Galerie St. Etienne, New York. *96* Brooklyn Museum of Art (left), BONB (right). *98* Wien Museum. *101* FFS. *103* ICCD (right). *104* Photograph by Sergio Martucci (bottom). *105* Photograph © 2004 The Gianni Mattioli Collection. *107* ICCD. *109* Marina and Antonio Forchino Collection, Turin. *114* © MMA/© 2004 Estate of Pablo Picasso/ARS. *115* YCAL. *116* Giraudon/ARNY. *117* Frederick R. Weisman Art Museum at the University of Minnesota, Minneapolis. *120* © 2004 Estate of Pablo Picasso/ARS/Rheinisches Bildarchiv. *121* MRT. *122* YCAL. *123* The Baltimore Museum of Art.

124 © 2004 Estate of Pablo Picasso/ARS (left), YCAL (right). *125* GEH (right). *127* YCAL. *128* Smith College Museum of Art. *129* YCAL. *130* FSP. *131–32* CU. *133* MRT. *134* William Kelly Simpson Collection. *136* © 1995 MMA. *139* SNDL. *140–41* Courtesy of the Academy of Motion Picture Arts and Sciences. *143* Archiv der Stiftung Deutsche Kinemathek Berlin.

Hahn Essay: *Frontispiece* Courtesy of The Library of The Jewish Theological Seminary of America. *150* VCBJ. *152* Library of Uppsala University, Sweden (left), VCBJ (right). *153* VCBJ (left), © Ursula Edelmann, Frankfurt am Main (right). *157* VCBJ.

Botstein Essay: *Frontispiece* BPK. *160–61* BPK. *163* Wien Museum. *164* SMB. *168–69* BPK.

Re Essay: *Frontispiece* BNF, Département des Manuscrits. *172* The New York Public Library/ARNY. *173* RMN. *175* APS, p. 100. *176* RMN, © 2004 ARS/ADAGP, Paris. *177* APS, pp. 33, 39. *180* The Jewish Museum, New York. *181* BNF, Département des Manuscrits. *184* CML. *188* YCAL. *189* YCAL (right).

Biographies: *Frontispiece* FSP. *196* Courtesy of The Library of The Jewish Theological Seminary of America. *197* Courtesy of The Library of The Jewish Theological Seminary of America. *198* BPK. *199* From *Anna Kuliscioff in Memoria* (Milan: Enrico Lazzari, 1926), p. 59. *203* ICCD. *204* GEH. *206* FSP. *207* BNF, Département des Estampes. *209* BPK. *210* SNDL.